Hannah Bradbury Goodwin

Sherbrooke

Hannah Bradbury Goodwin

Sherbrooke

ISBN/EAN: 9783337138745

Printed in Europe, USA, Canada, Australia, Japan

Cover: Foto ©ninafisch / pixelio.de

More available books at **www.hansebooks.com**

SHERBROOKE.

BY

H. B. G.,

Author of "Madge."

"There is a perennial nobleness in work."—CARLYLE.

"Through wisdom is an house builded; and by understanding it is established: And by knowledge shall the chambers be filled with all precious and pleasant riches."—PROVERBS.

NEW YORK:
D. APPLETON AND COMPANY,
443 & 445 BROADWAY.
1866.

ENTERED, according to Act of Congress, in the year 1866, by
D. APPLETON & CO.,
In the Clerk's Office of the District Court of the United States for the Southern District of New York.

TO

THE YOUNG WOMEN OF OUR REPUBLIC

𝕿𝖍𝖎𝖘 𝖁𝖔𝖑𝖚𝖒𝖊

IS MOST KINDLY DEDICATED, WITH THE EARNEST PRAYER

THAT THEY MAY GLEAN FROM ITS PAGES

STRENGTH, COURAGE, AND PATIENCE,

AND A LOVE FOR THAT WISDOM WHICH FILLS THE

CHAMBERS OF THE HEART WITH

"ALL PRECIOUS AND PLEASANT RICHES."

H. B. G.

CONTENTS.

Chapter		Page
I.	Leaving Home,	7
II.	Morning Clouds,	13
III.	Struggles with Pride,	21
IV.	Alice,	28
V.	Father's Letter,	34
VI.	Aunt Lydia,	38
VII.	March,	45
VIII.	Failure and Disappointment,	52
IX.	Foreshadowing of Grief,	60
X.	Only Waiting,	68
XI.	Aunt Lydia's Offer,	75
XII.	The Opening Way,	83
XIII.	The Mathews,	90
XIV.	The Day Before Christmas,	98
XV.	Spring Flowers,	107
XVI.	Virginia Thornton,	114
XVII.	Cameron Pond,	123
XVIII.	Night and Darkness,	134
XIX.	Carey Chapman,	142
XX.	The Brook and River,	151
XXI.	The Riding Lesson,	161
XXII.	Hope's First Party,	171
XXIII.	Stepping Stones,	186
XXIV.	Aunt Lydia's Letter,	194
XXV.	Hope goes to Hebron,	200
XXVI.	Aunt Lydia at Home,	210
XXVII.	Uncle John's Family,	219
XXVIII.	Caleb Hopkinson,	232

CHAPTER	PAGE
XXIX. The Shadow of Coming Events,	243
XXX. Ellen's Dream,	257
XXXI. Autumnal Storms,	265
XXXII. Brier Hill,	273
XXXIII. Mr. Hamlin's Library,	285
XXXIV. Aunt Lydia's Wedding,	299
XXXV. Rejected Love,	312
XXXVI. Home Again,	319
XXXVII. Dreams of Happiness,	328
XXXVIII. Hope Kendall's Christmas,	335
XXXIX. First Attempt at Authorship,	346
XL. Demolished Air-Castles,	354
XLI. Rachel Shaw's Story,	364
XLII. News from Hebron,	373
XLIII. Switzerland,	382
XLIV. What Might have Been.	394
XLV. Premonitions of Sorrow,	405
XLVI. Old and New Friends,	413
XLVII. Behind the Cloud,	422
XLVIII. Laurel Hill,	431
XLIX. Hope's Joy and Refuge,	441
L. Golden Threads,	449
LI. Conclusion,	457

SHERBROOKE.

CHAPTER I.

LEAVING HOME.

"Here is the place; right over the hill
　　Runs the path I took;
You can see the gap in the old wall still,
　　And the stepping-stones in the shallow brook.

"There's the same sweet clover-smell in the breeze;
　　And the June sun warm
Tangles his wings of fire in the trees,
　　Setting, as then, over Fernside Farm."
　　　　　　　　　　　　　　WHITTIER.

"You will consent to my going, Celia?"

"Not if any way can be devised by which we can raise the money and keep you at home."

"But we have thought of every thing, and this seems the only plan which promises success."

Mother made no answer. The plan which father had proposed seemed desolate and cheerless, but she was unwilling to hedge it around with womanly fears. I was the eldest child, not quite fifteen years of age, and yet no longer a child, for within the last week my feet had crossed the brook, and I was now standing in the deep waters of womanhood. And being no longer a child, I was permitted to be present when the fortunes of our family were discussed. One week had changed me so much—perhaps I should say the knowledge of one fact had so changed me, that from a careless child I had suddenly grown a thoughtful woman. I was no longer "Pet," or "Floy," as pleased the caprice of the household, but careful "Hope," troubled about many things.

I had returned from school one day to find my mother in tears. It was a strange sight, for she was an energetic woman, with a cheerful, courageous spirit, and tears rarely dimmed her clear gray eyes. She tried to hide them from me, and bade me go in search of my sisters, but I would not be sent away; I knelt by her side, entreating to be told what made her weep.

"I cannot tell you, Hope."

"Why, mother?"

"You are not old enough to comprehend."

"Just try me—do, mother; I shall be fifteen next month."

But there was no response until another violent fit of weeping had somewhat softened her grief, or the earnestness of my entreaties had exhausted her patience.

"Well, Hope, if nothing will satisfy you but knowing the cause of my trouble, sit down near me while I try to tell you. Do you know what the word mortgage means?"

"Yes, indeed, mother; a pledge of goods or chattels by a debtor to a creditor, as security for debt." I well remember how fluently the dictionary definition slipped from my tongue, but how meaningless were the words to my childish heart.

"You are right, Hope; well, two years ago last winter, when I was so very sick, and Dr. Ellis had to come from Wiltshire to attend me, your father got in debt. It was a hard winter—every thing was high; the doctor's bills were very large, and my sickness prevented your father from teaching, so he had to borrow money of Squire Thornton, and mortgage our dear old farm as security." Here there was another overflow of tears.

"Cannot father pay the debt?"

"No, my child."

"But Squire Thornton will not take our farm!"

"Not at present; your father has still another year to redeem it in."

"Then don't cry, mother; I'm sure father will find the money in less than a year; a year is such a long time."

"Oh, such a long time! if to earn this money your father must go away from home."

"Go away from home! Where will he go?"

"He has not decided yet, but to some place where he can earn more in teaching than he can get here. Go away now, Hope, and find your sisters. I want to be alone."

I obeyed, for a certain womanly instinct just dawning within me, told me that my mother's sorrow was beyond my power to soothe; but I did not seek my sisters. I wanted leisure to think; so I strolled into the orchard, where the shadows lay cool and thick upon the grass, and threw myself down in the grateful shade.

I remember well how long the shadows grew as I lay there—how uneasily fluttered a robin in the branches over my head, telling me as plainly as a fretful chirrup could tell, that there was no peace for him while I remained so near his nest. Then came the pleasant tinkle of the cow-bell in the lane near by, always a welcome sound to me until this evening; now it awakened no joy or happiness.

The knowledge I had just gained of debt and mortgage made a heavy burden for my young heart. What if father could not raise the money, and Squire Thornton should take from us our beautiful farm, the dear, old brown home, the fields where such luscious strawberries grew, the raspberry hedges and orchard? Ay, how dearly I had loved the orchard, and boasted of its golden fruit! Every girl in school had heard me say there were no such apples in town as our sweetings and pearmains, and it was dreadful to think Squire Thornton might have them all next year. I wondered if Virginia Thornton knew our farm was mortgaged, and if she would still be my friend. And then to think of my dear father, leaving us to earn money!

Here my sorrow found vent in tears, and loud sobs disturbed the evening repose of the robins, and floating on the quiet air of the summer twilight, fell upon my father's ear. He was just then passing through the lane from the mowing-lot beyond the orchard, and climbing the wall, he came with rapid steps to my side.

"What has happened to my little girl?" he asked so cheerily as he lifted me from the grass, that I felt almost ashamed of my tears; but the next moment came the thought that the hearty voice I so much loved would soon be where its tones could not cheer me; and pressing my face to his side, I wept as only those weep who are just beginning to know that life has sorrows.

Soon my father's gentle caresses and patient entreaties to be told the cause of my distress prevailed, and in answer to his often-repeated question, "What troubles my child?" I sobbed out, "Oh, father! must we lose our farm, and must you go away from home?"

"Who has told you, Hope?"

"I found mother crying when I came from school, and I teased her to tell me what made her cry. Must you go away?"

"Going away seems the surest way of earning money just now; but a year will soon pass, and then, please God,

I shall have secured my father's homestead to my own children."

He had drawn me gently along over the orchard path, as we talked, and now stood upon the stone steps of the cottage door. I saw how lovingly his eye rested upon the farm, and then wandered off to the beautiful scenery of our native town, and I knew that it was as hard for him to go as it was for me to be left; and I made a great resolve for a girl whose fourteen years had brought her so little self-denial, breathing a simple prayer that God would help me keep it.

I resolved to show no outward sign of my own sorrow, but cheerfully and courageously to help my parents bear their great trial.

It was not a month after the knowledge of debt had sobered my whole nature, before my father's plans for paying off the mortgage were matured. He proposed to accept a situation as teacher, which had been offered him in Ohio, and to occupy his leisure in writing; and at just this point in our family history my story opens.

When father had unfolded before us all his plans, there was silence for several minutes in the old kitchen, during which we could hear the ticking of the clock and the soft hum of insects that flitted past the open windows. He sat by the table, his broad, white forehead supported by a shapely hand which had upon it honest labor-stains, and mother, sitting near him, stitched upon a shirt. I was industriously engaged upon a stocking for the dear feet whose homeward coming I had so loved to watch.

Mother broke the silence by asking when he must leave. "This is the last of July, and I must be in Worthington by the first of September." Only a short month, and its hours would be so occupied with necessary stitching, that we should have no time to nourish regrets.

"Hope must leave school to look after the children and help on the sewing," mother said, with a regretful voice; and I tried to smile in answer, fearing to trust my tongue with words. School was a pleasure which I could not easily forego; not only because I loved my studies, but for the love I bore my young friend Virginia. If I remained away from school, I should miss the joy of daily meeting her.

"Hope will be willing to lend a helping hand, and will remain out of school cheerfully for our sakes," said father, with a fond, encouraging look at me, which I was forced to answer with another smile.

The golden August days flew by, and the last shirt was neatly finished, marked, and packed in father's trunk. He never knew how many tears had fallen upon those shirts and stockings; and then the morning came when we must say good-bye. Jonas Gould, our faithful friend and farm-servant, stood by the harnessed horse, waiting to drive my father to the city, where he would take a steamer for New York.

I must pause a moment to describe my father as he looked in that early morning light. He was in the prime of manhood, not yet forty years of age. Care had neither thinned his brown hair, nor ploughed furrows in his honest face—a face you would turn to look at in a crowd—so marked with noble purpose was the broad brow, so clear and full of kindly charity was the blue eye, so delicate and feminine the mouth, and then every movement of his fine figure denoted strength of will as well as of muscle.

Looking at him, you would not wonder that his wife hung in speechless agony upon his neck, when the hour for a temporary separation came, nor that his children clung in tearful tenderness around his knees.

"Celia, you make it very hard for me to go."

And my mother raised her head from his neck, left one

long kiss upon his lips, and thrusting back the tears into her heart, she said:

"God bless you, David, and keep you in the hollow of His hand!" But with the last sound of the retreating wagon, mother's strength again gave out, and, gathering us in her arms, her hot tears fell upon our heads.

CHAPTER II.

MORNING CLOUDS.

"What seems so dark to thy young sight
May be a shadow, seen aright,
Making some brightness doubly bright."

THERE were four of us. I, Hope, was the eldest, and though scarcely more than a child in years, I had a woman's new-born strength. Next in age was Sophie, a delicate child, fair as Mrs. Stowe's Evangeline, and with all the sunshine of her ten years garnered in her heart; William, a sturdy little fellow of six; and our baby Alice, just old enough to watch for papa's coming. Her three years could not comprehend the reason of his unwonted absence.

We had but one servant, or rather "hired man;" rough and uncouth, but strong, faithful, and honest, was Jonas Gould, and his willing hands performed the larger part of the farm work, while the labor in our small household fell entirely upon mother and myself; the servant-girl having been dismissed many months before my story opens. I was capable, and now that a purpose was given me, willing to work for mother and the children—at least, I was willing to do necessary housework; but mother was not a woman to sit in idleness and nourish vain regrets. While her husband, in self-condemned exile was toiling for his family, she, with her puny woman's strength, must do something in his absence to lift the great load of poverty from the household. Ay, but how could she help?—there were so few ways of earning an honest penny in our pretty village.

We sat considering in the autumn twilight, for since that day when I first learned of debt I had been taken into my mother's confidence. There was a shoe factory in the village, which was more than a mile from our farm, and several girls and women obtained employment in binding and stitching the shoes, but they were not people whom we knew.

We had always associated with the best families in our village, and had thought our social position to be quite equal to that of Squire Thornton's family. The Blakes and Chapmans, though living in much better style than we were, recognized us as friends and equals. Mother was a distant cousin of Mr. Chapman, the President of the Farmers' Bank, who owned the most beautiful farm and house in Sherbrooke.

Then we had a slight acquaintance with Mr. Clark's family, but had never quite liked them; they were showy, ostentatious people, without education, priding themselves greatly upon the position which wealth gave them. Mr. Clark was owner of the large shoe manufactory in our village, and it would certainly be very disagreeable to ask a favor of him, and my foolish young pride rebelled against it. But mother said we must be doing something in the long winter evenings that would at least assist in clothing the younger children, and we could think of nothing but binding shoes.

"You will send Jonas to ask for the work, mother, and then Mr. Clark need not know who does it."

"What harm is there in letting Mr. Clark know that we want work?"

"Why, he'll tell his wife, and then directly everybody in the village will know that we are binding shoes."

"And what if everybody knows it?"

"Oh, I don't want to associate with the Sampsons and Reeds, and all the rest of the people who bind shoes; and I'm afraid, when 'tis known that we work for money, all our old friends will drop us."

"Then, my child, we can afford to lose them, if their friendship cannot stand the test of honest poverty; but we cannot afford to sit idle when there is so much need for exertion; neither can we afford to stoop to the low deceptions which must be practised, if we attempt to do our work in secret. We will be honest and truthful, for self-respect will help us to bear many a burden."

"But do you think father would like to have it known that we work? I know that he never wanted me to go with Jennie Sampson or Mary Ann Reed."

"It was only because they were rude and ill-mannered; but binding shoes did not make them so. There is nothing degrading about labor, and no one need blush to own that the sweat of his brow procures his daily bread. There was not a more highly esteemed and honored man in town than your grandfather Kendall, yet his own hands helped clear this farm and till these fields, and you should be glad to add your little mite to help retain what he loved so much. If you continue to feel ashamed of helping your parents, you need not go with me to-morrow to ask for work at the factory. But we will not talk any more about it to-night. Get your history, and read aloud while I sew."

Father had decided that I should study at home during his absence; by doing so, I could amuse the children and assist Sophie, who was not strong enough to walk a mile to the village school; and then, being naturally fond of study, I did not need the stimulus of school. Mother heard our recitations, and was well qualified to direct my studies. I should have been perfectly content with her instructions, but for the loss of Virginia Thornton's society; and often during that autumn evening, while my head was bowed over the lesson in history, my thoughts wandered to the query, why Mr. Chapman and Squire Thornton should be so rich and prosperous, and we poor and in debt, and I speculated much on the chances of remaining intimate with Virginia.

The morning which followed mother's decision to apply for work, dawned cool and crisp. We were early astir, and under her active hands the household duties were quickly and neatly despatched. By nine o'clock she had seen Alice and Willie busy with books and toys, and carefully watched and guarded by Lottie. Then donning her neatly-kept bonnet and shawl, she called, " Hope, are you going to the village with me?" I had avoided the kitchen after my own share of the morning's work was finished, and stood idly swinging my sun-bonnet in the old porch, and gazing at the purple clusters of grapes which hung almost within reach of my hand. "If you wish it, mother," I replied; but her quick ear noticed the lack of cheerful, hearty response in my voice, and coming to my side she laid her hand upon my arm, and bent the clear light of her gray eyes upon my face: "I think you had better go with me, Hope; conquer a foolish and false pride to-day, and you may live to be proud of your victory."

She passed out of the porch through the gate, while I still lingered; but thoughts of the reproof which I should see in my father's face, if I yielded to this wicked, selfish pride, helped me to crush it, and throwing on my bonnet, my quick feet soon overtook mother.

She made no allusion to my lingering hesitation, but talked cheerfully as we passed along the familiar road, pointing out to me the beautiful colors of our autumn foliage, and telling me of the changes she had seen in the farms and houses we were passing, since she had lived in the neighborhood. And so, stilling the uneasy fluttering of my heart with her quiet tones and pleasant reminiscences, we passed the grave-yard, school-house, bank-building, and Mr. Chapman's handsome house; crossed the old bridge where I had lingered a hundred times to watch the rushing of the waters over the dam, and listen to the busy clatter of the mill; and then the new yellow-painted walls of Mr. Clark's factory met my vision, and before I had time to clothe my confused thoughts in words, we had crossed the threshold and were ushered into the counting-room, where sat the man I so much feared and dreaded.

He rose when we entered, and I remember well the blandness of his " Good-morning," and the suavity of his tones as he remarked upon the weather and made inquiries about my father; and then the quick, loud, and coarse tones in which he spoke to a hurried-looking clerk, and the eager, impatient look of his small black eye, as he turned again to my mother, saying almost as plainly as in words, " If you have any business with me, speak now." And mother spoke:

" Have you any stitching or binding to give out now, Mr. Clark?"

What an expression of astonishment and surprise came over his face as he glanced quickly at the lady-like figure before him, his eye resting for a second on the small, neatly-gloved hand! " You do not want work for yourself, Mrs. Kendall?" " Yes." " Bless us! you give me quite a surprise. I knew Kendall had been unfortunate, but never supposed it had come to this." And my keen wits discovered a petty triumph in his voice and face.

" My husband is obliged to make sacrifices, and I wish to share them; we do not look upon honest labor as degrading."

" Oh, no! no! of course not; but, you see, I had always looked upon you as above binding shoes—rather belonging to our aristocracy. Ha! ha!"

I did not like the laugh, nor the would-be jolly rubbing of his coarse hands; and the strong smell of leather, together with my feeling of fancied degradation in asking favors of such a man, almost overpowered me. I could have wept, only that pride held back my tears, and I wondered at the calm, quiet voice of mother, when she asked again, "Have you any work for me, Mr. Clark?"

"Well, we'll see; 'pon my word I'm sorry for you, Mrs. Kendall. Look here, Jenkins, can we give out any more work?"

The man addressed left off the packing of a box, and taking up an entry-book from a desk, seemed intently scanning its pages. "I think we might; we certainly could by limiting a few of our old customers. There's Jennie Sampson and Mary Ann Reed are earning more than five dollars a week. A round sum for women."

"That's a fact," responded Clark, "a round sum! We pay too much for our work, Jenkins; I found out yesterday that we are paying two cents more per dozen for binding shoes than Hollings & Dunn, of Wiltshire, pay; we must retrench. Why, only last Sunday Mary Ann Reed came out in a new flounced silk, as fine as a fiddle."

Again that disagreeable chuckle, more offensive than the smell of leather; and again mother reminded him of our errand.

"Yes, yes, Mrs. Kendall, happy to oblige you; certainly, always delighted to oblige; take a few pairs to-day?"

"If convenient, thank you."

"All in the way of business, ma'am; Jenkins tie up a dozen pairs for Mrs. Kendall. Carry the bundle yourself, ma'am? Yes, yes, our customers always do. All on a level here."

"How much do you pay for your work?"

"Two shillings per dozen, neatly finished."

We found afterwards it was the reduced price of Hollings & Dunn. "Good-morning, Mr. Clark."

"Good-day, ma'am, and success with your work. By the way, call on my wife all the same, you know; makes no difference with old friends."

My mother's "thank you" might have been dignified, but it was gentle and lady-like, and she gave no heed to the hot blush upon my cheeks, nor the angry tears which sprung to my eyes the moment we had gained the open air, but drawing me away from the highway, she proposed that we should cross the fields through a grove of maples; there was an old log bridge which spanned the stream a little further down, and we could reach our home by a pleasanter but longer route than the main road.

"Oh, mother," I sobbed, when we were fairly clear of the highway, "how could you be so cool when that man was so impudent? Just think of his saying we were all on a level, and asking us to call on his vulgar family!"

"Hush, Hope! he meant no offence, and although his family are not the kind of people I should choose to be intimate with, yet we might call upon them without injuring ourselves."

"But you will not, mother. It will not be necessary for us to call on Mr. Clark's family just because he furnishes us with work?"

"I shall have no time nor inclination to increase my circle of friends while your father is away; but Hope, why have you such an antipathy to Mr. Clark's family?"

"They are so ignorant and pompous, and Laura Clark talks so much about her new dresses, and tells the girls at school what they cost! Oh, dear! what would Virginia Thornton say if she knew we were working for Mr. Clark?"

"If Virginia is half as sensible as I have always

thought her, she will not love you less. Do not think of your annoyances any more to-day, but look around and see how much beauty God has spread over the woods and fields for our enjoyment. Truly ' He hath given us all things richly to enjoy.' Squire Thornton owns this grove, but he is obliged to share the beauty and fragrance of it with us."

How delicious the smell of the woods after that leathery counting-room! How soothing and cheering mother's words after my angry flow of tears had subsided; and then when we reached home, how pleasant and comfortable it looked! The old farm never seemed so dear before, never so well worth the sacrifices we were making; and after our early dinner was cleared away, and mother had given me a lesson in binding shoes, I grew quite cheerful over my work, and almost happy as I calculated the amount of our earnings.

"How many pairs do you think we can bind in a day, mother?" I asked, pricking the fore-finger of my left hand meanwhile.

"Perhaps if we are diligent, when we get accustomed to the work, we may finish a dozen pairs."

"Why, mother, we shall only earn three dollars a week at that rate, and Mary Ann Reed earns five."

"We can neither of us sit all day at our work. You must not neglect your studies, nor omit your out-door exercise, and I have a great many duties to my children besides house-work to prevent me from sewing steadily; but if we are only kept in health, I think we may earn quite a little sum while your father is gone."

And so the October day waned, and the radiance of its mellow sunset lighted up our kitchen and warmed our hearts, while a grateful smile rested on mother's face— caused, I was sure, by the happy thought that she was adding her mite to the maintenance of her family.

CHAPTER III.

STRUGGLES WITH PRIDE.

> "Angel of Patience! sent to calm
> Our feverish brows with cooling palm,
> To lay the storms of hope and fear,
> And reconcile life's smile and tear,
> The throbs of wounded pride to still,
> And make our own our Father's will."
> WHITTIER.

THREE mornings had dawned since my first introduction to Mr. Clark's counting-room, and the dozen pairs of shoes were stitched and bound. Something had whispered that it would be my duty to bring and return the work; but how I dreaded to hear mother say so, and how gladly I heard her bid Sophie prepare to walk with me the first time work was returned! The presence of my little fair-haired sister would make the ugly counting-room more tolerable. I had not conquered my aversion to Mr. Clark, nor my dislike to binding shoes, nor my fear that Virginia Thornton would look upon it as degrading.

Neither the beauty of the October day, nor the spicy fragrance of the woods, tempted me to avoid the highway, and take the path across the fields to the village, but rather the foolish fear that some one would see me carrying a bundle.

But gaining the sheltering shadows of the old woods, Sophie and I ran eagerly on, stopping now and then to pluck golden-rod and life-everlasting, or to watch the harvesting of the squirrels that were laying in their winter's store of nuts. The bundle was half-forgotten, and not till we had left the woods and the yellow walls of the hateful factory met my vision, did its presence vex me. And then, just as we were entering the building, a moment more and its door would have screened us from view, Virginia Thornton, turning a corner, saw us, and came eagerly forward.

"Why, Hope, Hope Kendall! is it you? Where have you kept yourself for a whole week, you little mouse?" And she held out to me her pretty right hand, and with the other drew Sophie to her side.

I did then, and I do now, almost venerate beauty—a beautiful woman, a beautiful tree, waterfall, mountain, blossom, or shell, have always seemed to me more particularly God's own handiwork than the more commonplace objects of His creation; and I have sometimes thought He might have commissioned angels to make the deserts, marshes, and prairies, while His own hand piled up the mountains, poured out the cascades, painted the rainbow and clouds, and tinted the flowers and shells.

Virginia was beautiful, and perhaps, until this morning, her beauty had been the secret of more than half my love and admiration for her; for, at fifteen, she was somewhat petted and spoiled—wilful and imperious, as I thought it it her prerogative to be, but generous and lovable; and, pausing on those factory-steps with my right hand in hers, I looked at Virginia with a more critical eye than ever before. I noted well the thick, wavy masses of her light hair, golden in the sunshine; the brilliancy of her blue eye, the transparency of her complexion, the straight nose and small mouth. I took in at a glance the well-rounded and elastic figure, and the small foot which tapped impatiently upon the stone step, and I thought of Squire Thornton's wealth and my bundle of shoes, and my heart uttered a sharp but silent cry, "Who maketh thee to differ?" What could it matter to this child of wealth, if my " Good-morning!" were a little cold?

"Good-morning! and nothing more? Why, you are not half glad to see me; and I verily believe you have tears in your eyes;"—and then, more quietly, "Is all right at home, Hope? Have you heard from your father this week?"

"Not yet; we have no mail until to-morrow."

"Come home with me now. Aunt Sallie will be glad to see you, and I have something to tell you—such pleasant news! I was longing to see you."

"Not to-day. I must see Mr. Clark, and then go directly home."

"What a business air and tone! One would think you dealt in leather; and perhaps that bundle under your arm, which I have been so curious about, is only shoes, after all."

She spoke in a playful, laughing tone, which grated so harshly on my heart, already full of tears, that they escaped, and, with a half-smothered sob, I exclaimed: "Oh, Virginia, they are shoes—shoes that mother and I have bound; and I have come for more." And then, hiding my face, tears dropped down on Virginia's hand. I could not look at her face, while she asked kindly why I cried about a bundle of shoes.

"Because you won't care for me any longer, if I bind shoes; and, oh dear! I must. Father's in debt."

"Why shall I not love you just as well? Will binding shoes make you like Jennie Sampson and Mary Reed?"

"Oh, no, no; indeed not! I study every day; and mother says there is nothing degrading about work."

"Of course not, you foolish girl. I hope I'm more sensible than to think less of you for that. Come, dry your eyes, and run in and do your business. I'm going to walk back with you as far as the old bridge."

I could have kissed Virginia in the fulness of my gratitude, as we stood upon the step; but mother had taught me that such salutations were not becoming on the street; so I pushed open the door, and with a comparatively bright face entered the counting-room, Sophie following with her hand upon my gown.

Still another trial was in reserve for my proud, sensitive nature; for, standing there, conversing with the shoe-manufacturer, was Mr. Chapman, president of the Farmers' Bank. What a contrast he presented to the keen-eyed, oily-mouthed Clark! this large, handsome man, with slightly silvered hair, broad brow, and honest eye. It seemed a long time that I stood there, not daring to speak while Mr. Clark conversed, regardless of my presence. What a cowardly, shrinking fear I had of that man! But, at last, Mr. Chapman turned, and seeing me, held out his hand.

"What brings you here, Miss Hope? and little Sophie too? all well at home?"

"Quite well, sir; thank you."

Here Mr. Clark, rubbing his coarse hands as usual, spoke in his patronizing way:

"Well, Miss! finished the work? Let me see," and unwrapping the bundle, he carefully examined each pair. "Very well done! very well for beginners—take a couple of dozen more to-day?" And then turning to Mr. Chapman, he said: "Sorry for friend Kendall, he's hard pushed, clever man too, but not quite sharp enough; has a nice family. I tell my women-folks to call upon them, if they do bind shoes; poverty is no disgrace."

How the words jarred and grated on my ear, worse than thorns in my flesh, and yet they were spoken in smooth, measured tones. Mr. Chapman made no reply, but stooping, kissed the fair cheek of my little sister, and said to me: "Tell your mother I shall bring Mrs. Chapman to see her to-day; we did not return from New York until yesterday," and bowing pleasantly he went out, leaving us to finish our business with Mr. Clark.

"If you please, sir, we would like more work."

"Yes, yes; I came near forgetting you. Jenkins, give this girl two dozen pairs, and be quick; I want you to carry this bill over to Davis, and tell him if 'tis not paid to-day I'll put it in Squire Thornton's hands."

There was no longer any blandness in his tones or suavity in his manners, only a dry, quick, business air from which we were glad to escape.

We found Virginia slowly pacing up and down in front of the factory waiting for us. At her suggestion we again took the by-path through the fields and woods, though I had lost the larger part of my false shame in exposing my package of work to the villagers. If Mr. Chapman and Virginia Thornton, knowing our necessities, could still treat us as equals, I cared little for the opinion of others.

"Shall you go nutting this fall, Hope, as we did last year?" Virginia asked, as we came in sight of a group of fine old chestnut trees, whose nuts had often helped make our long winter evenings pleasant.

"I don't know—yes, I think I shall, if I find time."

"How many hours do you stitch each day?"

"We have only worked two days upon shoes, but mother says I must only sew two hours in the morning and two after dinner. Then I've learned to help about house since last summer; I can make bread, and wash dishes, and look after the children almost as well as mother can."

"But when do you find time for study?"

"Oh, I have one hour in the morning, and one after dinner, and the whole evening."

"What a methodical little woman you are growing!"

"Mother plans my time and hears my lessons. She's the best teacher I've ever had."

"Oh, dear! if I only had a mother, perhaps she could teach me, and then I could stay at home."

"You are not going away, Virginia?"

"That is the secret which I wanted so much to tell you. Aunt Sallie has been making father believe that I'm growing up a dunce, and I really suppose that I am very ignorant for a girl of fifteen; so father decided a few days ago to send me away to school."

"What shall I do without you, Virginia?"

"You will miss me a little, then? I'm glad to be loved so much by you, Hope; but never mind now. I'm not going until after Christmas, and then I shall come back the first of July for a long vacation. You must promise to write a letter to me every week."

"You have not told me where you are going?"

"To a family school in Hampton, where they finish young ladies up splendidly. Aunt Sallie used to know the principal teacher. Next week I am going to Wiltshire with father to help select my new dresses." And the light-hearted girl rattled on about the dresses she would have, the style of her hat, the color of her ribbons, and the fashion of her cloak. Not that Virginia cared so much about the new things, but she saw that I was sad with the expectation of losing her, and tried to divert my thoughts.

We separated as we had often before at the log bridge, our old trysting-place, after many promises that we would meet often during the few autumn weeks that remained, and Sophie and I took the homeward path.

Again my thoughts were busy with the difficult query, Why God had bestowed his gifts so unequally? Why should Virginia's father be rich and honored, and mine oppressed with poverty? Why should she be so beautiful and I so brown and commonplace—so ugly that a neighbor once said in my hearing, "What a pity that child isn't a boy!" Why should Virginia have every advantage of a fashionable school—she who cared much less for books than I—and I bind shoes?

A few natural tears welled up again, as I drew the contrast between my friend's lot and mine; but I would not allow them to attract Sophie's attention, so as to cloud this bright October day for her, dear child, and I replied as cheerfully as possible to her merry prattle; turned aside from the path to see if the robins had deserted their summer's nest, and to look for a tame squirrel's hole; gathered a pocketful of nuts for Willie, and a large clump of mullein leaves for mother—she said they were good for croup; and presently my careful thought for the happiness of others caused me to forget the disadvantages which my Maker had placed in my path, and I began to think of some blessings which even Virginia did not possess. She had no mother. Ah, what was comfortable poverty like ours to such a loss as that? and then she had neither brother nor sister. Would I exchange mine for all Squire Thornton's wealth? I said Virginia had no brother; Squire Thornton had had a son, but he had been a wild, reckless lad, and three years before had suddenly left Sherbrooke in a fit of passionate rebellion against his father's restraint, and had not been heard from since. Some of the villagers had been heard to say that Squire Thornton needed just such a heavy chastisement as the loss of his only son, else he would have grown too proud and overbearing in his great prosperity.

The memory of my blessings, and the healthful glow of my morning walk, had brought cheerfulness to my heart before I reached the kitchen, where during the remainder of the autumn day the angel of patience sat enthroned.

CHAPTER IV.

ALICE.

"Only three, just three short years,
Since she came to me,
Nestling in my heart and arms,
Oh, so lovingly!
Now the rain drops on her grave,
Sighing wearily."

FIFTEEN years ago we had only two mails a week in our pretty village of Sherbrooke.

The post-office was more than a mile from our farm, and it fell upon me to go for the treasures which the mail brought us, as Jonas Gould, our man of all work, could rarely find time for such an errand.

Once every week we were blessed with a letter from father; and then, how short the distance to our home, and how happy the hearts and bright the faces that gathered around the table while mother read aloud!

Before the waning of the harvest-moon we had heard of father's establishment in his professional duties in the town of Worthington, all about his boarding-place, and much about his pupils.

"'Tis a glorious country," he wrote; "and if my precious wife and children were only here, I could be almost as happy as in Sherbrooke. Such a soil and such a climate have made a rich and prosperous State.

"Perhaps the intelligence and energy of emigrants from our old Bay State have had something to do with the prosperity of Ohio. But we need more of New England's school-houses and churches, and I sometimes think more of New England's hills, to make this region home-like. Perhaps even the old farm on the south side of Sherbrooke hill would have to be removed here, with all its stones, to make a home for me. By the way, tell Jonas, if the weather is mild in November, after the harvesting is finished, I want the old rail-fence at the lower end of the pasture removed, and a stone wall built instead; the stones to be taken from the field where wheat was sown last spring; and if Hope chooses, she may transplant raspberry-bushes on both sides of the wall, to make it look like an English hedge."

The wall was built, and, with the help of Jonas, raspberry-bushes were planted before the hard frosts came. How happy we were in the execution of any work which father suggested, and how many little pleasant surprises we planned for him!

The grape-trellis was getting old and broken, and Jonas must contrive to make a new one during the winter; but, first of all, the ugly stained paper must be removed from our kitchen walls, and replaced with a pretty pattern, which mother had seen in Mr. Davis's variety store. We paid for the paper with the first-fruits of our needles, and mother, with my help, hung it upon our low walls. How admiringly we looked upon the work when it was finished, and fancied father's surprise when he entered the kitchen and saw the change! I love to linger upon those pleasant autumn days, for the first snows of winter brought us a great sorrow. I cannot think of it now, though my heart has since grown familiar with grief, without an overflow of tears. It was Saturday night, and dark, threatening clouds had shortened the December day. Twilight had come on while I was waiting at the office for the mail to arrive, and the mile, which was not short in summer, would be long and dreary enough in the wintry darkness. There had been a light fall of snow the week before, but it only served to make the stones and stumps in a pasture by the roadside look grim and ghastly. And the grave-yard, which I never liked to pass alone after the winds had stripped the trees of their summer verdure, how could I ever walk by it in the gray twilight, when the pale, faded leaves would be rustling around the lonesome graves? But that letter, in my father's dear, familiar writing, strengthened my heart and gave me courage. I ran, with almost breathless haste, past the old mill and the grave-yard, but the road seemed long, and tears of joy almost blinded me when I saw the light in mother's window.

I think I never crossed that threshold with such an eager, joyous step again. Bounding in, I exclaimed: "Oh, mother, I'm so glad to get home! You cannot think how dark and dreary it is."

Mother's raised finger, and her " Softly, Hope, softly!" arrested my loud exclamations, and I saw that little Alice lay in mother's arms in an uneasy slumber—a feverish flush on her fair, round cheek.

" Is Alice sick, mother?" I whispered, handing her the letter, which she only kissed and put in her pocket.

" She is far from well; but I hardly know yet what is the matter. She is hot and feverish, and her breathing is unnatural, and she has played but little since noon; but I hope she will be better when she awakes. If you are not too tired, Hope, you may help Sophie set the table; 'tis already much past the children's supper-time. What made you so late home?"

" I had to wait for the mail, and I don't like to come from the village after dark."

" There is nothing to be afraid of, Hope, though I'm sure it cannot be pleasant; but the days will soon be getting longer. If you will draw baby's crib softly into this room, I will try and lay her down without waking her."

Relieved of her precious burden, mother stood by the

crib and read aloud that welcome letter, so richly freighted with love and hope, while I placed upon the table our usual supper of bread, baked apples, and milk; and after partaking of it in a strange, unusual silence, I cleared away the dishes and prepared the children for bed, while mother sat and stitched by the crib, watching the restless tossings of the little sleeper. Already the shadow of a great cloud hovered over us, and the few words that were spoken before Alice awoke were in half whispers. Once mother, with a smothered sigh, exclaimed: " The wind is getting stronger; and hush! there is sleet dashing against the windows. I'm sorry that I allowed Jonas to go home to-night."

" Why, mother?"

" If Alice should grow more unwell, I may want to send for Dr. Blake."

And just then a louder gust of wind shook the blinds, and with a low moan our sleeper awoke. " Alice wants papa," she sobbed; and oh, how often during that long, long night did that plaintive wail fall upon our ears, " Alice wants papa!" or " Alice wants water!"

By midnight the storm was raging with great violence, and our darling's breath was drawn in shorter, harder gasps. Mother had tried every simple remedy which the house afforded for her relief, and at last with anxiety that was almost agony painted upon her face, she turned to me:

" Hope, could you go for Dr. Blake?"

" Oh, mother, in this dreadful storm? and it is so dark! I should die of fear."

" Then keep these flannels wrung out of hot water on baby's neck; I must go myself."

" Oh, don't, don't! You'll perish in this storm, and I can't be left alone with Alice."

Mother was already tying a hood over her thick shawl. " Hush! you must do as I bid you, Hope; I cannot sit here and see my child die, until I've tried every means to save her." And then in a softer tone, " Do the best you can for Alice, and I will be back in the shortest possible time ;" and kissing in passionate haste the little sufferer's forehead, eyes, and lips, she was gone—not waiting to answer my frantic entreaties that she would wait until daylight, or wait one hour to see if Alice would not be better. And alone, in an agony of self-reproach, I watched the sick child.

Mother was hardly beyond call when I would have given my dearest treasure to have gone in her stead, and each low, wailing cry of the child was as an arrow in my heart. What an experience of sorrow, contrition, and shame was crowded into that midnight hour! What scalding tears fell upon the child's face, and what a length of time seemed mother's absence!

Did my aching heart deceive me? or were those piteous cries for papa, mamma, and water, growing fainter and more infrequent? Was not that husky breath more hardly drawn! And oh, was there not a film creeping over those sweet blue eyes?

I had kept up a mechanical habit of prayer ever since I knelt at mother's knee, and repeated, "Now I lay me down to sleep," as Alice did only last night; but a real prayer for help was never wrung from my heart, till I bent by that little crib, and entreated God to keep that gasping life till it could be breathed out on mother's bosom. My prayer was answered, for soon my straining ears caught the sound of wheels, and the next minute an eager step, and a "Thank God! she still lives," and mother was bending over the crib. She soon gave place to Dr. Blake, who, with hands gentle as a woman's, applied the usual remedies for croup, but only to soothe for a brief space the agonies of that conflict; for when the first gray light of morning dawned, our pet blossom lay pale and withered in mother's arms.

And mother, she did not sob aloud nor complain; but as she laid her dead baby back upon its little bed, smoothing the golden curls from the fair forehead, and straightening the pretty round limbs, even my young eyes could see that the restrained tears were dropping down upon her heart.

Once, only once during that long Sabbath, did her calmness forsake her, and the waters of her grief escape in tears. It was when Mrs. Chapman had dressed our baby in her best frock and combed out the tangled masses of soft hair, and gazing upon the still face, exclaimed, "Oh, if her father could only have been here!" And again, when the first shovelful of earth was thrown upon her little coffin, then mother's sobs rent the air.

She was buried in the orchard, by the side of a large rock, and under the branches of a tree where she had played. Mother said it must be so; and how often during the winter would she drop her work and look from the window at that little mound! It was a mild, open winter, and the light snows drifted past the grave, leaving it brown and bare. Well, we picked up with many a tear the little half-worn shoes, broken toys, and soiled picture-books, and laid them away:

> Only these were left us now,
>   And the house so still!
> Every thing seemed asking for her;
>   And our hearts, so chill,
> Asked for Alice, never thinking
>   Of our Father's will—
>
> Quite forgetting that the angels
>   Took her home to God,
> Only Alice's body resting
>   Under the brown sod:
> Help us now in our great sorrow,
>   Christ, to kiss Thy rod!

And I'm sure He did help us, for before Sophie and I had found the first spring blossoms to deck baby's grave, we could all speak of her and repeat to each other her broken, lisping words, and even hum softly in the twilight her little silvery tunes—not without tears, but tears are not always tokens of that grief which presses most heavily upon the heart. My grief for our lost Alice was sharper and more poignant because of the memory of the great selfishness which permitted mother to go out in that midnight hour; and though she always spoke tenderly and forgivingly of my faults, they were bitter remembrances.

CHAPTER V.

FATHER'S LETTER.

"Oh, smite us gently, gently, God!
Teach us to bend and kiss the rod,
And perfect grow through grief."
T. B. ALDRICH.

How should father be told of the death of his youngest child? I think next to closing the blue eyes of her baby, mother's saddest duty was to inform father of her brief sickness and death. Oh, how hard, how very hard to send such news to a friend sojourning in a strange land! but with many a heart-ache, and many a tear, my patient mother accomplished her task; and then with how much anxiety she awaited his reply! A whole month must pass, so tardy were our mails at that time, before we could receive an answer to that letter, and meantime the intervening weeks brought his usual letters, filled with loving messages to all, "and a kiss for my baby," when that baby's dimpled cheeks could never more be kissed. It came at last. I brought it from the office in the twilight of a wintry day, and with many long pauses between the sentences mother succeeded in reading it to her children.

I shall transcribe it here, because every thing from my father's pen is precious to my heart:

"Worthington, Jan. 15, 18—.

"My Dear Celia,

"Last evening, returning from my school duties somewhat tired, and longing for my sweet wife and precious children, I found your letter of December 29th upon my table. With what a thrill of glad, grateful joy I broke the seal, but how soon was my gladness turned to mourning, my joy to tears! Why was our child taken when I could not be with you, to support and comfort you? When God took our little Harry, we were a mutual support to each other; we knew how with tender care to assuage each other's grief; but how could you, my dear wife, endure this great sorrow alone? Alone! no, not alone, for the Comforter was with you, and Christ had gone before.

"I am glad to know that so many of our dear friends offered assistance in that dark hour of trial; and that Hope showed herself so capable and trustworthy. And surely it is a pleasure to know that the sufferings of our baby were so short, and pleasant to think she is one of the little ones who always behold our Father's face. To-day I can see that our affliction was tempered with mercy, but last night every thing was dark. I could only remember that my lamb was slain, and I not there to lay it upon the altar; that my blossom had withered, and I was not permitted to inhale its last perfume; that my harp was broken, and its last quivering music fell not upon my ear. Always when thinking of you, patient and lonely, I have seen you surrounded by our dear children. Hope, thoughtful and womanly, our happy Sophie filling the house with sunshine and music, Willie trying to be a man for mother's sake, while Alice with her thousand little winning ways was beguiling your heart of its sadness. How plainly have I heard her sweet voice in my dreams, and now to think its music will never fall upon my ear again, that her bright presence will be wanting in our home, if I should live to regain its shelter; that her quick, eager feet will never more run to meet me! Oh, it is hard to kiss the rod, and difficult just now to believe that our Father doth not afflict willingly, nor grieve the children of men, or I should rather say, it was difficult last night, but this morning I trust that I have a better spirit, and can think of our child as purified from sin, taught by Christ, and rejoicing in the presence of God.

"And then, dear Celia, after a few more years of patient waiting, perhaps a few more days, we may behold our child—

"'A fair maiden in our Father's mansion,
Clothed with celestial grace
And beautiful with all the soul's expansion '—

"It seems as though Longfellow must have written his beautiful 'Resignation' expressly for us. Dear wife, do not remain at home too closely this winter, brooding over your grief and loss, but accept the kind invitations of our neighbors and friends. This I am sure is unnecessary advice, for your own good sense will teach you the advantage of healthy, active employment for your heart and hands in this hour of affliction. Since commencing this letter, I have received notes of condolence from Mr. Chapman, Squire Thornton, and our good pastor, filled with kind expressions of sympathy. You will find these gentlemen firm friends; if any new trouble should arise, do not hesitate to call upon them.

"And now, commending you and our dear children to God, who 'shall supply all your need according to His riches in glory by Christ Jesus,' and praying that we may have an eternity of bliss in His presence,

"I am always most tenderly yours,
"DAVID B. KENDALL."

I could not help noticing that after the reception of this letter, every one received from father made some allusion to his hope of joining Alice in heaven. And as winter wore away, and we almost counted the days of his absence— we were expecting him in May—he said less of his return; but nearly every letter contained some instruction and laid out some plan that would be for our advantage in case of his prolonged absence. "If I do not get home in May," he wrote, "Jonas had better plant corn in the field where potatoes grew last year. Tell him to ask advice of Squire Thornton about his planting, and be sure that he is in season with his early vegetables." Then came hints and directions about my studies, and earnestly expressed hopes that we might all be kept together, that the homestead might be redeemed in case he did not live to see it.

When mother read these sentences, she would brush back a few tears and try to say, cheerfully, that father was getting a little homesick.

So we stitched away through the winter months, while I made some progress in algebra and history, and read old English poetry under mother's careful eye.

Then we built such pleasant air-castles for the future— that future which is usually so rainbow-hued to the eye of fourteen, and the chief corner-stone, the foundation of each charming castle was father's return. If he returned, then perhaps I might join Virginia Thornton at school—if only that great debt could be lifted—and far away in the future, almost hid in a veil of silvery haze, I could see a piano for Sophie, and I am sure our hearts could echo during that winter the beautiful words of Whittier:

> "Behind the cloud the starlight lurks,
>   Through showers the sunbeams fall,
> For God, who loveth all His works,
>   Hath left His hope with all."

CHAPTER VI.

AUNT LYDIA.

> "She stood straight and calm,
> Her somewhat narrow forehead braided tight
> As if for taming accidental thoughts
> From possible pulses; brown hair, pricked with gray
> By frigid use of life."   MRS. BROWNING.

I CANNOT tell you about my Aunt Lydia and her visit without revealing one fact in our family history which might else have remained a secret. My father's wife was my step-mother—my own mother, in as fond, as true, and as tender a relation as ever blessed a child.

My father's first wife lived only long enough to look upon my face, and pray for God's blessing to rest upon me. Before the close of my third summer, my father brought home his second wife, and bade me call her mamma.

I have but dim and indistinct memories of her bright face when she first lifted me to her lap, but I do remember that warm tears fell down upon my face when she kissed me, and that she murmured in a low, broken voice, "Father, help me to be true, loving, and faithful to my child!" I might not have remembered her first prayer, had I not so often heard it repeated as she knelt by my little bed. How

I loved my pretty, new mamma, and how that love strengthened with my growth, I will not tell you now, but will try to show you what a patient, self-sacrificing woman she was, and then you will see that I had abundant reason for my love.

Aunt Lydia was a sister of the mother whom I had never known. She had visited us rarely, for her home was distant more than a hundred miles, a formidable journey, made by stage fifteen years ago. Six years had passed since her last visit; and now, in answer to my mother's letter, telling her of Alice's death and father's absence from home, we had received from her an intimation that she would attempt to cheer our loneliness with her presence. We might look for her the first Tuesday in March.

I heard something like a sigh after mother had finished reading the letter, but she only said: "I am sorry that your aunt should take the time of your father's absence for her visit."

I did not ask her why she would prefer that my aunt should visit us when father was at home, for I did not remember that her last visit had given any of us pleasure. There was nothing attractive about Aunt Lydia to my childish eyes, and then she had taken undue advantage of my simplicity to question me about family matters, and my revelations had got me into disgrace with my father. He had called me " Silly goose," and " Tell-tale," and I knew Aunt Lydia was the cause of my trouble.

March came; and it seemed as though its chilling north winds might have blown Aunt Lydia straight from some frozen region into our home; only that my watchful eyes had seen her alight from the stage at our door with a large trunk, carpet-bag, and bandbox.

She was a most respectable looking person, as she stood there with the lingering sunset rays upon her slightly-frosted hair, assisting the stage-driver to find several bundles.

You could see that she was business-like and energetic, by the way that she paid the driver and gave him directions in removing her property into the house; you would know that she was neat and economical by the well-kept bonnet and cloak, which, from their fashion, must have seen already several years of service; and you would feel sure that she was critical by the keen, quick glance from her small black eyes, which looked as if they read a whole history of poverty, debt, and want of thrift, as she entered our kitchen:

> "Eyes that once might have smiled,
> But never, never have forgot themselves
> In smiling; cheeks in which was yet a rose
> Of perished summers."

And Aunt Lydia stands before us! Mother extended a most hospitable welcome to her guest, and hastened the preparations for the evening meal, remarking to Aunt Lydia that she must be tired and hungry after so long a ride.

"How far have you travelled to-day?"

"Only from Northville. I spent last night with Cousin Samuel's folks."

"And found them well, I hope?"

"In tolerable health, but poor. Samuel works hard; but there's a great leak somewhere. Are you making that tea for me?"

"Yes; for you and myself. I like a cup at night, but the children prefer milk."

"'Tis better for them; where are they? I haven't kissed them yet."

It was my mission to urge their reluctant feet forward. Sophie advanced shyly, offering her fair cheek for Aunt

Lydia's dry salute, and demurely answering her questions; but Willie required some forcible persuasions before he would accept her proffered kiss, and resisted most ungallantly when she attempted to lift him upon her lap.

"Ah, poor child, he has forgotten Auntie!" and an audible sigh escaped.

"He's a bashful boy; and then, you know, he was only a babe when you were here last.".

"Yes, I know, but Hope doesn't seem very glad to see me; I suppose you remember your aunt, child?"

"Oh, yes, very well. I was eight years old when you came to see us before."

"Then you must be fourteen now, almost a woman! Well, to be sure, how time flies! Come here, child, and let me see if you look like your mother."

I advanced a few steps, feeling uneasy under her searching gaze.

"You're more of a Kendall than a Hastings in looks; the eyes are like your father's, but you have Emily's hair and features."

And turning me toward the western window to complete her survey, she added: "You are much too brown; your mother was fair, with a beautiful color. What a pity 'tis that you cannot remember her, child!" Here another sigh escaped from some unfathomable depth, but mother, in cheerful tones, announced supper, and tried to divert her visitor's thoughts from unpleasant themes.

Supper over, the dishes washed, and the children in bed, I saw, with unpleasant forebodings, mother take up her basket of shoes, and drawing forward her small work-table, commence her accustomed stitching. Aunt Lydia's keen eyes were busy. "Do you make your own shoes, Celia?"

"No; these are sale shoes."

"You do not mean to say that you are obliged to do such work?"

"Perhaps there is no actual necessity for me to do it; I dare say we should have enough to make us comfortable if I sat still; but I have plenty of leisure, and I like to feel that I am helping David."

"Does David need any help in supporting his family?"

"He would not if we were free from debt. When that day comes, I can lay aside my needle, if I choose."

"How came David to get in debt?"

"That expensive sickness of mine that I wrote you about prevented him from teaching for nearly a year, and the farm never did yield enough for our support."

"Dear me, what a pity! I have such a horror of debt; but what sent David away from home? I never heard that he was gone until you wrote last month."

"He was offered a good situation in Ohio, and as he could earn more there than at home, he thought he could sooner redeem the farm by going."

"Redeem the farm? Goodness! Is there a mortgage on it?"

"Yes."

"For how much?"

"Five hundred dollars, and interest for three years."

Such sighs; such exclamations of pity; so many "Oh's!" and "Dear me's!" but mother sat quietly stitching upon her shoes, while I bent my crimson face over the chapter of history which I was trying to commit; and Aunt Lydia went on sighing, and commenting upon poverty in general, and ours in particular.

"How shocking! a mortgage for such a large amount on this old farm, that Emily was so fond of. Does David expect to redeem it?"

"He hopes to do so."

"Well, I never knew a mortgage cleared off, never! There was the old Bates farm in Hebron. Joseph was a thriftless fellow—lived high, drove a fast horse, mortgaged the farm his father worked so hard to pay for, and now the Bates girls are working in a factory to support their mother. And then there was the old Shelby place, had been owned by the Shelbys ever since the last war, until Tom got to speculating, and mortgaged it to raise money; and now they've moved to the city, and take boarders for a living!"

And Aunt Lydia enumerated several other cases, with dolorous sighs and interjections, all tending to show that a farm once mortgaged was lost. I thought of Job's comforters, but gazed steadily upon the page before me.

"I see you are not wearing mourning for Alice. Couldn't you afford the expense?"

"Not very well; and my friends all know that our sorrow is as deep as if we gave it an outward badge."

"But it looks so strange and odd! Now, as a family, we are all very particular about mourning. Why, I wore black three years after Emily died, and mother and I wore it quite as long when father died; and brother John has buried five children, and I always wore a black gown and bonnet at the funeral, and for several Sundays after. Is David willing that you should go without it?"

"I have not told him that we do, but I know he thinks very little of fashion in such a case."

"Well, I'm glad if you can afford to set at defiance the customs of society; for my part, I shouldn't like to be thought so singular." And then followed a list of Aunt Lydia's friends, who did or who didn't wear mourning, and what people said, together with a score of torturing questions about Alice's sickness and death; until at last mother's heart, so full of tears, overflowed, and bending her head upon her work-table, she wept in silence while Aunt Lydia poured forth what she termed the consolations of religion, by repeating such passages as—"The Lord gave and the Lord taketh away." "He doeth all things well." "As for man, his days are as grass; as a flower of the field so he flourisheth."

I listened to Aunt Lydia's hard, dry tone, as she repeated texts of Scripture; and I noted the look of satisfied self-approval on her face, and thought it was lip-service only which she rendered to her Lord; that her heart was a stranger to the beauty and inspiration of the words she quoted, and she never gave me cause in after-years to change the opinion formed that evening.

"Ay, nine o'clock, is it? Well, Hope, get me a candle. I'm tired, and then I always go to bed at nine; I'm very particular in all my habits. Shall I take the south chamber that I used to occupy?"

Very particular—how tired I used to be of Aunt Lydia's assurances that she was very particular! but she need not have taken the trouble to repeat it so often; the fact announced itself in the pinning of her collar, in the fit of her dress, in the precise folding of her work, in the cold, measured words she used. How it fretted my proud, impatient spirit to be told a dozen times each day that I walked too fast, and spoke too quick, and laughed too loud—that such manifestations of temper were unbecoming —all Kendall—no Hastings ever spoke or acted as I did; and then with a sigh she would exclaim, "Who'd think she was Emily's child?"

She always improved every occasion in mother's hearing to comment upon Emily's beauty, her sweet disposition, and my father's great love for his first wife. And my mother would listen with moistened eyes, never appearing to suspect that Aunt Lydia's words were intended to disturb her peace. She had married David Kendall with a full knowledge of his first love, and her heart was satisfied; while I believe my father could say, with Bayard Taylor:

> "No treason in my love I see,
>   For treason cannot dwell with truth,
> But later blossoms crown a tree
>   Too deeply set to die in youth.
>
> "The blighting promise of the old
>   In this new love is reconciled;
> For when my heart confessed its hold,
>   The lips of ancient sorrow smiled."

CHAPTER VII.

MARCH.

> "And in thy reign of blast and storm,
>   Smiles many a long, bright, sunny day,
> When the changed winds are soft and warm,
>   And heaven puts on the blue of May."
> BRYANT.

THE week after Aunt Lydia's arrival brought one of those delightfully clear days, when the March sky " wore the blue of May," and a look of kindly promise. Mother, glad of an excuse, I think, to leave for a couple of hours the stormy, March atmosphere which her visitor had brought to our kitchen, had prepared herself to go with Jonas Gould to the woods to assist in tapping trees, for the farmer's maple-sugar harvest was at hand. She had given me leave to accompany her, and we were standing in the old porch, hooded and cloaked, watching the loading of the sled with buckets, auger, axe, spouts, etc., when Aunt Lydia appeared.

"Where are you going, Celia?"

"To the maple-grove with Jonas, to assist him in tapping."

"Can't Jonas do such work without your help?"

"Perhaps he could, but not as easily."

"Then why not hire a man to help him?"

"I cannot well afford to; and besides, a couple of hours spent in this bracing air will do me good; I have often been with David to the woods."

"But of what use will Hope be?"

"There is no great need of her help. Hope, we can do the work without you, and you may remain at home to keep your aunt company."

"Oh, do take me along, please; I helped father last year, and I know just where the best trees are—better than you or Jonas."

"Waal, I reckon she does, Mrs. Kendall; she has a famous eye for picking out the best maples, and can do e'enamost as much of this kind of work as a man," said Jonas.

Aunt Lydia gave him a look from her black eyes which was intended as a rebuke for his interference; but the look was lost upon our good-natured Jonas, who, with a broad smile upon his honest face, called out, "All ready! jump aboard, Hope."

"You are brown as a nut now, Hope, and this March wind will spoil your complexion; stay at home, and read to me."

"I can read to you this afternoon; I haven't been to the woods since last November, and I want to go with mother."

"Very well; if you prefer the woods to my company, you can go, but 'tis very hard to travel a hundred miles to visit my only sister's child, and then find her so unwilling to oblige me." And Aunt Lydia walked back to the kitchen with an injured air, while mother came forward and placed her hand upon my arm, saying gently:

"Hope, you are not in a happy mood now; deny yourself this morning's pleasure, and go in and be social and agreeable to your aunt."

"I don't like Aunt Lydia, and I don't care to please her; she is always saying something to arouse my temper, and then she reproves me for my Kendall spirit."

"Hush, child, don't speak in that way. Bear with your aunt's peculiarities kindly and patiently, and you will find it a useful discipline. She is a well-meaning woman, and desires only your good. And now that I think of it, Hope, you can help me more by remaining in this morning and finishing those shoes, than you can by going to the woods. Then I shall be tired when I get back, and you can have dinner all ready for me. You know you must go to the post-office and factory this afternoon, and if you go to the woods you will be too tired for so long a walk."

"I shall stay if you wish it, mother, but I have a great dread of Aunt Lydia's remarks and questions."

"They are not always agreeable to me, but I try to remember that I too have traits of character which may be quite as unpleasant to some people as Aunt Lydia's are to me. Your father was always forbearing and patient with her."

Here Jonas again announced his readiness to depart, and I watched them move away, wondering who could ever detect faults in my dear, patient mother;-but after some minutes, remembering her counsels, I walked reluctantly back to the kitchen, where Aunt Lydia sat with a grave, reproving face. She was knitting. I had noticed, several times, that when she wished to show her displeasure, she made her knitting-pins fly with a sharp, monotonous click;

they might be heard in any part of the room when I entered, but not wishing to quarrel with my aunt, and my feelings being somewhat softened by mother's words, I asked her what she would like to hear me read.

"Nothing. I never wish to trouble anybody." Click, click, snap, snap, went the pins.

"Oh, I thought you wished to hear reading; but I'm glad you don't, as mother wanted me to finish this work."

"So you only stayed at home to please your mother?"

I made no reply, for certainly I had not remained in because my aunt desired it; but taking my basket of shoes, sat down to my stitching. A half hour passed, interrupted only by questions from Sophie and Willie, who were busy with their morning lessons. But a half hour was a long time for Aunt Lydia's tongue to rest, and Sophie's question about the Geysers in Iceland afforded a favorable opportunity to break the silence.

"Why doesn't Sophie go to school?"

"She isn't strong enough to walk so far; the school-house is a good mile from here."

"You walked that distance at her age."

"Yes, but I was strong and healthy."

"No more so than Sophie would be, if she were not spoiled by petting and indulgence."

I bit my tongue to keep it quiet, while Sophie's large blue eyes expressed surprise and wonder.

"How long since you have been at school?"

"Not since last summer."

"Well, it seems a great pity that a niece of mine should be growing up in ignorance, but I may as well be silent. My counsels have been set at naught ever since your father married again. Does he know that you are kept out of school?"

"Yes; he thought I had better study at home this

winter. You know mother is an excellent teacher; much better than they have in the village school."

"You get but very little time for study, with all your stitching and the care of those troublesome children."

"But I do study several hours each day, and mother never allows me to sew more than two hours at a time."

"She ought not to allow you to sew at all on such heavy work, and wouldn't if you were her child; it will make your hands coarse and rough. I didn't expect to find you so neglected: my only sister's child, that I've always looked upon as almost my own, kept at home to work, and deprived of all advantages that other girls enjoy."

Now I had a laudable pride in the proficiency I had already made in my studies, and pride in my mother's ability to teach; so I replied, somewhat hotly, "You are mistaken, aunt; I am not kept at home to work, and I am a better scholar than any other girl of my age in the village; much better than Virginia Thornton, who is a year older."

"Be not wise in thine own eyes, Hope; I'm sorry to see that you haven't conquered your Kendall temper. It is a great pity that you couldn't have had your mother's sweet disposition; but then a great deal may be owing to your bringing up."

"No girl ever had a better bringing up than I've had, and if my own mother was like you, I'm glad that I'm all Kendall."

My temper had reached a crisis, and, angry with myself for being unable to control it, and ashamed of speaking so disrespectfully to my aunt, I burst into tears. Sophie, not fully comprehending my trouble, leaned her head upon my shoulder, and wept in sympathy; while Willie, understanding just enough to think Aunt Lydia was in fault, shook his dimpled fist and thrust out his dumpy foot, muttering something about being a man.

This was more than the patience of a maiden lady, not particularly fond of children, could endure; and rising, she shook the young offender most vigorously, reseating him with a blow upon his little shoulder, which he bore like a hero, refusing to shed tears in the presence of his enemy, though I could see that his lip and chin trembled in his efforts to restrain them, but showing his Kendall temper by a flushed face and pouting lips.

Aunt Lydia's knitting-pins were clicking louder than ever, and my furtive glances at her face showed me that it wore a look of injured innocence. My own conscience condemned me for the last words I had spoken, but I could not ask my aunt's pardon while she wore that look, so I stitched on in silence till it was time to hear the recitations of the children. Their lessons over, Sophie and I prepared our early dinner.

How like a golden beam of sunshine upon an angry cloud was mother's face, when she came in from the woods, with a basket full of mosses, pine-cones, and evergreens! With what a cheerful, musical voice she exclaimed: "Jonas and I have had a delightful morning's work! I wish you could all have been out in this bracing air; the smell of the pines and spruces was better than medicine for me. If Sophie and Willie have been good children, they may go with me to-morrow. How is it, Aunt Lydia; do they deserve such a favor?"

"You had better ask Hope; I do not know what you would call good."

Mother turned her bright face to me with a questioning look.

"They have both had good lessons, mother; and Sophie has been a good girl; but I'm afraid that Willie and I have displeased aunt."

"Afraid! it is little you care whether I am pleased or not," said my aunt.

"Indeed, I'm very sorry, aunt, that I spoke to you in such a hasty way; and I think Willie is sorry for his naughty conduct."

But Willie, busy with a block house, made no response, and mother asked how he had offended.

"Oh, no matter now; I shall lay up no hardness against either of the children; but I would advise you, Celia, to take that boy in hand; he is getting to be very rude, and I should think him quite old enough to be taught respect for his elders."

"I have tried to teach him that; but you know children need many a line and many a precept, and then often go astray."

"I reckon, if the lines and precepts were sometimes enforced with the rod, they would not be so often forgotten. 'Chasten thy son while there is hope, and let not thy soul spare for his crying.'

Mother made no reply; but during the remainder of the day we both tried to amuse and conciliate her, and had the satisfaction before night of seeing her face assume a softer aspect. We knew she was in a more gracious mood, by the gentler click of the knitting-pins.

CHAPTER VIII.

FAILURE AND DISAPPOINTMENT.

"Count each affliction, whether light or grave,
God's messenger sent down to thee."

WE had many quiet, simple pleasures during the season for gathering sap; many days when a walk over the hard, crusted snow to the woods sent the blood in quicker, stronger pulses through our veins, and brought us forgetfulness of our petty cares and monotonous round of duties for a brief hour. Even Aunt Lydia had been persuaded more than once to put on thick wrappings, and, screening her face from all contact with wind and sun in folds of green barége, to go with us to the woods, "just to see if that awkward Jonas Gould hadn't spoiled the syrup by some carelessness."

She had plenty of advice to offer about the clarifying process, which Jonas did not always accept as submissively and gratefully as he might. He was a shrewd Yankee, and "guessed he knew a few things as well as most folks."

"Jonas, you ought to put the whites of at least six eggs in that kettle of syrup, to make it look clear and nice," said Aunt Lydia, as she watched the maturing perfections of the "sugaring off."

"Yes'm, I have, and a pint of milk too."

"I shouldn't have advised putting in milk, but there are some folks who don't ask nor take advice. You had better tie a string to a piece of salt pork and hang it to the bail of the kettle, so that when the syrup boils up it may just touch the pork; it will prevent it from boiling over."

Jonas muttered something about "the syrup all turning

to vinegar if her face hung over it much longer," and moved away to gather more sap.

And one bright morning Virginia Thornton, who was at home for a week's vacation, went with us to the woods, and returning spent the day in our kitchen, rehearsing the incidents of her school life. "We have such capital times at Irving Hall, that I'm always wishing you could be there, Hope," she said; "and oh! have I told you that Prof. Steinman says I shall excel in music? I'm very glad, because father will be pleased to have me excel in something."

I forgot for a moment our poverty, and exclaimed, "Oh, mother, don't you think it possible for me to go to Irving Hall next autumn?"

"It may be possible, Hope, but I do not think 'tis probable."

"But if father should be very successful, don't you think he can contrive a way?"

"You had better not think about it; make the most of each day's leisure, and you may possibly keep up with Virginia in every thing but music."

"Yes, indeed," quickly responded Virginia, "I should never go to school if I had a mother who could teach me at home, and then you know much more than I do now."

I made no reply, for I had become aware of the increased, ominous click of Aunt Lydia's knitting-needles, and felt sure that the severe look upon her face could only dissolve in words.

"No, Hope, you must not expect to go to school, nor to make any improvement at home; such ceaseless fagging and waiting, and so much running in the pastures and woods, never did make a lady of anybody yet, and never will."

"Aunt Lydia, don't discourage Hope," softly interposed mother.

"I had no intention of discouraging her, but I can't endure to see my sister's child nursing expectations that can never be realized. 'The wisdom of the prudent is to understand his way;' and it is better for Hope to know now that she is being fitted only for kitchen service, unless her mother's friends interfere. I should have offered her a home before this, where she could have the privilege of a good school, only that I knew she had been taught to look down upon her aunt as an old-fashioned, meddling woman, who had no right to offer advice."

The color that mounted quickly to my mother's forehead, and the light that flashed for a minute in her gray eyes, was more eloquent than words, and I saw that the strongest effort was necessary to keep her tongue from adding fuel to the fire. No bit or bridle could longer restrain mine, especially when I saw the look of surprise and astonishment on Virginia's face.

"You know very well, Aunt Lydia, that I study every day, and only work when I choose, and have no more exercise than I need, and no one can better teach me how to be a lady than my mother; father says so, and you know it."

I stopped for want of breath, when my aunt, with her most aggrieved look, as if she were unconscious of having said any thing to draw me out, replied:

"Very well, Hope, go on in that strain, and show Miss Thornton your lady-like training, and your Kendall temper. Show her your usual respectful manner of treating your aunt, and then ask her if she does not think a school might improve you. But, poor child, you have been neglected so long, that I'm afraid it would only be wasting my money to send you to school now." Aunt Lydia raised her handkerchief, to intimate that pity for me was moistening her small black eyes—eyes that had not been bedewed with drops of compassion and kindly charity for years, if ever.

"You have never thought of spending a cent of your money upon me, Aunt Lydia, and would see us all go to the poor-house before—"

Here my mother's hand was laid upon my mouth, and gently leading me from the room, she left me without a word, in the old porch with the gentle wind fanning my anger-flushed face.

A few minutes of calm reflection, with the memory of mother's reproving look, were quite enough to alarm my conscience and show me the wickedness of giving my passion the reins, and soon my hot temper had cooled under the influence of a shower of tears.

I had not been a half hour in the porch when Virginia came out, bringing my hood and cloak, followed by mother with a bundle of shoes, which must be returned to Mr. Clark that evening. She came to my side, and without appearing to notice my tears, moved the hair from my forehead in a gentle, caressing way peculiar to herself, and speaking in soothing, cheering tones, said:

"Hope, you may walk to the village with Virginia; 'tis the night for the mail, you know: go in and sit an hour with her, but return before dark."

I obeyed gladly, and soon the sprightly conversation of my friend, and the brisk walk in the open air, had changed my tearful mood to one more in harmony with the out-door world, though I could not rally my spirits to their usual buoyancy, nor forget that my besetting sins, pride and temper, had conquered me in the presence of my—friend, had gained a victory over many sorrowful, prayerful struggles.

Virginia had often walked with me as far as the door of the factory, but I had never asked her to enter, and did not wish her to this evening. When we reached the building she laughingly said, "I am going to have a sniff of your leather, so don't forbid me to enter."

Mr. Clark was in his counting-room, and made an effort to greet Virginia in a gentlemanly style. A curtly "good-morning" or "good-evening," was all the notice he had deigned to offer me for several weeks, and I greatly preferred his curt manners to his oily blandness.

I laid my bundle upon Jenkins' desk, who examined and paid me for the work, but did not bring forward any more shoes; so I ventured to speak:

"Mr. Clark, have you any more work for mother?"

"No, none at present; our business is falling off, and we cannot employ so many hands; sorry not to oblige you, but reckon your mother must find some more genteel work to do; this stitching will spoil your pretty hands. Good-day, Miss, I'm too busy to talk, but call again in the course of a month and we'll see what can be done for you. Good-day, Miss Thornton."

I plainly heard a coarse laugh follow our retreating footsteps. Tears of wounded pride and disappointment struggled to escape, but with a great effort were choked back; at fourteen, pleasure, sorrow, and anger alike caused the fountain to overflow. I was grieved and disappointed for mother's sake, as I knew she had counted upon our earnings during the spring to replenish our summer wardrobes, hoping that every dollar of father's salary might be used in paying off the mortgage. And then, I was annoyed because Virginia had heard our application refused by such a commonplace man. It was hard to ask a favor of one whom I regarded as an equal, but vastly more difficult to humble myself before an inferior. I had been taught to regard intelligence, moral worth, and good manners as the true basis of aristocracy, and I knew Mr. Clark possessed none of these. A little shrewdness and good luck had brought him wealth, for which he was barely tolerated in those circles which would have passed him by but for the glitter of his gold.

"I hope you do not mind the loss of work," said Virginia, as we moved toward her father's door. "I am afraid mother will be sorry," was the only reply I dared make, lest my friend should see how great was my disappointment.

Squire Thornton was at home, and greeted me cordially. He was a fine-looking, well-preserved man of fifty. Prosperity had not hardened his naturally kind heart, nor lifted him above sympathy for those less fortunate than himself. Perhaps the sorrow and disappointment caused by the waywardness of his only son had filled his heart with a more kindly charity for all.

He was in a particularly genial mood, and the cause of it was soon revealed.

The State Legislature had granted a charter for the continuation of a railroad, which would pass through Sherbrooke; and, moreover, a State loan had been secured, through the influence of himself and Mr. Chapman.

"But why are you so much interested and pleased, father?" inquired Virginia, after Squire Thornton had explained the difficulties that had been conquered in obtaining the charter and loan.

"Because the railroad will bring us so much nearer a large market, and make the products of our farms so much more valuable, and then Sherbrooke must be the shire town of our county before many years. We have a petition before the Legislature now, requesting the removal of the county buildings here, but do not expect our request will be granted before another winter, when we hope to hear the whistle of the steam-engine in our own village. Tell your mother, Miss Hope, that the name of David B. Kendall is talked of for registrar of deeds, and he'll get the appointment, too, if Mr. Chapman's influence and mine are worth any thing."

How grateful I felt for this bit of pleasant news to carry home that evening, for the letter we had so confidently expected did not come! I had never returned from the office empty-handed before since my father went away; and with two disappointments, no letter and no work, tugging at my heart, I should have made a sorrowful entrance into our kitchen, but for the kindly sunshine of Squire Thornton's message.

I tried to answer mother's eager questioning glance cheerfully, as I laid aside my wrappings, saying, "No letter to-night, dear mother; but I dare say there will be two next week."

A shade of sadness crept over her face, and a half sigh escaped from her lips, but she did not speak. She was standing by the window that overlooked Alice's grave, and watching the last lingering rays of daylight that rested upon it. I shall never forget how sweetly calm and patient was her face that night, nor how great the contrast it presented to the hard, querulous, world-soured visage of Aunt Lydia.

"No letter! Well, dear me! disappointments come to us all, sooner or later," sighed my aunt. "Most likely David is sick and couldn't write, or maybe he's dead! I had a strange dream only last night. I saw David as plain as day with Emily on his arm, looking, for all the world, just as they both looked the summer after they were married. Emily was in white, and they were coming toward me; 'tis a sure sign of disappointment or death to dream of persons coming toward you. I am always warned in a dream before a death occurs in our family. I remember now, as clear as can be, that I dreamed of seeing Emily riding toward me on a great white horse, only the week before she died; and I heard father call me, the night he was lost at sea, as plain as ever I heard a human voice."

At this point Aunt Lydia's voice became husky, and her spotless handkerchief was slowly drawn from her pocket and pressed to her eyes.

"I do not believe in warnings nor dreams, Lydia," said mother; "and though 'tis a sad loss to miss one of my husband's letters, I shall trust that some accident has deprived me of it, until I know certainly that his dear hand did not write it. I never like to borrow trouble."

"One would suppose you had enough without borrowing; but then I've always noticed that troubles, which would scarcely bend one person, would break another. Now I was in hysterics a whole night after Emily died, and it took two strong women to hold me in bed, and I've never recovered my spirits since." Here the handkerchief was again used as a shield for her eyes; and thinking the silence that followed favorable for opening my budget of news, I told of the projected railroad, the prospect of Sherbrooke being the shire town by another winter, and wound up with Squire Thornton's message.

Before I had finished speaking, Aunt Lydia's handkerchief had disappeared; and ere the pleasure which dawned in mother's face had time to form itself into words, my aunt had drawn a veil between us and hope's sunshine.

"Don't go and build any flimsy air-castles now, Celia, because of Squire Thornton's idle words. Wait until Sherbrooke is really the shire town and you see its county buildings, and above all, wait until you see David before you count upon his acceptance of office. Remember that 'the talk of the lips tendeth only to penury.' For my part I'd rather see David handle a shovel and spade all his life than dabble in politics or fish for office; you may mark my words, if he accepts of office, he'll never redeem the farm, never," and her words were rendered doubly emphatic by the sharp click of her needles.

I knew that mother's heart was struggling with no slight disappointment as she moved about, making preparations for our evening meal, but only a nice ear could have detected any suppressed grief in the tones of her voice, which were generally so cheery and genial. Even then I admired the heroism of her quiet heart, which could so unobtrusively thrust back its own sorrows, and, while bitterly aching under its burden, scatter upon all a fragrance as of crushed flowers. I did not fully comprehend how "her crucible of pain was watched by the tender eye of Love."

CHAPTER IX.

FORESHADOWING OF GRIEF.

> "'Tis very true my grief lies all within,
> And these external manners of lament
> Are merely shadows to the unseen grief,
> That swells with silence in the tortured soul;
> There lies the substance."
> — SHAKSPEARE.

ONE, two, and three mails had brought their treasures to Sherbrooke, and I had walked home empty-handed to see mother's eager, anxious face grow sorrowful, and to hear Aunt Lydia's prognostications of evil. April looked hopeful with her glintings of bright sunshine, her soft showers, and swollen buds. We had heard the robins sing, had found a few spring flowers; had noted that sunny banks wore a pale tinge of green, while a whisper of summer's promise seemed borne upon the winds; but this whisper did not bring its wonted joy and buoyant hope to our hearts. A cloud hung over the homestead, which the April sunbeams could not scatter.

It came at length—that letter. I saw the driver throw off from the coach the old black leather bag. I saw the postmaster adjust his steel-bowed spectacles to examine its contents, and I heard him say, "A letter for your mother, Hope Kendall." Hastily seizing it, I gave one quick glance at the superscription. It was not father's writing, but my young heart would not draw the darkest inference from that fact; he might be ill, or an accident might have deprived him of the use of his right hand; the letter would explain. Oh, yes, I must hasten home with it; but a strange, dizzy faintness had seized me; I nearly stumbled over the old horse-block by the office door, and must have fallen in my eager haste, if Mr. Chapman had not held out a hand to support me, and leading me across the way to his own door, he lifted me to a seat in his chaise, only saying, "My horse is harnessed, Miss Hope, and as you are not looking quite well and 'tis beginning to rain, I shall take you home; I have wanted to see your mother for several days."

He did not speak after I had shown him the handwriting on the letter which I held, until we reached the farm-house door, and then lifting me out, he said, "I must drive a little further up this road to make a business call, but tell your mother I shall drop in to see her in the course of an hour."

The sound of wheels brought mother to the door; there was no need of question from her: one quick, eager glance at my pale, hopeless face showed her that I was not the bearer of good news. Oh, how hopelessly she sank down on a seat in the old porch; what utter desolation there was in her colorless face; what a weight of misery in the sobbing, despairing cry, "My Father, prepare me for the worst!"

Flinging my arms around her neck, I cried, "Read the letter, dear mother; it may not be as bad as we fear." The sight of her grief had loosened my tongue, and I persuaded her to break the seal.

"Ah, no! 'Tis not as bad as I feared; your father has written himself—how nervous and foolish I've grown, to be so frightened because he did not direct it! Here 'tis, 'My dearest wife,' in his own writing," and mother pressed the words to her lips. "Let us go in and read it to Aunt Lydia and the children; but oh, Hope, I've had such a fright! I do believe it would have killed me, if there had not been one line from your dear father." Mother stopped to fold me in her arms before we entered the kitchen. I knew then that I shared largely in her love because of my resemblance to my father.

Sophie and Willie hung upon mother's knee, and I looked over her shoulder while she read:

"WORTHINGTON, April 4, 18—.

"MY DEAREST WIFE:

"You will be pained to know that I have been seriously ill. I was attacked with pleurisy three weeks ago to-day, and have suffered so much as to be unable to write before—"

"I told you he was sick," Aunt Lydia broke in upon the reading.

"Yes, but he's better now, almost well," answered mother, and resumed her reading:

"I am afraid you have been very anxious because of the failure of my letters; but I thought it best not to alarm you, by allowing some one to write in my stead. The attack was a most violent and dangerous one, and leaves me very weak—too weak to write all I wish to say to you.

Much as I know it will grieve you and the dear children to know of my illness, I think I ought to tell you now that I've had a bad cough for more than three months, but have kept on with my teaching until this attack of pleurisy. Dr. Sharp says I have some very alarming symptoms, though he's not without hope that I may recover, but he thinks I can never teach again. Oh, how I long to see you all, but when shall I be able to travel! The most trifling exertion brings me that troublesome pain. Celia, I need your strong, comforting, encouraging presence now; you know I am always despondent and low-spirited when I am ill. In my weakness and pain I fear I shall never see you again; but strange and incomprehensible as it may appear, a sweet peace almost invariably steals into my heart after these hours of depression, when God and heaven seem very near. Never has my faith been so strong, and whatever the result of this sickness may be, I know that every thing will be ordered in love and mercy.

"But if it be God's will that I linger here several weeks, unable to teach or to travel, do you think it would be possible for you to come to me? If not, then do not be anxious, for I have a most excellent nurse in my kind hostess, Mrs. Hill."

A postscript was added the next day by Mrs. Hill, who said her boarder had had an uncomfortable night, and the doctor had forbidden him to finish the letter.

Mother folded the letter and leaned forward upon the table, burying her despairing face in her clasped hands. Sophie wept in silence, and Willie, awed and sobered, but scarcely comprehending the cause of her sadness, attempted to comfort her in his childish way. Aunt Lydia essayed to offer consolation in her rasping, stereotyped manner.

"Don't give up till you know the worst, Celia. David is a Christian, and 'all things work together for good to them that love the Lord.' But God moves in a mysterious way! I should never have advised David to go so far from home and into such an unhealthy region too, but my advice wasn't asked. Why, even the water is so bad there that the kettles have to be burned out once a year to purify them, and I have seen ears of corn turned to stone by being in the wells for a few months." Aunt Lydia's emotions required the use of her handkerchief at this point, and the silence that followed was soothing, but of short duration. Such an opportunity as this for my aunt to show her aptness in quoting and her superior wisdom rarely occurred.

"Let me look at that letter, Hope. Dear me! 'a bad cough,' and his father's family were all consumptive—neglected, too, I dare say, when a little syrup of squills and spearmint might have cured it in the beginning. Men never will take care of themselves; like as not David forgot to put on his winter flannels. 'An attack of pleurisy!' Why, Sarah Fletcher died of that! and it almost always proves fatal, sooner or later."

"Don't, Lydia!" moaned mother,

"Well, I think 'tis better to be prepared for the worst. We never know what a day may bring forth. But what will become of his poor children?"

Another silence followed, broken by what was intended for a sob behind the handkerchief, and then came some of her favorite quotations: "One generation passeth away and another generation cometh, but the earth abideth forever." "And I said, Oh, that I had wings like a dove, for then would I fly away and be at rest." And with my heart aching and torn, my aunt's manner of quoting so exasperated me, that I could hardly refrain from wishing aloud that she had the wings, and would use them in such a way that we should find rest.

Mr. Chapman's entrance put an end to the quotations and dismal forebodings for a brief space, and caused mother to raise her face, upon which the last month had written so many anxious lines. I would rather have seen it bathed in a torrent of tears than have noted its quivering muscles, the dark rings beneath her eyes, and the hopeless expressions of each feature. "I was wishing to see you," she said, with forced calmness, as she exchanged greetings with her friend and kinsman: "I need your advice. We have heard from Mr. Kendall, and he's not well. Perhaps you had better read the letter; Hope, give it to Mr. Chapman." He read it without comment, and returning it to me, walked to the window, and looked out into the drizzling darkness. Mother was the first to speak.

"You see he has been very sick; but Dr. Sharp says there's hope, and perhaps you remember that David has had a cough before. Yes; he coughed last winter, and had a slight attack of this pain, but he said 'twas caused by fatigue; and I dare say this attack will pass off, if he has judicious treatment." Mother made a sickly attempt to smile, and look around upon us cheerfully.

"We will hope for the best," answered Mr. Chapman, but his words were hastily clipped by Aunt Lydia, who narrated with tedious minuteness the particulars of Sarah Fletcher's death, winding up with another quotation and sigh: "Our days are like a shadow that declineth."

No one replied to Aunt Lydia, and mother spoke again: "I must go to my husband, Mr. Chapman, and I must start to-morrow. Can you tell me just what route to take, and give me such directions as I need? I have never travelled alone."

Mr. Chapman, who had scarcely spoken since reading the letter, now turned from the window and addressed mother:

"It happens very fortunately for us both, that I have business which would take me to Buffalo in May; and since I came in I have been thinking the matter over, and have concluded that I may as well start to-morrow as to wait a couple of weeks, if I can get Squire Thornton to look after my business here. Perhaps I can make it convenient to go as far as Worthington."

Mother rose, and with a look which expressed a volume of thanks, she gave her hand to Mr. Chapman, saying, "We start to-morrow, then. At what hour?"

"As early as eight, to be in season for the boat; and as we shall both have many things to attend to, I will say good-night! Keep up your courage; 'tis never well to anticipate evil."

Mr. Chapman had hardly left the room, before mother was actively engaged in preparing for her journey, regardless of Aunt Lydia's remonstrances, who declared that "packing could never be done decently in the night—that mother needed a whole week to make preparations for such a journey—that David would be ashamed to see her in such commonish clothes—that the children would be sure to get sick in her absence—that Jonas could not attend to the planting without her—and finally, that she was a most unnatural mother to leave her children in such a way, and very disrespectful to her sister-in-law, who had travelled a hundred miles to see her." And then Aunt Lydia took refuge behind her handkerchief, and mother, with trembling hands, quivering lips, and eyes that looked like deep fountains of tears, went on with her preparations, only pausing to say:

"Why, Lydia, I can leave home more readily because you are here to look after the children, and be company for them; you would not have me remain away from David when he asks me to come. Jonas will do very well on the farm with Squire Thornton's advice, and Hope is so careful and womanly I can leave the children with her. You can spare me to go to your father, my child?"

I did not venture a reply; but I think mother must have seen registered upon my face the firm and courageous spirit, resolved to be her patient help and comforter at all times; for she drew me to her, and looked fondly into the eyes so like her husband's, kissing me as if to place a seal upon the unspoken contract.

How clearly comes up before me now the memory of that April evening, which formed one of the stepping-stones of my young life; I can hear the pattering of the soft spring rain upon our kitchen windows, and above all, the subdued, tremulous voice of mother, as she knelt in prayer; each petition knocks at my heart again, though her voice has been raised to God in my behalf many times since then.

It was late before every thing was in readiness for her journey, and then mother and I sat for a long time over the dying embers on the hearth, talking over the family interests, listening to the rain, and vainly trying to lift from each other's heart the heavy cloud.

CHAPTER X.

ONLY WAITING.

> "One, whose feet the thorns have wounded, passed
> that barrier and came back,
> With a glory on His footsteps lighting yet
> the dreary track."
>
> BRYANT.

THE April morning dawned brightly, bearing on its wings a faint perfume—a foreshadowing of coming flowers. Mr. Chapman came early in the carriage that would take himself and mother to the neighboring city. Very few words were spoken, but the embraces were long and tender, and I was glad to feel warm tears drop upon my hair and face, as mother held me for a moment locked within her arms, for I knew then that the first despair of her grief was softened, and that hope and faith were nestling in her heart.

We watched the carriage disappear around a bend in the road—Willie swinging on the gate, and wishing that he were a man, so that he could go along to take care of mother; while Sophie held my hand and vainly tried to hide the tears that obscured her vision.

Jonas, with an awkward air and troubled face, looked intently at the horse-shoe, which his strong arm had flung after the retreating carriage, to see if it had fallen on the side which betokened good luck to the travellers; and picking it up, he hung it carefully over the entrance to the porch.

Aunt Lydia, standing upon the steps, scolded Jonas for his foolish superstition, and me for remaining in the wind without a hood or shawl, and Willie for swinging on the gate. And coming in I took up the burden, heavy for a girl whose fifteenth summer was just dawning, and which must be borne alone in mother's absence, for who ever went to Aunt Lydia for sympathy? Advice she could give, and did give most freely; but I should pity the desolation of that heart which sought relief in my aunt's consolations. There was nothing done in the house or upon the farm, during the long month which followed that spring morning, but Aunt Lydia was ready with advice or remonstrance.

Jonas, instructed by mother and advised by Squire Thornton, gave no heed to her counsels. Hardly a day passed without an open altercation between them, but the shrewd, strong-willed workman was sure to come off victor.

"Wa'al, I guess I've a mind of my own," he would exclaim, "and don't need no telling. Ef I hain't planted as many pertaters and beans as most any man of my age, I'll give you my Sunday hat."

So hearty was his dislike of her, that I think if he had commenced planting potatoes in a field, and found that she approved, he would have altered his course and sowed wheat instead.

And it was little better within the house; Aunt Lydia was sure to rouse opposition in the children by proposing something different from what they were engaged in. If Willie were drawing pictures upon his slate the noise of the pencil disturbed her, and "Why couldn't he build a block-house in the porch?" The dispute was usually ended by my aunt, who would forcibly thrust him out of the kitchen, and then came a retreat behind her handkerchief.

If she saw me engaged in one kind of work, she invariably thought of something more necessary to be done; and though I would make brave efforts to keep my tongue quiet, alas! I am sorry to record that sharp, angry retorts often escaped my lips, almost always quickly followed by bitter, penitent tears. And when I begged my aunt's pardon, how very hard it was to listen to her favorite admonitions.

"Hope, that Kendall temper will be the ruin of you. Solomon says, 'Put away from thee a froward mouth;' and again, 'He that being often reproved, hardeneth his neck, shall suddenly be destroyed;' remember that, 'Whoso keepeth his mouth and his tongue, keepeth his soul from troubles.'"

If I had not so often heard my dear parents quote the precious words of the inspired writers, my aunt's frequent and ill-timed quotations would have fostered in me only dislike for that Book which has since become my wellspring of joy and consolation.

The days crept slowly on and the old earth put on a mantle of tender green to welcome in the May; and then the green grew deeper and the cherry, plum, and peach trees threw out their delicate, fragrant blossoms, mute expressions of spring's glad rejoicing.

How cheerfully we tended the tulips, daffodills, and pansies, in fact every spring flower that father loved, for my hope that he would return to the homestead was almost assurance. And while the breath of the apple-blossoms still lingered, and their snowy leaves lay upon the orchard grass and little Alice's grave, he came.

We had been looking for Mr. Chapman's carriage all the afternoon. He had sent orders for it to meet him in Wiltshire, and though he did not say that our parents would be with him, yet I had no doubt but his prolonged absence was an indication that he was awaiting the slow movements of an invalid.

He came—but oh, how changed! I caught a glimpse of his worn face and sharp features while Mr. Chapman and mother were assisting him from the carriage to the house, and I knew he had come home only to die. I could not speak to him then, with Mr. Chapman, Aunt Lydia, Jonas, and the children looking on, so I stole away to my own little room, where my tears might flow without adding to the grief of those I loved.

It was a dark hour, and my young heart was struggling with a great sorrow—all the bitterness and desolation of final separation swept over me, and I had no strength to contend against its deep waters. I lay for a long hour with my wet face pressed against my pillow, until I felt mother's cool fingers upon my forehead drawing the hair away with her tenderest caress.

"Hope, my child, you will make yourself ill, and then you cannot help nurse your father. Why did you run away here without speaking to us?"

"Oh, mother, I saw his face, and it was so changed."

"Poor child, and the great change brought you a knowledge which proved too much for your strength as it did for mine. But, Hope, look at me; the agony and weakness of my heart have given place to patience and submission. I count it a blessed privilege to be near your father and be taught resignation by him. He is so calm, so blissful in looking forward to an exchange of worlds, that we must not disturb him with our grief."

"But, mother, he cannot take us with him."

"No, but God will take us in His own good time, and the separation will be short. Come, Hope, your father has asked for you, and if you remain away longer it will grieve him."

That thought gave me strength to rise, bathe my tear-stained face, and follow mother to the kitchen, where father sat in a large easy chair, propped by pillows, and looking out on little Alice's grave, upon which the lingering, golden light of day was still resting.

I came and knelt by his side and hid my face in his lap before he was aware of my presence. He bent his lips to my hair and laid his thin, hot hand upon my head, while he breathed in a low and tremulous voice a short prayer. And then, after a minute's silence, he said in soothing tones, "'He shall cover thee with his feathers and under his wings shalt thou trust; his truth shall be thy shield and buckler.' My child, can you say that God is my refuge and fortress?"

"Oh, father, I try to love and trust Him."

"But is there no beauty and comeliness that you should desire Him?"

"I think I see the beauty of His character, but if He is infinite in goodness and infinite in power why does He so afflict his children?"

"Shall we receive good at the hands of the Lord, and shall we not receive evil? If only prosperity attended us here, we should never desire a higher, holier state of existence. I think I can look back upon what have seemed to me great afflictions, and recognize in them God's loving, merciful hand drawing me nearer to Himself. And I trust you will be able to regard this illness of mine as one of your stepping-stones to greater faith and purer love. Raise your head now, my child, I want to see what changes the months have made in you."

My father's wishes were always my law, and as quickly as possible I obeyed him, putting on the most cheerful look I could command.

"A little taller and a little fairer, with quite a thoughtful, womanly face for such young shoulders," he said, as I stood before him. "But you are too much of a Kendall still to please your aunt, I presume."

"I can never please her, no matter how hard I try."

"Your mother says you have been sorely tempted, and have sometimes yielded; but she says you have always had the grace and discretion to confess your faults, and she thinks you have struggled bravely to conquer your temper. I have a great many things to say to you, Hope, when I am sufficiently rested; but as I cannot talk any more to-night, you must leave me with your mother."

The June roses bloomed and faded, and, greatly to the surprise of Dr. Blake and our kind neighbors, our dear invalid lingered with but little apparent increase of weakness.

Indeed, there were a few days when he seemed stronger, and would take short walks and drives, and then his uniform cheerfulness often caused the breath of hope to flicker in our hearts.

Oh, if I could only record the gracious words that fell from his lips during these weeks—all intended to prepare us for the separation and soothe us for the loss; they are engraven upon my heart with a diamond point, but their chief interest and beauty could only be felt by those who knew and loved him.

Even Aunt Lydia was awed and subdued by his serene and cheerful trust, so that she rarely gave utterance to her dark forebodings and dismal quotations in his presence.

And mother watched over him with such calm patience, and even cheerfulness, that strangers would never have thought the light of her life was growing dimmer each day; but I knew that her grief was thrust out of sight and locked in her heart by her strong womanly will, that it might not disturb the quiet repose of father's last days.

August came with its sultry heat, and still father sat in his easy chair by the open door, and watched the reapers as they garnered the golden grain—too weak to walk or

4

ride now, but so quietly gliding down the dark river that we could not hear the ripple of its waves.

He had been talking even more cheerfully than usual; had called our attention to the rich, mature beauty of the summer day, and the waving grain, and then had repeated some lines, one stanza of which I remember—

> Summer speaks of those fair mansions
> Where there is no night;
> Where the beauty and the verdure
> Ne'er are touch'd with blight.

"Ah!" he exclaimed, "if such beauty crowns our summers here, what must be the glory of that city which hath no need of the sun, for the Lamb is the light thereof."

After a few minutes of silent meditation he spoke again, his wan features lighted with a celestial radiance. "Celia, the everlasting arms of mercy are around me!" Mother answered only with a smile; but when he closed his eyes again, I saw that mute despair and agony were stamped upon her face. Still, for some minutes she held his hand in silence, when, suddenly throwing herself forward upon his breast, she exclaimed, "He is gone!"

So noiseless was the approach of the death-angel that we knew not of his presence, and only mother had noted the ebbing of the life-flood from the hand she held.

He was gone, and the birds sang on, and the perfume of honeysuckle floated in, and the golden light of the setting sun bathed that dear, silent, pulseless form, all unmindful of our great sorrow, but from our hearts all beauty, fragrance, and sunshine had fled, I thought then forever.

I did not know that God could bid a new life bud and blossom over the ashes of our buried joys and hopes.

CHAPTER XI.

AUNT LYDIA'S OFFER.

"Sorrow must cross each passion-shoot,
And pain each lust infernal,
Or human life can bear no fruit
To life eternal.
For angels wait on Providence,
And mark the sundered places,
To graft with gentlest instruments,
The heavenly graces."
DR. HOLLAND.

THE great blow had come—the choking stupor of the hour had passed. We had seen my father's comely form laid beneath the apple trees, and had yielded to the tender, softening memories of our grief. The cares and burdens of life must be taken up and cheerfully borne for the sake of the living, and also in obedience to that honored voice, which had so faithfully endeavored to prepare us for this hour.

It was the evening after the funeral, when our kind neighbors and friends had left us alone with our empty home and aching hearts, when Sophie and Willie, worn out with sobbing for a loss which they could scarcely comprehend, had fallen asleep, and mother and I sat in silent thought, that Aunt Lydia, in her new bombazine dress, came in and seated herself near us. Her cambric handkerchief, with its deep mourning border, was freely used for a few minutes, and then, with a deep preparatory sigh, she spoke:

"Sorrow is better than laughter; for by the sadness of the countenance the heart is made better. Well, it's a comfort to think that every thing passed off so well. Mr.

Eveleth made some excellent remarks and a most touching prayer."

Mother grasped my hand, and leaned forward to hide her face, but made no response.

"It is a great consolation to know that every thing was done to make David comfortable and soothe his last days," added my aunt.

Now, deep as was my grief, and tender as was my heart at this hour, I could not but remember how little Aunt Lydia had done to relieve my dear father's suffering, or lighten mother's cares, and I could not help questioning her right to gather consolation from the fact that he was most tenderly cared for by others.

She had worn a flannel saturated with camphor around her neck, and had carried bunches of tansy, wormwood, and peppermint in her pocket to ward off contagion, and had advised me to do the same, as she knew "consumption was catching." Moreover, she had avoided coming into the room, where father usually sat as much as possible, only when she could make a display before visitors. The silence was again broken by my aunt. "I've made you a long visit, Celia; and as I can't do any thing more for David, perhaps I had better go back to Hebron."

"Do what will be most agreeable to yourself, Lydia," answered mother, without raising her head.

"I let my farm to Adoniram Staples for a year when I came here, and I don't suppose I am needed at brother John's. However, I have a house, and money enough laid up in the bank to afford me a comfortable living, only it is rather hard, at my time of life, to live alone, though to be sure I may marry. It is plain to be seen that my mission here is ended."

Mother was too truthful to attempt contradicting the assertion, or to ask her visitor to remain longer.

"Hope, you are an orphan now," said my aunt, after a short silence, which had been interrupted only by her own sighs, "and you do not need to be told that you are poor, and will soon have no shelter for your head, unless your mother's relatives provide for you."

"Lydia, she is as dear to me as either of my own, and will always share my home."

"Let Hope decide for herself. She is old enough to know that she has no natural claims upon you, and that a home shared with you must be one of hardship and poverty. There's a good school in Hebron, and if she will go with me she shall have a chance to educate herself and be somebody. I'll treat her as if she were my own child, for Emily's sake. Speak for yourself, Hope."

"Your aunt has made you a kind offer, my child, and her home in Hebron will possess many advantages. Make a choice without thinking of me."

"Oh, mother, I cannot leave you and the children. Father told me to try and be your help and comfort."

"You had better not decide to-night," said my aunt; "take time and think over the advantages of a good education and freedom from household drudgery and shoe-binding. I shall not go until next Monday, so there'll be time enough for you to make a decisisn. I think, Celia, we had both better leave Hope to choose for herself without influencing her. A girl of fifteen should have a mind of her own."

"Certainly," answered mother, rising and kissing me in her accustomed way of bidding good-night; "I will leave her free to choose; Hope knows my love will remain unchanged, whether she goes or stays." And mother left the room, while my aunt, regardless of the tacit compact which had just been made between them, approached and touched my cheek with her thin lips, a most unwonted caress for her to offer, and I felt the cold hand tremble which she laid on mine.

"Hope, what would your own mother say, if she could speak to you now? Would she not bid you accept a home with her only sister? You know I've told you how she put you in my arms when she was dying, and I named you by the last word which she uttered, thinking it would comfort your father; and I feel as though I had a right to claim you now."

"I think my own mother would tell me to remain with one who has in every way filled her place. You know, Aunt Lydia, that my step-mother has been loving and patient with me, and my father wished me to remain with her."

"But your father did not know what my intentions were. I did not tell him that I meant to adopt and educate you, because he was so weak and nervous when he returned that I thought it best not to disturb him; and then your step-mother had such unbounded influence over him, that she would have persuaded him to refuse. She cannot afford to lose your services, now that you are so capable and strong. Do you think your own mother would keep a girl of your age binding shoes when she ought to be in school? There, Hope, we'll say no more about it to-night, but to-morrow, after careful thinking, you will be able to decide."

My aunt left the room without giving me time to answer, and I sought my own couch with a disquieted and heavy heart.

For a long time conflicting emotions and desires kept me awake. I had often heard the school in Hebron spoken of in terms of commendation. My father had been preceptor there many years before; and my aunt's insinuations had filled me with doubts as to the utility of the education

I was receiving at home. Then I had always felt a strong repugnance to binding shoes, and had never taken kindly to the homely duties of housework. My dislike had been concealed as much as possible for fear of troubling mother.

Aunt Lydia promised freedom from these disagreeable employments; though knowing her habits of strict economy, it was natural to suppose I should be required to aid in performing the work of her household. Had not my nearest relative, my mother's only sister, into whose arms I had been placed, a wailing, helpless infant, had she not a right to claim a portion of my time?

But if scarcely a day of her long visit had passed without my temper becoming ruffled by her tongue, how could I become a dependent upon her bounty?

"No!" I mentally exclaimed, "rather bind shoes all my life than accept Aunt Lydia's charity. She would be sure to remind me of my dependence every day in her most irritating manner."

And then came up pleasant and soothing memories of the tender care which had ministered to my childhood—the love which had so patiently borne with my faults and aided me to correct them—the sweet companionship of the last year, like that of elder sister and mother blent in one. And could I leave my little sister and brother, when my dear father, only the week before he was taken from us, had said, "Your example as an elder sister, Hope, will have a great influence over the children; be faithful and tender to them, and loving and dutiful to your mother. She will find this world a weary place when I am gone."

With such memories fresh in my heart, how could I help deciding to share my step-mother's fortunes, even if ignorance, poverty, and labor were my only heritage?

The breath of the new day awoke us to a consciousness of burdens which must be taken up. There were many things besides that fresh mound of earth under the apple trees to remind us of our great loss—many things made sacred by his touch which must be gathered up and laid away, only to be looked at and wept over in secret; and some things to be kept just as he had used them, that we might feel his presence constantly with us. The Bible he had used for daily study, his escritoire and a few favorite books, must remain in their old places.

I can never forget the calmness and patience which marked mother's face, as she moved about gathering up these sacred relics, occasionally dropping a few silent tears upon some familiar article that seemed almost a part of him who had gone, but never giving away to violent grief.

And for many weary months after this day the pallor of her face and the dark rings around her eyes, when she joined us in the morning, showed that the larger part of her nights were spent in a sharp conflict with sorrow.

I dreaded an interview with my aunt so much that I kept as near mother as possible during the day, intending to have the support of her presence when I was obliged to give my decision; and the twilight had gathered, and we three were alone again, before Aunt Lydia found an opportunity to question me.

"Well, Hope, I am waiting to know if I shall have you for a companion in my pleasant home," she said, laying down her knitting, and fastening her sharp eyes upon me.

"I am much obliged for your kind offer, Aunt Lydia, but I prefer to live with mother."

"But I told you last evening that Mrs. Kendall would soon have no home for herself and her children, much less one for you."

"Then I can help her make a home; I am young and strong."

"No doubt she'll accept of your strength quick enough, but I wouldn't be a willing drudge for any one. I shall consult a lawyer to-morrow, to see if your mother's relatives haven't a right to interfere."

"You can ask Mr. Chapman; he is my guardian, and knows it was my father's wish that I should remain with mother."

"What did you want of a guardian?" asked my aunt in an exasperated tone.

"David thought it best that his daughter should have the advice and lawful protection of his faithful friend. Perhaps he anticipated some such emergency as this," mother answered in low, quiet tones.

"Very well, Miss Hope, you may abide by the choice you've made, and never apply to me, even if you haven't a crust to eat, nor a shelter for your head. You are a most ungrateful child, and blind to your own interests. But I know whose influence has prejudiced you against your mother's sister."

A hot, hasty reply was just bursting from my lips when I met an appealing look in mother's eye, and choking back my anger, I said:

"I do not mean to be ungrateful, Aunt Lydia, but I cannot leave mother and the children; and besides, I am afraid we could never live happily together. You know how my quick Kendall temper annoys you."

"'Foolishness is found in the heart of a child,'" answered my aunt, "'And anger resteth in the bosom of fools,' but I did hope that I might be allowed to make something of my sister's child."

The black-bordered kerchief was here used as a defence behind which to retire while she rallied her forces, and the silence that followed was welcome as the hush of a summer twilight, but of short continuance

"Solomon says, 'Make no friendship with an angry man,' and I believe you are right; we could not live in peace while your temper is so unbridled, and I suppose your faults have been neglected so long that it would be nearly useless for me to attempt to correct them. I see plainly that I'm not wanted here, and I would start tomorrow, only people will think it strange if I go before the Sabbath, as of course Mr. Eveleth will preach a funeral sermon, and ' it is better to go to the house of mourning than the house of feasting;' but I shall leave on Monday."

During the remainder of her stay, my aunt's face wore its most severe and injured expression, and she rarely spoke, unless some occasion for quoting a proverb or worn-out maxim occurred.

Mother maintained toward her, as usual, a quiet, polite demeanor, while I tried to be particularly attentive, so as to soften, if possible, any disappointment I might have brought her.

But, I think, it was a welcome hour to us all, when her trunks, bundles, and prim figure were finally adjusted in and upon the old stage-coach, and the horses were cheered into a brisk trot.

I am sure that Jonas Gould failed to throw a horseshoe; and notwithstanding the sorrow which had shadowed his face of late, a most satisfactory smile lighted it as he gazed after the retreating stage. "I guess as how she wouldn't come again in a hurry, if she waited for my asking," we heard him mutter, as he closed the gate, and took the path to the wheat-field.

"Has she gone a long way, mamma?" asked Willie.

"More than a hundred miles."

"I hope she'll not come again till I'm a man."

We dared not give utterance to Willie's wish in words, but I'm sure they found an answering echo in my heart.

Before the last of that summer's flowers were faded, I could more clearly understand the loving Providence which makes—

> "The springs of time and sense
> Sweet with eternal good."

CHAPTER XII.

THE OPENING WAY.

> "She asked for patience and a deeper love
> For those with whom her lot was henceforth cast,
> And that in acts of mercy she might lose
> The sense of her own sorrow."

SQUIRE THORNTON had extended the time of redemption on our farm before father's death; and when the expenses of his illness and travelling had been paid, there was left of his salary, while in Ohio, but a small sum. With this mother had paid the interest on the mortgage, and bought us decent mourning. She had yielded to the prejudices of Aunt Lydia and the neighbors, who thought outward badges of mourning absolutely necessary when a family was bereft of its head.

Then came anxious thoughts for the shelter and daily bread of her children. And perhaps it was well that, during the autumn and winter that followed father's decease, mother's sorrow was somewhat absorbed in anxiety for her family.

Had there not been a multitude of perplexing cares about the present and future of her children to occupy her thoughts, she might have been crushed by the weight of her grief; but when the necessity for exertion was so great, her woman's will locked up her sorrow in a secret chamber of her heart as a luxury too expensive for use, when poverty must be met and grappled with; it was only brought out and wept over in the silence and darkness of the night.

But "grief hallows hearts, e'en while it ages heads," and there was a sweet purity, an utter forgetfulness of self in mother's character after the plough-share of grief had passed through the tender soil of her heart, which wrapped her about like a mantle, and brought forth an abundant harvest of kind words and charitable deeds. She came forth from her crucible of pain stronger and more beautiful in spirit, as every sick, destitute, and neglected person in Sherbrooke knew, before the pitying earth had covered with grass and flowers her husband's grave.

She made the memory of father fragrant and precious to his children by keeping constantly before them his many Christian virtues. "Praising what is lost makes the remembrance dear."

We had not asked for work at Mr. Clark's factory since early in the spring; but as mother looked forward to winter and saw the numberless wants of her family, she decided to make another effort to obtain shoe-binding.

And the October sun looked down upon us and the faded forest leaves through a soft yellow haziness quite in keeping with the melancholy of the days and our hearts, as we threaded the familiar path through the woods to that disagreeable factory. I was accompanying mother uninvited, bent upon sharing whatever annoyances might beset her; and as we walked along, I could not help contrasting my present emotions with those of one year ago. Then I had regarded the application as degrading, and my proud heart had rebelled against the hard requirements of poverty. I had looked enviously upon the ease and luxury of the Thorntons, Chapmans, and Blakes. But the discipline of the past year had taught me lessons of self-control, humility, and content. I had learned to recognize His hand, who made me to differ, to accept His appointments with simple, unquestioning faith, and to believe that if He hedged up our paths with obstacles, He would, in His own good time, lead us into green pastures. The windows of my heart had been opened to the gentle, revivifying influence of that charity, "which hopeth all things, endureth all things."

We found Mr. Clark in his counting-room, bustling and noisy as ever; and though he tried to assume something of his first condescending suavity in his greeting of mother, it seemed an ill-fitting cloak.

"How d'ye do, Mrs. Kendall, how d'ye do? haven't seen you for several months," was the greeting of the manufacturer as we entered, but I anticipated no good from his uneasy eye and the constant rubbing of his hands.

Mother gave him a simple, quiet answer, and her pale face, deep mourning, and subdued tones seemed to touch for a moment, with something akin to kindly feeling, the yellow, sapless substance that served him for a heart, for he jerked out with some difficulty: "Sorry for you, ma'am; your loss is one the whole town feels. A nice man, a very popular man was Mr. Kendall; should have called upon him when he was sick, but was full of business—and then I didn't think he'd go so soon—run down very fast, didn't he, ma'am?"

Mother murmured something in reply, but her trembling voice and downcast eyes, from which no tears were allowed to escape, deterred him from offering any more sympathy.

"You know we are in embarrassed circumstances, and there is an urgent necessity for us to do something for our support—" Mother was interrupted by Mr. Clark's "Sorry to know it, ma'am, very sorry: hoped your husband had been lucky enough to pay off that mortgage. He must have earned something handsome in Ohio, didn't he?"

"He was not able to teach quite six months of the time he was absent; and his sickness, and the expense of going and coming, consumed the larger part of his earnings. I called this evening, Mr. Clark, to see if you could furnish us with any more work?"

"Sorry, ma'am, but am afraid we can't. Business dull—market full—lots of old hands can't be employed; like to oblige you, ma'am, but it isn't quite the genteel thing for ladies like you to bind shoes: ha, ha!"

"We did not look at the gentility of the work, but simply at the honesty, and our necessities."

"Well—sorry to disappoint you, ma'am: times may be easier in the spring, and then we may want more hands. Good-day, ma'am, good-day;" and Mr. Clark bowed us out of his dingy counting-room, with a great diminution of the politeness which he showed a year before.

I think, if we could have lifted the veil of the future for a moment, and seen Mr. Clark, after the lapse of a few years, a cringing, crest-fallen applicant for our bounty, we should not have left his factory with a more independent tread, even though a bitter load of disappointment lay heavily on our hearts.

We turned to take the by-path through the woods, not because we had any hateful bundle to conceal—how gladly would I have carried a bundle of shoes up the main street of our village that day!—but because the faded forest leaves seemed to rustle in harmony with the subdued and tender memories of our grief.

We had not left the main road, when Mr. Chapman's pleasant voice was heard, calling mother's name. He came up, and, holding a hand to each of us in his pleasant way, said:

"I'm glad to see you out, Mrs. Kendall; the air of this charming Indian summer day must do you good. Mrs. Chapman and I were intending to call upon you this evening, to talk over a little matter of business; but, if you can spare the time, turn back, and we will talk it over in my parlor."

We were soon seated in a pleasant, handsome room, chatting with our kind friends, with an ease and freedom which seemed to me almost marvellous after our recent rebuff.

As I listened to the quiet tones of Mr. Chapman, the easy and intelligent flow of his words, and remembered the abrupt, bustling manners, and broken sentences of Mr. Clark, I could not help making a comparison in favor of the dignified Christian gentleman.

Mrs. Chapman was genial and motherly, not as intelligent and polished as her husband, but possessing a large fund of good common sense. They had two children. William Carey, the eldest, usually called Carey, out of regard for his mother's most excellent family, was studying in a German university. I scarcely knew him, so little had he been in Sherbrooke since he first entered college; but Maria was the friend and playmate of our Sophie, and was often at our farm.

After an abundant exchange of kind inquiries about family matters, harvesting, etc., Mr. Chapman asked mother if she had any leisure time to dispose of.

"I have leisure which I am very desirous to turn to good account. You know so well the circumstances in which we were left, that you do not need to be told that I am anxious to be earning something. I have met with a severe disappointment this very afternoon. Mr. Clark told me that he had no work to give us."

"I am sorry you asked him, Mrs. Kendall; he is a hard, over-reaching man. I have a plan which will be more profitable than binding shoes, if you are willing to assume the care which it involves. Did you ever hear your husband speak of an old college friend by the name of Mayhew?"

"The lawyer who settled in Philadelphia, and married a beauty and an heiress?"

"The same. I met him in Wiltshire yesterday, and he told me that he was just ready to sail for Europe with his wife, whose health is delicate. He has two children whom he does not wish to take abroad, and he is desirous of placing them with some person of intelligence and refinement, who can instruct them, look after their manners, and, in short, be a mother to them for the next two years. He had made arrangements to leave them with his sister, who lives in Wiltshire, and would have been off by the last steamer, if she had not been thrown from a carriage, and so seriously injured that she cannot take charge of her nieces."

"Why does he not put them in a boarding-school?"

"I asked him that question; but both Mr. and Mrs. Mayhew think their girls too young for school; they are only ten and twelve years of age. I spoke of you to their father, and he was so much pleased and interested in what I said of you, that he is going to drive his wife over here to-morrow to call upon you. I know Mayhew is able, and will expect to pay liberally for the board and instruction of his daughters. How does the plan look to you?"

"If I had confidence enough in myself to think I could make them a pleasant home, Mr. Chapman, it would appear an easy and agreeable way of supporting my own children. But you know that I have not sufficient knowledge of music and French to teach them, and those branches would be considered most important by your city friends. Then my house, and whole style of living, is so simple that I much doubt if I could make them feel at home."

"I would trust you for that, Mrs. Kendall," said Mrs. Chapman; "there's nobody on earth I'd as soon my Maria should live with, if I was going to Europe, which, thank Fortune, I'm not. Why, Maria is as fond of you as can be, and is always teasing to spend a day with Sophie."

"I am very grateful for the kind opinion of you both," said my mother, rising to go, "and I shall look at this plan in all its bearings."

"Remember that Hope is old enough to lend you a helping hand in this enterprise. She is growing to look more like her father," added Mr. Chapman.

There were pleasant last words and good-byes, and then we were out upon the street again, taking the highway, because of the rapidly waning light.

"Yes, I'm sure I could lend a helping hand, mother," I said, after we had walked for several minutes in silence on our homeward way.

"Ay, Hope, then you think favorably of Mr. Chapman's plan?"

"It will make you a great deal of work, and add to your cares; but I've been thinking in how many ways I can help you."

"Just like my thoughtful child; but tell me some of the ways."

"Why, I can keep their room in nice order, and look after their clothes, and take them out for walks and help amuse them."

"You can certainly do all you have said, and if I decide to take them, I shall make great claims on you for assistance. But they are probably petted, spoiled children, and would subject us to many annoyances."

"Yes; but would there not be some pleasure in helping correct their faults, and a great deal in teaching them? It seems to me a much more agreeable way of earning money than binding shoes."

"I think it would please your father better. Oh, if we could only consult him in such an emergency as this!" But, alas! we already knew that—

> "We may call against
> The lighted windows of thy fair June heaven,
> Where all the souls are happy, and not one,
> Not even my father, look from work or play,
> To ask, 'Who is it that cries after us,
> Below there in the dusk?'"

CHAPTER XIII.

THE MAYHEWS.

> "It was late in mild October, and the long, autumnal rain
> Had left the summer harvest-fields all green with grass again;
> The first sharp frosts had fallen, leaving all the woodlands gay
> With the hues of summer's rainbow, or the meadow-flowers of May."

THE home so dear and valuable to us never looked to me so humble and commonplace as it did that morning we were expecting the Mayhews. Then I saw that the ceilings were low, the furniture old-fashioned and simple, and the walls brown and bare; and I began to fear that Mr. Mayhew would desire a more stylish boarding-place for his children. But as I looked about I gathered hope from the consideration that every thing was neat, and that if we had no pictures upon our walls, we had charming views from our windows, painted this morning " with the many tints of the season gay."

The day being mild, I had the vanity to open the door of our best room, which had been rarely used since mother had dispensed with a servant. This room opened out of our pleasant, tidy kitchen, and its floor was covered with a well-preserved carpet. It had a straight-backed sofa, a few prim-looking chairs, a well-filled book-case, and a small table upon which stood a few simple ornaments. One engraving, the pride of our home, representing Mount Vernon, hung upon the wall.

After throwing up the window, that the fragrance of the late honeysuckle and the ripening grapes might enter, and placing upon the table a basket of the purple fruit and a vase of asters and autumn leaves, I waited with restless expectation the call upon which so much depended.

It was near noon when Willie announced the approach of two carriages.

"They've stopped at our gate, mamma;" he called. "One is Mr. Chapman's chaise, but the other I don't know." A minute more, and mother had welcomed her guests, and was performing the duties of hospitality with the ease and self-control of a gentlewoman.

"You have a fine prospect here," remarked Mr. Mayhew, declining the proffered seat, and remaining near the open door. I could see at a glance that he was a gentleman, and his remark gave him a high place in my estimation, for not to have admired the view that I regarded as so charming would have been an unpardonable breach of good taste.

"What mountains are those on the left?" he asked; and mother being engaged in conversation with Mrs. Mayhew, I stepped forward, and answered:

"They belong to the Berkshire range, sir."

"And that sheet of water?"

"Is Cameron pond."

"This pretty village in front is Sherbrooke, of course?"

"Yes; and away to the right, where you see a steeple, is North Sherbrooke."

"Chapman, a man might travel a long way, and not find so charming a picture spread out before him as may be seen from this door."

"I have always thought the scenery in this portion of our State remarkably fine, and artists are beginning to find it out: there were a couple from New York here, making sketches, last summer. Mrs. Kendall has one of the pleasantest situations in town."

"I should think it must be," answered Mr. Mayhew; and his eye continued to drink in the beauty of the October day, while he spoke of the landscape, the ripening fruits, and autumnal dyes.

At length, apparently satisfied, and pleased with his impressions of the out-door world, he turned to take a survey of the room and its occupants. His clear, well-trained, intelligent eye appeared to take in, at a glance, our struggles with poverty; for it was quickly withdrawn from the room, and rested with a pleased smile upon mother, who still entertained Mrs. Mayhew. My eye followed his, with a nervous, undefined dread; but as I looked upon mother's neatly fitting black dress, her rich brown hair, partially covered with a widow's cap, her soft gray eyes, and pleasant face, I thought the elegant-looking strangers must be satisfied with her appearance.

"I should not need to be told that this was a daughter of my old friend Kendall," said Mr. Mayhew, as his glance rested for a moment on my face. "Are you his eldest child?"

"Yes, sir; I'm fifteen."

"Standing with reluctant feet
Where the brook and river meet,"

he repeated, in a low, musical voice: "Chapman, can you tell me why this girl resembles her father so closely? Her features are not his, and she has darker hair."

"But her eyes, and the whole expression of her face, are her father's; and I trust she has inherited his noble, generous spirit."

I gave my old friend a grateful glance for the compliment, but I could not summon words to thank him. Mr. Chapman now engaged Mr. Mayhew in conversation, and I turned to the children, who had been standing by him. Both were pretty, showy girls, much alike in features and expression. They might have been *more* than pretty, if they had looked pleased and happy; but a cold, haughty look rested on their childish faces, giving them a prematurely old, artificial expression. The innocent, trusting simplicity of their years had given place to a proud, conscious air of superiority. I drew the eldest one near me, and asked if the long ride had tired her.

"No. It was only twelve miles. I ride as far every fine day."

"Then you must be fond of riding?"

"Not in a carriage: 'tis pleasant enough to ride on horseback, if one has nothing else to do."

"You have been at school?"

"No. We had a governess—a hateful old thing!"

"She wasn't always disagreeable," added the younger girl, speaking for the first time since her entrance, but apparently not so much to clear the character of her governess, as to dispute with her sister; for a lively discussion immediately ensued as to the merits and demerits of the governess, which had to be checked by their father.

I endeavored to put them in good humor by offering

them some grapes, which they accepted in sullen silence, while I, not daring to open another subject with the girls, which might lead to a dispute, listened to their mother. She had just commenced a history of her physical ailments, describing most minutely and pathetically the beginning and progress of her disease, and the different medical treatments to which she had been a martyr. We finally learned that her last physician had recommended a residence for several years in the south of Europe.

"And I'm quite worn out with the trouble of getting off," she added. "Just when I thought every thing was ready, Mr. Mayhew's sister met with that unfortunate accident, and upset all our plans for the children. But if you will take them, I think we can feel quite safe to leave. I'm sorry for them to give up French and music, but Mr. Chapman thinks there will be a good music-teacher here in the spring, and, I dare say, you can keep them busy through the winter with English studies. Haven't you a piano?" she asked with some consternation, looking around.

Mother did not have time to reply before Mr. Mayhew spoke. "Mary, Mr. Chapman says he will superintend the removing of our own piano here, and then, if Mrs. Kendall will oblige them to practise regularly, I think they will do very well without a teacher until Spring."

Turning to mother, he added:

"I am much more anxious about their English at present than I am about accomplishments. Can you teach Latin?"

"Yes."

"Then you will find enough to do for the next three years, if you are so kind as to take them in charge, and I must say that, since I've seen you and your pleasant home, I am very desirous of leaving them with you."

Mother thanked him, and said, "I will try to make

them happy, Mr. Mayhew, and will do every thing for them that I could for my own; but I'm afraid they will find this too quiet a home."

"They will soon enjoy country pleasures as much as your own children do. Here, Dora, Annie, come tell Mrs. Kendall that you will try to please and obey her, if she will be so very good as to take charge of you."

The girls thus addressed approached mother, who drew them gently within her arms, asking, "Which is Dora?"

"The elder one replied, "I am called Dora, but I was named Deborah May, after papa's mother. I don't like Deborah, and so I'm called Dora, and sometimes Dora May, because I was born in May."

"And she likes that because it isn't old-fashioned," said the younger one, with more vivacity than she had manifested before, though I thought she evinced a spice of malicious fun in exposing her sister's foible.

"Papa chose queer names for us all," she added, while Mr. Mayhew looked at her with an indulgent, pleased smile; "I am called Annie Priscilla, and my eldest sister, the one who is going to Europe, is Rachel June, but we call her June, because she looks just like the June roses."

"At least, her partial little sister thinks so," interrupted her papa, while her mother with a languid smile remarked, "You are talking nonsense, Annie," and brought the child's communications to a sudden termination, by rising and asking to see the room which would be given her children. She was forthwith conducted to Aunt Lydia's favorite south chamber, whose windows overlooked the village and pond.

It was a large, sunny room, but furnished cheaply, with a straw carpet and ugly furniture.

The proud lady drew up her handsome silk, as if she thought there were contamination in such coarse, homely surroundings, but she only said, "This would be a very pretty room if it were furnished in better style. I suppose you would be willing to refurnish it?"

"It would be impossible for me to do so, Mrs. Mayhew; my means are very limited."

"Perhaps, then, the furniture which belongs to their room at home might be brought here with the piano; I'm sure they could never be contented in a room like this. You see, Mrs. Kendall, they've always been indulged and petted, and I'm sometimes afraid they are half spoiled. I've never seen a well day since the youngest was born, and with my weak nerves and constant company they've been left almost entirely to their maid and governess. I don't know how you'll manage them, but Mr. Chapman says you can do every thing, and we've already had so much delay on their account—lost one steamer, you know—that I think we shall decide to leave them with you. Then what the poor things will do without their own maid, I'm sure I don't know; but Mr. Mayhew objects to their having one, and says they are quite old enough to learn to depend upon themselves, and that you are just the person to teach them how to do it. I'm sure I never could."

Mrs. Mayhew had probably forgotten that she was the daughter of a good, honest farmer, who had made his money late in life, and that in her own girlhood she not only managed without a maid, but had helped her mother wash, bake, and sew, as was the fashion for farmers' daughters. She could now say with one of Shakspeare's fair creations:

> "Sure, this robe of mine
> Does change my disposition."

It had doubtless sifted from her memory the golden wheat of her early years.

"They are delicate girls, Mrs. Kendall," added the

fashionable mother, "and not used to country ways; you must watch them very carefully, and not allow them to run about in muddy lanes and wet grass, and be sure that they always wear broad-brimmed hats; I should be wretched to come back and find them brown as gypsies."

But not a word did the fair lady say about the moral and religious tints which must be given to their souls during her absence from them, though there were minute directions about the care of their bodies and their outward adorning.

The preliminaries were at length settled, and our visitors after partaking of a lunch of fruit, cake, and genuine country milk, departed.

It was decided that the children would come to us immediately after their parents had sailed, and Mr. Chapman would go to the city for the purpose of bringing them. Not many days elapsed after the visit of Mr. Mayhew, before the piano and furniture arrived, and the old south chamber could hardly be recognized in its new appointments. A pretty carpet, with green ground and crimson vines and flowers, and a set of light, graceful cottage furniture, with neat muslin draperies, changed the entire aspect of the room—even the landscape I thought looked lovelier from the windows.

Then our barn had received an inmate, much to the delight of Sophie and Willie, who were never weary of admiring and feeding the beautiful brown pony, which Mr. Mayhew had sent from the city for the use of his children. It was to be a surprise for them, and would, he thought, help reconcile them to the great change in their style of living, as well as afford them a healthful exercise in the open air.

The piano would effect a change in our domestic arrangements very pleasing to me, inasmuch as space could not be found for it in the kitchen; therefore the "front room" must be kept warm for a study and music-room; but as wood was abundant on the farm, and Jonas Gould strong and willing, mother did not object to the expense of another fire.

Six hundred dollars per year had been offered for boarding and instructing the children, and the sum had been accepted. What astonishing things we proposed doing with the money which we thought might be saved after defraying expenses! First and foremost in all our plans was the paying off that mortgage; then came some much-needed repairs for the dear old house; and then—but the vision was shadowy—we hoped for the accomplishments of music and French for Sophie and myself.

"Only that you may be better prepared to earn your own livelihood," mother said, as we built castles and anticipated our release from many of the petty annoyances of poverty.

The buds of hope were already beginning to burst from the ashes of our grief.

CHAPTER XIV.

THE DAY BEFORE CHRISTMAS.

"Childlike though the voices be,
And untunable the parts,
Thou wilt own the minstrelsy,
If it flow from childish hearts."
KEBLE.

"DORA, if you stand idling by the window, you will not have your lessons in time."

"I can get them in the evening."

"But you know I must insist on having regular hours for study. The evening will not suit me as well."

"I like to see Jonas Gould shovel the snow."

"That is a childish excuse, Dora, and unbecoming a girl of your age."

Mother spoke mildly; but there was decision in her quiet tones, and the petted child turned from the window with a cloudy face, and took up her arithmetic. The parlor looked cheerful and pleasant that winter's morning, with the bright wood fire upon the hearth, and the sunshine streaming in upon the faded carpet and fair young heads. It was late in December, only the day before Christmas, and the first fall of snow lay clean and white upon the earth. Every tree and shrub glistened with a crystal coat of mail, and the old stone wall looked grim and sombre beneath its sparkling crown of white. Winter wore its loveliest garb, and many young feet were tempted out upon its slippery paths. A walk to the village and a call upon Maria Chapman had been promised our pupils for the afternoon, if lessons were satisfactorily committed.

"I don't understand this arithmetic."

It was Dora who spoke again.

"What part of it?" asked mother.

"All this about five-eighths of three-fourths."

Mother took up an apple, and cutting it into four parts, simplified and illustrated the lesson, till even the sullen Dora was obliged to confess she understood. But her temper was still cloudy, for presently she threw down her book, exclaiming, "I never shall like arithmetic, and I can't see the use of studying it."

Mother had been all over that ground with her so often that she took no notice of the remark.

"Miss Lathrop always allowed us to study what we chose."

"Indeed! but you see I am not Miss Lathrop, and my method of teaching is different," mother answered pleasantly. "And your dear papa told me that I must insist upon your doing whatever I thought for your good. We will not waste time in talking, Dora; but if you wish to please your father, and gain a pleasant recreation for the afternoon, go to work with a determination to conquer these little difficulties, and I'm sure you will succeed."

Dora was a child of much quickness and natural ability, but idle, wilful, and perverse, because of petting and indulgence. There was a generous, genial element, too, beneath the thick crust of selfishness which twelve years of neglect had fostered; and though she had been under mother's tender training but two months, the germs of her better nature had several times shown themselves in spite of her selfishness and sullen temper.

Annie was much like her sister in temper; if her faults were less annoying, it was simply because she was younger by two years, and not because of better impulses.

After much patient encouragement on mother's part, accompanied by a kind, unwavering decision, the lessons were conquered and recited. Then came dinner, and generally another hour of study, but on this day they were to have a whole afternoon for recreation. Mother wanted the leisure to visit two or three poor families, who had always been remembered by father in our more prosperous days; and soon after dinner she took me with her into the bright, frosty out-door world. We had turned and repaired several garments, which Sophie and Willie had outgrown, for the small children of poor widow Reed, whose eldest daughter, Mary Ann, spent all her earnings on fine clothes.

We found the widow fretful, complaining, and overworked. In answer to mother's question, "How are you getting along, Mrs. Reed?" she replied, peevishly, "In the old way, from hand to mouth; the little I can earn scarce keeps us from starving."

"You have some kind neighbors who remember you at this season?"

"Yes. Squire Thornton sent me a barrel of flour last week, and Mrs. Chapman gave me some apples and potatoes; but, with six such hungry mouths to feed, it will all be gone in no time. And then folks see my Mary Ann dressed out so gay, and they think there's no need of giving. If she'd only pay her board it would be some help; but she puts every thing on her back, and runs in debt, too, and that worries me." Mother attempted to say something hopeful and comforting, but was interrupted by Mrs. Reed with—

"Goodness me! you don't know any thing about trouble, Mrs. Kendall! I know you've buried the best husband that ever a woman had, but he died like a Christian; and you could watch over him, while my poor man died at sea. Then, your children are a comfort—prettybehaved little things; and Miss Hope grown up quiet and steady, while my Mary Ann thinks of nothing but beaux and smart dresses; and Tom, who is old enough to be helping me, is so lazy and dishonest that nobody will employ him; and the youngest ones are saucy, and full of tricks. I don't believe anybody ever had such a hard life as I have."

Three of the children stood near, with uncombed hair, soiled faces, and mouths ajar, listening to their mother's hopeless account of them.

It was useless to offer comfort, for Mrs. Reed met every suggestion with—"La, it sounds well enough. You just try it with my children;" or "I haven't time to learn my children manners; 'tis more'n I can do to get 'em bread; there's nothing for me but hard work and poor fare. No! you don't know how to pity me, nor nothing about my troubles! Goodness! when you was a little straightened, didn't good luck send you a couple of nice children to teach, and handsome pay for it, too?"

"Don't call it good luck, Mrs. Reed; but a kind Providence. The same loving, watchful eye cares for us both, and knows all our wants. He sends you health, and work to employ your hands, and I wish you could learn to go to Him with your troubles."

Mother was answered only with complaints and fretful repinings. Even the comfortable garments we had spent hours in making, were received with scarcely a thank. Mrs. Reed said, "They'll help keep the children from freezing; but I sometimes think the sooner they are all dead and buried, the better it will be for them; they'll never be any help or comfort, if they live to grow up."

We left the miserable, untidy home of Mrs. Reed, thinking how truly happy those must be who have no need to pray, "Feed me with food convenient for me, lest I be poor and steal, and take the name of my God in vain."

Some one has said that "a losing struggle with life crushes the gentle and hardens the rebellious;" but the souls that accept sorrow and misfortune submissively, having "buckled on the whole armor of faith," come forth from the ordeal purified and strengthened.

We called next upon two poor lone women, who lived in a couple of small, meagre rooms over a joiner's shop. Miss Shaw, in her youth, had been the village schoolmistress; but the infirmities of her bed-ridden mother had prevented her from teaching for many years; and now the sole subsistence of these two women depended upon the needle of the younger one and the charities of the villagers. What a pleasant contrast they presented to Mrs. Reed! Their plain room and scanty furniture were neat, though every thing bore marks of Poverty's relentless hand, and both faces were lighted with that "hope which, like an anchor, sure and steadfast, entereth into that within the veil."

The faded, care-worn face of the daughter looked almost brilliant as she welcomed mother, and she could hardly find words to express her gratitude, when she saw a nice hood which mother had quilted out of a breadth of old silk, and a pair of stockings which my fingers had knit, while my eyes had been employed with Latin grammar.

"You are so kind to think of us, when you are in so much trouble, Mrs. Kendall, and have so much to do for your own family! God will abundantly reward and bless you."

"He has tempered my great affliction with mercy; and though His chastening has been grievous, I trust it will work out for me eternal good."

"I am sure it is already yielding the peaceable fruits of righteousness. You have no common loss to mourn, Mrs. Kendall; and it is a wonder to everybody how you bear up under it so well."

"But I must keep up my strength and courage, Miss Shaw, for the sake of the children; I sometimes think that the necessity of working for them is one of my greatest blessings; for had we been left with abundant means, I'm afraid that I might have sat down and nourished my sorrow, until I should have been unfit for any duty; but now, with the great need there is for exertion, I have no time for repining."

"And with so much anxiety for your children, and a heart so full of trouble, you find time to think of poor neighbors, and do something for them, too."

"You were always a particular friend of my husband's, and I shall never forget those who knew and loved him."

"Ay, none knew him better, or loved him more, outside of his own family, than we did. He was a little flaxen-haired boy, with large blue eyes, when he first came to school to me, and always a good boy and a good scholar. I took great pride in teaching him; and then, when he grew up to be a man, he was a kind, generous friend, always sending us something to make mother comfortable. It is a blessing to have known such a single-hearted man, and a pleasure to remember his unselfish life."

A half hour was spent in kind, sympathizing, encouraging conversation, showing

> "How beautiful the law of love
> Can make the cares and toils of daily life;"

and then we bade them good-bye, and returned in the gathering twilight to our own humble home. And how cheerful and comfortable it looked compared with the wretched home of the Reeds, or even with the threadbare poverty of the Shaws! Reader, if ever you are inclined to complain of God's gifts, or fret under the burden He has laid upon you, or if life seems to you an insipid, tasteless draught, go into the neglected lanes and alleys of your town, and seek out homes humbler than your own; call upon the poor, sick, and neglected, and then, if your heart is not softened, your love increased, and the whole tide of your being stirred with stronger and more generous impulses, why, stay at home and turn discontent, like a sweet morsel, under your tongue.

We found the kitchen tossed into a pleasant froth of excitement by the arrival of a box, directed to the Misses Mayhew, and bearing unmistakable marks of travel. Jonas Gould, with hammer and chisel, was making an awkward attempt to remove the cover, when we entered; he was hindered in his work by the impatient hands of Dora and Annie.

"Only think, Mrs. Kendall—a box from Paris! Such

a surprise! and filled with Christmas presents, too, I've no doubt; only Jonas is so slow, we shall never get at them," exclaimed Dora, in an impatient voice.

"Wa'al, Miss, I reckon if you'll let me do the work in my own way, you'll see the inside a heap sooner than by pulling and hauling with your own hands. Stand back a minute, and give me elbow-room."

Mother drew away the eager girls, and Jonas quickly revealed the tempting contents of the box. Into the midst of it plunged Dora and Annie, with an earnestness which mother made no effort to repress. Such exclamations of delight had rarely been heard in our kitchen, and, indeed, the old walls might almost have been moved to speak, so marvellous was the display.

There were winter hats, blue velvet, with soft white feathers, for the petted children of wealth, and a variety of Parisian knick-knacks. A beautiful little globe, "To make geography pleasant," as the card attached to it said, and several well-chosen illustrated books of natural history and botany; and, to crown their happiness, there was a coral bracelet for each.

Mr. Mayhew had not forgotten the family of his old friend; and the appropriateness of his gifts showed alike his good sense and delicacy of taste. There was a book of choice engravings, with mother's name in gilt letters upon the brown morocco cover, and an exquisite mourning-pin for her also—a beautiful little work-box for Sophie, and a Chinese puzzle for Willie—while I was made happy and grateful by a complete set of drawing materials, a pretty collection of studies, and a box of water-colors.

Then, Mr. Mayhew had written mother such a kind letter, showing his appreciation of the care she was giving his children, that she gathered new courage and strength for her labors.

That was a cheerful Christmas, even though the withered leaves and light snows lay upon the graves in the orchard, and despite an ever-present consciousness that the voices we best loved would never again mingle in our Christmas greetings. Cheerful, because with the eye of faith we saw him, who had hitherto been the joy of our hearts, rejoicing in the presence of his risen Saviour.

We were content, because

> "All the jarring notes of life
> Seemed blending in a psalm,
> And all the angles of its strife
> Slow rounding into calm."

CHAPTER XV.

SPRING FLOWERS.

"Here's flowers for you—daffodils
That come before the swallow dares, and take
The winds of March with beauty; violets, dim
But sweeter than the lids of Juno's eyes
Or Cytherea's breath—pale primroses
That die unmarried, ere they can behold
Bright Phœbus in his strength."
       SHAKSPEARE.

"MRS. KENDALL, it's a wretched shame for me to waste an hour in planting-time to ride with the girls—there's a heap to be done, and only one pair of hands to do it all. So I've just saddled the pony and tied him to a post, and when they've had enough of riding they can leave him there."

"But, Jonas, do you think it will be safe for them to ride alone?"

"Safe as a wooden rocking-horse if they'll just keep on the road between here and the mill."

And Dora, coming in dressed for her ride in a blue habit, with a pretty cap of the same color, looking as bright and spring-like as the month whose name she bore, declared it would be fun to ride alone.

"I never could see the use of having Jonas along, on that lumbering old farm-horse."

Mother hesitated before granting permission, but yielded at last to Dora's persuasions to try her "just this once," stipulating that for this morning she was only to ride up and down the length of road that bordered the field where Jonas was at work. The child had been growing quite docile and sunny under mother's gentle treatment; for the last month there had been very few violent outbreaks of passion and fretfulness; and when seated upon her pony this morning, I could not help noticing how much more amiable the expression of her face had grown since the previous autumn.

"I am really beginning to love her, mother," I said, as she rode out of the gate and down the road, looking back with a happy, pleased smile.

"It would be strange if you did not love her heartily by this time; she has been with us more than six months."

"But don't you think she is improving in looks and manners?"

"Yes, very much; the simple and regular routine of study and exercise, which has been enjoined upon her, together with the habit of obedience, has softened her temper and her pride. I think their father will find them both greatly improved, if he lives to return."

"Do you suppose Mrs. Mayhew will like the change?"

"She would be very unwise to regret it, as they will still be young enough to learn all fashionable arts and accomplishments. Hope, I think we may spare an hour for garden-work this morning; if you will bring me a trowel, I will transplant some roots and shrubs to the orchard."

She rarely allowed a day to pass without speaking of some trait of our father's which she wished us to imitate, and I knew she was now going to plant something which should tell of her constant thought and love, that

> "Those grave-mounds might be bathed in balmy bloom
> With loving memories eloquently dumb."

She did not speak while removing from the soft, clinging soil a few rose-bushes, perpetual bloomers, and a root of heliotrope; then she asked:

"Is there any flower that you wish to see growing by their graves, my child?"

"Pansies, mother—let me have a large clump at the foot of each grave. Father loved them; they are hardy, too." And so we removed them to the soil made sacred by our beloved dust and watered them with our tears.

"He loved these flowers, and I believe he knows how sacredly dear to me is every thing he loved."

Mother spoke in a low voice, as if communing with herself; but I saw that love and holy faith filled her heart by the light that rested on her face, by the tender, almost caressing way in which she handled the roots and shrubs which he had planted.

Our pleasant gardening was interrupted by the sound of a horse's quick tread, and in a moment more the chestnut pony bounded to our gate, riderless. Mother gave me a hurried glance of alarm, and sprang toward the gate; but I reached it first, exclaiming:

"I can run faster—let me go," and fear lent me wings. I flew down the road toward the mill, only pausing to hail Jonas, and bid him follow. Half the distance had been measured in breathless haste, when I saw the child sitting upon the grass, supported by a kind neighbor, whose house was near, and who had seen the accident.

"It's not much of a hurt, I reckon," said the woman; "more fright than any thing. You see that idle Tom Reed was loitering around, and the devil tempted him to throw a stone at the pony, which hit him on the leg, and made him jump; and the girl, not being prepared for it, was thrown from the saddle. How are you now, deary?"

"I'm so faint!"

"Yes, I dare say: a great fright is apt to make folks faint. Miss Hope will hold you, while I run for some water."

I took Mrs. Berry's place, soothing the faint, frightened child with all the tenderness I could summon, until the water arrived, quickly followed by Jonas and mother, whose fears would not allow her to wait. After a copious draught of the cold water, and free bathing of her face and head with the camphor which Mrs. Berry had brought, Dora was so far revived as to make an effort to stand, but quickly sank again on the grass, exclaiming:

"Oh, my ankle! it aches so that I cannot stand."

Mother examined, and found the ankle of the stirrup foot already much swollen. So she despatched Jonas for Dr. Blake, with a request that he would come with a vehicle which could convey the injured girl to her home.

Hardly a half hour had passed before our good doctor arrived, but the time had seemed much longer while we listened to Dora's moans, unable to relieve her. The doctor, upon examination of the injured limb, found it only a sprain, but a serious one. He lifted her into his buggy, and bade mother get in to support her; and then, seated upon a stool which Jonas had brought from the farmer's, he drove gently toward our house.

"Wa'al, I guess, if that shiftless Tom Reed don't find something to do besides throwin' stuns, the gallows will have its due before many years," muttered our thrifty farm-hand, as we turned to follow the doctor's carriage.

I was in no mood to talk to Jonas, so I lingered to gather blue violets, that grew by the roadside, and to pluck the delicate white blossoms of the wild cherry, that grew luxuriantly by the way, while I inhaled large draughts of the sweet-scented air. And, standing by the hedge, pulling sprays of hawthorn-buds, I heard my name called from the road. Looking around, I saw Mrs. Reed, in most untidy garments, her head covered with an old gingham sun-bonnet, and her face wearing a wild, hurried look of fear.

"My goodness! Miss Hope, what has my wicked Tom

gone and done now? He came home a while ago, and said as how he'd throwed a stone, which had frightened Dora Mayhew's pony. I scolded him soundly for idling round and throwin' stones, but was too busy to think any more about it, till we saw your man, Jonas Gould, ride off with the doctor; and then poor Tom begged so hard that I'd come and see what had happened to the girl, all along of his mischief, that I run right off, all in a hurry and flutter. Do tell me, now, what's the matter?"

"She was badly hurt, but Dr. Blake says 'tis only a sprain."

"Well, Goodness knows, I'm thankful it's no worse. She might have been killed; and then I s'pose poor Tom would have been hung or shut up in jail. And sometimes I think he'd enough sight better be in jail than idling about town, getting into all sorts of scrapes. Dear me! I'm in hot water all the time; if 'tain't one trouble, 'tis another; and now I shall be worrying about your mother's fagging over a sick child, all along of Tom's wickedness."

"Do not worry about that, Mrs. Reed; mother has had trials so much greater, that this will seem a trifle to her."

"Goodness! what should I do with a sprained ankle in my house? It's lucky that it falls to your mother to take care of her instead of me; I should just fret myself to death about it. Wa'al, now that I've hearn what the matter is, I may as well go back to my sewing. I've wasted an hour already just for that idle boy—poor fellow, he feels bad enough about the mischief he's done this time."

"Won't you take my nosegay, Mrs. Reed?" I asked, as she was turning to leave.

"Law, child, what good would flowers do me? They ain't food nor clothes, and I've no time to look at nor smell of them, and no vase nor tumbler to put them in; they'd just wither away in our dirty, stifled room."

Still she took the flowers, and a softer, more womanly look crept into her hopeless face as she held them, and her voice had a mellower tone, as she said:

"I used to pick violets when I was a girl like you; they used to be thick as hops on my father's farm. Dear me! what an age since I've picked a flower; poor folks don't find time to run after flowers."

"Mother thinks we gain time by taking walks and bringing home flowers or evergreens to make our rooms look cheerful, because we can work so much faster afterwards."

"Your mother has queer notions; but she's a good soul, if there's one living. She don't know nothing about poverty and trouble like mine; if she did, she wouldn't find the heart to care for flowers; but I'll keep these, and may be find a broken mug to put them in. Good-bye."

I gathered another handful of violets, hawthorn, and cherry-blossoms, and hastened home to assist mother. Dr. Blake had just finished dressing the injured limb when I entered, and was saying:

"You must be patient, little girl, and lie upon the sofa, till I give you permission to run about—meanwhile, Miss Hope will read to you and bring you flowers, and tell you how to be courageous. But I must look after Tom Reed; he's on the high road to ruin, and when a boy gets too old to mind his mother, the neighbors should interfere. I think the best thing we can do for him now is to send him to the Reform School."

It was hard for Dora to lie on the sofa while the spring flowers bloomed and the fragrance of apple-blossoms stole in through the open windows; hard to hear the whinney of her pony when he was brought out for Annie's use, and harder still to keep her impatient, fretful temper in restraint;

but I think she profited much by those weeks of pain; they taught her many useful lessons of self-denial and control.

Mother never chided her for the disobedience which had been the primary cause of the accident, though once she gently reminded her that had she ventured no further down the road than she had been told to ride, she would not have encountered Tom Reed.

We sought in every way to amuse her, and in order to keep her mind occupied, encouraged her to study a little each day; and the monotony of her confinement was often relieved by a ride in Dr. Blake's gig, or Mr. Chapman's chaise. By the time she could limp around the garden and farm with the help of her little crutch, the haymakers were cutting the waving grass, and the wild strawberries were red and luscious on the pasture-knolls, and her own face wore a more amiable, happy look, as if the patient love which had watched over her hours of suffering had taken root in her heart.

CHAPTER XVI.

VIRGINA THORNTON.

*"Women will love her that she is a woman,
More worth than any man; man that she is,
The rarest of all women."*

SHAKSPEARE.

Two years had flown since Dora limped upon her crutch to gather the summer flowers, and the earth was beautiful again, as if fresh from the hands of the great Architect. Mother and I had worked on hopefully,

"Through all the bristling fence of days and nights,"—

had gathered to our home two more pupils from our own village, Maria Chapman and Agnes Blake, and by careful economy had paid the interest on the mortgage and lessened the amount by some two hundred dollars; but there was still a debt of three hundred dollars, and means were sorely needed to make repairs upon our house and improvements on the farm, if we hoped for any income from it in the future.

Mr. Mayhew had written, asking mother to retain Dora and Annie another year, as his wife's health was so much better in the south of France, that he had decided to remain abroad for the present. Mother was very glad to keep the girls, because of the remuneration, and because we were both strongly attached to our capricious but steadily improving pupils.

Virginia was at home again, and gazing upon her fair, bright face, I almost forgot the beauty of the midsummer day. Her voice, "like the clear trill of singing birds," brought music and gladness into our humble home.

"And you are not going back to school?" I asked, when the first glad greetings were over.

"No, father says not; you know I have been away nearly three years, and I have been so well taught, that he thinks I can get along by myself. Besides, he wants me for company. Aunt Sallie is going to be married."

"Aunt Sallie going to be married! You are joking, Virginia."

"It is really so. I wouldn't believe it till Captain Wynne himself appeared yesterday. But Aunt Sallie isn't as old as we've always fancied her; she is so very sedate and proper, and dresses so prim, that she has never seemed likely to marry, but father says she isn't forty."

"But only think of not loving until one is middle-aged!"

"Oh, as for that, Aunt Sallie has been engaged to Captain Wynne ever since she was a girl, but she has such a horror of the water that she couldn't be persuaded to go to sea with him; and then when my mother died I was left to her care, and her conscience wouldn't allow her to leave me until I could take care of myself and make father a comfortable home. I never knew how much reason I had for loving and honoring Aunt Sallie until I talked with father last evening."

"Will she go to sea with Captain Wynne now?"

"No, he has laid up money enough to retire upon, and is going to build just the prettiest little cottage close by the village; we were deciding upon the plan for it this morning, and the mechanics are going to work upon it this very week; so you see I'm not likely to lose the benefit of Aunt Sallie's good counsels. Now tell me what you've been doing since the Christmas holidays."

"A little study, a little teaching, and some sewing and housework. You know I assist in teaching and taking care of our pupils."

"Yes, but what are you studying now?"

"I am reading Horace with mother; she is an excellent teacher of Latin, but doesn't know much about French. Mr. Eveleth has helped me a little in learning to translate it, so that I am reading a few pages of Corinne each day. Then mother says I've reached the end of her mathematics, which only finishes up arithmetic and algebra. I am doing something in history, and you know I am learning to play the piano."

"Indeed, how does that happen?"

"Why, I suppose Mr. Chapman told Mr. Mayhew that I had some musical talent, for he wrote mother that I might use his piano to practise upon; but I didn't commence until last fall, when mother thought it might encourage Dora and Annie if I took hold earnestly and learned to play."

"But you've had no teacher?"

"Not exactly a teacher, but Mrs. Eveleth has helped us along. She cannot perform very brilliantly, but she understands the science, and has been of great assistance to Dora and Annie, and has been so kind as to come here once a week ever since last fall, just because she is so desirous to help mother make an attractive home for her pupils."

"I always knew she was the very essence of goodness. But, Hope, you make me ashamed of myself! With all your hindrances, you have been advancing more rapidly at home than I have at school."

"You over-estimate me, Virginia, and don't do yourself justice. You know I have a great deal to encourage me to study; poverty is a most inspiring stimulus."

"Your mother has made it so, but I reckon Mrs. Reed has never found any thing inspiring in poverty. Do you enjoy having the Mayhews with you now?"

"Much more than I thought we ever could when they first came; they've grown quite studious and obedient."

"I thought them very ill-tempered and disagreeable during my last summer's vacation; but I cannot imagine how they could do otherwise than improve under your mother's training."

"It has been a good thing that mother had the care of these girls, because she has had to spend so much time and thought upon them; and I'm sure it has been a good thing for me."

"Why good for you, Miss Wisdom?"

"Well, their faults have called into exercise my patience and charity, and in trying to be an example for them I have been more diligent, more watchful of my temper and manners, so that I trust I am a little stronger than last year."

"A very Samson in every thing but physical strength, I've no doubt; and your wisdom so astonishes me, that there is no more spirit left in me."

"Now, you are joking."

"No; but a little extravagant, perhaps. Here comes your mother, with her pretty flock."

It was a pretty flock, and my untutored eye saw that it would make a charming study for an artist: mother in her mourning garments, with a womanly grace and beauty which time could never quite despoil, leading Willie on one side and Annie Mayhew on the other, while Dora and Sophie, their hands full of delicate wild flowers, were just behind; the lengthening shadows and the soft, golden light of the midsummer evening bathing all.

Virginia received a hearty greeting. She was a universal favorite; no one could look upon so fair a creature without admiration. One writer says:

"The beautiful are never desolate,
For some one always loves them;"

but I doubt if mere physical beauty inspires an emotion strong enough to be called love. It may captivate the fancy, but there must be beauty of soul and purity of heart to kindle and feed the sacred flame. There was enough of amiability and generosity in Virginia's character, aside from beauty of face and form, to win the love of those who knew her well; and then her apparent unconsciousness of personal attractions added much to their power. She never appeared to know that

> "Her cheeks had the pale, pearly pink
> Of sea-shells—the world's sweetest tint,"

and that, looking in the blue depths of her eyes, one thought of violets, and all things pure.

"Dear Mrs. Kendall, I'm not feeling very amiable just now, for I've been cross-questioning Hope, and I'm jealous of the progress she's made, and more than half wish father had never sent me away to school, but had persuaded you to teach me. I know my education is called finished, still I'm sadly deficient in every thing but music."

"You have time enough before you to make up for many early deficiencies, and I shall always be glad to assist you, though you'll find me a poor substitute for the accomplished teachers you have just left."

"I shall claim the privilege of reading history two or three times a week with Hope, if for no other reason than an excuse for coming here; but I'm afraid I shall have neither time nor patience for any harder studies. I mean to keep up a thorough knowledge of music, and take lessons again as soon as we can get a good teacher here. Father thinks the cars will run by October, and then a master can come from Wiltshire. Come, Hope, get your hat and go with me as far as the corner. Aunt Sallie will expect me before dark."

We were both in a gay, glad humor as we took the road to the village, and chatted and laughed with an *abandon* quite unlike my quiet, every-day demeanor. There was something inspiring and contagious in my friend's breezy laugh and rippling, musical voice; and her presence banished for the hour all thoughts of our hard, struggling existence.

Such happy, gorgeous castles as we built, while the tired hay-makers walked past us, and the heavy carts of fragrant hay lumbered along, and the birds sought their nests, tenderly twittering, only seem attainable to young eyes.

We had reached the corner, and were lingering for a few more last words, when we were startled by the approach of a horseman, and I saw that Virginia recognized the rider; but before I could ask his name he had checked his horse and raised his hat, bowing to my companion.

"Good-evening, Miss Thornton."

"Good-evening, sir;" and Virginia bowed with a stately grace very unlike the free, careless air she had worn a minute previous.

"I hardly know whether to call your friend Miss Kendall; but I believe 'tis the little Hope that I used to see in Sherbrooke before I went abroad."

"Hope Kendall, don't you remember Carey Chapman?" asked Virginia, by way of introduction.

"Oh, yes, very well; but I had not seen him for so long that I did not know him at once;" and I offered my hand, while a half cousinly greeting must have shone in my face, for the young man said:

"Let me remember; are n't you some far-away cousin of mine?"

"My step-mother is distantly related to your father."

"Ay, yes, well I may venture to call you cousin Hope, when we get better acquainted. I see now that I should have spent more of my vacations in Sherbrooke; even my little sister is half afraid of her grown-up brother. Which way are you walking, young ladies? And may I have the honor of dismounting to bear you company on foot?"

"No, indeed not, Mr. Chapman, we are used to this road, and besides we are going different ways; we were just parting as you came up."

"Ay, in that case you make it difficult for me to choose my own way, either would give me so much pleasure; but as I am the bearer of a message to Mrs. Kendall from my mother, perhaps your friend will allow me to return with her."

I had rarely spoken to a young gentleman before, and I was painfully conscious of an awkward, confused air as I parted with Virginia, and turned toward home. That elegant figure walking by my side with his horse's rein thrown carelessly over his arm, so embarrassed me, that at first my tongue almost refused the utterance of words. But soon the easy, careless flow of his conversation upon familiar topics put me so much at ease, that I could answer his questions about the neighbors whose farms we were passing; and before we reached mother's door, he had touched a subject upon which I could always find words, my friend Virginia.

"It seemed natural to meet you with Miss Thornton this evening; I remember you were great friends when you were little girls."

"Yes, we've always been friends, but Virginia has been away nearly three years at school."

"And getting high notions of her beauty and the importance her father's wealth will give her, I suppose?"

"She isn't proud, and she does not appear to know that she's beautiful."

"She cannot help knowing that. She has a rare combination of beautiful features; but after all, they would look tame, if they only covered ignorance, conceit, and pride."

"But Virginia isn't conceited, and she isn't ignorant."

"She certainly has a warm defender in you. It is not a common thing for a beautiful woman to be admired by her own sex. Has Miss Thornton any accomplishments?"

"She reads French, plays the piano, and draws."

"She has probably a school-girl's smattering of those branches; she could get little more in the time she has been at school; but 'tis no business of mine. Have you been at school?"

"No, I have studied with mother."

"And learned much more than you would in school, I'll warrant. I remember that your mother used to impress me as a sensible, highly cultivated woman."

I felt grateful for his compliment to mother, and glad to see his deferential manner of greeting her. She was standing in the vine-covered porch as we approached, and gave him a quiet, graceful welcome,

"Will you not fasten your horse and come in, Mr. Chapman? We can give you some excellent raspberries and a glass of milk."

"Thank you, not to-night, Mrs. Kendall, but I shall claim, by right of our distant kinship, the privilege of renewing my acquaintance with you and your family at an early day. I have been in Sherbrooke so little for the last six years that I feel quite a stranger. Mother sent me here with a very earnest request that you would give your little school a holiday for to-morrow, and join a small picnic party, which proposes to visit Cameron pond. I was especially enjoined to say that every member of your family was included in the invitation, and that father had provided means for your conveyance."

"He is very kind and thoughtful, but I do not go into society."

"This will be a very sober affair, Mrs. Kendall—only Mr. and Mrs. Eveleth, Dr. Blake and his wife and daughters, Squire Thornton and his family, and Captain Wynne, and Mr. and Mrs. Crowell, who are visiting us. Don't say no."

Mother turned a hesitating look upon my eager face, and answered:

"I don't know—perhaps for the sake of the children I ought to go—they have so few pleasures."

"Certainly you will go. I shall tell mother you have accepted; and to-morrow morning about nine o'clock father's carriage will take you up, while a hay-cart, drawn by four trusty farm-horses, will convey all the young people."

"But I'm afraid the hay-cart will carry too much sail, unless a grave matron like myself goes as ballast."

"The hay-cart shall be convoyed in a most dignified manner; I give my word of honor."

The young man bade us good-evening, mounted his horse and rode away, while mother and I still lingered in the porch.

"Carey Chapman seems greatly improved. I hope he will make an upright, useful man, for his father's sake, as well as his own," mother remarked, still looking at the fine figure of the retreating horseman.

"He must be very learned, I think. So many years in college, and abroad."

"I dare say he has a good education, but superior advantages do not always make a man."

"Do you think him handsome, mother?"

"He would generally be called very fine-looking; but there is not quite strength enough in his face to please me, and a little too much hauteur and self-conceit. He has a good figure and a pleasant address."

We went in, and the hour that followed was devoted to a critical reading of Milton's "Comus;" but the grand old English poet did not quite thrust from my thoughts pleasant anticipations for the morrow.

CHAPTER XVII.

CAMERON POND.

"Summer, clad in regal beauty,
 Crowns the sloping hills;
Sleeps in quiet, shady valleys,
 Laughs in rippling rills;
Summer, with her wealth of fragrance,
 Floats on every breeze,
Whispering in her mystic language
 To the listening trees."

MOTHER announced the anticipated picnic pleasures at the breakfast table.

The glad joy of the children made itself so noisy that it was with difficulty held in check.

"Oh, mamma! am I to go?" asked Sophie.

"And I, too, mamma?" almost shouted Willie. "I've never seen the pond. May I take my fish-hooks and little canoe?"

"Oh, Mrs. Kendall! won't it be lovely? Shall I ride my pony?"

"You are all to go in a hay-cart, with Maria Chapman and Agnes Blake."

Then came such a clapping of hands and clatter of eager young voices as only mother's "Hush, children, hush!" could restrain.

"Mrs. Kendall, may I wear the new silk mamma sent me from Paris?" asked Dora, followed instantly by Annie, who exclaimed:

"I shall wear my pink muslin and white hat."

"No, girls, you will wear your green ginghams and common straw hats."

"And look just like dairy maids? Why can't I wear what I choose, Mrs. Kendall?"

"Because it would be unsuitable, Dora; finish your breakfast and get ready as soon as possible, so that we may not keep our friends in waiting."

"I'm not going if I must make a fright of myself." Dora spoke in an angry tone, with knit brows.

"If I wished to punish you, I should certainly forbid your going, after such a manifestation of ill temper. I trust you will quickly see how foolish and disrespectful you have been. Go, now, and make yourself ready."

Dora moved off in a more disagreeable mood than she had shown for some months; and even the sight of the hay-cart and her young friends failed to restore her to good humor.

But Squire Thornton and his fair daughter were in the cart, and their keen enjoyment of the morning's pleasures was contagious. Perhaps, too, the neat simplicity of Virginia's dress—a blue cambric, with linen collar and cuffs—had a pacific influence upon Dora; for soon the sullen frown melted into a pleased smile.

Captain Wynne, Aunt Sallie, and the Eveleths took the lead in Squire Thornton's carriage, followed by Dr. Blake, his wife, and two daughters. Then came the hay-cart with its freight of children, baskets, pails, and hampers, followed by Mr. Chapman's carriage, containing his wife, Mr. and Mrs. Crowell, their visitors, and my mother. Mr. Chapman and his son were mounted on excellent saddle-horses, and cantered gayly along within chatting distance of the carriages. If the young man's chestnut horse was more frequently seen at that side of the hay-cart where sat my friend, it seemed only a matter of course ; for Virginia never looked lovelier, or more unconscious of her charms, and never rolled from her tongue so glibly before those pretty little nothings which are laughed at and admired if they fall from beautiful lips.

Cameron pond was nearly four miles from the village, but within the limits of Sherbrooke—a short ride past thrifty-looking farm-houses, fields of waving wheat, and rich pastures, when the ripe beauty of midsummer crowned the earth, and the air was fragrant with the spicy aroma of evergreens and ripening fruits.

Even the hedges were dressed in holiday attire, with clumps of elder and wild roses in full bloom, modestly regaling us with their soft hues and sweet scents. How delicious the smell of the newly-mown grass, and the buckwheat that " whitened broad acres ; " and how in harmony with the perfume, the beauty, and the chirrup of birds, was the lulling hum of myriads of insects! Inharmonious, and yet increasing the general harmony of the day, we heard at intervals the clicking sound that mowers make in sharpening scythes.

I can hear now the echoes of those glad young voices, that startled flocks of timid sheep from their quiet grazing, and sent them scampering in a huddled group over the pasture-knolls ; and even the mowers paused to look at us, resting upon scythe-handles and rakes, and many a straw hat was waved in sympathy with our holiday mood.

Raspberries and blueberries grew abundantly in the pastures which skirted the pond ; and one of the chief delights of the excursion, to the younger members of the party, would consist in gathering these berries. Virginia and

I were not too old to enjoy the berrying; and, provided with baskets, we took the children under our especial care and started for the pastures, very soon after arriving at the maple-grove, which would be our rendezvous for the day. The gentlemen prepared their lines and bait for sport upon the water, while the ladies made for themselves comfortable seats upon the mossy knolls with the carriage cushions, and took out their knitting and embroidery.

"Miss Thornton! Miss Kendall! you are not going toward the pond—this way, if you please," called young Chapman.

"We are going with the children for berries; we do not know how to catch trout," answered Virginia.

"But I promised myself the pleasure of teaching you. Come with us to the boats, and leave the berries to the children. Miss Belinda and Esther and Mrs. Crowell are going out on the pond."

"Thank you; the sail would be pleasant, and the fishing, too, I've no doubt; but I see by the look on Hope's face that the children must not be allowed to go by themselves."

"Is the face of your friend your moral barometer?"

"I dare say it would be a safe one. You will be glad of our berries when dinner is served. Come, Hope;" and the blue dress and pretty hat disappeared amongst the trees, followed by the children and myself.

The berries were ripe and plentiful; and eager hands soon filled the baskets. Then there was a fresh pleasure in searching for flowers to adorn the dinner-table, which was to be laid in the grove. In our happy, frolicsome mood we did not notice how short our shadows had grown upon the grass.

"I suppose, young ladies, you have verified the truth of these lines to-day:

'Like the swell of some sweet tune,
Morning rises into noon.'"

We had been so busy with our flowers, we had not heard Carey Chapman's step.

"Is it really noon, Mr. Chapman?" asked Virginia, springing up, and letting fall an apron-full of wild roses, pale blue lobelia blossoms, and scarlet cardinal flowers.

"Really noon; but do not spoil your floral treasures, Miss Thornton. Allow me the honor of ornamenting your hair?" And the young man, without waiting for permission, took several of the delicate pond-lily buds which he had brought with him, and twisted their stems around Virginia's large coil of golden-brown hair, allowing the buds to droop upon one side. The effect produced was charming, and Mr. Chapman saw it; but he only said, "Solomon, in all his glory, was not arrayed like one of these."

For a minute Virginia seemed confused and half annoyed, but laughingly exclaimed:

"Mr. Chapman, I will not be the only one to wear flowers. 'Crown Hope, or I will tear these lilies from my hair."

"Certainly, with your friend's permission;" and picking up a scarlet flower and a spray of fern, he fastened them into my hair with such a half playful, half serious way, that I could not summon courage to forbid him.

"If I read your face aright, Miss Hope, you care little for outward adorning, but much for that meek and quiet spirit which is woman's brightest adornment."

I could not answer, but turned to call the children, asking Virginia if we should not start at once for the grove.

"I was sent to call you. The fishing-party are impatient for dinner."

"Were you successful in your sport this morning?" Virginia asked, as we turned toward the grove.

6*

"Not enough so to tempt me out of the shadows of the woods again to-day. I think you were wise to join the berrying-party; but if you have spent all the morning in picking berries, you must be tired."

"Oh, no," answered Virginia, "we spent a long time in search of flowers, and then sat down in the shade to arrange them and talk."

"Had I been there, I could doubtless have said—

> 'Thy talk is the sweet extract of all speech,
> And holds mine ear in blissful slavery.'

Pray what did you find to talk about?"

"Oh, a multitude of little things—such as men never condescend to think of. But Hope turned aside my stream of nonsense by telling me about a new book she has been reading. What was it, Hope?"

"'Queechy,' written by Miss Warner."

"Mark how accurate she is, Mr. Chapman: now if I had read the book, I should never have asked who wrote it, or remembered the title; but little Miss Wisdom can begin with the first chapter, and tell you the whole story."

"Did you like Miss Warner's book?" asked Mr. Chapman.

"Very much, sir; more than any story I have ever read. Do you like it?"

"Quite well, but it has some grave faults."

"Tell me what they are, please."

"And so spoil your pleasant memories of the book?"

"I think not, but rather teach me how to form correct opinions of another."

"You see what a sober, blue little woman she is, Mr. Chapman: not content to give this one day up to pleasure, she must be gathering up something useful to lay away in her wise head. But tell us, Mr. Chapman, what are some of the faults of the book?"

"There are some very good descriptions of every-day life in it, but many more distorted, unnatural scenes; for instance, Mrs. Evelyn's persistent annoyance of her guest, and Mr. Thorn's persecution of the lady whom he wishes to win. Then Fleda was too pretty and pious, too astonishingly capable for an ordinary mortal—"

"Not too pious, Mr. Chapman?"

"Well, I didn't mean to speak lightly of genuine piety, or affirm that a person could have too much of it; but it seems to me there is such a thing as making too great a parade of it. Mr. Carleton pleased me more than any other character, but he was only a reproduction of John Humphreys."

"But you like Miss Warner's style?"

"It has some excellences; it is simple, unpretending, and not too ornate, but it wants strength and vigor. The long conversations dilute and weaken it; she would have made a much more readable book by compressing it nearly one-half."

"How it must spoil one's pleasure to know as much as you do, Mr. Chapman! Now with me, 'ignorance is bliss;' when I read a book that pleases me, I cannot detect its faults, so I gather only pleasure, where you and Hope would be annoyed with faults of style."

"Are you sure, Miss Thornton, that you do not lose more than you gain? There are scores of books rich in thought and style, which yield a mine of wealth to the careful gleaner, but which a superficial reader might not detect."

"I dare say my pleasures might be increased even in reading, if I would only be more critical. I ought to be, just to please Aunt Sallie; she has had a deal of trouble with my careless habits. Look! there she comes, leaning on Captain Wynne's arm, looking as rosy and happy as a girl in her teens. They are in search of us, most likely, and have made our loitering an excuse for a stroll by themselves. We must hail them, else Captain Wynne will mistake the pond for an ocean, and your fishing-smack for his brave ship Alacrity, and will smuggle Aunt Sallie off to some fairy isle where lovers are immortal."

Virginia moved on with quick steps, swinging her pretty hat, and calling in clear, musical tones:

"Halloa! Captain Wynne, you have lost your reckoning; this pasture is a long way off from the Bay of All Saints, or the Cape of Good Hope."

"And you are a long way off from your dinner, young lady. How many tugs are needed to bring you into port?"

"Were you and my aunt sent for that purpose?"

"We came without sending, for we thought young Chapman had got becalmed. I shall take you in charge and make sail for the grove."

"I doubt if you would have thought of dinner, or remembered what you came in quest of, if I had not hailed you."

"I shall not quarrel with you, Miss, but turn you over to your aunt for reproof.

It was a merry party at the dinner-table, and the trout, sandwiches, berries and cream were relished by all, while the larger part of the company were regaled with something better than what appealed to the palate. Politics and Mrs. Stowe's new novel were discussed calmly and sensibly by the elders. Several of the gentlemen were excellent talkers; could differ in a spicy, pleasant way without getting angry or heated.

All agreed that Mrs. Stowe had drawn a truthful picture of slavery's brightest and darkest side; all but the young New Yorker, who, in a loud and pompous manner, declared:

"The book is a gross misrepresentation from beginning to end. I have seen slavery in the border and Gulf States too, and I have never known one instance of cruel whipping. I tell you the negroes are an inferior race, lazy, and good for nothing, without an overseer's lash, and much better off, owned by intelligent white men, than when left to shift for themselves. Mrs. Stowe had better have spent her time in knitting sale socks than in weaving such a tissue of falsehoods to rouse and embitter the South, and to make abolitionists out of Northern parsons and women."

"If Mrs. Stowe's pictures are false, why need they embitter the South?" asked Squire Thornton; "when a people have truth for their shield, they can afford to be patient under misrepresentation."

"I tell you the whole spirit of the book is repugnant to the South, and is working like leaven amongst the ignorant masses of the North and West. It is all false, and I defy any one to speak from personal knowledge of a single act of injustice to the blacks."

"I have spent days and weeks in almost every Southern port, and have often visited the plantations in the Gulf States," said Captain Wynne, in a calm tone, though we saw an unwonted fire in his eye, "and if I may be allowed to speak from personal observation I will say that I have seen some ignorant and cruel masters, who would be tyrants anywhere, and I have known honest, generous, wholesouled Christian men, owning slaves and vainly trying to protect them from the horrible evils that necessarily attend the system. Mrs. Stowe's masters, Shelby and Legree, faithfully represent the two classes."

"But I asked for facts—instances of cruelty that have been witnessed by any one."

"Let me give you one," answered the captain. "Three years ago last December, I took an orphan nephew of mine, who was wasting away in consumption, to New Orleans; and while my ship was getting ready for a return voyage, I spent a few days with the lad in a private boarding-house, especially recommended for its high-toned respectability. A young mulatto girl, not more than sixteen, had the care of my room, and one of her duties was to bring a pitcher of water to me every morning. Occasionally she forgot or neglected to do it, and at such times I rang for a servant. One morning, when Susan had failed to bring the water, and I had just opened the door to receive it from the hands of a little black boy, the proprietor of the house happened to be passing in the hall.

"'How is this?' he asked; 'doesn't Susan wait upon No. Four?'

"'Usually,' I answered; 'but this morning she has forgotten the water.'

"'Has it occurred before?'

"'I think so; but the omission was of trifling consequence.'

"'It will be no trifle to her,' I heard him mutter, as he walked angrily away; and within ten minutes after I heard the girl's cries and entreaties for pardon, issuing from a large room over the carriage-house. I threw up the sash of my window, which was within a few feet of that room, and distinctly heard blow upon blow fall upon the young girl. The sound almost froze my blood; and, shutting the window, I moved as far from the scene as possible, grieved and humiliated that I could not rescue her from such cruelty. The next morning Susan appeared, moving slowly, as if each step were an effort, and wearing upon her neck a heavy wooden yoke, a badge of her disgrace. How long she was compelled to wear it I do not know; for my ship sailed that afternoon, and I took my nephew on board, glad to be away from a city, the very air of which was heavy with the sighs of an oppressed people."

"A solitary instance," growled the New Yorker, "and one which may be written on the same page of history with a New England abolitionist's treatment of his family, which I have positive evidence was so barbarous, that the neighbors were often obliged to interfere."

"Come, come," cheerily called Mr. Chapman. "We will not allow any subject discussed under such a sky as this, that does not increase the general harmony and pleasure of the party. I hold myself in a measure responsible for the happiness of each one for this day. There are still some important items on the programme of pleasures, which have not been discussed; such as a game of Copenhagen for the children, under the direction of Captain Wynne."

Mr. Chapman's summons was obeyed with alacrity, and soon all were engaged in merry, noisy games.

We were all sorry to see the shadows growing long, though many of our party were too young to know the truth of Tennyson's lines—

> "The tender grace of a day that is dead
> Can never return to me."

CHAPTER XVIII.

NIGHT AND DARKNESS.

> "The wise and true
> Crave not for lofty tasks, but turn the small
> To greatness, by the great heart doing all
> For God."

THE children had gone to sleep, tired with pleasures and play, and we sat, mother and I, by the southern window of her sleeping-room, looking out upon the still night. The earth looked as if

> "Lulled upon an angel's lap
> Into a breathless, dewey sleep."

The light of the full moon brought out clearly a field of wheat, just beginning to turn pale, as if in fear of the reaper's sickle, glistened upon the gurgling waters of the brook, and stealing through our open window, showed me every feature and expression of my mother's face.

"I have some news for you to-night, Hope—something that will make the memories of this day more than pleasant for us both. Mr. Chapman says the railroad will be finished before winter. There are only six miles more to build. And he says the company wish to change the original location of the road as it approaches the village, to avoid an immense ledge of rocks near Cameron pond, and the new survey will take the road through our back lot. Mr. Chapman says it will save the company a large amount of money to locate on our land, and they will be willing to pay me liberally for that field—enough, he says, to lift the mortgage from the remainder."

"Oh, mother, I am so glad, so happy!"

"I cannot tell you, Hope, what a load of anxious care is taken from my heart, nor with what great thankfulness I see the way for securing this home to my children. If your father could have lived to see this day, my joy would be complete and full."

"His faith was so great in God's promises, that he hardly needed this knowledge."

"Truly, 'God is a shield unto them that put their trust in Him.' You can say to-night, 'He is my refuge and defence.'"

"Never with so much confidence and gratitude before."

We sat silent for some time, looking out upon the orchard and fields, which we could now call our own. Mother spoke again:

"This railroad which has been so long desired by our villagers will be a great help to us, because it will bring us much nearer a large market, and make our fruit and vegetables more valuable."

"Don't you think we can make some repairs to the house by another spring? It needs painting so much, and the parlor ought to be refurnished."

"I am more anxious about your education and that of the children than I am about repairs at present."

"But, mother, we are all doing very well now."

"Yes, but the time is coming when you will need instruction which I cannot give. I was talking over my affairs with Mr. Chapman to-day, and he wishes me to take at least four more pupils into my family."

"Where would you put them?"

"I should be obliged to finish off two rooms over the kitchen and porch. I have thought of this plan before Mr. Chapman spoke of it. He thinks he can secure the pupils for me as soon as the rooms are ready. One of my greatest inducements to adopt this course, is the wish to secure employment for you at home, because six boarding pupils and a few day scholars will give us both as much work in teaching as we ought to do. Then the railroad will bring us so near the city that I can hire a professor to come out two or three times a week and teach you and our pupils those branches which I cannot. Do you like this plan?"

"Oh, very much—'tis better than binding shoes."

Mother smiled—a smile that told me she still saw some traces of my besetting sin, but she only said:

"I think it will open the way for us to do more good and earn more money than we could in binding shoes. Hope, look toward the village. Is it moonlight that makes the old church tower so red?"

We both looked at the tower, and while we gazed saw tongues of lurid flame creep stealthily up into the soft moonlight, and then recede as if rebuked by the pure, white light, and again dart angrily and in broad sheets upward, as if defying heaven's light and man's puny resistance.

"Is the church on fire, mother?"

"I think not; 'tis only the reflection of the fire that we see upon the tower, but the flames are really a little west of the church. I'm afraid 'tis Mr. Clark's factory."

"Indeed, if some building must be burned, I would rather it should be that factory than any other."

"Hope, you do not mean what you say! The loss of Mr. Clark's factory will deprive a great many poor people of the means of getting bread. Why did you speak so, child?"

"Oh, mother, for a minute I was all wrong, and remembered only his sharp, overbearing manners to me, without a thought for the poor people who would be turned out of employ by his loss."

"I trust you do not wish Mr. Clark any harm. Revenge cannot dwell in the same heart with that charity which thinketh no evil."

"The feeling is gone now, and I would gladly save Mr. Clark's property if I could."

"I am afraid the fire is making too swift progress to be stayed. Look! see how grand and awful those flames mount upward! The clouds are beautifully tinged."

For a few minutes my eyes were too full of tears to permit of clear vision—tears of regret and pain that a sin like revenge had not been conquered, and only thoughts of His strength who could give me the victory dried my eyes.

"What spell is upon the village!" exclaimed mother. "It seems as though nothing is doing to stay the fire, and at this hour the people cannot all be sleeping—'tis not eleven o'clock yet."

"The bell is ringing, and hark! I have two or three times thought I heard the shouts of people. Do you think we could be of any use if we ran to the village?"

"No, we should only be in the way. What a grand display that fire would be, if we could know that it was injuring no one!"

Grand and awful, but not in harmony with the dewy stillness of the summer night, the flames leaped, glared and flashed out defiantly, and then sank sullenly away like a dissatisfied avenger.

The next morning dawned bright and beautiful, and the sun came up and kissed the dew from the grass and flowers, and looked smilingly down upon the black and smoking cinders of Mr. Clark's factory. I walked early to the village to carry Mrs. Reed and Miss Shaw a part of the berries and flowers which we had gathered the day before, and arrived at Mrs. Reed's miserable cottage before I came in sight of the ruins.

I found the widow in great distress, rocking to and fro in a creaking chair, and sobbing out disjointed sentences, apparently grieving and complaining in the same breath; while Mary Ann sat by the window in a flounced pink muslin, with bare neck and arms, and three or four untidy children clamored for breakfast.

"Good-morning, Mrs. Reed," I called, advancing into the room.

"Dear me! there's no good morning for me anywheres, Hope Kendall. Such a trouble as has come now would break any mother's heart, let alone all as has gone before. Did you know as how my Tom went and did it?"

"Did what, Mrs. Reed?"

"Set fire to Mr. Clark's factory! Goodness, I'm all in a shiver when I think what his poor father would 'ev said. It's lucky he was drownded before this came upon us. Oh, my poor Tom! my wicked boy!" And for several minutes the distressed mother could not articulate for sobs. I had never seen such an exhibition of violent grief before, and was astonished that Mary Ann could sit gazing into the street so indifferent to her mother's suffering and her brother's guilt.

"What made Tom do it, Mrs. Reed?" I asked, thinking the recital of her trouble to a sympathizing listener might be a relief.

"Oh, Miss, Tom has been a wicked boy ever since his father died, more'n four years ago; but there was a time, just after he throwed the stone at the young lady's pony, when Dr. Blake and Mr. Chapman talked to him and persuaded him to work in their gardens, when I think he tried to do better. But he got worse again last winter, and wouldn't go to school, and the farmers all knew what a bad boy he was, and wouldn't give him jobs to do, so he tried to get work at the factory. Mr. Clark was real sharp with

him, and told him as how he was a thief and a vagabone
and stole his cherries, and that he oughter be in jail, and
that the gallows would bring him up—and a lot more he
said that made Tom awful mad, and he came home and
swore Mr. Clark should suffer for it. And oh, dear, I only
made it a sight worse by telling him as how Mr. Clark had
served him right, and that decent folks couldn't be expected
to hire such an idle, dirty boy. Dear me! if I had held
my tongue and not added fuel to the fire, or if I had allowed
Dr. Blake to send him off to the Reform school a year ago,
this mightn't have happened."

Mrs. Reed gave away again to loud sobs and groans,
rocking her body and wringing her hands in real distress,
and Mary Ann still sat speechless and stolid.

" Did any one see Tom do it?" I ventured to ask again.

" Not as I knows of," groaned the poor mother. " Only
everybody said at once as how he must have; and Jenkins, him as works for Clark, you know, said he heard Tom
say as Clark should eat his words. And then Square
Thornton came as soon as ever it was light this morning,
and asked if Tom slept at home. Dear me! I thought
my own words 'ud have choked me; but I told him as how
I didn't know, for Tom was nowheres to be found."

" Then, perhaps, Mrs. Reed, Tom didn't do it, after
all."

" Mercy on us! If I could think so! but he did, for I
heard him tell the Square so. Tom came slinking home
soon after sunrise, and I s'pose the Square was watching;
for right after, he came in and sat down by Tom; and, instead of swearing and scolding at him, he only says,
'Tom, my poor boy, what made you set fire to the factory?' and Tom turned pale, and tried to speak, but couldn't.
And at last he broke out, and he says, 'Who saw me do
it?' and the Square says, 'No matter who saw you, Tom;

tell me all about it; for I'm your friend, and if anybody can help you, I can.' The Square's voice trembled, and great tears fell down from his face, and dropped on Tom's hand; and, poor boy, he burst out with a loud sob, and says, 'I did it, Square, because Clark swore at me, and called me thief, and vagabone, and 'liar, and I swore he should be sorry for it.' Then the Square says, 'Tom, did you know it was a great crime to set fire to a building, and that you must be shut up in jail if you did it?' And Tom said he didn't care any thing about that—he only wanted to hurt Clark—and he was idling round by the counting-room window yesterday, and he heard Clark swear at Jenkins—something about insurance papers—and say as how they'd run out, and he must go to Wiltshire about 'em the next day; and then he made up his mind to do the mischief last night, so that Clark shouldn't get his insurance.

"Law, Miss! I can't tell you how soft and kind the Square spoke, nor how bad it made Tom feel to see tears in such a big man's eyes; and then while the Square was talking just like a minister, the constable came and took poor Tom away." Here Mrs. Reed was again choked with sobs and tears, and I wept, too, remembering that when I first saw the fire my feelings were much akin to those which prompted poor Tom to commit the deed.

"And now, Miss Hope, as if I hadn't trouble enough with Tom, Mary Ann says as how she's going to wash her hands of the whole thing. She won't stay here in Sherbrooke to be disgraced by us; and, only think, she's packed her trunk, and is waiting now for the stage; it will kill me quite; and, dear me! what's the use of my living?"

At this point Mary Ann turned her face from the window, and drawled out, in saucy, defiant tones: "Why should I stay here to have Tom's actions flung in my teeth, and listen to your frettings? There's nothing for me to do, now that the factory is burned, and I'm going to Wiltshire. Me and Sarah Sampson settled that at the fire last night. But folks won't know, there, that ever my name was Reed, you may depend on that. Once out of this place, and I'll see if I can't get into decent society."

"Oh, Mary Ann, if you go off now, right on top of all my troubles, you'll break my heart, sure," sobbed Mrs. Reed.

"Law, mother, I've heard that old story more'n a thousand times, and your heart is as good as new still. Save your breath, I say, to cool your broth; for I'm bound to go. There's nothing here for me to do."

"Didn't Mrs. Chapman say, not an hour ago, that she'd pay you well for doing her sewing, and that she'd get the other ladies to give you work too, if you'd stay with me?"

"It's no use talking, I tell you," growled Mary Ann. "I'm not going to sew for folks who think they're such a mighty ways above me; and every time I went for work they'd ask, 'When did you hear from poor Tom?' I'll leave the Sherbrooke sewing for you to do." And Mary Ann bounced out of the room, slamming the door.

The widow's sorrow, after a few minutes of unrestrained sobbing, broke out in complaints at her hard lot, and regrets for Tom; and not knowing how to offer balm to such a bruised heart, I was glad to see Mrs. Eveleth approaching the house.

I only waited to receive the kind greeting of our minister's wife, and to say good-bye to Mrs. Reed; for I longed to exchange the disagreeable odor of the widow's cottage for the sweet breath of the summer morning; longed, too, for a quiet minute in which to thank God that He had not permitted my unkind thoughts to work out deeds of dark revenge.

CHAPTER XIX.

CAREY CHAPMAN.

"I was glad that day;
The June was in me, with its multitudes
Of nightingales all singing in the dark,
And rose-buds reddening where the calyx split;
I felt so young, so strong, so sure of God!
So glad! I could not choose be very wise."
MRS. BROWNING.

LEAVING Mrs. Reed's miserable home, I took the by-path across the pastures and through the woods to our farm. I was humbled and dispirited by the knowledge of sin and sorrow which I had learned at the widow's, and needed a solitary walk. The fragrant breath of summer stole into my heart with a message of peace and forgiveness—the old pines whispered soothingly as they swayed sleepily in the warm air—but above all came the still, small voice of my Master, assuring me that I sought not in vain the light of His countenance; and very soon my heart was in sympathy with the glorious summer morning, and I was walking lightly over the forest-path, thinking how I might comfort the poor widow, and assist Mr. Clark's family.

Stopping for a moment to enrich the bouquet of wild roses which I had gathered with some sprays of sweet fern, I was startled by the quick, sharp crackling of bushes near; and before I could collect my thoughts, either in fear or surprise, Mr. Chapman's large house dog sprang to my side. The animal knew me, and spoke his gladness at meeting me as plainly as any dog is permitted to speak, wagging his tail, and rubbing his nose upon my hands and dress.

I caressed and soothed him, wondering why he should be at this distance from the village alone, and attempted to start toward home, calling the dog to follow. No; an angry bark, and a seizure of my dress with his teeth, prevented me from taking a step upon the homeward path, or toward the village; but every look and motion told me that I must follow him into the woods. It would not be pleasant, but, choking back the fear and dread which crept over me, I decided to be guided by the dog.

It was not an easy path over decayed trunks of trees and jagged rocks, through tangled blackberry-bushes, buckthorn and briers, and it seemed to my throbbing, aching heart a long way that the excited and determined dog led me; but he paused at last, just when my tired feet seemed no longer able to obey my will, just when the last drop of courage seemed oozing from my heart, paused where a tall clump of blossoming elders hid the brook from my sight, whose rapid gurgling murmur I could hear. But only for a minute did the dog stop, while he could smell the ground and listen, when seizing my gown with his teeth he darted through the bushes, regardless of my torn hat and clothing. When the brook-side was reached the object of the dog's eager haste and impatient solicitude was discovered. Carey Chapman lay across the rocks in the narrow bed of the brook, whose shallow waters, wasted by the midsummer heat, fortunately could not reach his head, which rested upon a rock higher than its neighbors. He was not dead, though my first sight of his pallid face had almost frozen my blood with fear, but the second longer, steadier glance showed me that he breathed.

I forgot my weariness, my torn dress and scratched hands, forgot my shy fear of the handsome young man, forgot every thing but that a human being was suffering and perhaps dying, and, springing upon the rocks, in a moment

I was by his side, unmindful of the water which flowed over my feet and drenched the hem of my skirts.

Dipping my hand into the cool current, I dashed it upon his head and face, chafing his hands and arms meantime as vigorously as my strength would permit, encouraged and assisted by the dog, which, as if conscious of the danger of his young master, would lick the hands I had rubbed, looking into my face as if for confirmation of his hopes. I never knew how long I stood in the cold stream, and I could never tell the depth of that anxiety and fear which lent me such unnatural strength and courage, but at last we were rewarded; the dog certainly showed that he was repaid, by the slow, intelligent opening of the young man's eyes, and by the faint, almost inarticulate whisper—

"Where am I?"

"In the woods, and in the water."

"How came you here?"

"Your dog brought me."

"What has happened to me?"

"I do not know, but think you must have fallen and afterwards fainted."

He lay for a minute with closed eyes and contracted brows, as if trying to collect his scattered thoughts, and then said:

"Yes, I have it now: I was out hunting with the dog, and attempting to cross the brook, my foot slipped upon a rolling stone. I must have fainted or been stunned by the fall; but tell me what good angel sent you to my rescue?"

"The dog was your good angel to-day, sir."

"Ay, where did the dog find you?"

"If you will put your hand upon my shoulder and rise up, sir, I will tell you when you are seated upon that dry, sunny bank."

He attempted to rise without the aid of my shoulder, but his proud strength of an hour ago was not obedient to his will, and with manifest reluctance he accepted the proffered support.

"I believe no bones are broken," he said, gently shaking the water from his light summer garments, "but I have a strange sensation in my head—a dizzy faintness, which will oblige me to lean on you. Can you half carry me to that sunny bank?"

"I will try, sir; do not be afraid to lean upon me, and be careful how you step."

We had just reached the bank when I saw that he was again overcome with faintness, and allowing him to sink upon the soft moss of the sunny knoll, I dipped my handkerchief in the cool water and laid it upon his head, and then bruising the pungent leaves of the sweet fern I held them to his nostrils, rubbing his hands and arms meanwhile as before. The sunlight, the cool water, and the fragrant herbs, combined with my vigorous rubbing, quickly restored him, and soon I had the happiness of seeing a faint glow creep over his face, a conscious light into his eyes.

"Carlo," he called softly, "come here, old fellow, and lend me your strength;" and beckoning the dog to his side, he threw an arm around his shaggy neck and raised himself to a sitting posture, still leaning upon the dumb friend that had rendered him such good service.

"So you have been my good angel this morning, old boy," addressing the dog and stroking his ears in a caressing way, "at least I have Miss Kendall's testimony to that effect. Will you tell me now where my dog found you?" turning toward my face a clear blue eye.

"I was returning from the village through the pastures and woods, and had walked nearly half the distance, when your dog sprang out of the bushes and told me as plainly as he could that some one needed my services."

" Were you not afraid to follow him?"

" Yes, sir; but he gave me no choice: he would neither allow me to advance or retreat upon the path, but pulling my gown in his teeth, obliged me to follow him through the bushes."

" Your brave courage brought me relief—perhaps life—how shall I thank you?"

" I do not wish to be thanked, sir."

He reached out and took my hand—a small brown hand with an ugly scratch upon its back, made by a resisting blackberry-bush; he saw the wound and guessed its cause.

" My dog brought you over a rough road?"

" Yes, sir." I could not meet his questioning eye, for I was painfully conscious of my torn, wet, and soiled dress, muddy boots, and ribbonless hat.

" Sit down and rest your tired limbs upon this sunny knoll. Your errand of mercy has brought you only fatigue, I fear."

" Something more, sir."

" May I ask what?"

" Pleasure and gratitude that I brought you relief."

He raised the scratched hand, which he still held, to his lips, and said:

" I am very grateful for the kindness, strength, and courage you have shown, and glad that I am indebted only to you."

We sat in silence some minutes, so long that the awkwardness of my situation was becoming painfully oppressive; and springing up, I seized a long, velvety mullein-leaf, and twisting it into a cup, I passed it full of cool water to Mr. Chapman.

" Hebe, not content with services already rendered,

would still be cup-bearer. Thank you for the draught; may it prove a refreshing nectar! And now, my young friend, I think we must be moving toward the path; 'tis dangerous for us both to remain longer in our wet garments."

"But, Mr. Chapman, you are not strong enough to clamber over those logs, and through the bushes; wait here, and I will go to the village and send help to you."

"No, I cannot allow you to go alone, Miss Hope. I think I was only stunned by the fall, and am fast regaining my strength. You should sit here while I go for help, only that I am sure exercise will be better for you than sitting still in damp clothing. I will guide you more gently through the bushes than my dog did. It will not be necessary to regain the path; I can take you an easier way to your mother's door, by following up this brook for half a mile or so."

We started up the brook, often pausing to rest where the sunshine shimmered softly through the trees, and to examine ferns, mosses, and lobelia-blossoms, while Mr. Chapman told me of the beautiful variety of flowers which he had seen in our own country and in Europe, talking with so much ease and intelligence that I soon forgot my awkward embarrassment, my weariness, and torn clothing, and found myself talking freely with him about the books I had read, and the few pleasures of my quiet life.

I was almost sorry to recognize our own pasture bars and the western gable of our house, sorry for myself, as the pleasure and excitement of talking with a well-read, cultivated man were new to me; but when I saw that his face had not lost its pallor nor look of pain, I was glad we were so near a haven of rest.

"I will leave you here, Miss Hope, with your permission, and regain the road as quickly as I can. My soiled clothing and weakness will be a sufficient excuse, I trust, for my want of gallantry in not taking you to your mother."

"Come home with me and rest; mother will be glad to see you, and Jonas Gould will drive you to the village. There he is now with the farm-horse and cart; he is coming to this field for a load of hay."

"I will not go to your mother's house in this plight, my little Hebe, but I will accept of Jonas Gould's services, and thank you, too. May I call at your mother's to-morrow, to inquire after my brave preserver?"

"We shall be glad to see you," I answered, timidly accepting the hand which he held out to assist me over the bars. My own was taken and carried again to his lips, gratefully I knew, but the act only increased the awkward confusion with which I hailed Jonas, and explained to him Mr. Chapman's condition, desiring him to drive that young gentleman to the village.

"Wa'al, I s'pose I oughter, but there's a heap of hay to be got in afore night; and besides, this old cart is hardly the thing for so smart a young chap to ride in."

"Never mind the cart; I shall be very glad to ride in it," answered the young man, climbing to a seat in the uncouth vehicle, while I walked slowly to the house, thinking over the strange accident which had rendered my services so important to Mr. Chapman, and wondering what mother would say to the part I had acted. Then arose in my heart a fear of what others would think, and an anxious desire to conceal the whole affair from every one but mother. Even the children must not see me in this plight, for I could not be questioned by them, nor rehearse before them the incidents of the morning. So I stole cautiously into the house by the back entrance, crept softly up the back staircase to my chamber, and then called mother.

She came at my summons, with surprise upon her face and in her tones.

"Why, Hope, what has kept you so long?" and glancing at my torn and wet dress, "What can have happened to you, child!"

I told her carefully and truthfully all I knew of the accident, and the part I had been obliged to act; and with her keen, searching eyes upon me, I repeated the conversation which had beguiled the latter part of my walk, only omiting such phrases as "My little Hebe;" neither did I speak of the kiss which the young man's lips had left upon my hand, though no other occurrence of the morning so burned into my memory; and then I wound up my recital with a very abundant overflow of tears.

Mother took me in her arms, caressing me in her own quiet way. "Poor child," she said, "I do not wonder that you are overcome with fatigue and excitement, but you have done nothing which calls for tears. You have shown a brave, generous courage, which only endears you to me, and which would make your father proud of his child. Thank God that He has permitted you to save the life of a human being, and then try to banish the incident from your thoughts."

"Oh, mother, I never want to hear it spoken of again! Please do not tell the children, nor our friends."

"You may trust me, Hope; I will not allow your name mentioned as a heroine."

"Do you think Mr. Chapman will tell his friends?"

"He will be obliged to account for his soiled clothing and his fatigue, but I doubt if he mentions your name. Get up, now, and let me help you take off your wet garments. I shall insist on your keeping in bed for the remainder of the day, and shall bring you some hot herb tea directly."

My long and rapid walk in the heat, followed by standing in the cool waters of the brook, proved too much even for my healthy, vigorous young frame. The morrow found me feverish, faint, and dizzy—too ill to rise; and for the next fortnight a severe influenza, accompanied by a low nervous fever, kept me prostrate.

I saw no one during this time but mother, Sophie, and Dr. Blake, though I received daily proofs of the remembrance of my friends in the shape of jellies, fruits, and flowers, and heard young Chapman's voice more than once in the parlor below my chamber.

Mother never mentioned his calls, though she told me of Mrs. Chapman's, Mrs. Eveleth's, and the Blakes'. Virginia was away from the village, visiting with her aunt some distant friends, else it might have been a difficult matter to exclude her from my bedside, or evade the questions she would have been sure to ask about the cause of my illness. It seemed strange to me that when mother brought to my room bouquets of uncommon beauty and rareness, such flowers as I knew were only to be found in Mr. Chapman's conservatory, that she left them in water, without a word.

Once only did she mention young Chapman's name, and then it was when she brought me several neatly-bound books, among which were Longfellow's "Evangeline" and "Hyperion," Tennyson's "Princess," and a volume of Mrs. Browning's poems.

"Carey Chapman brought these," she said; "and I find he intends them as a gift, for he has written your name in them. I suppose he wants to show his gratitude to my little girl for the kind service she rendered him; but he need feel under no obligations to you, especially as you did not know to whom the dog was leading you."

"No, mother; I want him to forget it."

"I told him so, dear child."

I could not help noticing that mother had never called me "child" and "little Hope" so often since my father's death, as during this illness; and I thought she intended to show me that other people, too, looked upon me as a child. But if a woman's hopes, aspirations, cares, and anxieties had not touched my heart before, I am quite sure that kiss upon my poor scratched hand would have heralded the dawn of womanhood. Certainly I looked upon the hand, as long as the scratch remained, with a tenderer glance than I had been wont to bestow upon it; and though

"He only kissed
The fingers of this hand wherewith I write,
Yet, ever since, it grew more clean and white,
Slow to world-greetings.
A ring of amethyst
I could not wear here, plainer to my sight
Than that first kiss."

CHAPTER XX.

THE BROOK AND RIVER.

"And some that smile, have in their hearts, I fear,
Millions of mischief."
SHAKESPEARE.

WHEN, at last, I had Dr. Blake's permission to leave my chamber, the ripened wheat was trembling under the reaper's sickle. Marigolds, asters, and hollyhocks told me that Summer had passed the noontide of her glory; but life's sweet spring-time current was flowing in my veins, and joyous gratitude for returning health gave brilliancy to my eyes and animation to my features.

Had mother asked why I dressed with such unusual care it would have puzzled me to frame an answer in words; but my plain, simple wardrobe had never looked so meagre as when I examined it for my afternoon toilet on that first day of my return to the parlor. I selected a white lawn, kept for a holiday dress in summer, and, sighing that I had not just one little ornament besides my sash of blue ribbon, presented myself below-stairs, receiving hearty and noisy greetings from the children, and a quiet kiss from mother, who made no remark upon my dress. Dora, Annie, and Sophie could not restrain their curiosity.

" Why, Hope, you are dressed for company; and I'm so glad! We've had lots of company, too, since you've been sick—Belinda and Esther Blake, and Mrs. Chapman, and Mrs. Eveleth, and ever so many more. Carey Chapman has been here every day, and has given me lots of beautiful rides upon my pony."

" Wouldn't some other word answer your purpose as well as 'lots,' Dora?" asked mother.

" Dear me! I never can think of the best words when I'm talking fast; and Carey Chapman told me, only yesterday, that I mustn't say 'lots,' and 'jolly,' and 'guess.' But, Hope, what made you get sick?"

" A bad cold."

" Yes, I know; but how could you get cold that delightful day?"

" What day?"

" Why, the day we had such a jolly picnic."

" Isn't 'jolly' one of your forbidden words?"

" To be sure! How could I forget? But, Hope, you look ever so much prettier since you were sick, and I wish you'd wear that white dress every day. It would be lovely, if only you had a breast-pin or knot of ribbons. Mrs. Kendall, I have several brooches—may I give one to Hope?' asked Dora.

"Hope does not care for a brooch, Dora," answered mother; "and then, perhaps, your father would not like you to give away his presents."

"I have one that Miss Lathrop gave me—a real beauty—but I never wear it, because I didn't like her. Let me give it to Hope, please, because I've never given her any thing, and I'm so glad to see her down-stairs." The eager child flew off to her room, without waiting for an answer, quickly returning with a pretty coral brooch, which she fastened triumphantly in my dress.

"Do let Hope wear it, for my sake, Mrs. Kendall. It is mine to give away, if I choose."

"Why do you wish Hope to wear it?" asked mother.

"Because she has been so kind and patient with me, and because I'm so glad she's down-stairs again, and because I love you both."

The child's head was drawn for a moment to mother's bosom; and when it was released, I saw that she had conquered—that I was free to accept the ornament—a fact which gave me more pleasure than I could have explained to mother. My personal appearance had suddenly become a matter of consequence to me.

The afternoon did not wane without callers, as something had whispered it would not. Belinda and Esther Blake came first, driving themselves in the doctor's old-fashioned chaise. They were several years my senior—had been young ladies ever since I could remember—were both much alike—fair blondes, with pale-brown hair, and light eyes—girls who were always quoting their city relatives, showing off boarding-school manners, and were always ready to display their accomplishments—girls who thought the end and aim of existence was to marry. Belinda, the elder, always led off in conversation, her sister responding in a mincing, affected way.

"Down at last!" exclaimed Belinda, after greeting my mother. "Who gave you leave to get sick?"

"Just now, too, when everybody is here?" chimed in Esther.

"And we were to have such a gay time after the picnic," added Belinda.

"Horseback excursions, and parties for Mrs. Crowell," said Esther.

"But they haven't all come off yet. You'll be in time for our party next week. Won't she, Mrs. Kendall?"

"You forget that Hope is hardly old enough for such a party," said my mother.

"Oh, you've kept her such a child!" said Belinda. "And she's taller than I am, and looks so young-ladyish to-day! How old are you, pet?"

"Eighteen, a month ago."

"Bless me! I had finished school at sixteen, and was quite come out—went everywhere—especially when we were visiting at Governor Fairchild's — he's mother's cousin, you know."

Yes, we knew—as did every one who knew Belinda.

"You must let her come, Mrs. Kendall, and wear this very white dress, and pretty coral pin. She looks twenty this minute, and so womanly! You would like to come to our party, Hope?"

"I believe so, if mother is willing."

"Hear that, now, puss!" exclaimed Belinda, addressing her sister. "'I believe so!' You and I could have told with certainty at her age whether we liked a party, could we not? But sometimes I think ma allowed us to go out too young. It made us appear older than we were."

This was an important item to keep before people when young ladies were twenty-five, and single.

They kept up a lively, meaningless rattle of words for a half hour, which required few responses from us, and then left, after extorting a conditional promise from mother that I should attend their party.

Then came Mr. and Mrs. Chapman and their city guests. They paused but few minutes, as they had started for a drive to North Sherbrooke, but long enough for our good friends to express their pleasure that I was released from my chamber.

"And wasn't it curious, Hope, that Carey should have had that dreadful fall just the day after we were all kept awake by the fire?" said Mrs. Chapman. "I told husband that every thing was happening all at once—the picnic, the fire, Carey's fall, and then, in a day or two, we heard of your sickness."

Mrs. Chapman's words and manner gave me pleasure, because they assured me that she knew nothing of the part I had acted in her son's rescue.

The sun was throwing long shadows upon the grass while I sat watching at the south window, hoping and expecting that other callers would come from the village. Mother sat near, plying her needle, and remarking upon the book which Sophie read aloud. It was "Hyperion," and a few sentences in the fifth chapter particularly interested her. They drew my own thoughts in from the village road, and from the fragrant honeysuckle which I pulled through the open window; and as these sentences, and the conversation which followed the reading of them, formed one of the stepping-stones of my life, I will quote them:

"The sword of his spirit had been forged and beaten by poverty. Its temper had been tried by a thirty years' war. It was not broken, not even blunted; but rather strengthened and sharpened by the blows it gave and received." Mother interrupted the reading, by asking:

"Hope, if poverty proved a stimulant, a sharpener to the intellect of this great man, why may it not to yours?"

"I suppose his spirit could overcome all obstacles; but can we be sure that he might not have written better if he had been surrounded with ease and luxury? It seems to me that poverty shackles the mind with petty and trifling cares, and that very few can become great or famous while they must be occupied with anxious thoughts about daily bread."

Mother did not answer, for at that moment Sophie exclaimed, "Oh, look!"

It was a sight well worth seeing. Virginia Thornton and Carey Chapman, on horseback, had just paused at our gate. Virginia, on a small cream-colored horse, had never looked prettier. Her dark-blue habit and white hat, with its drooping feather, were admirably suited to her style of beauty. She placed her hand upon Mr. Chapman's shoulder and sprang lightly to the ground, and the next minute was looking into my eyes and kissing my cheeks.

"Hope, what made you get sick when I was away?"

"I couldn't avoid the illness, nor choose the time."

"But, then, if you had waited until I came home, I would have taken such excellent care of you!"

"When did you return, Virginia?" asked mother.

"Only last night, and we've had such a splendid time! Come and see my beautiful horse, a present from father. He was sent home last week, but this is the first time I've tried him."

My friend pulled me to the open door, within a few feet of the horses, which Mr. Chapman had just secured. He came forward with a pleased smile, and offered me his hand. If mine was held a moment longer than was necessary in an ordinary greeting, it was not long enough to attract the notice of mother or Virginia, who was chatting gayly about the good qualities of her horse.

"I am glad to see you out again, Miss Hope."

The words were simple enough; but when I timidly glanced at his face, I fancied there was a warmer greeting in his eyes than in his words. He turned to mother, saying, "Your daughter will be strong enough to take a riding-lesson next week."

"I hope so," mother answered.

"Yes, indeed; Hope must ride, or else I shall but half enjoy my new pleasures," said Virginia. "She can have my horse almost any day; but how can we manage to ride together?"

"Hope can ride my pony," said Dora.

It was strange to hear such an offer from the lips of Dora. The use of her pony had been grudgingly allowed her sister, who had an equal ownership right with herself; but Annie had more than once been obliged to yield her claims to Dora's selfish exactions. Her offer was received with most hearty approval by all, and we soon turned from our examination and discussion of horses, habits, and caps, to the simple parlor, the plainness of which always disturbed me when our more prosperous neighbors were seated in it.

"You have not told me yet what made you ill," exclaimed Virginia, when the chat about riding was dropped. "Were you too much fatigued with picnic pleasures?"

"Miss Thornton, do you require of all your friends explicit reasons for health or sickness?" asked young Chapman, before I could frame an answer.

"Of course not; but when Hope gets sick, I've a right to know."

"There are moods, both of mind and body, which we cannot always account for."

"Mr. Chapman, have you not felt a cheerful, healthy tone of mind after reading certain books, for which you could hardly give a reason?" asked mother, with the intention of turning the conversation from me, and I heartily thanked her for it.

"Often, Mrs. Kendall. I have in my memory now several books which have left upon my mind a deep coloring for months; and yet, at the time of reading, I was scarcely conscious of their influence. Mitchell's lectures on astronomy produced a clear, vigorous tone of mind, and a habit of concentrated thought which I felt for some time. Then Ik Marvel's "Reveries of a Bachelor" gave me such a habit of living over the past, that often the duties of the present were neglected. 'Hyperion,' which I see open on your table, gave me an earnest longing to travel, to see the Rhine, which Longfellow says, 'Like the stream of time, flows amid the ruins of the past;' and yet, at the time of reading it, I was only conscious of the beauty, rhythm, and melody of the book. Do you like 'Hyperion,' Mrs. Kendall?"

"I like the few chapters which we have read very much. Longfellow has given me a strong desire to become acquainted with the writings of Jean Paul Richter."

"May I bring you a translation of some of his writings?"

"Thank you; I shall be glad to read them. Virginia, your face has a story in it. Will you give it a voice and words?" asked mother.

"I was only thinking of what Mr. Chapman said about books, and wondering if any thing I have read gave tone and coloring to my mind."

"And what conclusion have you reached?" asked Mr. Chapman.

"That I have read too carelessly to leave any lasting impressions."

"You have still time enough to correct careless habits," said my mother.

"Perhaps so; but I'm too much like Dorothy Dalyrimple—somebody that I read about once, who wanted to know every thing, but didn't want the trouble of learning. I shall never be careful and scholarly like Hope."

It was so archly and prettily said, that one could hardly determine whether, underneath the playfulness, lay a shadow of regret.

"Miss Hope is to be a teacher, I believe," said Mr. Chapman, addressing his words to mother. "She looks grave enough for such an office; and you are to have quite an addition to your family school, father tells me."

"Yes; and I could not manage them all without the help of my little girl."

There it was again, "Little girl!" What could mother mean by thus forgetting the respect due my eighteen years? I felt the hot color dying neck and cheeks as she looked toward me with a pleasant, approving smile.

Perhaps, to hide my confusion, she bade me go with Sophie and bring some fruit, cake, and milk to our guest. I was glad of the opportunity to cool my flushed face; but the color had hardly faded, before it found another excuse for a more violent return.

"My cup-bearer again," said Mr. Chapman, in a voice too low for any ear but my own, when Virginia and the children were engaged in such a noisy play of words. "It has grieved me very deeply that my little Hebe should have suffered so long for the services she rendered me. Are you quite recovered now?"

"Not quite strong, but almost well."

"And have felt no ill-will toward me, as the cause of this dreary confinement in summer-time?"

"How could I, Mr. Chapman? Please forget all about that morning, sir."

"You ask an impossible thing. I shall endeavor to show my grateful remembrance of it in every possible way."

Again there seemed to me a deeper meaning in his tones and eyes than in his words; and again, for a single moment, my right hand lay in the clasp of his. The occupants of the room were all too busy with talk and refreshments to notice this little by-play, which consumed scarcely two minutes, but was long enough for me to draw flattering inferences, and store them up.

Long, level rays of golden light stole through the honeysuckle vines before our guests rose to depart. I watched the floating feather of Virginia's hat disappear amongst the willows which fringed the road, and then drew a low chair so near that I might lean against mother, too tired and too happy to talk—too happy even to ask my heart what had so quickened my pulses and sweetened life.

CHAPTER XXI.

THE RIDING LESSON.

"Moreover, something is, or seems,
That touches me with mystic gleams,
Like glimpses of forgotten dreams."

WITH returning strength came a keener enjoyment of summer pleasures than I had ever known before. A daily drive with Virginia in her father's carriage, usually accompanied by her aunt and Captain Wynne, did wonders toward restoring the hue of health to my cheeks; and rarely a day passed that Carey Chapman did not find an excuse for calling—perhaps only a book was left for Miss Hope, or Mrs. Chapman had sent a message to mother; and then it seemed an easy and natural thing for the young man to linger and talk with mother. She talked well, and was, moreover, his distant kinswoman. More than a week slipped away after my return to the family circle, before I was deemed strong enough for a riding-lesson. Meantime, mother had spent her leisure in preparing me a riding-habit. She could not afford the expense of buying one, and so contrived to make a very pretty one out of an old green merino dress of her own.

"But what will you do for a hat?" she asked, when the habit was completed, and we had both admired its neat fit.

"Wear my old straw one, I suppose. How pleasant it would be, if we only had money enough, so that we might buy every thing we needed, without spending so much time in contriving!" I spoke with a little sigh, which did not escape mother's notice.

"Hope, you are not allowing your old false fear of poverty to revive? Struggle against a complaining spirit, my child, and remember that God has placed you in just those circumstances which will best develop your spiritual nature. Think of the great mercies of the last two years—the employment in teaching so providentially sent us both, and then this last great relief, in clearing off that mortgage."

"Oh, mother, I had not forgotten those blessings; and I often feel so strong, that poverty seems no evil; but just then I was thinking of Virginia's beautiful hat, and how she has only to ask for whatever she fancies—"

"And just a little envy of your friend's position crept into your heart unawares?"

"I cannot help sometimes contrasting my lot with hers, but I do not think I envy her."

"I trust not, my child. If you make a right use of all God's gifts to you, I think you will be quite as contented and useful a woman as Virginia; but you must be willing to see your friend noticed and caressed in society much more than yourself, and if your love for her is unselfish you will take pleasure in seeing her admired, unless you find that admiration makes her vain. Guard your own heart carefully, Hope, lest an undue love for the pleasures of society, which you are just beginning to taste, should creep into it. You may bring me your straw hat, and let me see what I can do with it."

We both grew quite merry over the process of rejuvenating the hat which had served me so faithfully for two summers, and which would still have been respectable but for its last encounter with the blackberry-bushes. Mother found that she had enough of the old green velvet trimming of her dress to give the hat quite a stylish air.

"There, who says that contentment, faculty, and tact are not better than money?" she exclaimed, when her task was completed. "Make yourself ready now, Hope, while I give Jonas orders about the pony; 'tis almost time for Virginia and Mr. Chapman to appear."

It was a happy group that stood upon the old stone steps and in the yard, to see me lifted into the saddle, and watch the gentle movements of the pony up and down the yard, while Mr. Chapman, the elder, taught me how to use the rein and curb, how to sit at ease, and how to carry my shoulders. Virginia and Carey Chapman sat upon their horses near the gate, watching the progress of my lesson. Willie, astride the fence, looked on, and told how he should ride, when he was a man. Dora laughed at my awkward seizing of the saddle's pommel whenever the pony trotted, while mother's pleased face encouraged and gratified me. I knew her pleasure in my ride was greatly enhanced by the presence of the elder Mr. Chapman, who was to accompany us.

When my kind, fatherly friend was satisfied with the confidence I had gained from his teaching, he mounted his own horse, and we started at a gentle pace up the road leading to North Sherbrooke. The scenery for many miles around our town was beautiful, as all know who are familiar with Western New England; and seen when the mature beauty of summer crowns it, with a silvery mist, like a delicate gossamer veil, shrouding the hill, and the golden-rod and silken-tasselled corn nodding in the fragrant air, it was lovely—especially lovely to the eyes that had seen nothing more majestic or beautiful than what might be seen in the vicinity of Sherbrooke—young eyes, too, that had not been sated with pleasures.

"You are enjoying the ride?" asked Carey Chapman, coming so near my pony that he could reach down and draw the reins more tightly through my fingers, while his father rode forward by Virginia's side.

"Yes, more than I can tell." He smiled in a pleased way, and said:

"Ay, 'tis pleasant to be young and sad to know that—

'The world's air warps our way,
And crops the roses from the cheek of day.'"

I mused upon his words, conscious that his eye rested upon my flushed face.

"Do you mean, Mr. Chapman, that as we grow older and mingle more with the world, we shall lose the keen enjoyment of pleasures?"

"Just that, my little friend, but I see you are sceptical."

"I should be sorry to think this exercise on horseback would never give me as much pleasure again, and sorry to know that my own Sherbrooke would ever look less lovely."

"And I should be sorry to mar your happiness of to-day, by the faintest prophecy of what the world may bring you. I was speaking in general terms. There are doubtless hearts that always carry about with them the dews of youth —so pure and truthful that the world's air never crops their roses; I could even venture to predict that you are one of the favored few."

"You have seen the Rhine, Mr. Chapman?"

"Yes, and the Alps."

"Does your remembrance of the Rhine rob our New England rivers of their beauty? and is there no longer any grandeur or loveliness in the Berkshire Hills for you, because you have looked upon the Alps?"

"I see you are intent upon making me prove that 'the world's air has not cropped my roses.' Well, to be candid, I must admit that gazing upon grand and majestic mountains has not made our own New England hills less fair for me, neither has the Rhine stolen from the Connecticut its loveliness. I think that acquaintance with European scenery has only made me more keenly alive to the beauties of our own; but I rarely meet a person who has travelled much, who does not speak contemptuously of the rivers, lakes, and mountains of his own country."

"I should think such persons gained but little and lost a great deal by travel."

"Have you not met people, who are constantly depreciating the pleasures within their reach, because they do not compare favorably with those they have enjoyed at some former time?"

"I remember, when I told Belinda Blake how much I liked to hear Mrs. Eveleth sing, she told me if I had heard Jenny Lind, I should never care for Mrs. Eveleth's voice; and I thought then how much better it would be for me never to hear Jenny Lind, if her voice would spoil my ear for Mrs Eveleth's singing, because you know I must hear Mrs. Eveleth every Sabbath, and could not expect to hear Jenny Lind more than once in a lifetime."

My companion rode on in silence for several minutes, and then asked, abruptly:

"Do you sing?"

"Only a few hymns with mother."

"Your friend Miss Thornton sings uncommonly well."

"Yes, I like her voice."

"'Tis sweet and flexible both in singing and talking. Miss Hope, could you contrive to carry a few of those blossoms, which I see near that wild grape-vine, if I dismount and gather them?"

He did not wait for a reply, but swinging himself from his saddle, threw his bridle-rein over his arm, and walking to the hedge, gathered a few of the flowers and some sprays of sweet fern, which he bound together with a tendril of the grape-vine and then presented to me.

"Do you know the name of these flowers?" he asked, as I secured the bouquet to a button of my habit.

"The evening primrose—'tis common in our pasture, and lovely, but it withers very soon; these will be faded to-morrow."

"Yes, the flower fadeth and the grass withereth; there is nothing substantial and enduring."

"But the word of the Lord abideth forever," I ventured to add, in a timid voice.

"We are told so," he answered in a dreamy, abstracted manner, as if the beauty and truth of the words had never taken root in his heart. Shy, shrinking, and fearful of expressing my thoughts before any one but mother, something gave me courage to say:

"Every word of God is pure; He is a shield unto them that put their trust in Him."

"I see that your father's faith has wrapped you like a mantle, my little friend. Be thankful that you are never vexed with doubts about the authenticity of the words you have quoted."

"Did you know my father, sir?"

"Very well—as well as a lad of eighteen years may know a mature man; he helped prepare me for college, but I seldom saw him after I left home for Yale. He always impressed me as a man of generous culture and rare refinement—a man whose faith in Christ and His religion amounted to knowledge."

"His last words were, 'I know that my Redeemer liveth,' and 'The everlasting arms of mercy are around me.'"

My voice was choked with emotion, and only the strong desire to impress upon Carey Chapman's heart the reality of my father's faith would have induced me to mention his last words.

He saw the tears which could not be repressed fall down upon my flowers, but with a delicate kindness, which I appreciated, made no allusion to them. He strove in a careless way to divert my thoughts, pointing out the beauties of the landscape, and chatting about our mutual friends, until his father and Virginia drew rein in front of a farm-house, and awaited our approach.

"Hold my horse a minute, Carey; I have some business with Farmer Hutchins, which will only take a minute's time. Halloa, here comes the farmer himself; I shall not be obliged to dismount. Good-evening, Mr. Hutchins!"

Mr. Chapman's last words were addressed to a stout, tanned, resolute-looking man, in blue cotton overalls, who approached us with a sickle in one hand and a rake in the other.

The rake was dropped upon the neatly-kept greensward, that he might shake the extended hand of Mr. Chapman.

"Glad to see ye, Square, and the young man too. It's easy to see with half an eye as how he's a chip of the old block."

"Carey, do you remember Farmer Hutchins?" asked Mr. Chapman.

"Perfectly—how do you do, sir?" extending a neatly-gloved hand to meet the farmer's huge, brown one.

"Tolerable, so as to be stirrin', as ye see. What have ye been larning in them foreign schools, young man?"

"Things that will be of use, I trust."

"Umph! not half as useful as a knowledge of farmin', I'll bet. But I don't keer what ye've larned, if ye've only steered clear of them foreign notions, as I've heern tell of, and stuck fast to the gospel as Elder Eveleth preaches. Come home now for good?"

"I shall settle somewhere in my native State, I think, but I am not sure that Sherbrooke will furnish me with employment."

"What kind of work are ye fitted for?"

"I have studied the profession of law."

"Ye'd better hire out with me till after havestin'. It'll take off that pale, sickly look, and give ye a wholesome coat of tan, and mebbe some blistered hands. I don't ask nothin' for my advice."

"Mr. Hutchins, are you in want of more help?" asked the elder Mr. Chapman.

"Wa'al, me and the boys calculate to do up the harvestin', but Andrew, he's taken a notion as how he must have more larnin', and so he's a goin' to North Sherbrooke 'Cademy, and we don't get a great sight of work out of him."

"I'm trying to get places for the Widow Reed's two boys, lads of twelve and fourteen, and it occurred to me, Mr. Hutchins, that an energetic, determined man like you, would know exactly how to manage one of them. On so large a farm there must always be plenty of work for such a boy."

"Plenty of work, no doubt of that; but I reckon it would take the hull of a man's time to keep one of them lazy chaps busy."

"No, I think Matthew is naturally a better boy than Tom, and he is pretty thoroughly frightened now by the result of his brother's mischief, and promises to be industrious and obedient if he can get steady work."

"I tried Tom a couple of days when I was plantin', and his idle, ugly ways would have tried the patience of Job. You would hardly believe it now, but I caught him chasin' my young turkeys into the wet grass and stonin' the sheep; and the next day he pulled up more'n half my onions, pretendin' as how he thought 'em weeds. I reckon I don't like the blood well enough to try another one of them."

"But, Mr. Hutchins, you'll find Matthew better disposed than Tom, and if you'll take him on trial a couple of days, you'll certainly be doing a most charitable deed. His poor mother is over-worked and fretful—her eldest daughter gone off, and the whole family are about as miserable as 'tis possible for people to be. Don't answer me now, but think the matter over until to-morrow."

"Wa'al, I'll talk with my old woman; if she's a mind to be plagued with him, I don't know as I keer. There'll be a heap of apples and pertaters to pick and corn to husk, and then I s'pose I could keep a chap busy in pickin' stones from the hill-side lot. Mr. Chapman, won't you walk in and eat some of my Bartlett pears? They're just prime now."

"Thank you, I should like to do so, but 'tis getting near sunset, and these young ladies must be trotting toward the village."

"I didn't know as you had any galls so large. That one on the light horse is as large as my 'Cindy."

"That is Squire Thornton's daughter, and the other is Hope Kendall."

"David's gall, I see by her eyes! I hope, Miss, you are like your father in more things than eyes. He was a man as a gall might be proud to call father."

Involuntarily I reached out my hand to the bluff farmer, and thanked him for his kind words.

"Take keer, Miss, keep a tight rein on yer pony. He don't like the hissing of my old gander."

But Farmer Hutchins' warning was not in season. The pony, restless with standing and glad of an opportunity to show off her spirit, danced and reared, and before the farmer could seize the check-rein, sprang forward and flew off on the road leading to her stable. I heard, as in a dream, "Cling to your saddle!" "Use the curb!" from two or three voices, and was conscious that my safety depended on keeping my seat and using the check, as Mr. Chapman had taught me.

The pony, though restless and spirited, was not vicious, and when she found that the hissing gander was not in pursuit, and that a firm hand held the check-rein, she gradually slackened her pace, so that Carey Chapman overtook me after a brisk gallop of over a mile.

"Are you frightened?" he asked, riding alongside, and seizing the pony's reins with so firm a grasp that her gallop was changed to a gentle trot.

"Not much; but I'm glad that you have come."

His face said that he was more than glad, but his words were few.

"We will pause here until my father and Miss Thornton overtake us." And he checked both horses, taking the two sets of reins in his left hand, and reaching out, he took my trembling hand in his firm, steady one.

"You have shown courage and presence of mind in managing the pony, but no more than I should have expected of you. With your mother's permission, I shall put you on this horse of mine, after a few more trials of your skill. Will that please you?"

"If it will give you pleasure, if you think I can manage him, I believe I should have courage to try."

"You would have courage for any thing which is right, would you not, my little Hope?"

I made no reply, for at that moment the sound of approaching horses caused Carey Chapman to release my hand, and place in it my pony's reins, and in a minute more the questions of my friends had to be met and answered, and their congratulations accepted. I was glad of the escort of my elderly friend back to my mother's door, glad that his grave words needed only short replies, and glad that the clear, ringing laugh and musical voice of my friend Virginia were so near. There was also a pleasure, which I could not have described, in listening to the voice of Carey Chapman, even when his words were not addressed to me.

CHAPTER XXII.

HOPE'S FIRST PARTY.

"The life of man upon this fair earth is made up for the most part of little pains and little pleasures. The great wonder-flowers bloom but once in a lifetime."—LONGFELLOW.

" And all the rooms
Were full of crinkling silks, that swept about
The fine dust of most subtle courtesies."
MRS. BROWNING.

I AWOKE with the early dawn on that September morning, whose evening hours were to bring me the pleasures of my first party—awoke with a dim, delicious half-consciousness of some happiness in store for me; and contrary to my usual custom, I lay for several minutes, before making my toilet, indulging in the new luxury of a day-dream. My busy, practical life had furnished me with neither warp nor woof for such dreams, before the present summer.

I remember distinctly the delicate perfume of the honeysuckle, which floated in through my open windows; and never since that morning have I seen or inhaled honeysuckle without a momentary return of that sweet daydream.

I remember, too, that a robin poured forth his song from the branches of the linden-tree, that leaned protectingly toward our western windows; that Jonas Gould's shrill whistling of "Hail Columbia" mingled with the bird's song.

But mother's voice calling cheerily to the children broke the golden chain of my fancies and brought me down to the simple routine of my quiet life. I always assisted her in preparing breakfast and making the house tidy; then came the children's lessons; and I usually sat with them during their hours of study, busy with my own Latin or history.

Even with the pleasant anticipation of an evening party these duties must receive attention. So I plodded mechanically through them, until the sun threw long shadows into our little parlor.

Mother had not mentioned the party during the day; but when I had put away school-books and finished my tasks, even to the methodical spreading of the tea-table in our tidy kitchen, she followed me to my chamber.

"You would be disappointed not to go to the party this evening, Hope?"

"I should like to go; I thought you were willing I should."

"I have given my consent to your going, but I have some anxieties about the effect this party will have upon you, and I do not like a few of the people whom you will meet."

"Why, mother, I thought the Blakes were very exclusive."

"They try to be, but this party is made for Mr. and Mrs. Crowell, whom I do not like, neither would

I choose Belinda and Esther as companions for my little girl."

"I will stay at home if you say so, but I thought father approved of small parties, and I remember he often went with you to Dr. Blake's."

"You forget, Hope, that our age and experience taught us to cull only the flowers and reject the weeds of such conversation as we must listen to. And then, your father had the rare faculty of giving a high and pleasing tone to the conversation and amusements of such parties. I shall not forbid your going, and perhaps 'tis well that the monotony of your quiet life is to be broken up; but you must remember that such pleasures will be very rare, and that any little attentions you may receive will be more for your father's sake, than because his little girl is attractive, wise, or old enough to receive them."

She kissed my lips, looking into the eyes that every one said were like my father's, and added:

"If he were only here to go with you, child, I should have no anxieties about the result."

We both stood for some minutes in silence, looking out upon the fair landscape, which had lost none of its summer beauty, watching the clouds as they floated in the western sky—

"Like golden down on some high angel's wing,"

and then changed to purple, and faded in the twilight.

"Night shows us stars, as sorrow shows us truths," mother said softly, quoting from an author whom I did not read, as two or three stars shone out upon their dusky background; "sorrow has taught me many a lesson of trust and reliance, which I could never have learned in the bright noontide of prosperity."

Mother turned from the window, lighted my lamp, and

went down to the parlor. She knew my wardrobe left me no choice for my evening dress, and in its simplicity required no aid from her.

I was quickly attired in a white muslin, beautifully ironed by mother's own hands, with the very childlike adorning of sash and pin; but she had taught me that neatness and simplicity were more suitable ornaments for a young girl than jewels, and I was quite satisfied with her teachings, if not with my simple dress.

Dr. Blake's servant came for me with the old horse and chaise, and as mother carefully secured my wrappings, her lips touched my forehead with a caress and a blessing.

"I shall sit up for you, Hope, and you must not remain after eleven. Tell Mrs. Blake I said you must return at that hour."

Dr. Blake's house was one of the most pretending in its style and surroundings that our village could boast. Standing a little removed from its neighbors, old-fashioned, square, its three-story front had quite an imposing effect upon one who had never so much as seen the neighboring city of Wiltshire.

My happy courage forsook me for a minute as I entered alone the wide hall, and was told by a servant to walk up a flight of stairs. However, I was met upon the landing by Belinda and Esther, who seized me with noisy demonstrations of pleasure, which even then seemed to me unreal, and while they pulled off my wrappings, told me what guests were expected, and made comments upon my dress.

"Do you always wear white?" asked Belinda.

"And never so much as one flower in your hair?" added Esther.

The young ladies were dressed alike, in lemon-colored, gauze-like material, made in the extreme of fashion, with flounces and low corsage, their pale-brown hair in drooping curls and ornamented with a profusion of flowers of every hue, while showy bracelets sparkled upon their thin arms.

"Aren't our dresses lovely?" asked Belinda. "They were sent from Wiltshire only yesterday."

"And we were in such a fright lest they shouldn't be in season," said Esther; "we had them made like the one Mrs. Crowell wore at Mrs. Chapman's party, only hers was pink. Did you know we had all our dresses made at Madame Florian's, in Wiltshire?"

"No, I didn't know it."

"Governor Fairchild and his wife, and Cousin William are coming to our party," said Belinda.

"And Cousin William is splendid," added Esther, surveying herself in the mirror, pulling her ringlets out, rearranging her flowers, and shaking out her flounces.

"How do you know? It has been three years since we saw him!" retorted Belinda in a sharper voice than I had supposed could issue from such colorless lips.

"Oh, I know. I peeped through the blinds when the carriage drove up—he wasn't in the carriage, but on a splendid black horse, and he has an elegant figure. Hark! I hear their voices now in the hall! They've gone down to the parlor."

"Goodness! what will they think not to see us there? And pa and ma are so old-fashioned! Why, they never would have made this party but for us, and pa never talks about any thing but his stupid patients, and ma thinks only of the Reeds and their troubles."

"Come along, Esther! You needn't be a bit afraid, Hope, we'll find some one to talk with you." And Belinda good-naturedly shook out the skirt of my muslin, and seizing some pink blossoms from a sweet-scented geranium in the window, she fastened them in my hair without heeding my protestations. It was an easy thing for her to be amiable to a little girl, whom she did not fear as a rival; and so shielded and half-hidden by Esther's ample flounces, I followed the girls into the parlor, and received the kind greetings of Dr. and Mrs. Blake, while the daughters with affected raptures greeted their city relatives, entirely forgetting in their excess of hospitality to the Fairchilds to introduce me, which omission gave me for the moment unnecessary pain and confusion.

While the large, cheerful, old-fashioned parlors are being filled with guests, I must describe a few of them. Ex-Governor Fairchild shall sit first for his picture—the dignity of his social and political position gives him the precedence. Tall, with iron-gray hair, white whiskers, thin, decided lips, and broad, high brow, a marked man, even if one had not seen the steel-gray eyes, quiet and steady this evening, but which could emit almost dazzling rays when occasion fanned their fires. He talked more freely than he smiled, and was gravely polite to all.

Mrs. Fairchild was not the mother of the tall young man, who called her by that sweet name, I saw at a glance. Her sunny blue eyes, abundant brown hair, fair complexion, and light, girlish figure could not have seen more than thirty-five years. Sprightly, intelligent, and amiable, she could not be otherwise than attractive; and whenever the ex-Governor's ear was arrested by the silvery tones of her voice, the stern lines of his face unbent, and the gray of his keen eye melted into blue, reminding one of gray morning clouds, softened by the sun's rays till they were lost in the blue depths of the sky.

William Fairchild had, as Esther told me, an elegant figure, but he appeared quite too conscious of it, and bore

himself with a haughty air, as if he thought his social
position and worth could not be known unless announced
in this way. He appeared easy and affable with Esther,
who apparently regarded it as her especial prerogative to
entertain him. I wondered how an educated man could
find so much amusement in the frivolous topics which they
chose to converse upon. I have since learned that sensible
men generally treat women as if they were incapable of
conversing upon any thing but the fashions, the weather,
and the peculiarities of their neighbors.

Mr. and Mrs. Eveleth were the next arrivals: Mr.
Eveleth, dignified and taciturn, rarely allowing a smile to
light up features that were positively handsome with such
an illumination; kind and faithful as a pastor, his people
feared and reverenced rather than loved him, and only
those families, whose thresholds had been crossed by heavy
afflictions, knew the depth of tender human sympathy that
throbbed beneath his cold exterior; with a highly-polished
intellect, and finely-strung, sensitive nature, he was often
depressed by his people's lack of appreciation. Mrs. Eveleth was a genial woman, whose face always wore an
encouraging smile. She had been an accomplished teacher
of music for many years before her marriage, and still
retained a clear, musical voice, singing soprano in our
village choir, and pathetic old ballads and hymns in our
social gatherings. Her presence was always warmly welcomed in every home, but it was light, warmth, and medicine to the poor.

Captain Wynne, Aunt Sallie, Squire Thornton, and
Virginia followed our pastor and his wife. They need no
introduction. Indeed, words could never describe the
bright beauty of Virginia; dressed in soft blue silk, her
faultless arms exposed, the golden wealth of her hair coiled
simply in a knot upon the back of her head, and delicate

white lace fastened with a cross of pearls upon her neck, she was a fair vision.

I was no longer shy, timid, and alone—the presence of my friend always encouraged and exhilarated me. Standing by Virginia's side, I could meet the eyes of Carey Chapman, when he addressed me in a lower, graver tone than he had used in speaking to my friend, or the Misses Blake, who hovered around the young, unmarried men, as I have seen butterflies hang around flowers, poising their gay wings over first one and then another fragrant blossom, as if uncertain which would yield most perfume or honey.

"You are late, Mr. Chapman!" said the fair Belinda, with a smile, which was intended as a gentle rebuke for his having withheld himself from her charming society so long.

"I beg your pardon, Miss Blake, but I did not intend to be a laggard. Your rooms certainly present attractions enough to draw one at an early hour almost against his better judgment. My father and I were detained in Wiltshire until near sunset."

"Oh, I know, 'tis court week, and that horrid Tom Reed is to have his trial. If I were judge, he should be sentenced to the penitentiary for life."

"Why, Miss Blake! Who would suspect that so much sternness could dwell beneath so fair an outside?"

Miss Blake simpered and pulled her flowers, but still asserted that Tom Reed was a vagabond, and past all hopes of reform.

"Who is counsel for the poor boy?" asked Mr. Eveleth, who had overheard the conversation.

"Squire Thornton has offered his services, and although he neither wishes nor expects to clear the lad, he hopes his sentence of imprisonment may be only for a short term."

"Dear me! and then he'll be sure to come back and burn us all up out of spite. If I only knew the judge, I'd tell him what a mischievous fellow he has always been."

"You forget, Miss Blake, that his surroundings have not been favorable to the growth of any thing but evil—upbraiding and neglect at home, and no regular employment for his hands or mind; we should have looked for just such fruit," said the clergyman.

"You surely would not have him released, Mr. Eveleth?" questioned Belinda.

"I would have his term of imprisonment short, and then place him in a reform school. I believe, with judicious treatment, the boy may yet be reclaimed."

"Well, I'm glad you've more faith in human nature than I have. But as I tell ma a dozen times a day, I'm tired of the very sound of Reed. There's always something to be done for the widow and her family, and they are such an ungrateful set there's no pleasure in doing any thing for them."

The clergyman turned away, and Carey Chapman said:

"Your charities must needs be appreciated, then, Miss Blake, else you take no pleasure in giving?"

"Certainly; I should never give away any thing just for the pleasure of giving, and the Reeds never know the worth of one's gift's. Only last week I gave Martha Jane a dress of my own, and if you'll believe me, in less than an hour she came back, and said as boldly as could be, 'Mother says as how if you'll give me a shawl to go alongst with the gownd, mabbe I might go to Sunday-school;' and mind you not so much as a single thank did I get for my gift."

"You gave her a shawl, of course," said young Chapman.

"No, you may be sure not! but ma heard the polite begging, and the next day my old Stella shawl was missing, and last Sunday I saw it on the shoulders of the ungrateful Martha Jane."

It would be impossible to describe the pretty little tosses of Belinda's curls and fan during this recital, or the manner in which she fluttered off to chat with Mrs. Crowell.

Carey Chapman turned, and described to Virginia and myself poor Tom Reed's appearance in court; and then Squire Thornton joining in the conversation, the gentlemen soon found themselves discussing Fremont's chances of election.

Soon there came a hush in the general buzz of conversation, for the sweet tones of Mrs. Eveleth's voice, which had lost none of its tunefulness, floated out through the rooms. She sang "The Harp that once through Tara's Halls," with genuine pathos, playing her own accompaniment. Belinda and Esther appeared to think they could only show their superior knowledge and appreciation of music by simpers and winks. "Horrid, old-fashioned, isn't she?" whispered Belinda, behind her fan, to Carey Chapman; "but she must be asked to sing because she's the minister's wife, you know. I get enough of her voice on Sundays."

"But I must acknowledge that I like her singing, Miss Blake, even if you set me down as deficient in musical taste."

"How strange, when you have had such opportunities to hear good music! Now Hope likes Mrs. Eveleth, because she's never heard any thing better; but you've heard Jenny Lind?"

"Yes, and many another celebrity; but Mrs. Eveleth's

voice stirs a deeper fount of feeling than almost any one I have ever listened to."

Belinda passed on, and I heard her criticising and depreciating the singing to Mrs. Crowell, who was a ready listener.

Mrs. Eveleth rose, after singing one song, answering the urgent entreaties for more by saying—

"No, I only opened the way for the young ladies; my songs are all old-fashioned."

"But if you always sing them in that way, your hearers will not complain," said the ex-Governor, leading her to a seat.

Mrs. Crowell next astonished her listeners with a noisy, clashing selection, played with considerable skill and brilliancy, but without taste or feeling; and then the daughters of our host, after affected hesitation and excuses, consented to play a duet, the chief attraction of which was noise.

"Lovely, charming!—that must have been Mozart's composition," exclaimed Mrs. Crowell. "Don't get up; pray give us something more."

Thus entreated, Esther sang a sentimental song, in a weak, thin voice; Belinda playing an accompaniment, while their delighted friend made wry faces behind her fan for the amusement of her husband.

"Won't some of the gentlemen favor us with a song?" asked Belinda, rising from the piano. "Oh, Cousin William, you used to sing delightfully! Do give us just one song."

"I'm not in tune to-night. Pray excuse me, and beg Miss Thornton to be my substitute."

"How cruel!" murmured Belinda, giving her cousin a little tap upon his arm with her fan, to enforce her words. "And I have told Mrs. Crowell what a superb tenor you sing."

Then followed a playful war of words about his unwillingness to oblige, the hard-heartedness of men in general, and the cruel exactions which they made upon all ladies who could sing and play.

I saw that Belinda did not mean to ask Virginia to sing, and I heard her refuse Carey Chapman's request; but good Mrs. Blake, who was unmindful of her daughter's desire to keep Virginia's beauty and accomplishments as much in the background as possible, urged her with so much genuine good nature, that Virginia yielded, and sang "Comin' through the Rye," in a sweet, unaffected way, which arrested every ear and silenced the hum of voices, which even Mrs. Crowell's noise had failed to do.

"Bravely sung, my Scotch lassie!" called out Captain Wynne, " I do not wonder that—

'All the lads they smile at thee.'"

Virginia rose, blushing and confused at the blunt captain's compliment, but he drew her back to the piano, saying, "One more, my bonny lass; sing 'Are there Tidings,' just as you sung it for your father and me last evening;" and a chorus of voices exclaimed, "One more, Miss Thornton."

Belinda and Esther whispered to their cousin and Mrs. Crowell during the entire performance. I occasionally heard such sentences as, "What a pity her voice hasn't been cultivated!" and "She sings only old, worn-out songs;" "Never has heard any good music."

Virginia was not permitted to rise after her second song. The captain declared she had sung that so well, that every one wanted to hear "The Pilot."

"But that is really very old-fashioned, Captain Wynne," pleaded Virginia. "I only sing it to please you and father."

"Old-fashioned!" called out the captain in a voice nearly as loud as if he had been giving orders on board the Alacrity, "so are the Psalms! and I've no doubt the birds sing just the same old-fashioned things that charmed Adam and Eve; but who dares to say the robin's song is not as sweet and welcome as if we had not heard it every summer of our lives?"

Mrs. Fairchild seconded the captain's request, laying a small, jewelled hand upon the young singer's arm, and saying, "Do sing 'The Pilot,' Miss Thornton; my father used to sing that nearly thirty years ago, while I sat upon his knee."

Virginia needed no further urging, and "The Pilot" was followed by "Kathleen Mavourneen," to please the ex-Governor, whose eyes lost their gray during the singing—only the deep hue of a midsummer sky shone in them.

The announcement of refreshments relieved Virginia from the piano, and she was escorted to the supper-room by Carey Chapman, who had listened to the music with an eagerness which I had noted well, but which had given me only pleasure and pride.

I was kindly looked after by Mr. Chapman, whose wife had been carried off by Squire Thornton.

"So this is your first party, is it, Miss Hope?" asked my elderly friend, helping me to the tempting delicacies. "Are you enjoying the company?"

"Very well, sir."

"I am sorry your mother is not here. A little more variety in her life would be a great benefit to her. Tell her that Mrs. Fairchild will call upon her to-morrow, to talk about her school. She has two little girls about as old as the Mayhews, and she wants to leave them in a good school for the winter. She is going to Washington with her husband. How soon will your new rooms be ready?"

"Not before the last of October; the workmen have but just made a beginning."

My elderly friend chose grave, practical themes to converse with me upon; but as he often turned to talk with other friends, my ear caught many bits of the conversation around me. Mrs. Crowell was describing her gay New York life to the delighted Belinda. Carey Chapman, Virginia, and Mrs. Fairchild were discoursing upon music, and gayly chatting about little nothings, in an easy, sparkling, off-hand way, that seemed mysterious and unattainable to me. Esther favored me with her company long enough to assure me that "the supper was got up in the best Wiltshire style," and to ask if I had ever tasted such jelly or ice-cream before, or seen such a splendid bouquet.

"Splendid" was Esther's great word, applied indiscriminately to jellies, custards, flowers, fashions, and sunset clouds, and was second only, in her list of. adjectives, to "sublime," which she used a trifle less sparingly.

We were moving from the refreshment-room, when my eyes caught sight of the clock. It was eleven, and my dear, patient mother sitting up at home waiting for me. I ran to Mrs. Blake, and asked her if she could send me directly home.

"As well now as at any time," she answered, "but it is not late, my dear. Why must you go so early?"

"Because mother will sit up for me."

"Well, you are a good girl, and I'll send for Patrick and the horse at once. I hope you have enjoyed your first party?"

"Oh, very much."

"That's right; go up to Belinda's room, and put on your shawl and slip down the back stairs; you will find

Patrick waiting at the side-door, and be sure and give my love to your ma."

"Passing through the library, I found a group surrounding Mrs. Crowell and Belinda, and saw at once, by the animated looks and tones, that something novel and exciting was under discussion.

"Capital fun," exclaimed Belinda.

"Won't it be splendid?" cried Esther.

"But what if the gentlemen do not accept our invitations?" asked Virginia.

"You needn't fear; they'll be glad enough to accept our escort for once."

"Did you hear what Mrs. Crowell proposes, Hope?" asked Belinda. "A horseback excursion to Switzerland for next Saturday; the ladies inviting the gentlemen because it is leap-year. Won't it be rare fun? But of course you can't go, as you never ride."

"You should have seen Hope ride last week," commenced Virginia, but her voice was drowned by a chorus of exclamations and questions from the eager sisters, who were delighted with the prospect of an excursion, which would give them an excuse for showing their preferences by inviting their escorts.

I slipped away into the hall, but, before reaching the staircase, encountered Carey Chapman.

"Going so soon?" he asked, looking kindly into my eyes, and taking my hand in his. "I am afraid this party has cropped some of your roses."

"No; it has only given me fresh buds."

"May their blossoms never wither! How are you going home?"

"With Patrick, in the doctor's chaise. Good-night, Mr. Chapman."

"Good-night, my little Hebe."

CHAPTER XXIII.

STEPPING STONES.

"The lesser griefs, that may be said,
That breathe a thousand tender vows,
Are but as servants in a house
Where lies the master newly dead."

TENNYSON.

SWITZERLAND was a hilly district of Sherbrooke, west of the village nearly five miles. Winding through the rugged rocks, with many a plunge and leap, flowed one of the numerous streams that feed the Connecticut. Its hurrying waters had once turned a mill, the ruins of which still stood in Switzerland, adding much to the picturesque beauty of the place, and forming one of the principal objects of attraction to visitors. I had been there only once, when business had called my father to that district; and I had a strong desire to see again the rapid stream, the lonely mill, and the wild beauty of the rocks, and a natural wish to join the equestrian party which proposed visiting the district on Saturday. I gave mother a careful history of the pleasures of my first party, which I must say lost some of their brilliancy rehearsed in the clear light of morning, but enough of the evening's glamour remained to make the prospective ride very tempting, and I was very cautious in approaching the subject.

Something intuitively told me that mother would not approve of my joining a party of ladies who invited their cavaliers, and if she did approve the plan, whom should I invite?

My thoughts wandered from studies on that bright September day, far away from the smoothly flowing lines of Horace to the musical whirl of the mill-stream. I thought more just then of the sermons which might be read in the stones of our rugged Swiss district, than of the rhythm and melody of Latin poetry.

"Mother, do you think leap-year gives ladies any particular privileges?" I asked, as soon as the children were released from morning tasks for an hour's recreation in the orchard.

"No, real ladies do not wish for any liberty during leap-year, that would be a stain upon the modesty which is a woman's brightest ornament and surest shield at all times. Why do you ask such a question, Hope?"

"Because when I left Mrs. Blake's last evening Mrs. Crowell and Belinda were talking about an excursion to Switzerland; the ladies were all to go on horseback, and to invite the gentlemen."

"And you wish to join such a party?"

"I should like the ride, and I should like to see Switzerland again."

"You can have both those pleasures without laying aside that maidenly reserve which becomes your years. If Mrs. Crowell and Belinda choose to get up such a party, I would not give my sanction to it by joining."

Mother drew up her work-table to the southern window with an air that plainly said further talk upon such a theme was idle and useless, and I went about the preparations for our noonday meal with more sullen dissatisfaction in my heart than had visited it before for months.

Nourishing my discontent, I soon began to think that mother had in some way cruelly restricted my pleasures, had robbed my simple, monotonous toil of something which might have given it color and life. And what right had she to deny me this gratification? She had no natural claims upon me, as Aunt Lydia had often assured me; and now that I was eighteen, I had a right to choose my own resources of happiness, and was no longer obliged to render obedience to a step-mother.

What if she had been kind, patient, and forbearing?

During father's lifetime her love for him would have stimulated an affection for his child; and since his death, had I not made myself so useful that selfishness would cause her to keep up a show of tenderness and love? Aunt Lydia had suggested such thoughts, but at the time I had thrust them aside as wicked and heartless; now when a pleasure was denied, these hints assumed shape, vague and shadowy, but still substantial enough to annoy me, and disturb the even, cheerful flow of my spirits—a cheerfulness which I had attained after many prayerful struggles.

My irritation sought a variety of ways to show itself, aside from my clouded face and curled lip; I knew mother noticed it, and once or twice I caught a look of grief and surprise upon her patient face, as she sat stitching in the window.

It did not soften my mood to see that she was busy in altering a plaid silk dress of her own for me—a silk that father had bought her in our more prosperous days. But when reason and judgment were brought to bear upon my angry mood, when I remembered that I had received no invitation from Mrs. Crowell and Belinda, that really mother had placed no restrictions upon me—she had only told me clearly how she looked upon such a party—when I remembered the purity of her life and teachings, the tender forbearance which she had always shown me, I was melted, and longed to throw myself upon her neck and confess my fault; but the children had again resumed study, and mother and I sat with them; I could not humble myself before them, and when they were released Mrs. Blake came with Mrs. Fairchild.

The meeting was a mutual surprise and pleasure to both ladies.

"It must be Celia Dinsmore!" exclaimed Mrs. Fairchild, holding mother's hand and scanning her features.

"Yes, and you are—"

"Mary Humphrey."

"The little Mary who was our pet at school—I certainly ought to have recognized your eyes and hair, but I was looking for the ex-Governor's lady and not for my little friend."

"I am Mrs. Fairchild, but the same little Mary, somewhat grown and changed with years. Pray tell me how long you have lived in Sherbrooke?"

"Nearly fifteen years—ever since my marriage."

"Are your parents still living in New York?"

"They are both dead."

"Ah, excuse me! but England is so far away, and I had not heard. Where are your brothers, Horace and Leigh?"

"Horace was a colonel in our army, and was killed in our war with Mexico. Leigh is a politician—has been a Senator from New York, and I believe is now canvassing the country for Buchanan."

"I knew Leigh would be a politician and an honored man. Has he a family?"

"He has a wife, but I do not know if they have children. Have you never heard that my marriage was displeasing to Leigh, and that he has never forgiven me?"

"Indeed, no! I should have supposed that Leigh Dinsmore would have been a most generous, forgiving brother, especially to an only sister."

"What fault could he find with your marriage?" asked Mrs. Blake; "I'm sure David Kendall was good enough for any girl."

"He was far too good and noble for me," mother answered, with a little patient sigh and a glance at the western window, from which could be seen the orchard and the graves. "But Leigh did not like his politics, nor his poverty, nor his family; he did not want me to be a stepmother. You know this is my husband's daughter by his first wife, and mine because her father gave her to me and my heart accepted the gift." Mother looked at me with a fond smile, which brought tears to my eyes.

"I do not see how 'tis possible for Leigh to resist coming to you now. You have informed him of your husband's decease?"

"Yes, I wrote him a note, and he answered it, expressing sorrow for my affliction, and saying that he would try and find time to visit me; but I'm afraid his public duties and pleasures will always prevent him from finding time. The loss of my only brother's love is a bitter grief to me, but He will soften it who has taught me how to bear a greater loss. You have children, Mrs. Fairchild?"

"Yes, two girls, eleven and thirteen years of age, and I want to place them under your care for the winter—perhaps for a longer time."

And then followed questions and answers about the habits, studies, and dispositions of the children, an examination of the room which could be given them, and an agreement upon terms.

"Mrs. Fairchild looked pleased when the preliminaries were arranged to her satisfaction, and rose to leave, expressing in a most cordial manner her desire for an intimate acquaintance with the friend of her school-days and the teacher of her daughters. She turned kindly toward me, asking if I was my mother's assistant, and without waiting for an answer, added—

"You are very grave for a young girl, and I dare say you are an excellent teacher. Do you join the riding-party on Saturday?"

"No, ma'am."

"Ay, that's a pity, but perhaps you do not ride. Belinda and Esther are talking of nothing else to-day, and are very anxious lest the weather should not favor, or suitable horses be obtained. Mr. Fairchild has been persuaded to remain, and there will be two vacant seats in our carriage, unless you and your mother will consent to occupy them."

"Oh, you must, Mrs. Kendall," said Mrs. Blake. "The girls charged me to make you promise to join the party. You see the doctor did not like Mrs. Crowell's plan for the ladies to invite the gentlemen, and he wouldn't allow the girls to go, unless two or three carriage-loads of older people went along; so we are to have a picnic party like the one at Cameron Pond. You will join us, Mrs. Kendall?"

"Thank you, I will think about it, and send you word in the morning."

Our visitors were gone and we stood in the porch looking out upon the village road.

Now is the time, I thought, to ask mother's pardon for my unkind, irritable humor during the day.

"Oh, mother," I whispered, drawing close to her side and hiding my face upon her shoulder, "can you forgive me?"

"Forgive what, my child?"

"You must have noticed how angry I have been, and how uncomfortable I tried to make you."

"Oh, yes, I remember now—I have been grieved all day because you were annoyed for so slight a cause."

"But you forgive me now?"

"With all my heart," and she touched my hair and forehead with her lips. "Have you lost your angry mood, and do you see the justice of my remarks about the party?"

"I knew that I was wrong before Mrs. Fairchild came, but when I heard you tell her about your brother Leigh, I felt so sorry that my behavior had added a drop to your trouble, that I could hardly wait to ask your pardon until she was gone."

"You are my comfort and happiness, dear Hope; think no more about the mistakes of this day, only try to gather courage and strength for the future."

"But, mother," I asked, when we were seated in the parlor with our stitching, "why did you never tell me about your brother Leigh?"

"Because the loss of his affection was so great a grief to me that I could never speak of it to any one but your father; and I should not have mentioned it to-day, if Mrs. Fairchild had not known us both before my marriage."

"Did your parents die before you knew my father?"

"Yes; soon after mother's death, I came to spend a few weeks with Mrs. Chapman, and met your father. Our meetings were frequent, for he was an intimate friend of Mr. Chapman's, and our acquaintance with each other soon grew into love. I had promised to marry him before I returned to New York, never thinking that Leigh would object, as I was quite old enough to make an independent choice. I think my brother opposed my marriage more because he thought me unfit to assume the cares of a large family, than from personal dislike to your father. You know your grandparents were living with your father at the time of my marriage; they were aged and infirm, and

Leigh knew that I should have cares and anxieties for them as well as the responsible duties of step-mother. Looking back now upon the way in which we had been living, and remembering my brother's pride, and his strong will, I do not wonder that he opposed me, but I do think it strange that he should withhold his forgiveness now. If Leigh could have known your father intimately, known how bright and beautiful his love made my life, I am sure he would have relented long ago."

"I wish he would come now and see how happy and comfortable we are, and what kind friends you have in Sherbrooke."

"And what a loveable daughter and companion the little child has made for me, whom he held up as such a formidable incumbrance; ay, well, I wish so too sometimes, but after all my chief happiness in this world must come from a faithful discharge of my duties and a patient waiting for joys that are eternal. Hope, you had better take the children to the village for a walk, and start at once, so as to get back before dark. Call at the post-office and mail this letter for Mr. Mayhew. I will have a basket of nice things packed for Mrs. Reed by the time you are ready."

The letter which I brought home in the waning light of that September day was from Aunt Lydia, and must form the subject of a new chapter.

CHAPTER XXIV.

AUNT LYDIA'S LETTER.

"I could wish no surer index of character, especially a woman's, than to read a letter from her pen."

"HEBRON, Sept. 8, 18—.

"MY DEAR HOPE:

"'As cold waters to a thirsty soul, so is good news from a far country.' Truly, my heart could echo the words of the wise king last week, when I met Mr. Eveleth at our Association, and learned from him that you were well, and had chosen like Mary the 'better part.' When I last saw you I feared that the foolish and hasty temper, which had gained such an unbridled control over you, would separate me forever from my dear sister's child; but I am rejoiced to know that you have at last given heed to my reproofs, and have sought that understanding which is a well-spring of life. Mr. Eveleth says you appear to have made good use of your odd bits of time by studying. Remember, Hope, that 'through wisdom is an house builded, and by understanding is it established.'

"I hear that Mrs. Kendall has several pupils in her family, and that she is expecting more. You must be of great service to her now; and I'm afraid she will not consent to gratify a wish of mine, which I have been constantly cherishing ever since Mr. Eveleth said so much in your praise. I want to see my only sister's child; and since my fall upon the ice, last winter, I can't travel by stage, or I might come to Sherbrooke: but if Mrs. Kendall has filled her house with boarders, she can't spare me the old south chamber, which always was mine when my precious Emi ly, your mother, was alive. But she will be very unjust and unfeeling if she doesn't allow you to visit me now, when I'm lame and lonely, and longing for a sight of my own niece, who was dear as a child to me for the first three years of her life.

" You must be needing a little change of scene and air. I dare say you haven't been a dozen miles from Sherbrooke since your father died. Poor David! I often wonder what he would say if he could be told that you are kept mewed up at home, minding children and drudging about house, when other girls of your age are in school.

"If you hadn't inherited an uncommon intellect from your mother's family, you would have been crushed in spirit, and moped to death. Mr. Eveleth thinks you might be a teacher now, in some respectable school; it is greatly to your credit, if you have picked up any thing like a decent education. I shall expect you next Tuesday night, and have enclosed five dollars to pay your fare. It won't be enough to buy you a dinner, but of course Mrs. Kendall will allow you to take a lunch of bread and cheese, or cold meat. Doughnuts always taste good on a journey.

"I wish you could contrive to bring me a basket of Bartlett pears from that corner tree, close by the lane, and a peck of damsons for preserves. I suppose Mrs. Kendall won't object, as she can't possibly use them all.

"I was shocked to hear what an awful wicked boy that Tom Reed has grown to be. I remember of admonishing Mrs. Reed, the last time I saw her, to 'withhold not correction from the child.' She must have learned to her sorrow that ' a foolish son is the heaviness of his mother.' But I hope his sad example will be a warning to the youth of Sherbrooke, especially to your half-brother William. Tell him, from me, that 'even a child is known by his doings, whether his work be pure, and whether it be right.' I wonder what Mr. Clark will do, now that his factory is burned up? Poor man! he has learned that 'an inheritance may be gotten hastily at the beginning, but the end thereof shall not be blessed.' I've always understood that he oppressed the poor to increase his riches, and now he may expect to come to want.

"Your Uncle John, whom you've never seen, sends his love, and hopes you'll come next week; and your Cousin Lydia is thinking a sight of your coming. Mind, we shall all expect you next Tuesday; but if you don't come, we shall know whose fault 'tis. I've written a long letter for me, so I'll close here.

"Your affectionate aunt,
"LYDIA HASTINGS."

"What a provoking letter!" I exclaimed, after reading it. "Aunt Lydia always rouses every bit of resistance in my nature. How thankful I am that I'm not obliged to listen to her proverbs every day! I mean to borrow her own style, and tell her that 'even a fool, when he holdeth his peace, is counted wise; and he that hath knowledge spareth his words.'"

"Hush, Hope—do you not remember that 'the discretion of a man deferreth his anger, and it is his glory to pass over a transgression?'"

We both laughed heartily over the contagious spirit of quoting which had seized us; but mother's merriment quickly subsided as her eye ran over Aunt Lydia's letter. She read and returned it to me with a graver face than she was wont to wear.

"Will you visit your aunt, as she wishes, Hope?" mother asked.

"If you think such a visit a necessary penance for my besetting sins; but not because I am needing change of air, or the sound of Aunt Lydia's quotations, or the sight of her face."

"I do not know how to part with you, even for a month's visit; but your aunt has claims upon you which I would not like to set aside; and, as she says, the journey and change of scene may refresh you."

"I am sure I do not need any such refreshing, and you cannot spare me; there is work enough for us both, and how could you manage it alone?"

"I should be obliged to hire help; but you know we have decided to do that before the Fairchilds come. I am going to ask Mrs. Reed to let Martha Jane come in and help us, until I can obtain a more capable girl."

"Are you really in earnest about sending me off?"

"If you do not go, your aunt will think you are unjustly detained by me; and I've no doubt the journey will be a benefit to you. Your home and your duties will seem more pleasant after a short absence."

"I do not need to go away from home to learn its value; but if you think Aunt Lydia has any claims upon my gratitude because of the care which she took of me when I had no mother, I will go and make her a visit. Father said I must always show her kind attentions when I could. But what if she should insist upon my remaining with her?"

"It is not likely she will attempt to detain you against your will; but if she should, your guardian can claim and place you under such protection as he thinks best. If you reach Hebron Tuesday evening, you must leave here on Monday, and spend the night in Wiltshire. I do not like the idea of your travelling alone."

"And I do not want to go alone, and I do not want any of Aunt Lydia's hints about my Kendell temper, and my defective education, and my artful step-mother; and you need me at home; so I think I had better remain, and write Aunt Lydia a dutiful letter."

Mother sat in silence for several minutes, stitching upon the plaid silk, while I weighed in the scales of knowledge and imagination the pleasures of home, and the pleasures of a short journey. It would be very pleasant to see Wiltshire and the country through which I must pass, pleasant to see Uncle John's family, pleasant to show Aunt Lydia a kind attention even if I did not love her, but I hardly dared enumerate the pleasures even in thought which must be left at Sherbrooke; the chances of meeting Virginia and the Chapmans, of riding on horseback, of another party, and, more than all, I must lose the daily pleasure of assisting mother.

"I have been thinking your aunt's letter over, calmly, Hope," said mother, after a half-hour of silent stitching; "and I think if your father could speak to you he would say 'Go.' It may require a little self-sacrifice on your part, and it certainly requires a great deal on mine to bid you go. I will walk to the village in the morning, to see if Mr. Chapman does not know of a trusty person who will be travelling toward Hebron next week, in whose care we can place you."

Mother had not spoken of the excursion to Switzerland after Mrs. Fairchild's visit; and I could not help hoping that the presence of older people in carriages would give the party such a different character, that she might be induced to join it. But as she returned from the village on Saturday morning without making any allusion to the party, my hopes faded.

"You had better lay aside your books, Hope, and get ready for your visit," said mother, taking off her shawl and preparing for work. "You will need the whole day for your preparations. Mrs. Fairchild has kindly offered to take you in her carriage to Wiltshire on Monday, and her husband will try to find you an escort for the remainder of the journey. By giving the children a holiday, I can finish the plaid silk for you, and with your gray merino for a travelling-dress, I trust your aunt will think you are respectably clad."

"She will be sure to find fault with something, but it had better be my dress than my temper. I do hope I shall be able to keep my tongue under control. But, mother, I shall be afraid to ride with Mr. and Mrs. Fairchild in their carriage."

"What will make you afraid? I presume the horses are well broken, and the carriage is strong."

"I didn't think about the horses nor the carriage; but you know I am such an ignorant country girl, and the Fairchilds have travelled so much and seen such elegant society, that I shall be afraid to speak before them."

"Then you will be very foolish. They will not expect to find you mature and accomplished, but artlessness and good sense are always attractive to well-bred people. Act naturally, without assuming airs, or attempting to talk about things of which you are ignorant."

"Shall you go to Switzerland with the party this afternoon?"

"No; I declined the invitation for us both; if only our own friends and neighbors were going, I might accept, for the sake of giving you pleasure; but I do not like Mr. and Mrs. Crowell, nor the manner in which the party was got up, and we shall both be so busy in making ready for your journey that we shall have no time for the excursion."

For a minute my proud, strong will rebelled against mother's decision, but only for a minute, and walking up to her side I leaned my flushed cheek against hers. She drew me closely to her, with an embrace which soothed my ruffled temper, and strengthened my weak heart—an embrace which told, in language more convincing than words, that her watchful love sought only my permanent good. It was something of a trial to see the gay party drive past our house soon after noon. I gazed through the vine-shadowed window until the last carriage disappeared, and a little sigh and a few natural tears escaped, when I saw my friend Virginia with the equestrians; but I brushed them resolutely away and returned to my work, comforting myself with the thought that happiness might be found at home as well as in Switzerland.

CHAPTER XXV.

HOPE GOES TO HEBRON.

> "All common things, each day's events,
> That with the hour begin and end,
> Our pleasures and our discontents,
> Are rounds by which we may ascend."
> LONGFELLOW.

MONDAY morning found my simple preparations for travelling completed, and an hour of leisure which I could spend in walking to the village to bid Virginia good-bye. Mother wished me to call first on Mrs. Reed. I found her, as usual, in the most untidy confusion, working hard, without any system or tact. Martha Jane was lazily clearing away the remains of breakfast, her uncombed hair half concealing a stupid, purposeless face. Three half-dressed, unwashed children sat upon the floor, quarrelling over a frightened kitten. My entrance called from Mrs. Reed a torrent of complaints, mingled with ejaculations and threats to the children.

"You find us all in the suds, Hope Kendall, but that's no new thing. Martha Jane, hand her a chair, and make haste with them dishes. Hope has done more work this morning than you'd do in a whole day, I'll be bound. I never could see why all my children should be so shiftless. Goodness knows as how there ain't a lazy bone in my skin. How's your mother, Hope?"

"She's well, and sent you this small basket of pears."

"Mrs. Kendall has always something nice to send, while I've never a bone to give a hungry dog. Put the pears in the cupboard, Martha Jane, and mind, you are not to touch one now."

The prohibition was useless, for Martha Jane slipped a pear into her sleeve, and went about the washing of her battered cups and plates, munching it.

"Mrs. Reed, I'm going to Hebron to visit my Aunt Lydia, and mother wants to know if you can spare Martha Jane to help her, while I'm away."

"Spare her! as well as not, if she's a mind to go; but your mother'll find her next to no help at all. She's strong enough to do a woman's work, but loiters over a few chores all the forenoon. What in the world can you want to visit that preaching old aunt of yours for?"

"Aunt is lame, and wants to see me, and mother thinks I ought to show her some kind attention."

"Well, I s'pose your mother knows best; but I never could bear your aunt's tongue. She called here two or three times, and preached about 'sparing the rod and spoiling the child,' as if I hadn't whipped my children as long as whipping was of any use. I remember as how she warned Tom to turn over a new leaf—poor boy! he's fast in jail for five years, learning a shoemaker's trade, Square Thornton says."

"Have you heard from Mary Ann?"

"No, and never expect to, unless it's some bad news. There's no good could happen to such a disobedient girl."

A few tears rolled down the poor widow's hard, hopeless face, and fell upon the coarse overalls she was making. Perhaps she remembered when Mary Ann lay in her arms a tender, innocent babe, but neither the tears nor the memories softened her mood.

"Tell your mother she's welcome to try Martha Jane, and I hope she'll make her earn her board. Farmer Hutchins is trying to keep Matthew out of mischief. He came in yesterday, and brought me these overalls to make, and a present of garden-sarce and apples."

"Mr. Hutchins is a very kind-hearted man."

"Well, I s'pose so; but it's easy enough to be generous when a man has more turnips and beans than he knows what to do with, and heaps of apples rottin' on the ground."

I turned to the daughter, a stout girl of fifteen, and asked if she would go to mother in the afternoon.

"I hain't nothin' fit to wear."

"Any gown which you can work in at home will answer."

"Them proud Mayhew girls will laugh at me."

"No—I think not; and if you try to please mother, I am almost sure she will give you a dress of mine. Will you go?"

"Well, I reckon I'd rather work for your marm than anybody else."

"You will come, then?"

"If nothin' happens."

I was glad to leave the small, stifled room, tainted with the odor of fried pork, onions, and cabbage, and breathe the invigorating air of the September morning.

Virginia gave me her usual hearty welcome.

"What sent you to the village, Hope, this bright Monday morning?" she asked.

"I came to see Mrs. Reed, and to bid you good-bye for a few days. I am going to visit my Aunt Lydia."

"Oh, Hope! not just now, when we are to have a wedding in the house? Aunt Sallie is to be married Thursday evening, and I was going to invite you and your mother to-day. You can put off visiting your aunt until next week."

"Not very well; for Aunt Lydia wrote that she should expect me to-morrow evening, and Mrs. Fairchild is going to take me as far as Wiltshire this afternoon."

"What in the world have you done, that you should punish yourself by visiting your aunt? I'm sure you don't love her well enough to travel a hundred miles to see her."

"Mother thinks I should go. You know my aunt took care of me after my own mother died; and she is lame now, and wants to see me."

"And wants a fresh ear to pour her quotations into. I'm glad that I am not her dutiful niece. She would kill me in a month's time. She always reminds me of one of her own dismal quotations—something about a contentious woman and the continual dropping of a rainy day. Now, Carey Chapman quotes quite enough to suit me; but there is usually some aptness and beauty in his quotations. I wish you could have heard him repeat some of Bryant's lines last Saturday, when we were at Switzerland.

"What were they?"

"Oh, I never can remember poetry, but something about the death of the brier-rose, violet, and golden-rod:

"'The wind-flower and the violet, they perished long ago,
And the brier-rose and orchis died amid the summer glow;
But on the hill the golden-rod, and the aster in the wood,
And the yellow sun-flower by the brook in autumn beauty stood,

Till fell the frost from the clear, cold heaven, as falls the plague on
  men,
And the brightness of their smile was gone from upland, field, and
  glen.'

Have I given you his quotation?"

"A part of it; but how could you know what Carey Chapman repeated at Switzerland?"

"You gave me a clue; and as I learned the poem only last week, it is fresh in my memory."

"I should think you and Carey ought to be firm friends, you are so much alike. Now, you can appreciate all his fine quotations, but the larger part of them are lost on me. You should have seen his shocked look when I asked him who wrote the lines you have just repeated; and when he said 'Bryant,' I gave his nerves another jar by asking if Bryant was an Englishman."

Virginia's light, musical laugh rippled out as she recalled her blunders; but though she treated them as amusing trifles, I could see that the memory of them annoyed her. And, moreover, I discovered upon a table near us an open volume of Bryant's poems. Pointing to it, I asked:

"Are you correcting the faults of your education?"

"So far as to find that Bryant lives within a hundred miles of Sherbrooke," she replied, with a conscious blush, and plunged at once into an amusing description of Saturday's pleasures.

"I wish you could have gone to Switzerland with us, Hope. It was capital fun to listen to the raptures of Belinda and Esther over the beauties of the place; and Mrs. Crowell lisped out her adjectives and murdered her grammar in a most delightfully unconscious way. You know, if I am ignorant, I make no pretences, as some people do. And then Mrs. Crowell put on such a fine-ladyish air, and pretended to be afraid of an honest-looking cow that was grazing by the roadside, so that William Fairchild had to lead her horse past the proximity to her horns; and when we reached the old mill and dismounted, Mrs. Crowell and the Blakes could not manage to walk in their riding-skirts, without a man's arm to lean upon. I despise such affectation of helplessness. Mrs. Fairchild was as independent and courageous as she is lovely. She's more like your mother than any other lady I've ever seen; and I'm so much in love with her that I almost envy you the pleasure of riding to Wiltshire with her."

I rose to go, and Virginia, protesting that she hadn't seen the old log bridge over the stream for a whole month, seized her pretty hat and bore me company. She was a fluent talker about trifles, and I could not help noticing that this morning her words flowed with the rapidity of a mountain brook; and what Carey Chapman had said and done since we met, seemed of much greater importance to her than I thought needful or proper. But if thoughts of this young man crept more frequently into my own heart than they did one month ago, why not into Virginia's?

Ah, but Virginia had not torn her hands with blackberry-bushes, nor perilled her life for his sake, and I doubted if his lips had ever touched her hand, however tempting its fair beauty might have been. I was sure he could never have called her "My little friend," nor "Little Hebe;" those phrases were for me alone, as was also the delicious memory of that morning's accident, which brought the current of our lives into such pleasant harmony for a blissful hour.

Much as I loved Virginia, I could not force my tongue to speak of that accident to her; it was a sacred passage in my quiet life, locked in a secret chamber of my soul.

"It seems like the days when the 'sound of dropping

nuts' is heard," said Virginia, as we stood upon the log bridge, the half-way resting place between the village and our farm. "I'm sure the woods are still enough to hear the fall of a nut, and this stream is seen through a 'smoky light.' You see the wise spirit of my friends is contagious. I am beginning to read poetry, but I hope never to fall into the habit of frequent and affected quotations."

"You do not mean I should infer that your friends are guilty of that fault?" I asked.

"Never draw inferences from my rambling remarks, Hope. And now for a few days, good-bye. Be sure and come back before the 'south wind searches in vain for the flowers,' but do not allow your aunt's proverbs to make you any graver than you are now."

And the rippling music of her laugh floated out into the still woods, startling the echoes from their dreamy quiet, while her buff morning dress and white hat disappeared amongst the old pines, and I turned my steps homeward, stopping now and then to gather late blossoms and fragrant fern, and pausing by the pasture bars which Carey Chapman had assisted me to cross, while I looked with fond, loving pride upon the fields, orchard, and roof that we could now call our own. The soft beauty and aromatic breath of the day invited me to linger by the bars under the shade of a large maple, long enough at least to indulge in a sweet day-dream, but the short shadows upon the grass forbade me such a luxury.

It was nearly noon when I entered our kitchen, and soon after Mr. Fairchild's carriage stopped at our gate.

"Only for a few days, my child," mother whispered, looking tenderly into my tear-filled eyes; "and remember, you are going upon a mission of kindness and charity that would meet your dear father's approval."

I could not trust myself to answer, but received in

silence the good-bye kisses of the children, and sprang into the carriage.

Mr. and Mrs. Fairchild were too much occupied with mother to notice my quietly-dropping tears. The visit I was proposing to make promised little compensation for the pleasures I was leaving, but the ride to Wiltshire was over a richly-cultivated farming country, and the scenery after the first few miles entirely new; my eyes were soon attracted by the beauties spread out before me, and my thoughts divested from unpleasant themes by the intelligent conversation of my new friends.

We reached their residence in the suburbs of Wiltshire before nightfall. It was a large, unpretending family mansion, surrounded by tastefully-cultivated grounds, which overlooked the river. Mrs. Fairchild was met at the door by two well-grown girls, who were somewhat boisterous in their greetings.

"Why, girls! what a noise you make!" said their mother; " there, you have kissed me times enough, Edith! One would think we had been gone a month."

"You have been gone five days, and Meroe and I have been stupid as owls, with nothing in the world to do."

"You had your lessons and your practice?"

"But lessons and practice are not company. We had nobody to speak to but Miss Grey."

"Here, Edith, Meroe, this young lady is Miss Kendall, from Sherbrooke, who is to be one of your teachers this winter."

Both of the misses looked and bowed.

"Edith, you may show Miss Kendall up to the west chamber, and when she is sufficiently refreshed, bring her down to the dining-room. I hope Hepsy has prepared for us a substantial supper, for the invigorating air and long ride have given me a keen appetite. Has William arrived?"

"Yes, he came before dinner; but he wasn't a bit pleasant, and wouldn't tell us about the party."

"I'm afraid you teased him with questions; I will tell you about the party in good time. Run off now with Miss Kendall."

They led the way to a pleasant chamber, which looked out upon the river. There was an air of substantial comfort about its furnishing that made me feel quite at ease; and once alone with me, the girls commenced chatting in an off-hand way.

"Have you come here now to teach us?" asked Edith.

"No, I'm not coming here, but you are going to Sherbrooke to board in my mother's family."

"Oh, won't that be dull and stupid?"

"I think not—there are two misses from Philadelphia boarding with us, and a sister of mine, all near your age."

"That alters the case. Are you the only teacher?"

"No, my mother teaches more than I do."

"Is she young and nice?"

"I think so, but your mother can answer that question better than I can."

"I shall ask her this very night, for I don't like old teachers; they are always cross. Miss Grey must be fifty at least, and her hair is the color of her name. Indeed, she's all of a color, gray hair, gray eyes, gray skin, gray name, and gray gowns."

"Mamma wouldn't allow you to speak so, Edith. She says Miss Grey is an excellent teacher," said Meroe.

"Well, Miss Kendall will see for herself when supper is ready. I hope you don't always wear gray," she said, glancing at my gown as she spoke.

"Why, Edith, I shall tell mamma," Meroe said, without giving me time to answer. "I'm sure Miss Kendall's dress is pretty, and she has a pink bow and lovely hair. She's not a bit like Miss Grey."

"I didn't say she was. Come down now, that's the supper bell, and mamma said she was half starved."

"Mamma never said so. You know she tells us that such expressions are vulgar and foolish exaggerations."

"How precise we've grown!" said the elder sister, tossing her short, thick curls, and showing volumes of mischief in her merry, dark eyes.

She will not be the most easily managed of pupils, I thought, as we walked to the dining-room, and I noticed that she was pulling her precise sister's dress awry as we passed along.

There was an ease about the hospitality of the Fairchild family which made me feel quite at home with them. I forgot their position and wealth, forgot the poverty of our own home, and listened with more interest and pleasure to the conversation than I had supposed it possible to feel with comparative strangers.

The young man appeared more affable at home than at Dr. Blake's party, laughing and chatting with his young half-sisters and singing at their request several popular airs, playing his own accompaniments with a fine, delicate touch. His manner toward his lively step-mother was an odd mixture of playful familiarity and affectionate reverence. He called her Mary more frequently than mother, using both names often, as if the pronouncing of them gave him pleasure.

Much as I had dreaded riding to Wiltshire with the Fairchilds, and accepting their hospitality for the night, I parted from them in the morning with real regret, and not without promising Mrs. Fairchild and her daughters that I would make them a longer visit on my return to Sherbrooke.

Mr. Fairchild put me on board the cars which would

take me the larger part of the way to Hebron; the last twenty miles must be made in a stage.

I was lonely and cowardly when I found myself for the first time in a railroad car, rapidly whirling away from home on a most unwelcome mission; but the dreary day wore to a close, and the sunset saw me receiving my aunt's welcome on the steps of her stiff-looking red cottage.

CHAPTER XXVI.

AUNT LYDIA AT HOME.

"Alas! dear friends, the winter is within us,
Hard is the ice that grows about the heart,
For petty cares and vain regrets have won us
From life's true heritage and better part."

"So you've come at last?" said my aunt, leading the way into her parlor, and untying my bonnet. "I didn't half expect you, though I told Jane not to put the tea on the table till the stage got in."

I was surprised to see her moving about with precisely her old manner, when I had imagined her lameness would require a cane.

"How is the lameness that you wrote about, aunt?" I asked, not daring to look at her, but smoothing my hair in front of a little mirror, which had an uncouth adorning of painted egg-shells and branches of asparagus.

"Not much better. I've a terrible pain in my left shoulder every time there is a storm brewing."

"Then you were injured in your shoulder? I somehow fancied the lameness affected your walking."

"You should never fancy things, child. I am often so lame that I can scarcely step; but I always make the best of every thing. The fall jarred and sprained me in every limb, and I've no doubt most women would have laid abed ever since ; but I'm not one of the nervous, whimsical kind, and I've kept about. How's Mrs. Kendall?"

"Very well; and the children are well. Mother sent her love."

"It didn't increase the size of your baggage, I reckon. Did you bring the pears and damsons?"

"No—we were sorry that I couldn't; but I rode to Wiltshire with some friends of mother's, and we didn't like to give them the care of any thing but a valise."

"You didn't come a hundred miles to make a visit with only a valise, I hope?"

"You shall see what a quantity of things mother packed into it—enough clothes to last me a month."

"They'll have to last longer than a month, or you'll send home for more. Move your chair to the table; you must be hungry."

"Yes—the ride has given me an appetite, and your supper looks tempting."

"Come back to the table, Jane," called my aunt to a young woman who had brought in the tea, and was moving away. "Hope Kendall gets her own meals, and is my sister's child. She's not to be treated like company."

"I'm glad to hear you say so, aunt; I want to feel at home with you."

"I'm sure I don't know where you should feel at home, if not in the house where your mother was born, and which your gran'ther built."

"I didn't know I was coming to the same house that mother lived in when she was a girl."

"I dare say not. Some folks have tried to keep you ignorant of your own mother's family."

I felt the hot blood in my face, and the angry tears in

my eyes, because of the unjust insinuation; but remembering that my mission was a peaceful one, I swallowed my tea and my annoyance, and tried to think only of my bountiful supper.

"Your baked pears are excellent, aunt."

"Well, I hope they are eatable; help yourself to another. How many boarders has Mrs. Kendall?"

"Only two now, but there will be more before winter."

"What in the world will she do with them all?"

"We are having rooms finished over the kitchen."

"And of course running in debt, instead of trying to clear off that mortgage?"

"Oh, aunt, I've such pleasant news to tell you! Mother has sold our back field to the railroad company, and paid off the mortgage."

"Sold the back field, child? Why, Mrs. Kendall must be crazy! What will she do for a pasture?"

"There was grazing enough without that, since mother sold the oxen and sheep. We keep only two cows and a farm-horse, and Dora Mayhew's pony."

"Well, times have changed! As for me, I've a great respect for Solomon's injunction, 'Remove not the ancient landmarks which thy fathers have set;' but I suppose Mrs. Kendall couldn't be expected to care much for the farm. Emily set her eyes by it, and would as soon have parted with her right hand as a foot of that farm. I should have advised keeping it for David's children; but my advice wasn't asked. She may find that ' without counsel purposes are disappointed.'"

"But, aunt, you forget that mother was obliged to sell that one field in order to keep the house and the fields around it. We have more land left than Jonas can till profitably."

"So she keeps that blundering, self-conceited Jonas

Gould yet? He reminded me daily of the words, 'Folly is joy to him that is destitute of wisdom.' There were no such prating fools about the farm when Emily was alive, and no boarders in the house either. I suppose Mrs. Kendall couldn't contrive to get work enough out of you in any other way but by filling her house up with children?"

"Mother takes the hardest part of the work upon herself. I assist her in house-work and teaching, but I always find time for study."

"Yes—but no thanks are due Mrs. Kendall for that. If it were not for your Hastings blood and spirit, you'd never have the heart to study. Take another cup of tea."

No—not another swallow of tea or bit of cake could be forced down with that uncomfortable rising in my throat, which constantly threatened to break out in tears or angry words; so I rose hastily from the table and walked to the front door, which remained open to admit the mild evening air.

Twilight was gathering up the shadows; but enough of sunset's golden clouds remained to show me dimly the village and surrounding scenery.

Hebron was a small hamlet, hardly worthy the name of village. There was a river which afforded water-power for a saw-mill, and an abundance of pine logs, boards, and slabs lying around. A chair-factory gave the village an appearance of activity, and a two-story brick building, labelled "Hebron Academy," a variety-store, and a meeting-house with an ambitious spire, won for it respect and dignity in the eyes of the neighboring farmers. Thrift and industry were plainly written upon a few two-story white houses, as well as upon several cottages of humbler pretensions. Beyond the village, in the purple mists of the twilight,

I could see a yellow farm-house and a wooded hill. The more distant scenery was wrapped in night's mantle.

I was in no hurry to encounter my aunt's tongue again, so I stepped from the door into the primmest-looking garden I had ever seen. Tall sun-flowers and hollyhocks stood in stately rows upon each side of the path, and exact, diamond-shaped beds were filled with bachelors' buttons, sweet-williams, asters, and verbenas. Marigolds, sage, saffron, and wormwood, and several kinds of mint were allowed a generous space, in consideration of their usefulness, and regaled me with pungent odors.

Aunt Lydia had daguerrotyped herself in the garden: even the two uncomfortable-looking old poplars by the gate seemed to be mysteriously muttering her dismal quotations to each other as their stiff branches crackled in the evening breeze.

"Hope, come in out of the damp night air," called my aunt from the doorway. "You'll catch your death by such carelessness. Come, child, sit down and tell me about yourself. What have you been doing since I saw you?"

"Growing tall for one thing, you see."

"Yes—you're more of a Hastings than a Kendall in size, and have your mother's small hand. How do you manage to keep it so white, with all your kitchen drudgery?" she asked, taking the hand nearest her, and bringing it directly under the rays of the oil-lamp for inspection.

"Oh, kitchen-work leaves no permanent stain; and then, I've been very idle for the last month. I took cold, and was feverish and ill for a few days; and since then mother hasn't permitted me to see much of the kitchen."

"Poor child! I'm glad you were allowed a little rest when you were sick. What does Mrs. Kendall expect to gain by boarding and teaching girls?"

"An honest living for us all, and in time a good education for me and the children. Before winter sets in she expects to have a master come from Wiltshire to teach me and the pupils French and music."

"What possible good can music do you, without a piano?"

"We have one in the house, which I can practise on; and one of the things which we hope to earn by teaching, after we have repaired the house, is a piano for myself and Sophie."

"You'd much better lay the price of it away in the bank, for a rainy day. It seems to me vain and self-conceited for Mrs. Kendall to set herself up for a teacher of girls at her time of life. Tell her, from me, that 'wealth gotten by vanity shall be diminished.'"

"We never expect to get wealth. Our highest aim has been to be out of debt, to own the homestead, and to be well educated."

"Well, 'the desire accomplished is sweet to the soul!'" Aunt Lydia drew out the words with a heavy sigh, as if our desires compassed impossibilities. "I hope Mrs. Kendall isn't filling your head with ambitious vanities. She was a gay, worldly person when your father got ensnared with her artful wiles. Who are the Mayhews that you've mentioned?"

I gave her a minute and careful account of their family history, as we knew it—described their looks, their dresses, their studies, and the improvement in their manners; and then told her what I had heard and seen of our expected pupils, glad to dwell as long as possible upon any theme which would prevent Aunt Lydia from insinuating disagreeable things about mother.

"And now, aunt, tell me about your fall upon the ice," I asked, when I had finished my narration.

"It was last February that I fell; there had been a

snow-storm, which turned into rain, and then it froze, making the roads one sheet of glare ice. I had started for brother John's—he lives in that yellow house that you saw on the hill—and your Aunt Abby, that's John's wife, had sent for me to help her get a quilt into the frame. Abby never could do any thing without help. She's always sending for me to show her about making preserves, or pickles, or sausages, or some other thing that she should have known about years ago. And that very morning I had told Jane that we would pick over our apples, and boil down cider for Shaker apple-sauce ; but I put my own work by when Abby sent for me, and drew on some old stockings over my boots, to keep me from slipping. I've always believed that I should have got along without falling, if I hadn't dodged to get out of the way of Nathan's sled— Nathan is your cousin, and Abby had sent him over for me. I never could see the use of dragging about a sled, as Nathan always will in winter; but, as I was saying, I dodged so that the sled shouldn't strike my ankles, and the skirt of my gown caught in the runner, and down I went, cutting a pretty figure on the ice, and spraining my ankle, besides almost putting my left shoulder-blade out of joint. I didn't put that foot on the ground for more than one month. Then, when I tried to pick myself up, I could scarcely move for sprains and bruises; and who should come along but Mr. Hopkinson, our new minister, and he had to help Nathan lift me on to the hateful sled that had done all the mischief, and walk by the side of it, holding me on, while Nathan dragged me back to my own door. It was such an awkward thing for our minister to be seen half carrying me into the house, and he a widower, too! His wife hadn't been dead three months, poor thing! I saw she was going into consumption when they came here from York State, last fall, and I spent more'n half my time in running back and forth, between here and the parsonage, and in making her broths, custards, and jellies. She had just no appetite at all, and got weaker every day, till the last of November, when she died.

"I always carried a camphor-bag about with me, and kept sprigs of sage and peppermint in my pocket, to prevent me from catching the disease. How many times Mrs. Hopkinson looked up with a sweet smile, when I was smoothing her pillows and giving her drinks, and said, 'What should I do without you, Sister Hastings?' And once, it was the very day she died, and I could scarcely hear the words, but she drew down my head and whispered, 'Be a friend to Caleb and the children, when I am gone.' And I've tried to be," Aunt Lydia added, pausing, either for want of breath, or because her narration had brought up reminiscences too tender and sacred for words, and which she seemed to be living over in memory.

I inferred, from her gentle sighs and the shadow of a smile which crept over her hard features, that there was nothing unpleasant in the memory of that death-bed scene, nor in the events that succeeded. I longed to break the silence by asking my aunt how old a man Mr. Hopkinson was, how many children he had, and if he were really so guileless as to be deceived by her quotations and ostentatious piety, her attentions to himself and his motherless children, as to think of giving her the deceased Mrs. Hopkinson's place in the family; but I could not manage to frame a single question upon that subject in a manner to suit my notions of delicacy, and Aunt Lydia was the first to speak.

"How often have I said to Brother Hopkinson, when we were speaking of the sainted dead: 'The memory of the just is blessed.' Dear man, he has accepted the chastening of the Lord, and has come forth purified. He comes in often of an evening now, and I can see that he is comforted by my presence, and he sends his dear little girls in almost every day to ask my advice about something."

Again there was silence in the room, and what seemed to me a delicious reverie in my aunt's mind, and feeling very tired, I arose and asked to be shown my room.

"You go to bed early, Hope. I haven't told you yet about the long confinement that followed my sprain, nor how Mr. Hopkinson was so kind as to come in and read aloud to me every day. He read the Memoir of Mary Lyon, and a whole book full of Dr. Huntington's sermons. I often told him that the great doctor's sermons were not equal to his, but at such times he said I was a partial listener."

"I am glad you have such a good minister, and glad that he has been such a kind friend to you. To-morrow you must tell me more about your sickness, and introduce me to Uncle John's family. You know I've never seen them."

"No, and it's a wicked shame that you have been kept in ignorance of your mother's family until you are a grown-up girl. You must be eighteen now?"

"Yes, eighteen last June. But you know, aunt, we have not been able to indulge in the luxury of visiting. It has been hard, up-hill work with us, ever since father went to Ohio. I cannot tell you how happy we are to be out of debt."

"You have been a foolish girl to share the hardships of poverty, when your mother's relations would gladly have taken care of you. But you may make up your mind for a long rest now; we shall not allow you to go back to Sherbrooke in a hurry."

I was in no mood for contradiction with my aunt, and taking up my lamp, followed her to the chamber, receiving from her a cold, formal kiss, and an injunction to remember my dreams. She left me in a tidy room, and the solitude and rest were so gratefully accepted, that I was soon wrapped in a slumber too sweet and refreshing for dreams.

CHAPTER XXVII.

UNCLE JOHN'S FAMILY.

"Actions, looks, steps, words, form the alphabet by which you spell character."

WHEN I awoke, the sun was stealing through the small panes of my window, and lighting up the curiously-contrived patch-work coverlet of my bed. The great wheel in the saw-mill was moving, and a whizzing, rasping sound saluted me; the dam and saw-mill were so near my aunt's house that the whirr of the wheels and clicking of the saws could be heard even when the doors and windows were closed, and these sounds seemed to me a fitting accompaniment for her voice and knitting-pins.

I prepared myself to meet Aunt Lydia's scrutiny with as much neatness and despatch as I could command, and then threw up my sash to strengthen and fortify myself for her presence, with a few breaths of the clear, mountain air, and a view of the scenery which as I approached the village the previous evening had looked charming and picturesque. Distant mountains and wooded hills, dotted here and there with the bright hues of the soft maples, which were putting on their brilliant autumn garb, met my vision; and close at hand, the thrifty village, rapid stream, and piles of new boards made a pleasant picture.

Even the old poplars looked less stiff and sentinel-like in the morning light, and the garden smiled up with a prim but honest air, as if conscious that the sun shone upon no new-fangled vanities within its precincts.

Aunt Lydia, in an ugly green sun-bonnet, bent over the bed of marigolds, clipping their yellow blossoms into her apron. I was in no hurry to meet her, but remembering her methodical habits, and fearing lest I had already kept her breakfast waiting, I ran down to the garden and bade her good-morning.

"Good-morning, Hope! There, you've nearly broken a branch from my oleander, and mercy on us! you're stepping on the strawberry-vines! Do be careful."

"I will try to be. What are you doing to the marigolds, aunt?"

"Cutting off the blossoms to keep for sickness; they're excellent for canker-rash and scarlet fever, but I suppose you've never learned how to make flowers useful."

"I don't know much about their medicinal qualities— I know they are useful in making a room look bright and cheerful."

"That's one of the vain and silly notions you've got from Mrs. Kendall. I remember she would always have a vase of flowers in David's room, though I told her that they poisoned the air. Some folks always have the asthma and rose-cold when roses are in bloom, and I dare say your father's end was hastened by breathing the scent of flowers so much."

I made no reply, but moved down the garden-paths, gathering the prettiest blossoms I could find, determined that for at least one morning they should adorn my aunt's breakfast-table and parlor-mantel. When Jane called us to breakfast I ran in, and while Aunt Lydia was disposing of her marigolds and mints, I seized a couple of tumblers and arranged my flowers. When we were seated she looked at them with a grim smile and said:

" 'Vanity of vanities,' saith the preacher, 'all is vanity.' The psalmist tells us, of the grass, 'in the morning it flourisheth and groweth up; in the evening it is cut down and withereth.' Hope, help yourself to buckwheat cakes, while I pour out the coffee."

The breakfast was not finished without several more quotations, interspersed with instructions to Jane about household matters, and a careful laying out of farm-work for Adoniram Staples, the "hired man," who occupied a seat with us.

Breakfast finished and Jane and Staples dismissed, aunt took down, from a corner of her mantel, Barnes' Notes and her Bible, and read in a most solemn tone a long chapter, with commentary notes. The prayer that followed, though I tried to raise my heart with each petition, seemed to me a cold, mechanical sacrifice, rather than a grateful thank-offering, gushing from a deep fountain of love in the heart.

I was left to amuse myself while Aunt Lydia assisted Jane for a couple of hours, and taking from her small collection of books the most readable looking one, the Memoir of Mary Lyon, with the name of Caleb Hopkinson written on its fly-leaf, I went to my chamber, and after putting it in the same prim order as I found it the previous evening, sat down and wrote my dear mother a description of my journey and welcome from Aunt Lydia. Mother never seemed to me so lovable, womanly, and polished as when I thought of her in contrast with my aunt's narrow angularity.

My letter was a long one, and before I had finished it Aunt Lydia came in to the room, equipped for a walk.

"Who are you writing to?" she asked.

"To mother."

"It seems to me you are in a great hurry to send off a

letter the very day after you reached here. Does Mrs. Kendall require an exact account of every thing that happens when you are out of her sight?"

"It is my pleasure to tell mother every thing that interests me."

"Hope, why do you persist in calling your father's widow by the name that belongs to my dear sister? Can you not see that it annoys me to hear you call Mrs. Kendall 'mother?'"

"She has been the only mother I have ever known, and I'm sure she deserves that title, she has always been tender and faithful to me."

"Well, we won't have any more words about it, for I can see that your Kendall temper is getting the better of you. I suppose I ought not to expect you to heed my reproofs, when you've never been taught to respect me. Are you ready to go over to your Uncle John's now?"

I brushed away a few tears that would come, and put aside my unfinished letter, but meantime my aunt's busy eyes had discovered my valise.

"What! your valise still unpacked, child? Your dresses will be pressed in a thousand wrinkles; let me help you unpack it," and I was obliged to see my aunt's hands pull out every article of my wardrobe, and hear her ungracious comments upon it.

"Well, to be sure, you've nothing in your valise that close packing would hurt! Mrs. Kendall's old things altered over for you, I see. Does she wear mourning yet?"

"Yes."

"You may be thankful for that, else you wouldn't get as much as her old dresses. My! if here isn't her old plaid silk! You must look like a fright in it. Has she never bought you so much as one new thing since your father died?"

"Oh, Aunt Lydia! she does for me all she could possibly do if I were really her child. My clothes are better than hers or Sophie's."

"Poor thing! if I had known you were kept so shabby, I would have furnished you with something decent. Come along now, or we sha'n't get over to John's before Abby commences to get dinner; and she may like to know we are coming. Country folks are not always ready for strangers; but 'better is a dinner of herbs where love is, than a stalled ox and hatred therewith.' We shall find the love at Abby's, if we don't find the stalled ox." That, at least, was a comforting assurance.

We walked down the main street of the village, over the bridge, from which we could see the great water-wheels in motion, past the meeting-house, parsonage, and academy, Aunt Lydia giving me as much of the village history as time would allow, while we were walking up the gentle ascent that led to Uncle John's yellow farm-house.

We were met at the door by a pretty, bright-looking young woman, whom Aunt Lydia introduced as my cousin and her namesake. Her greeting was awkward and embarrassed, and not unlike my own; for my acquaintance with Aunt Lydia had not prepared me to love one who bore her name.

The tall, thin woman with sad, brown eyes and gray hair, who came from the kitchen and greeted us in a low, pleasant voice, was my Uncle John's wife.

"I came right in from my butter-making," she said, "because I am not going to make a stranger of Emily's child. She don't resemble her mother; does she, Lydia?"

"I often tell her she's more of a Kendall than a Hastings," answered my aunt.

"She has David's eyes, but darker hair. Make

yourselves at home, while I finish moulding my butter. Lydia," addressing her daughter, " blow the horn for your father."

" No, Abby, let John alone till dinner-time ; we are going to spend the day, if 'tis convenient to you," said Aunt Lydia.

" That's right. Of course you'll take us country folks as you find us," said Aunt Abby, turning toward me. " We all work for a living, and are not always prepared for company."

" I guess Hope knows as much about work as any of us," said Aunt Lydia. " Poor child! she has seen little else for the last three years."

" I've had work enough, Aunt Abby, because I chose to share mother's ; but it has always been made easy and pleasant for me."

" You do not look as if you had seen many hardships," said Aunt Abby, with an agreeable smile—a smile that gave so much beauty to her sad face that I knew at once we should be friends.

Before the day was over, I knew the reason for the shadow which lay on Aunt Abby's face might be read on five little marble slabs in the old graveyard, where lay Simeon, Benjamin, Edward, Mary, and Naomi, children of John and Abigail Hastings.

I found my cousin sensible and well-informed ; she had attended school at the academy several terms, and before dinner was ready we had made rapid strides toward an acquaintance.

Uncle John answered the summons of the dinner-horn, and came in with Nathan and his workmen to partake of the noonday meal. He was a keen, shrewd-looking man, past fifty, much like his sister Lydia in features and expression, but with a less self-righteous manner, though one could see that his own opinions were valuable to himself, and were maintained with much tenacity.

"How do you do, Lyddy?" he called out in a nasal, but not unkindly voice. "So we've succeeded at last in getting a sight of Emily's child; and she's worth seeing, too," he added, shaking my hand vigorously, and leading me to a seat beside himself at table. "More like David than Emily," he continued, helping me generously to pork, cabbage, and potatoes, and scanning me most sharply with his keen black eyes, "and quite as tall as our Lyddy, though not as stout. How do you like our town?"

"Very well, what I've seen of it. I came only last evening."

"Lyddy must harness up and take you to the Ridge after dinner, and round by the old meeting-house at the four corners, where your marm used to go, before ever she saw David Kendall. She sat in the singing-seats, and I shall always remember her just as she looked that first summer, when David came to keep the academy. She almost always had on a white gown of a Sunday, and her pink cheeks and bright eyes were a sight worth seeing; weren't they, Lyddy?"

"She certainly had a fair countenance; but our Emily knew that 'favor is deceitful and beauty vain,' for she was one of the Lord's chosen."

"That's a fact; she was the flower of our family, and good enough for David Kendall, which is saying a great deal; for he was one of a thousand. If he'd only had a trifle more of shrewdness, he might have gone to Congress; or, at least, he wouldn't have mortgaged his farm."

"But if a man has an extravagant wife, whose head is filled with high-flown city notions, he shouldn't be blamed for selling his birthright for a mess of pottage. David didn't mortgage his farm in Emily's lifetime."

I winced under the insinuations of Aunt Lydia, and longed to defend my step-mother's character, but decided to wait until I could be alone with my uncle and his wife. I turned my flushed face toward Uncle John, who had answered his sister's last words by saying, "That's a fact," a stereotyped answer of his, as I quickly learned, to my aunt's emphatic assertions.

"Do you live in the old house still?" he asked.

"Yes, and own it, too, free from debt."

"You don't say so! Tell us how it came about."

I told, with some misgivings, about the sale of the field, for Aunt Lydia's deep sighs rose above the clatter of knives and forks, and I noticed that my uncle suspended his operations on the pork and cabbage during my narration.

"Humph! it's always a pity to sell off one's cattle and pasterin'—a farm runs out in a little while if the hay is sold off, instead of being fed out to cattle on the land. Who advises your marm?"

"Mr. Chapman, the president of the railroad company."

"Yes, yes—interested, of course. I smell the rat. But it's none of our business, Lyddy. I reckon we can take care of Emily's girl, if ' bad comes to worse.' "

"We should be worse than infidels if we provided not for our own households," aunt replied, " and I look upon Emily's child as my own now."

"That's a fact, Lyddy; but how will the elder like to have Hope in the family? or haven't you come to terms yet?"

All laughed, and Aunt Lydia looked confused. Something resembling a flush spread over her sallow face, and quickly retreated, followed by a severe and injured expression.

"John, you are too old to indulge in the unprofitable

habit of joking, and you must have forgotten that 'he that refraineth his lips is wise.' It would be a pity if Brother Hopkinson couldn't sometimes spend an evening in a friend's house."

"That's a fact, and it's nobody's business; if he wants to marry some sensible woman, I've no objections to his taking my sister."

Aunt Lydia tried to look severe, but it was very evident the subject was an agreeable one, and that Uncle John had committed no grave offence in alluding to it. The conversation turned upon crops and harvesting, which proved a sufficiently fruitful theme to last through the second course of apple-dumplings and cheese, and then Uncle John and his workmen returned to the cutting up of corn-stalks, and Aunt Abby and my cousin cleared away the remnants of dinner; after which they came into the parlor with their sewing, and talked over housekeeping and neighborhood affairs with Aunt Lydia. As neither of these topics interested me, I examined the shells that my grandfather had brought home from foreign shores, and counted the stripes and colors of the bright, home-spun carpet, and thought of Sherbrooke, wondering how long Aunt Lydia would manage to keep me away from my home.

I was startled from my reverie by the agreeable voice of Aunt Abby.

"I trust you will be happy in Hebron, Hope. Your aunt is determined to keep you here, and I suppose there is no reason why you cannot stay."

"Indeed, there are plenty of reasons why I cannot; my mother needs me, and the children love me, and my father wished me to remain with them, and I like my home."

"Hope, you forget that you have no claims to what you call home; it belongs to your step-mother and her children," said Aunt Lydia. "But, Abby, I think we had better not discuss this matter with her now; wait until she has been with us a month, and she will be better able to choose for herself. Lydia, isn't it time for you to harness the horse and take your cousin to the Ridge?"

Lydia started for the pasture where the old farm-horse was feeding, and I followed, glad of an excuse to cool my irritation in the September air, which was fragrant with the smell of ripening fruits.

The horse was quickly caught and led to the barn, where Lydia harnessed him into a light, open wagon, with her own hands, showing an acquaintance with straps and buckles which seemed quite wonderful to me. She apologized for her dexterity in this kind of work by saying:

"You see, Cousin Hope, mother and I have been obliged to learn how to harness, because father and the men are always so busy."

With the reins in my cousin's hands we were soon driving over a rough, hilly road, which commanded a fine view of distant mountain scenery.

The town of Hebron was cut into abrupt hills, over which the roads passed in an honest, straightforward manner, as if ashamed of any contrivance which would take the traveller around a sharp hill, instead of over its summit. I was reminded of Whittier's lines:

"And round and round, over valley and hill,
Old roads winding as old roads will,
Here to a ferry and there to a mill."

The Ridge was a natural pass, thrown up between two narrow ponds, known in Hebron by the name of the "Twin-basins." There was a wild, rugged beauty about this part of the town, unlike any thing I had seen in my native State, and I was glad when my cousin drew rein upon one of the highest hills, and pointed out to me some of the most remarkable features of the landscape.

"Do you see that high mountain away in the distance? In this light it looks almost like a purple cloud—that is Bald Eagle; and that old gray meeting-house to the right is where Aunt Emily used to sing. I don't believe we'll have time to go there to-night, this horse is so slow. Down in that little red house in the valley lives an old, deformed woman, who tells fortunes and gathers herbs for the Shakers. We will go and have our fortunes told before the pleasant days are gone. I'm glad that you are going to live with us in Hebron, and I want you to like the town and people as well as I do."

"But I'm not going to live here, Cousin Lydia; I only came to make a short visit, because aunt wrote in such a way about her lameness, that mother thought I ought to come."

"Poh! she's been cured of her lameness for a long time. She only used it for a trap to catch you; and if I didn't want to stay with Aunt Lydia, I'd never let her frighten me into the notion of staying. She's well enough in her way, and father thinks a world of her, but she's too dreadfully pious to suit me. She always frightened me into doing the ugliest and most disagreeable things. Won't she make Mr. Hopkinson's little girls wish she had been in Van Diemen's Land, before ever she wheedled their father into thinking she was such a sweet saint?"

"Is she really going to marry Mr. Hopkinson?"

"Everybody thinks he's going to marry her, or at least that she means he shall. He is a sight too good for her, though his sermons are a little dull; but she'll put so much spice and vinegar into him, that she won't be obliged to eat caraway seeds to keep her awake when he's preaching. You'd laugh to see her pet his girls; her words are sweet as June butter, and she kisses them and plays with their curls, when I know she abominates curly hair."

"Isn't Aunt Lydia too old to think of marrying?"

"Capital! I'll tell her of that;" and my cousin's loud but hearty laugh provoked the hill-side echoes. "Too old? Why, she's only a little past forty, and Elder Hopkinson must be more than fifty. I suppose it will be a good match for him, for Aunt Lydia has quite a snug little property, and you know ministers are always poor as church mice."

"But what kind of a step-mother will she make?"

"Well, if the elder and his girls always have as much faith in her piety as they seem to have now, and never contradict her, she'll do well enough. But I'm glad she isn't to be my step-mother. It must be horrid to have to mind a woman and call her mother when you know she isn't. I should think you'd be glad to get away from yours, if half Aunt Lydia says is true."

"If you knew my mother, your only wonder would be that I could consent to leave her even for a short visit. There never lived a more faithful, loving, self-sacrificing woman, and I believe I am quite as dear to her as either of her own children; sometimes I think she loves me better, because I am more like my father than they are."

"Well, I am astonished! We've all got the notion from Aunt Lydia that your step-mother kept you drudging for her and her children till there was no spirit left in you. Mother has always said that we should make great allowance for the jealous way in which Aunt Lydia would look at things. You know she was terribly disappointed because your father didn't marry her after his first wife died, and perhaps that's the reason why she can't see any thing decent in the woman he did choose."

This was news, indeed, and accounted for many things which had seemed a mystery before. Poor Aunt Lydia!

if she had really loved my father, it was natural that she should look with jaundiced eyes upon her successful rival, and even grudge the love that her sister's child gave to her. I determined that the knowledge of my aunt's disappointment should so soften my feelings for her, that I would try to pour some little balm into her bruised heart by kind and delicate attentions. And zealously desirous of practising my good resolutions, when my cousin left me at Aunt Lydia's gate, I ran up the garden path and into her little parlor, surprising her beyond measure by throwing an arm around her neck and kissing her."

"Law, Hope, how you frightened me! you made me drop a stitch, right in the instep too! What a fright the wind has made of your hair! Go and make yourself decent, for I'm expecting Mr. Hopkinson will call, and I want to introduce you to him."

"As my future uncle?"

"Go off with your silly romancing. Girls always do make fools of themselves at your age."

But I stopped long enough to take a good look at my aunt's face and dress; she had exchanged the brown gingham, worn through the day, for a lilac muslin, and a coquettish-looking head-dress of black lace and pink ribbons took the place of her ordinary cap; and either her pink ribbons or her rose-colored anticipations softened and lighted up her hard features so that she looked—well, almost agreeable.

CHAPTER XXVIII.

CALEB HOPKINSON.

"At church, with meek and unaffected grace,
His looks adorned the venerable place;
Truth from his lips prevailed with double sway,
And fools who came to scoff, remained to pray."
GOLDSMITH.

"He walked the dark world, in the mild,
Still guidance of the Light;
In tearful tenderness a child,
A strong man in the right."
WHITTIER.

I PUT ou the plaid silk, which my aunt had predicted would be so unbecoming, and coaxed my hair into as much smoothness as its stubborn, curly nature would permit, and sat down to watch the sunset glories from my window. The pleasant chirp of crickets fell on my ear, but did not drown the deep, bass voice which replied to my aunt's cracked treble. Neither did the pungent, pitchy odor of a pile of newly-sawn boards quite despoil the delicious scent of a summer sweeting, whose boughs, laden with ripening fruit, were in reach of my open window.

I watched the fading of the sunset until I was summoned by my aunt to join her in the parlor.

Presenting myself with more than my usual timid reserve, I was hardly prepared for the kind, assuring glance of a pair of blue eyes bent upon me.

"Mr. Hopkinson, this is my niece, Hope Kendall."

"I'm glad to see you in Hebron, Miss Kendall, and hope you may like the place and people well enough to make a permanent home here."

I thanked him for his kind wish, but did not think it

necessary to inform him that I did not intend to like any place but Sherbooke, or find a home under any roof but my step-mother's.

After a few commonplace questions and remarks, Mr. Hopkinson turned from me, and conversed with Aunt Lydia upon church matters. He was a grave but kindly-looking man, and the deep furrows upon his face and Time's silvery footprints in his hair, told the tale of at least half a century.

A dreamy, abstracted look in the blue eyes and the undecided expression of the lips assured me that, however learned he might be in theological lore, he was not well read in a knowledge of his fellow-men.

He impressed me as an honest, generous man, who had a better acquaintance with books than with human nature— a man who would endeavor to win souls by presenting before them the love of Christ rather than the terrors of the law—a man whose hearers would be better acqainted with Calvary than Mount Sinai.

I liked him none the less when I observed a general air of rusty untidiness in his ill-fitting black garments, carelessly-tied white cravat, and clumsy, patched shoes ; but woe to his negligent, scholarly ease and peace of mind, if ever Aunt Lydia acquired the right to straighten out his wardrobe and clip his heavy, ragged eye-brows ; and that she aspired to this honor, even my limited knowledge of womankind enabled me to perceive. I could read it in her nicely-modulated tones of voice, in the coquettish tosses of her pink ribbons, and in the careful, motherly way in which she spoke of Mr. Hopkinson's children.

" How is Ellen's cough?" she asked, when Deacon Sanborn's obstinate refusal to commune with the church until it had excluded Smith Perry for pro-slavery sympathies, had been discussed.

"Ay, Ellen's cough? Well, really, Sister Hastings, I've been so busy in preparing a sermon upon the text, 'Bear ye one another's burdens, and so fulfil the law of Christ,' that I've scarcely noticed the child for a week. The object of this discourse is to enforce the beautiful doctrine of Christian charity upon our members. I find there is much strife engendered by this antislavery discussion, and great danger of our having two opposing parties in our little church, unless the hearts of our people can be filled with the loving, forbearing spirit of our blessed Christ. Has your own mind been especially exercised upon this important question of slavery, Sister Hastings?"

Now Aunt Lydia took an eminently practical view of things, and would much rather have given her reverend friend a recipe for his daughter's cough than have answered his last query; but she could not allow him to suppose her uninterested in a theme of such magnitude, the discussion of which was threatening the peace and harmony of both Church and State; and, putting on an expression of unusual wisdom and charity, she replied:

"I've been more or less interested for several years, and have been praying that the Lord would raise up a deliverer for his people; but I've never taken an active part in the Antislavery Society in our own village, because I couldn't see clearly what they expected to accomplish in their sewing-meetings. And then, my heart has been bound up in the cause of the poor and sick and needy in our own town. Charity begins at home, you know, Brother Hopkinson, and our Lord said, 'The poor ye have always with you.'"

"Certainly, and your time and charities have been most worthily bestowed; but I've no doubt you'll soon find your heart accepting a larger field for your benevolence. Our oppressed colored brethren will need much teaching before they will be ready for general emancipation. I sometimes think they will need to be led through the wilderness as long as were God's chosen people, before they will be ready for the inheritance of freed men. Are the good people of Sherbrooke moving in this great cause, Miss Kendall?"

I had been so engrossed in speculations upon the probable amount of Aunt Lydia's charities to the sick and destitute, that I was quite unprepared for the minister's question, and had a most vague and visionary idea of what the "great cause" might be, but ventured to stammer out, "I believe so, sir."

"My niece has been confined so closely to a hard and narrow sphere of duties, Brother Hopkinson, that you must not be surprised to find her entirely ignorant of the great benevolent movements of the day. I hope, in time, we shall be able to correct the faults of her education." But the sigh that followed spoke of the vanity of such a charitable hope.

"It is never too late to learn, Miss Kendall, and I am rejoiced that you are to have the benefit of your aunt's wise counsels this autumn, as well as the instructions of Mr. Hamlin, at the academy. Your aunt tells me you have never been at school."

"I have been studying at home for three or four years. My mother is an excellent teacher, sir, and I think I have advanced as rapidly in my studies with her as I should have done in school."

"'Whoso boasteth himself of a false gift is like wind and clouds without rain,'" answered my aunt; "you had better let others judge of the advancement you have made, than proclaim it yourself." Then, turning to the minister, she added: "My niece inherited from her mother an ambitious desire for knowledge, and I've no doubt she has managed to pick up much more after her hard tasks were finished than most girls would. I shall be greatly obliged if you will take a spare hour one day this week, and find out what she has learned, and advise her what studies to pursue. You see I am taking the liberty of a friend with you."

"And giving me great pleasure by doing so. I can never forget your self-sacrificing devotion to my late wife and my motherless girls; and if I can serve you by assisting in the education of your niece, I shall be most happy. Miss Kendall, what progress have you made in your studies?"

"Mother says I am prepared to teach the common English branches; but it will be unnecessary for you to advise about my studies, Mr. Hopkinson, for I am going back to Sherbrooke in a few days to assist mother in teaching, and to receive instruction from Professor Roeder."

"Ah, perhaps I had misunderstood your aunt."

"No, Mr. Hopkinson, I made my plans without consulting Hope; for I knew her step-mother would never allow her to come to Hebron, if she suspected that I wished to improve the condition of my sister's child. She has always managed to frustrate all my efforts in behalf of my niece; but I trust that Hope has too much good sense not to yield to our united persuasions for her good. She ought to know that 'he that refuseth instruction despiseth his own soul.' Perhaps we had better say nothing more to her about it, until she has been here a few days, and has become acquainted with Mr. Hamlin and some of our young people."

"You are right, Sister Hastings; old prejudices and associations cannot be overcome at once; but your niece doesn't look as if she would make any stubborn resistance to benevolent designs for her good."

Then I was sure my face was not a faithful mirror of

my heart, for I had not the slightest intention of submitting to benevolent designs. My whole nature rose up in rebellion to my aunt's assumed authority, and her wicked insinuations about my dear mother's oppression of me.

It was unjust to my father's memory for me to sit in silence and hear his cherished wife so misrepresented, but how was I to combat, single-handed, my aunt's quotations, and her provokingly meek and injured look, when I ventured to contradict her in the presence of a third person?

I had not sufficient courage to attempt my mother's vindication in Mr. Hopkinson's presence, fearing lest my tongue should betray too much of my Kendall temper, but I resolved to tell him the whole truth before leaving Hebron.

Aunt Lydia had taken up her knitting—it was a small sock, which must be intended for some poor, stockingless child—and the minister had taken up the difficulty between his two obstinate members; their belligerent position appeared to lay heavily upon his heart; and while my aunt's needles softly clicked, he was rehearsing to her the reasons for and against retaining Deacon Sanborn, and excluding Smith Perry; so I slid noiselessly out of the parlor, that I might gain time to finish the letter which I had commenced in the morning.

The village clock struck the hour of nine before I heard Mr. Hopkinson's voice upon the steps, bidding my aunt good-night.

"Good-night, Brother Hopkinson; remember to tell Ellen that I have made a syrup of squills, spearmint, and honey for her cough, and she must come over in the morning and get it."

"You are too kind, Lydia! What would my poor, motherless children do without your thoughtful care?"

The reply was indistinct, but I was almost sure that the

parting upon the steps was more tender than the ordinary relations of pastor and people require. I did not see Aunt Lydia until the next morning, and then there was nothing in the immovable gravity of her face to tell tales of the previous evening, and nothing in her manners toward me showed that she remembered the expression of my determination to return to Sherbrooke.

After breakfast she told me that she should be very busy during the morning, as she had invited friends to tea. "If you would like the walk, Hope, you may go over and ask your Uncle John and his wife and Lydia to come and drink tea with us. Tell them that Mr. Hopkinson will be here, and Mr. Hamlin."

It was an errand I was glad to execute—not only because I should enjoy the walk in the clear, bracing September air, but because it might afford me the chance of enlisting the favor of Aunt Abby. I seized my hat in " the most unbecoming and hoydenish haste," as Aunt Lydia assured me, and running down the garden-path, half stumbled over a pretty child, whose dreamy blue eyes were an exact copy of Reverend Caleb Hopkinson's; so that, without her ugly mourning-frock, I should have known she was the motherless little Ellen, coming for my aunt's syrup of squills and spearmint. I stooped and kissed the child's innocent, wondering face, telling her where she would find Miss Hastings; but the meeting with Ellen had sobered my pace, and as I moved slowly along toward the yellow farm-house I wondered how long she would wear that calm, sunny look after Aunt Lydia had the ordering of her steps.

I found my aunt and cousin ironing in the tidy kitchen of the farm-house. Though every thing about the farm and buildings betokened prosperity, they kept no help, and the systematic neatness of the household arrangements could hardly be exceeded.

"Sit down here, Hope; I suppose you are not afraid of a kitchen, nor of hot smoothing-irons," said my aunt.

"No, indeed; I have a pleasant acquaintance with both. Mother has shown me how to work so handily, and has taught me that there is so much dignity about all kinds of honest labor, that I feel quite proud of my skill, and can come down from the translation of a Latin ode to the washing of dishes, without any jar to my nerves."

There was a smile in Aunt Abby's brown eyes.

"Your mother has taught you both Latin and housework?"

"Yes, and almost every thing else that I know; and her teachings have been so tempered with love and gentleness, that all knowledge seems beautiful and sacred to me."

"All but a knowledge of sin," suggested Aunt Abby. "I should like to know your mother."

"Oh, Aunt Abby, if you would only go to Sherbrooke and see her in her family and in her school, I am sure you would like her. Why did you never come when my father was living?"

"I visited him once before his second marriage, but after that I always had a young child, or sickness in my family—something to prevent me from visiting; and then your Aunt Lydia gave us such an account of your stepmother that we had no desire to see her. But, Hope, you do not look as if you had been uncared for and treated like a hireling."

"My looks would belie me if I did. I do not believe a daughter was ever more tenderly cared for. Mother has always been more patient with me than with her own children."

"Why should she be?"

"I think my resemblance to father made me her favorite, and perhaps my motherless infancy won her sympathies. She has always treated me in such a way that I have never known the want of a mother's love."

"Your father was very much beloved and respected here and in Sherbrooke. Do you see the best society in your village, now that you and your mother are known to be poor?"

"The very best; and mother's pupils belong to what are called old, aristocratic families. Now that our debts are paid off, we shall keep help, and I shall have more leisure for study and the instructions of a professor from Wiltshire. Why should Aunt Lydia be so unwilling to believe that I know any thing?"

"We have a good school here, and I suppose 'tis natural that your aunt should wish to keep her only sister's child near her; and perhaps 'tis not strange that she should think you must have been neglected after your father's death, when she knew of the mortgage on the farm and the severe economy it was necessary for your mother to practise, and it may be that her interest in Mr. Hopkinson has persuaded her that you will be useful in helping take care of his girls."

"She has some selfish motive, I am certain, for I have no faith in her love for me. But I shall not stay in Hebron, Aunt Abby, because it would be unjust to mother. She will need my assistance in her school, and will pay me as much as I could earn elsewhere. And then, Aunt Lydia and I could never live harmoniously together, not even under the minister's roof. She always had a remarkable faculty for exasperating me when she visited us, and my Kendall temper has been very near the boiling-over point several times since I came. You would not advise me to leave mother now, Aunt Abby, just when I can begin to repay her, in some small degree, for the tender care she has always given me?"

"No, your Uncle John said this morning that you were old enough to make your own choice; and after what you told Lydia, we both concluded it would be for your interest and happiness to remain with your step-mother. But before you came, Hope, we supposed that, once removed from your mother's influence, you would gladly accept a home with your aunt."

"Perhaps she will be consoled for my obstinacy in the love of the Hopkinsons. I came over to invite you to drink tea with the minister at Aunt Lydia's this evening, and must run back and help her prepare for company; but I am so comforted because you think I am right in returning to mother, that I think I can keep my temper in check and make myself agreeable to my aunt all day."

"You should certainly try to do so, for she is a good woman in her way, and has had many disappointments to sour her. I hope there is not another great one preparing for her. But stay, Hope, and tell me about your father's last sickness. He was preceptor of our academy for more than a year before he was married, and we all loved him like a brother. Your aunt will not need any help but Jane's in preparing for company."

And Aunt Abby put her smoothing-irons upon the stove and sat down, with her sad brown eyes upon my face, while I gave her a simple history of the poverty which made it necessary for father to go to Ohio; of little Alice's death; of mother's patient sacrifices for us all; and then of father's illness, his faith, and his triumphant entrance into life.

It was not told without tears, and Aunt Abby's clean apron was often lifted to her eyes, while Cousin Lydia's hot iron went up and down over the snowy folds of linen in an uncertain and tremulous way.

"May God bless your mother, and make her children

worthy of her and of the father whom He has taken! Come with me to the cornfield, Hope, where your uncle is at work; I am going to carry him a pitcher of home-brewed beer." And Aunt Abby, in her white sun-bonnet, and I in a straw hat, were soon seated by Uncle John's side upon a stone, and, by careful questioning Aunt Abby soon drew from me the history which she had just heard in the kitchen. Uncle John's shrewd black eyes often seemed busy, during my narration, in counting the pumpkins, which were scattered in rich, yellow beauty over the field, yet I knew they more frequently were fastened upon my face.

"Bravely told, my girl! Your aunt would say you had the pen of a ready writer, or the tongue of a ready speaker—which is it, Abby? I am always getting her proverbs mixed up—cart before the ox, or horse behind the plough. But don't go and use that tongue of yourn in speaking on woman's rights and spiritual influences, like a young woman did in our town-hall last spring. My! her words ran as fast as the stream over the mill-dam, and sounded wonderfully smooth and pretty, but when I got home I couldn't remember nothing at all of what she said. When I saw my old woman coming to the field, I knew she had something for me besides beer, and I feel as if I'd heerd the elder read a psalm. I believe if our Emily could speak, she'd say, 'Go back to the woman who has been more than a mother to you,' and that's all the advice I have to offer you, Hope."

"Thank you, Uncle John."

"I don't know as I've said any thing worth thanking for, but if you're paid for tramping out here over the sharp stubble, I'm glad of it. Your Aunt Lyddy is a terrible nice woman, smart as a steel trap, and knows a heap more about the Scripters than most ministers do; but somehow

you and she looks at things from a different stand-pint, as
the woman lecturer said, and there's always two sides to a
story. Now, you're too wise a girl to go and let on to
your aunt that I said so, but really, I do suppose she took
a mighty fancy to your father, when he was courting our
Emily, and was awfully disappointed that he didn't marry
her instead; and then when Emily died she felt sure of
him, and tried her best to comfort him by taking care of
you; but it would not work—and so you mustn't think it
strange that she could never see any good in Celia Dinsmore. Go off to the house now, or I'll set you both to
cutting up corn-stalks. You've wasted an hour of my daylight already, and where will your dinner be, old woman?"

The last sentences were said with a look and tone that
contradicted his words, and I left the cornfield with more
love in my heart for my rough, uneducated, but honest
uncle, than I had supposed it possible to give a brother of
Aunt Lydia's.

CHAPTER XXIX.

THE SHADOW OF COMING EVENTS.

"There is no wind, but soweth seeds
Of a more true and open life,
Which burst, unlooked for, into high-souled deeds
With wayside beauty rife."
LOWELL.

The remembrance of what Uncle John and his wife had
said about Aunt Lydia's disappointments would take, I
thought, much of the stinging harshness out of her words,
and make a veil of charity through which to look at her

in future. And returning from the yellow farm-house, I entered my aunt's kitchen with a lighter heart than I had carried since leaving Sherbrooke. I saw at a glance that my services were not needed: two loaves of cake, with just the right shade of brown, were sending their tempting perfumes through the room, and Aunt Lydia's hands had just completed wonderful results in the heaped-up froth of her custards.

"Can I help you, aunt?" I asked.

"No, the last stroke of work is done until it's time to set the table. I always keep my house in order for company, and when there's a place for every thing and every thing in its place, it doesn't take me long to make a loaf of cake and a few custards. It isn't every one that has my faculty, though."

"May I cut some flowers and arrange them in the parlor?"

"There are no vases to put them in, and what good would flowers do, except to remind us of the frailty of all things?—and we don't need them for that. Almost every day the death of some one tells us that 'here we have no continuing city.' Just after sunrise this morning the bell tolled a long time; I tried to count the strokes, and reached seventy, when I got confused by the roar of the dam, and couldn't make out whether it struck seventy-six or seventy-seven times; but Prudence Styles came in a little while ago, to tell me that her grandma'am died this morning at sunrise. Poor soul! she had a cancer on her neck, that eat clear away into her vitals. She was seventy-seven last May. Prudence wanted to borrow my black delaine dress and thibet shawl for her mother to wear at the funeral, and of course I had to lend them, though I told her to be careful of them, as there was no telling how soon I might be called to put on mourning myself. The Styleses are shiftless folks, always borrowing; the old lady has been sick more'n a year, and there has been plenty of time for them to get mourning and grave-clothes ready since Doctor Houghton told them she must die, but now they've got to hurry up a shroud before to-morrow evening. Prudence had the boldness to ask me to go over and help make it; as if I hadn't done enough when her grandma'am was living, in making broths and jellies for her! But the more you do for some folks, the more you may."

"You have no objections to my cutting flowers, if I can find some tumblers and dishes for them, aunt?"

"No, not if you can find pleasure in such vanities."

But though the permission was coldly given, I felt that I had achieved something of a triumph. From my aunt's homely abundance of flowers I selected enough of the more delicate and fragrant to soften the aspect of her stiff little parlor. The string of painted egg-shells, that hung over the small mirror, was hid with a wreath of climbing honeysuckle, hop-vines, and verbenas; and bouquets of honest-looking pink and white asters, with a fringe of green, made bright, cheerful spots for the eye to rest upon.

A faint smile of pleasure lurked for a moment around my aunt's mouth when she saw the effect of my adorning, but it was quickly swept away by the hard, stern lines of her every-day expression. "Only 'grass of the field, which to-day is, and to-morrow is cast into the oven,'" she quoted with a sigh.

"But, aunt, you know that even our Saviour noticed the lilies of the field, and it cannot be wrong for us to love them and decorate our rooms with them."

"If we have the ornament of a meek and quiet spirit, we shall think little of outward adorning." And my aunt moved gravely away, to assume the lilac muslin and pink ribbons, showing by her air that she considered my vanity justly rebuked.

Aunt Abby and my cousin came early in the afternoon, prepared for a long talk, with knitting for an accompaniment, and I brought down the hood of scarlet and white wool which I was knitting in anticipation of the coming winter, while Aunt Lydia took from her basket the unfinished little sock.

"For whom are you knitting such a small stocking, Lydia?" asked her sister-in-law.

"For Adoniram Staples' boy, and there are plenty of feet that will need such stockings before the snow flies. Hope had better be spending her time on something useful, than in making such a flummery for her head."

"This will be a hood, aunt, and very becoming when 'tis finished;" and to convince her, I threw the bright, soft folds over my hair.

"Isn't it a beauty, mother? and so becoming! I wish Hope would teach me how to make one," exclaimed Cousin Lydia.

"You had better wish for some useful knowledge, child! A quilted silk hood like what I made you last winter is much warmer and more sensible-looking."

"I don't care if my things aren't all sensible-looking— I mean to have a hood just like yours," whispered my cousin, with just enough defiant mischief in her eyes to make them irresistible.

Aunt Abby, apparently fearful that the hood would lead the stream of words into some disagreeable channel, asked how Adoniram Staples' family were getting along.

"As comfortably as most people do, who live from hand to mouth, I suppose. Mrs. Staples is nervous and sickly, and has no faculty to make the most of Adoniram's wages. He's always in debt, though I've paid him twenty dollars a month ever since last April, and have given them a sight of apples and potatoes and garden sauce."

"Tell him to call at our house on his way home to-morrow night; I have some things that will be useful in his family."

The sisters-in-law, who were very unlike, conversed amiably together upon the poverty, sickness, and thrift of their neighbors, Aunt Abby adroitly turning the tide of talk when it approached some threatening sand-bar, snag, or rock, until the minister came in, when there was no longer need for her watchfulness; Aunt Lydia's words flowed as smoothly as a meadow brook, and her temper appeared as serene and unruffled as the calmest inland lake in a midsummer day.

Mr. Hopkinson's dreamy eyes rested upon her, when she quoted sacred passages and applied her handkerchief to her eyes in alluding to the death of old Mrs. Styles, as if he thought her the embodiment of all womanly virtues.

Uncle John's entrance was a little noisy, but he was evidently on the best of terms with his minister, and they soon were engrossed with the merits of the Sanborn vs. Perry case. Uncle John appeared to take a most practical view of things, alleging that Smith Perry's subscription was of more worth to the church than the deacon's good-will.

"You see I can't quite make out what harm will come of Smith's communing with slaveholders, as he says he did when he went to Petersburg to visit she that was Naomi Perry."

"You forget the pernicious example, Brother Hastings, and the countenance that his communing with slaveholders would give to their heinous crimes."

"Solomon says, 'Enter not into the path of the wicked, and go not in the way of evil men,'" quoted Aunt Lydia.

"That's a fact, Lyddy, and you and the parson together

will be too much for me; but after all, I can't see how Smith's communing with them slaveholders will hurt us, and I can see just where the shoe will pinch, if we lose his subscription."

"But, Brother Hastings, if we exclude Smith Perry for an act of his, which sanctioned the barbarous system of slavery, will it not be the protest of our church against that awful sin?"

"Yes, most likely; but it seems to me, that the voice of our little church up here in the Green Mountains will scarcely be heard in the South. We shall fail to convince them of their sins, while we lose an honest, paying man. You know Smith stands a good chance of being our next representative from this district."

"It is not good to have respect of persons in judgment, Brother John. 'He that saith unto the wicked, Thou art righteous, him shall the people curse. But to them that rebuke him shall be delight, and a good blessing shall come upon them.'"

The minister listened to my aunt's quotation with a smile of approval, as if he were calculating the advantages of having such a ready tongue constantly near him; while Uncle John, with a look of wonder upon his shrewd face at the aptness of her quotation, exclaimed, "You do beat all, Lyddy, for Scripter texts, that just hit the nail on the head. I've no doubt if you had Deacon Sanborn and Smith Perry where you could rap them with your proverbs for an hour or so, you'd set them both right."

Mr. Hamlin, the teacher, entered, and the tide of talk turned upon school matters, while Aunt Lydia slipped out to put a few last finishing touches upon her bountiful supper-table, and I taught my cousin how to knit a hood, and listened to the conversation between the minister and the new-comer.

There was an open, honest manliness about his words and manners that involuntarily won my respect, though I had felt certain, before seeing Mr. Hamlin, that I should dislike him, because Aunt Lydia commended him so highly. He was not handsome, compared with Carey Chapman, the only young man whom I could call a friend, but there was strength in his square forehead and heavy eyebrows—honesty and intelligence in the large, dark eyes, that beamed with a steady light—firmness and purity in the well-cut lips. Every thing about his face and figure denoted strength rather than elegance, native intelligence rather than outward polish. When he spoke, his voice had a clear, healthy, metallic ring. There was authority and self-respect in his tones, and I was sure there might be tenderness, if he were speaking to mother or sister, and hearty sympathy in both hand and voice for every one that needed help.

I noticed that he appeared disinclined to converse upon the theme which Mr. Hopkinson was constantly bringing forward; but when asked for an opinion, gave it in few words.

"Mr. Hamlin, you have not told us what action the Church ought to take in reference to Deacon Sanborn and Smith Perry," said the minister, after we were seated around Aunt Lydia's supper-table.

"I would not dare dictate if I had the right to, but I think it would be vastly better for the Deacon and Mr. Perry to talk over their difficulties alone in the spirit of Christian charity, than compel the Church to array herself against either of them. I have no doubt they would be surprised to find how nearly alike they think—how slight a barrier separates them."

"Very likely; but ought not the Church to array herself on the side of truth in this important crisis?"

"There can be but one opinion, sir, on that point, and there ought to be but one on the question of slavery: its evils are sufficiently manifest; but I do not feel certain that any action your Church could take would soften its aspect, or carry conviction of its unrighteousness to the hearts of those whose moneyed interests are involved in it."

"Every way of a man is right in his own eyes," sighed my aunt from behind her large, old-fashioned tea-urn. "Mr. Hopkinson, do help yourself to cold chicken. Is your tea agreeable?"

"Perfectly, madam," responded the minister, with an abstracted air and smile that told me his thoughts were far away from the fragrant beverage by his plate.

"Hope, help Mr. Hamlin to some currant jelly; it is always nice with cold chicken;" and Aunt Lydia, in her careful provision for the material wants of her guests, soon gave the conversation a practical, every-day tone, which still admitted the weaving in of an occasional proverb. Sitting opposite the clergyman and Mr. Hamlin, I could see that two pairs of eyes were invariably raised to my aunt's face when the words of the wise king flowed from her lips— Mr. Hamlin's with a curious smile in their brown depths, and Mr. Hopkinson's with an expression which plainly said, "She openeth her mouth with wisdom."

I was pleased and surprised with the shrewdness and intelligence of Uncle John's remarks. He met the two educated men half way, and though his opinions were always clothed in blunt, common words, and his grammar was defiantly independent of text-books, yet he showed a better acquaintance with history and politics than many men of greater pretensions. There was no cowardly shrinking in him from any theme of general interest, and I could see that both minister and teacher respected his honest, unscholarly way of talking and thinking.

Supper over, we returned to the parlor, and to the discussion of those great moral and political themes which, in small communities like Hebron, where there are few accidents and but little neighborhood news, form much more general topics of conversation than in cities. Those who are always laughing at the ignorance and awkwardness of country people, who imagine that all knowledge of books and all refinement is confined to cities and large towns, would do well to correct their opinions by taking lessons of our New England farmers.

Cousin Lydia and I sat apart, busying our hands with the scarlet and white wool, and chatting upon such topics as girls of eighteen usually talk about; while my thoughts often wandered to the sober talk of our elders, and my ears were often arrested by the pleasant, healthy voice of the teacher.

"Your aunt tells me that you are to be a pupil of mine soon, Miss Kendall," and Mr. Hamlin drew his chair near mine, that his conversation might not interrupt the flow of words on the opposite side of the astral lamp. I looked up at the speaker's face, in doubt how to answer: that a generous fund of knowledge and a ready ability to impart it, lay behind that square forehead and heavy brow, I felt sure, but how to frame an answer which would not look doubtful of his attainments, or disrespectful to my aunt, puzzled me.

"Have I made a mistake? Are you not the orphan niece whom Miss Hastings was expecting?" he asked, with a smile which beamed in his eyes rather than played around his lips.

"I am her niece, but I have a home and a mother in Sherbrooke"—there I hesitated, conscious that his questioning eye rested upon my face.

"And you are not inclined to drink from such springs as may be found among our hills?"

"If I do not remain, it will be from no distrust of the springs, Mr. Hamlin, but because my mother needs me. She is a teacher too."

"Ay, and you are preparing for that profession?"

"Yes, but only as an assistant in our family school."

"Your aunt will be disappointed; I inferred from what she said that your remaining with her was a settled thing."

"I shall be sorry for my aunt's disappointment, but I cannot remain here; my mother and her family need me."

"That consideration should have weight with you. How do you like Hebron?"

"The town is beautifully located, and the scenery is more grand and rugged than any I have seen before."

"Has your cousin shown you the Ridge yet?"

"Yes, we have been there once."

"If you are a good walker, I should like to show you Brier Hill on Saturday. You will have no objections to seeing it again, Miss Lydia?"

"Oh, no—it will be lovely at this season of the year, and I want Hope to go there."

"'When woods begin to wear the crimson leaf,
And suns grow meek'—

Do you remember Bryant's lines on October, Miss Kendall?"

"No." I couldn't summon courage to tell him that I knew any thing about Bryant.

"You ought to be familiar with his writings; the hills and woods which have inspired him must be neighbors of yours."

"His native town is more than fifty miles from Sherbrooke."

"Ah, I thought it was nearer. He seems to me more thoroughly American than any other poet of ours; his descriptions of seasons and scenery belong exclusively to New England. What other region would his graphic picture of winter so truthfully portray?"

He paused for an answer, but I bent my eyes perversely upon my knitting. Had Carey Chapman spoken of Bryant's word-pictures, I might have shown him my knowledge of them, but I did not mean to allow Aunt Lydia's favorite the chance of becoming familiarly acquainted with me.

Mr. Hamlin, however, seemed determined to make me talk, and came down from the poetical to the real, telling me some amusing incidents of his teacher's life; and though his voice was pleasant, his words well chosen, and his whole manner earnest and cheerful, yet he failed to unloose my tongue, only as replies to direct questions were necessary.

Aunt Lydia's guests left at an early hour—all but the minister, and he was listening with apparent interest to a minute and circumstantial account of the sickness and poverty in Adoniram Staples' family, and therefore excusable for prolonging his stay.

I went to the garden-gate with my cousin, and after bidding her good-night, stood for a half hour in the clear, silvery moonlight, thinking, oh, how lovingly of mother and Sherbrooke! I might have stood there, leaning upon the gate, unconscious of time, an hour longer, so completely lost was I in idle and delicious reveries, soothed too by the monotonous fall of the waters over the dam, had not the sound of voices upon the steps arrested my attention.

The tall stems of hollyhocks and lilac-bushes hid me from the view of any one standing upon the steps, but the distance did not prevent the tones of a deep and tender bass voice from reaching me. I could see through the clustering leaves my aunt's prim figure in the doorway and Mr. Hopkinson by her side; and yes—I was sure, he was holding her hand.

"You have made me inexpressibly happy, dear Lydia," I heard him say in a low voice, but so distinct that the words floated out upon the still night air as far as the gate. What could I do? If I moved or ran to the house, I should disturb an interesting scene, which my womanly instincts told me would be ungenerous; but I could not be an eaves-dropper, that would be more ungenerous still; so I coughed and fumbled at the latch of the gate to give warning of my approach, and then walked boldly up the path to the door, where I said something about the beauty of the night having tempted me to remain out in the garden, and, bidding them good-night, ran up the flight of stairs to my room. It was not long before Mr. Hopkinson passed out of the gate and my aunt presented herself in my room with an expression on her face very unlike any thing which had greeted the minister's vision.

"So, Miss Hope, you've been proving the truth of the proverb, 'Stolen waters are sweet, and bread eaten in secret is pleasant?' How long had you been listening?"

"Aunt Lydia, you don't think I could be so wanting in honor as to listen? I unwillingly heard just one sentence, and then I coughed, and walked directly up to the door."

"Don't fly into a passion, child, but tell me what you heard."

"Mr. Hopkinson was saying something about your having made him happy."

"What in the world could have made you stand moping in the night air?"

"It was so lovely in the moonlight, and there was so much harmony in the night; you know Shakspeare says—

'There's not an orb which thou behold'st,
But in his motion like an angel sings.'"

"Stuff! what did that old heathen know about angels singing? Your head is filled with silly nonsense, which you must have got from Mrs. Kendall. When your mother and I were girls, we didn't quote sentimental poetry."

"Tell me just what kind of a girl my own mother was, Aunt Lydia," I asked, hoping to rouse the slumbering tenderness of her nature, and divert from myself the severity of her displeasure.

"She was sensible and industrious, and everybody spoke well of her. She had a pleasant temper, too, which I wish you had inherited."

"I'm sorry that I fail to please you, aunt, but I hope Mr. Hopkinson's girls will make amends for your disappointment in me."

"Poor, motherless things!" sighed my aunt, in a softer, more womanly voice than she had used before. "Well, I shall try to bring them up in the fear of the Lord. I suppose I may as well tell you now as at any time, Hope, that I've decided to marry Mr. Hopkinson."

"I'm glad of it, aunt, and I wish your decision may bring you great happiness."

"I don't look for great happiness in this world, but I hope to do my duty by Caleb and the children; the girls need some one to look after them. Ellen has a bad cough, and Mary squints and has a stoop in her shoulders, while neither of them has learned to knit, or sew, or do any thing useful. I was telling their father this evening, after John's folks went away, how much little Ellen needed careful nursing, and what a pity it was for Mary to form such idle habits. The dear man is so bound up in his books and sermons, that he had no idea of the sad state of things around him, but I felt it my duty to tell him. And then he flustered me so, by asking if I would take care of his dear children, that I hardly knew what I said, but something about being unworthy of such a trust, and that a prudent wife was from the Lord. He seemed quite overcome, and wept like a child; but after a minute, he took my hand and asked me if I loved him and his children well enough to take the place of the sainted dead. I had been expecting an offer for several weeks, but somehow I wasn't quite prepared for it when it came, or perhaps the sight of his tears overcame me, for I could scarcely stammer out a word. I just laid my head on his shoulder and cried, too; and then he soothed me and talked in such a comforting way, that I couldn't help saying to him, 'Pleasant words are as an honeycomb, sweet to the soul and health to the bones.'"

"How soon will you be married, aunt?"

"You're amazing simple, Hope, for a girl of eighteen! to think every thing could be settled in an interview of half or three quarters of an hour. He said nothing about the day, and it's not likely he will for several weeks, though he's sadly in want of a wife, poor man! I noticed his wristbands were ragged, and his button-holes were fraying out this very afternoon. I shall have my hands full until I get things straightened out, but I long to clear his premises of that shiftless Matilda Crockett, with her long curls."

"Has Mr. Hopkinson any thing to depend upon but his salary?"

"It's not at all likely that he has; but I have a comfortable income, and 'better is a little with righteousness than great revenues without right,' as I was saying to Caleb not an hour ago. I've rattled on like a love-sick girl to you, but it's all owing to your moping in the night air, so that you overheard Caleb, though I suppose you must have known it sooner or later. I only hope you've not caught a cold that'll end in fever. I should be in a fine muss with sickness in my family, just now, when I need four hands instead of two. There'll be house-cleaning, and preserving, and quilting to do before winter sets in, for I don't believe Caleb will wait for a wife many weeks longer. Now, Hope, I shall get you a dose of my spearmint syrup, to throw off the effects of standing in the dew."

I took the syrup, thankful to escape with so mild a punishment, and went to sleep, wondering how much more harshly my aunt would have treated my offence, if Mr. Hopkinson's timely proposal had not softened her mood.

CHAPTER XXX.

ELLEN'S DREAM.

"The blessing of her quiet life
Fell on us like the dew;
And good thoughts, where her footsteps pressed,
Like fairy blossoms grew."
WHITTIER.

"I did hear you talk
Far above singing; after you were gone,
I grew acquainted with my heart, and searched
What stirred it so!"

THERE were no traces of Aunt Lydia's new happiness to be seen in the business-like air with which she went about her morning's work—no softer light in her keen black eyes, and no unbending of the hard lines about her mouth, as she gathered her marigolds and mints; they were only common herbs for her—good for coughs and fevers.

Love had not heightened nor transformed the common things around her, nor made an Eden out of her rugged New England farm.

There was no dreamy abstractedness about her, as she

laid out work for Adoniram Staples, nor later in the day when she brought out her quilting-bars and prepared her bright patchwork for its oak-leaf pattern. But when little Ellen Hopkinson stole shyly into the kitchen, and asked if she might help Jane gather the crab-apples, there was a tenderer gleam in Aunt Lydia's eyes, as she drew the child to her side, and lifted for a moment her golden-brown curls. It seemed as though the purity and delicacy of the little face had touched some hidden spring of kindliness beneath the hard crust of her nature.

"How's your cough, Ellen?"

"Not much better."

"Have you taken the syrup?"

"Yes, ma'am; but I coughed just the same, and it hurts me so right here!" placing a thin little hand upon her narrow chest.

"Poor child!" exclaimed Aunt Lydia, with a sigh, taking the little hand into her own hard palm; "you have too much fever about you. Do you sleep well nights?"

"Not very well. I'm so hot, and I have so many dreams, that I feel tired when morning comes."

"I shall come over to-night and bathe you in weak poppy-tea, and make you a pillow of hops, and put a soothing plaster on your chest. Are you tired now?"

"Yes, ma'am. I'm almost always tired."

"Then you'd better lie down on the sofa here, and see me quilt, instead of helping Jane pick crab-apples. Hope, you may bring a pillow from my room."

The child was soon arranged to my aunt's satisfaction upon the sofa, and a drawer, full of curious shells, corals, and Chinese flowers, drawn from the quaint old maplewood bureau and placed upon two chairs by the side of the sofa for her amusement. It was strange to see Aunt Lydia do even a little thing for the gratification and comfort of a child—she who had so mercilessly swept away Willie's block-houses and paper soldiers; and I almost involuntarily breathed a prayer that the tender spell might continue to rest upon her, when she took the vacant chair by the minister's hearth.

"Where did you get these beautiful shells, Miss Hastings?" asked the child.

"My father brought them home from sea; he was a captain, and the last time he came he brought those Chinese flowers. I remember now how disappointed he looked, when I told him they were useless things. Poor man! it was a sad voyage for him, for Emily died while he was away, and never saw the white crape shawl and dove-colored silk which he brought her from Canton."

My aunt raised her handkerchief to her eyes, though no visible moisture seemed to require it; but the quilting would not allow her many minutes for the show of grief, and she was soon actively engaged in drawing the oak-leaf pattern upon her patchwork.

"You must let me help you, Aunt Lydia."

"Well, I shall be glad of any help. At your age I could put a quilt in the frame, and draw the pattern, and do every stitch of the work. Emily and I made nearly all the quilts that Mrs. Kendall is wearing out. It was precious little that she brought into the house, though her relations all turned up their noses at David because he was poor. Hope, go to the pantry and bring a baked pear for Ellen, while I finish marking this pattern."

I brought the pear and sat down near the child while she ate it, telling her meanwhile such stories as had pleased my own childish fancy, and describing the delicate shells and corals to her, until the long, dark lashes closed over her blue eyes, and "sleep held her in his downy thrall."

"She's the exact image of her mother," whispered Aunt

Lydia, bending over the couch and gazing at the little sleeper's face. "And what's more, the winter snows will fall upon her grave, unless Dr. Houghton can do more for her than I think he can. I shall have him sent for to-morrow. Poor Caleb! he will feel her loss—he always calls her his 'little lamb,' and 'Violet.' I'm glad that I shall have the right to comfort him when the blow falls." And Aunt Lydia returned to her quilting, with an expression on her face which plainly said she would do her duty by Caleb and his children. The oak-leaf pattern came out with remarkable exactness from under my aunt's nimble fingers; and while her needle flew, her tongue was not idle. She told in half whispers, and with most painful particularity, the incidents connected with the sickness and death of all her relatives and friends, and from her great store-house of death-bed memories she drew many dark prophecies for the little sleeper.

"It's consumption that ails her, I'm almost sure, though I never thought it was any thing but a bad cold until to-day; but do you see that hectic flush on her cheek? She caught it of her mother. I shall take care to have plenty of fresh camphor-gum and herbs about me when I'm waiting upon her; and you must do the same. She ought to go home now, before the dew begins to fall. Hope, wake her up gently, while I roll up this quilt, and then you may walk home with her, and go on to your Uncle John's, and ask Abby and Lydia to come over to-morrow and help get this quilt out of the frame."

The slight noise which I made in moving my chair awoke little Ellen, whose innocent eyes seemed just recalled from a fair, beautiful vision, so filled were they with a joyous, peaceful light.

"How long have I been sleeping?" she asked.

"More than two hours, I think. Are you refreshed?"

"I cannot tell, till I've walked about. Has anybody been here with lilies?"

"No—you must have been dreaming."

"Then it was the loveliest dream I ever had. My own mamma, whom Miss Hastings knew, came in with a silvery dress, and her hands full of lilies, which she was holding out to me when I awoke."

"How did your mother look?" asked the hard, practical voice of my aunt.

"Not a bit as if she were sick or dead, but just as young and pretty and loving as could be. How I wish she had spoken to me!"

"It was only a dream, child. If you are rested now, Hope may walk home with you. Tell your father I will come over before your bed-time and make you comfortable for the night;" and Aunt Lydia actually stooped and left a kiss upon the child's cheek.

"Do you think it was only a dream, Miss Hope?" asked Ellen, as I led her down the garden-path and out upon the soft turf of the roadside.

"Only a dream, but certainly a very pretty one. You know your mother can never come back."

"I know; but papa says if I am good, I may go to her some day. The time seems so long since mamma went, that I'm afraid I shall not know her, unless she looks as she did in my dream. Do you think if I live ever so many years, and grow up to be a tall woman, that my mamma will know me when I die?"

"I hope so. Did you ever ask your papa that question?"

"Oh, no—papa is so busy. Mary and I talk things over by ourselves since mamma died. Won't you come in, Miss Hope?"

"Not to-night, thank you, but some other time." I stooped to kiss, with almost reverential awe, the pale lips, which something instinctively told me would not return love's pressure many months, and then with quiet, sober steps, and thoughts far away from Hebron and the autumn evening, I walked toward Uncle John's.

A quick, manly step brought back my thoughts from their wanderings. "Good-evening, Miss Kendall. I am glad to find we are walking in the same direction. May I have permission to keep within talking distance of you?" No one who had ever listened to Mr. Hamlin's voice could mistake it.

"I am going to my Uncle John's, and you will find me a poor talker to-night, and at all times."

"Well, there is always a pleasure in talking to an intelligent listener. I observed you were that, last evening."

Very cool, I thought, not only to observe my listening habit, but to comment upon it; he certainly should not be flattered by any attention which I would give his remarks in future.

"Didn't I see you leave little Ellen Hopkinson at the parsonage gate?"

"I left her there, on my way to the bridge."

"And I saw you, from my school-room steps, stoop and touch her face. I am glad that you are her friend. She is a delicate little plant, fading like these leaves, and her father is too much absorbed in books and parish duties to see it; and your aunt is strong and practical, and will not know how to nourish the child's pure and sensitive spirit, though she will take excellent care of the body. You could understand her wants, and sympathize with her weakness."

"You mistake, sir; when I left Ellen, she was in want of sympathy, which I did not know how to give. She had dreamed that her lost mamma approached her with lilies in her hand, and I dared not offer her comfort, by telling her that perhaps God had sent the beautiful vision."

"Ellen already bears a lily in her hand. Will you remain in Hebron until after she has crossed the dark river?"

"I think not—certainly not, unless my aunt is very desirous that I should nurse Ellen; I am impatient now to be at home."

"Unless your mother's claims upon you are imperative, would not Christian charity prompt you to remain and comfort the sick child with your strong presence?"

"She can have no claims upon me, Mr. Hamlin; I've only seen her once before this evening; and even if I were willing to care for her, she would probably choose some one whom she knew better for an attendant."

"There are very few who would know how to take care of Ellen—just how and when to read to her, sing for her, and soothe her with gentle caresses. I think you are one of the few."

I looked away at the purple clusters upon the elderbushes by the roadside, that I might show a want of interest in his talk. What right had he to assume such a knowledge of my capacities, and why should Mr. Hamlin be so interested in the motherless little Ellen? I paused to pluck some blue gentians and life-everlasting that grew near the path, more to show my indifference to his company than because I cared for the late flowers.

"Shall I tell you, Miss Kendall, what lines the blue-gentian always bring to my memory?"

"If you please."

"They are from Longfellow's hymn on flowers—

'Everywhere about us are they glowing,
  Some like stars to tell us Spring is born;
Others, their blue eyes with tears o'erflowing,
  Stand like Ruth amid the golden corn.'

"I think if by any chance I should find this flower in a crowded city alley, it would bring me a vision of cornfields, crimson maples, and ripening fruits. I was a farmer's boy, and the very smell of the freshly ploughed soil is a grateful perfume to my heart. Perhaps you might think me wanting in ambition, Miss Kendall, if I should tell you that one of my greatest desires is to own a few acres of this fair footstool, that I may realize upon it my ideas of a home."

There was a question in the tones of his voice, which I might have evaded, had not my eyes chanced to meet his, and seen in them an earnest questioning more emphatic than his words.

"I think it would be pleasant to own land and beautify it with shrubs and trees, and build upon it a home, but my ambition would hardly be satisfied then."

"May I ask what it craves?"

"I should wish for some nobler work than could be done with the hands alone. I could not be a hewer of wood and drawer of water."

"No. One must have something to occupy both heart and head as well as the hands—some sweet human sympathies and some work which will assist our fellow-travellers over the rough and thorny paths."

We had reached the gate of Uncle John's garden, which Mr. Hamlin opened for me to pass, and then, with a grave bow, bade me good-evening.

I had decided, before seeing Mr. Hamlin, that I should not like him because my aunt did; but there was an honest, intelligent manliness about him which seemed very likely to batter down my determination, unless I used proper care to strengthen it.

The half-dictatorial way in which he laid out work for my autumn was disagreeable to an independent nature, which acknowledged no authority but a step-mother's.

And yet, standing by my uncle's gate, and looking upon the purple hills, I thought of an authority and a will which might be like golden fetters to my heart; but it was a foolish day-dream, a fanciful cobweb, which the hearty laugh of Cousin Lydia brushed from my thoughts.

"Come in," she called from the door, "and tell me what new beauty you have discovered in Hebron. I am sure you have stood by that gate, since Mr. Hamlin opened it, as if you were reading a sermon."

"I was looking at the hills; they are beautiful in this sunset light."

"Have you no hills in Sherbrooke?"

"Yes; but yours are higher, and have the added charm of novelty."

"You are a queer girl, Hope; not a bit like any one I've ever seen before. Come in, and let me see if you are substantial enough to eat a supper of hominy and milk."

There was certainly enough of the substantial on Aunt Abby's supper-table to bring my thoughts down to material things, and far away from sunset glories.

———◆◆◆———

CHAPTER XXXI.

AUTUMNAL STORMS.

"Ah! well-known woods, and mountains and skies,
   With the very clouds ye are lost to my eyes;
   I seek ye vainly, and see in your place
   The shadowy tempest that sweeps through space."
                                        BRYANT.

WHEN I saw the leaden-colored shadow that lay athwart the heavens on Saturday morning, I knew there would be no walking to Brier Hill. Heavy folds of clouds hid the distant mountains, and the earth looked up as if " dismayed and dumb," and shuddering with some nameless fear. There would be nothing for me but stitching upon my aunt's quilt, and listening to her oft-told family traditions and gloomy forebodings. Before noon the old poplars were creaking in the gale; their stiff, rheumatic branches wheezing as if with pain under the hand of some huge giant, while the more pliant branches of the apple-trees swept the ground and unloosed their golden fruitage. Grape and hop vines were stricken down, sun-flowers bowed their yellow faces to a level with the marigolds, blinds were shaken from their fastenings, and every thing bent and swayed beneath the gale. The rain fell in blinding, drenching gusts.

"It's the equinoctial storm—a little later than usual," sighed my aunt, as she raised her eyes to the drenched windows. "Such storms always put me in mind of the time when your gran'ther was wrecked off Cape Ann. It was in November, and his ship was driven on to the rocks by a terrible northeaster. It was so cold, that nearly all his sailors perished before they could be got off the wreck. Father's hands and feet were awfully frozen, and it's a wonder that he hadn't died, but his time hadn't come. He made three successful voyages after that, and then was washed overboard in a gale, which nearly capsized the ship —so his mate told us, who came all the way from New York to break the tidings. It was in May the news came, just after your father's second marriage, and when the young man came to the door I was out in the garden sowing lettuce-seeds.

"He was on horseback; but he got off, and leaned on the gate while he talked, until he came to say, 'Your father was washed overboard in a great gale, just as we were entering the British Channel,' when I fainted clear away and dropped down on the ground. Old Mrs. Avery lived next door, and she heard the young man call out for help, and she run right over, and threw water on my face, and rubbed me with camphor until I opened my eyes; but it was as much as they could both do to get me into the house and on to a bed, and I wasn't myself again for more'n a week. Hope, take more pains in fastening your threads. You're an amazing poor quilter for a girl of your age."

"This is my first lesson in quilting."

"Mrs. Kendall ought to be ashamed of your ignorance, but I dare say she never made a quilt in her life. Emily's house was filled with nice bedding, that ought to have been kept for her child, instead of being worn out on boarders."

I knew it was unsafe for me to venture a reply, so I stitched in silence upon the quilt, only raising my eyes to watch the progress of the storm.

My aunt's reminiscences, told with tedious and unnecessary digressions, flowed nearly as uninterruptedly through the day as fell the rain; neither had a cheerful effect upon my spirits, or diverted from their sober channel my homesick thoughts. With the evening shadows the storm seemed to gather violence and force, but sunshine and strength to defy it came to me in two letters from Sherbrooke, brought in by Mr. Hamlin, who stood for a few minutes in front of my aunt's crackling wood fire, shaking drops of water from his hair and coat upon the braided rug, and telling her what ravages the storm had made.

"You have not been home since school and back again?" asked my aunt.

"No. I was detained in the village so long, that I waited for the mail. Your niece looks as though her letters had brought her pleasant news."

"They have, Mr. Hamlin; and I'm greatly obliged to you for them."

"No thanks are due. I knew you could not walk to the office in this storm. Have you seen Ellen to-day?"

The question was addressed to me; but my aunt saved me the trouble of replying, so I bent my head over the contents of my letters.

"I meant to have gone over to-day; but the wind was so high that I thought I couldn't carry an umbrella. I left her comfortable last night."

"I met Dr. Houghton there when I ran in from school. He recommends cod-liver oil, and a blister for her side; but I haven't much faith in such remedies. I'm afraid our good minister has another great sorrow to meet soon. Miss Hastings, you'll hardly thank me for soiling your rug with the drippings from my coat, and my sister's tea will be waiting for me. I must say 'good-night.' " And yet he seemed in no haste to leave the warmth and cheer of Aunt Lydia's wood fire, but lingered to tell her of his sister's crippled boy. I did not raise my eyes from my mother's closely written pages until Mr. Hamlin's second " good-night" forced me to look up and accept his outstretched hand. His coming was like a health-giving, aromatic breeze, lifting and carrying away the cloudy atmosphere of my aunt's parlor.

"Come, Hope, finish your letters after supper—Jane's muffins are cooling. What's the news from Sherbrooke?" Aunt Lydia asked, while pouring her tea.

"I haven't quite finished reading mother's letter, but there's no news in it."

"What in the world can she find to fill four pages with, if she doesn't tell you the news?"

"Mother always finds enough to say, but she hardly ever talks or writes what people would call 'news.' Virginia's letter will be filled with it."

And what a contrast I found in the two letters! Mother's was quiet, tender, filled with anxious solicitude for my welfare, and showing on every page glintings of her watchful love. And Virginia's letter was easy, off-hand, and filled with bits of gossip and a lively description of her aunt's wedding, while the name of Carey Chapman, as if by accident, was often woven in.

"Carey has decided to settle in Wiltshire," she wrote, "and will be established in an office there next month. It will be so pleasant for the Chapmans to have him near home, and then he can come to Sherbrooke for all our parties! I think we shall have a gay winter, and I'm going to coax you out to all our merry-makings. Carey says you are too sober and practical; but he doesn't know much about my little brown mouse. Won't he be surprised if ever he finds out what a mine of poetry there is behind your demure face? Oh! I mustn't forget to tell you that Belinda and Esther are coming out in the character of blues. They called here this morning, and chatted like magpies about books, which I'm sure they've never read. You would have laughed to see the surprise they affected when they saw Carey Chapman in our parlor, though I've no doubt they knew he was there before they thought of calling. Mrs. Crowell has gone back to New York, and I'm heartily glad, for I think she flirts with unmarried men much more than is becoming; and how such a dear, good, common-sense woman as Mrs. Chapman could tolerate her, I don't see. She was only second-cousin to the Chapmans, but she made as free with Carey as if she were his sister, and monopolized his attentions whenever she could."

The letters carried my thoughts most effectually away from my aunt's parlor, but they filled my heart with an intense longing for home.

"Let me read your letters, Hope," said my aunt, when we were seated in the parlor. It being Saturday evening, all signs of work were laid aside, while my aunt had been for some minutes apparently occupied in studying "Barnes'

Notes." "I've never seen one of Mrs. Kendall's letters to you, and I'm curious to see how she writes."

I handed the precious pages to her, hoping their spirit of love and tenderness might soften her jealous heart toward my dear mother, but she read the letters through without other comment than—

"It's easy for her to write, but if she'd spend more time in useful work, and less in reading and writing, it would have been better for David and her children. No one could ever say of her, 'She looketh well to the ways of her household, and eateth not the bread of idleness,' which to my thinking had much better be said of a woman, than that 'she has the pen of a ready writer.' Let me see Virginia's letter."

I made no answer to my aunt's unkind remarks, but gave her my friend's letter, and took up "My Schools and Schoolmasters," by Hugh Miller, a book which I saw Mr. Hamlin lay upon the table when he came in. He had probably forgotten to take it; and soon the book had so won my interest, I was glad of the forgetfulness which had given me pleasure.

"Virginia writes what I call a letter," said my aunt, interrupting my reading. "She tells about things that one likes to hear of. It seems her Aunt Sallie Thornton is married at last! I never could make much of her when I was at Sherbrooke, she was so hard to get acquainted with. She always looked as if she was worried to death about something, and no wonder, if she's been waiting all this time for Captain Wynne. Why didn't you tell me that Carey Chapman had got home?"

"I didn't know that you remembered him."

"What was there to hinder me from remembering him, I'd like to know? You seem to forget that I spent two years and a half in Sherbrooke, taking care of you, and got acquainted with nearly everybody in town. The last year I was there, Carey Chapman came almost every day to recite to your father. He was a handsome boy, and behaved like a gentleman when David's eye was on him, but he was full of mischief. I never did like one of the Chapmans; and if it hadn't been for them your father never would have married Celia Dinsmore. So Carey is a lawyer, and settled in Wiltshire? Well, to be sure, how time flies! It's fifteen years since I saw him, and he must have been as much as twelve years old then. Most likely he'll marry Virginia Thornton. She'll have money; and young men now-a-days think more of money and beauty than of that wisdom 'whose price is far above rubies.' She mentions his name often enough in this letter—a dozen times, at least."

"Yes; but you know the families are neighbors, and have always been intimate."

"And girls are always silly enough to be talking and thinking about any young man who flatters them with a little notice. I hope you'll know better than to be dazzled with Carey Chapman's good looks and soft speeches, though like as not Mrs. Kendall will be trying to make a match for you there. He's a relation of hers, I believe."

Was I already dazzled? No—I thought not; my judgment was cool and clear, but I had no reply for my aunt.

"I might have been married more'n once, if I'd been as easily pleased as most girls are," resumed my aunt, after a few minutes of welcome silence. "It's not for the want of chances to marry that I've lived along alone, till some spiteful folks call me an old maid. There was Andrew Bennett, always hanging around here when your father was courting Emily; but I didn't encourage him, and he went off to the Sandwich Islands, where he's made a mine of money, I've heard. And after that, Abner Slocum would have given his eyes if I'd have married him; but he was lame, and folks called him 'Do-little,' because he was shiftless. He married Sarah Fletcher, and they lived in that old house next to the bridge, till she died of pleurisy, poor thing! and the last I heard of Abner, he was peddling essences and little nick-nacks. And now I'm going to be a minister's wife! Well, 'the steps of a good man are ordered by the Lord, and he delighteth in His way,' as I said to Caleb, when he told me how his thoughts had been directed toward me ever since his wife died."

I fervently hoped the good minister would never have occasion to wish his steps had been differently ordered.

The Sabbath broke bright and calm, and the blue skies bore no traces of Saturday's storm; but many a broken bough and prostrate tree, and many bushels of dislodged fruit, told tales of the giant's strength. Aunt Lydia could not help casting wistful and anxious glances at her apple-trees as we walked to church, and I'm afraid that thoughts of her bruised and injured fruit prevented her from gaining the instruction and benefit which she ought to have received from Mr. Hopkinson's most excellent discourse. It was the sermon on Christian charity, which he had labored so faithfully to prepare, and fortunately his opposing members were there to hear it.

The minister appeared a stronger and more cultivated man in the pulpit than out, and listening to him, I was more than ever surprised at his choice of a wife. Cousin Lydia's pleasant voice was prominent in the village choir, and the rich bass which accompanied her soprano, I soon learned to know was Mr. Hamlin's. Aunt Lydia intercepted her niece and the teacher as they came down from the gallery, and took them home with her to luncheon; and the intelligent conversation of Mr. Hamlin, between the morning and evening service, made for me the pleasantest day I had passed in Hebron.

CHAPTER XXXII.

BRIER HILL.

"There is a beautiful spirit breathing now
Its mellow richness on the clustered trees,
And, from a beaker full of richest dyes,
Pouring new glory on the autumn woods,
And dipping in warm light the pillared clouds."
LONGFELLOW.

THE autumn days wore on with little diversion or attraction for me, save occasional letters from my mother and Virginia; and though I was conscientiously trying to make myself useful to my aunt and little Ellen, yet I was impatiently longing to be summoned back to Sherbrooke.

Mother had written, after hearing through me of Aunt Lydia's approaching marriage, advising me to prolong my visit, if I could be of service to my aunt; and in order to drown my home-sick thoughts, I had quilted, stitched, and crocheted with desperate energy—had learned to make broths and jellies, and a wonderful variety of teas and syrups for little Ellen, who was growing more wan and weak with the fading of the flowers. Wisely-chosen books, left upon my aunt's table by Mr. Hamlin, helped beguile my leisure; and a portion of each day was spent in the low, square parlor of the parsonage, partly to please my aunt, and partly because my presence was so agreeable and soothing to the sick child.

As Mr. Hamlin had predicted, she could find rest in my strength, and solace in my voice, when the awkward tenderness of her father and the practical matter-of-fact nursing of my aunt failed to please. She was never tired of listening to the hymns which I had learned of my mother, nor weary of the books which I read, if she could be permitted to sit upon my lap, or lean her head upon me during the reading. Mr. Hamlin was a favorite in the parsonage, and was always welcome to little Ellen. We often met by her couch, though I chose those hours for my visits when school-duties usually confined him to the red-brick building, nearly opposite the minister's; but I was often detained by the child's entreaties or necessities until school-hours were over, and the young man at leisure to make his daily visit.

He would enter the parsonage parlor, where his little friend had a low couch, as softly and tenderly as if his life had been spent in attending the sick, always bringing something which gave the child pleasure; flowers, bright leaves, or some of the choicest fruits which the orchards of Hebron afforded, but more than all bringing to her presence a cheerful face and voice. I carefully avoided meeting Mr. Hamlin, but it appeared as if accident or design of his was almost sure to bring us daily together; and before I had been my aunt's guest a month, I knew that she too was devising ways and means to bring about these interviews.

Little as she loved me, it would be a gratification to her if I became interested in any one who would separate me from my step-mother. And then there was that in Mr. Hamlin's bearing which gave almost a sure warrant of happiness to the woman whom he honored by his choice; and even Aunt Lydia's selfish heart would desire happiness, protection, and an honorable position for her sister's child. He called frequently upon my aunt, usually directing the larger part of his conversation to her, but never leaving without obliging me to express an opinion about some book or author, or some commonplace event, so that every day I grew more and more conscious that he was becoming acquainted with my habits of thought and study, much against my will; for though I could not help liking the man, I was resolved not to cultivate an affection for one whom Aunt Lydia was constantly holding up as the embodiment of manly excellence.

"He's what folks call a self-made man," said my aunt one day, while we sat in her tidy kitchen, sewing together the narrow strips of a braided rug, which was destined to cover a worn place in the minister's carpet. "A farmer's boy, who worked his way through college without asking help from anybody, and Caleb says he knows a sight more'n most young men do who've been to college. He's always studying now, Mrs. Craig says, and sits up so late nights, that she's worrying lest he should get sick. It's remarkable how much he contrives to do, and yet he always finds time to visit the sick and say a kind word to the poor. Little Ellen takes to him wonderfully, and likes his reading better than her father's. He has been a great friend of the Hopkinsons ever since they came here from York State."

"Is he a native of Hebron?"

"Yes; his father and mother used to live in the same house where Mrs. Craig lives now—it's on the ferry-road, about a half mile beyond your Uncle John's; they died ten years ago this fall, of typhus fever—both in the same month. You see Mrs. Hamlin had got all worn out, waiting on her husband, when the fever took her, and it made short work. Elizabeth—that's Mrs. Craig, you know—had been married, about two years before, to a shiftless spendthrift, who took her to Montreal, and treated her so badly that she had to leave him soon after her parents died, and come back to the old farm with her little crippled baby. Folks say that her husband, in a drunken fit, threw the baby out of bed, and lamed it for life, and that Elizabeth couldn't stand his abuse after that. Philip is just as tender of her and her little boy as a man can be, and stays here in Hebron that he may board with her, when Caleb says he might be a professor in some college, and earn a sight more than he can in Hebron. It's a small farm where they live, and belongs as much to Philip as it does to his sister; but he doesn't count any part of it his because Elizabeth has been so unfortunate, and I suppose she couldn't any more'n make a living off it for herself and boy. I've been intending to go and call on Elizabeth ever since you came; but with Ellen's sickness and the fall work I've had my hands full without calling on neighbors. If it's pleasant we'll go to-morrow afternoon, and take tea with John's folks on our way home. Mr. Hamlin is poor, but a 'good name is rather to be chosen than great riches,' and everybody gives him a good name. You had better go and read to Ellen now, and take over the bowl of calves-foot jelly which I made this morning."

"Aunt, I would rather stay with Ellen to-morrow than go with you to see Mrs. Craig. I don't like to visit strangers."

"You're a foolish girl, Hope, and haven't a bit of forethought for your future, nor the least desire to please your mother's family. Remember, 'he that troubleth his own house, shall reap the wind;'" and Aunt Lydia laid down her braids and held her handkerchief to her eyes, to show me that my opposition to her wishes was causing her grief. So, without more words, I took the bowl of jelly and walked out into the mellow light of the October day, lingering as long as possible upon the path between my aunt's and the parsonage, that the hazy beauty of the day might steal into my heart with its softening influences, and fit me for the task which love for little Ellen usually made agreeable. I found her worn and nervous, with only her awkward little sister for an attendant.

"How is Ellen to-day?" I asked, taking the place by her couch which Mary had vacated.

"Oh, my cough has been so bad! and I thought you would never come. Papa is away since morning, and Matilda has been cross, and Mary can't read to suit me."

"You have certainly had troubles enough to vex a well person. Now tell me what I shall do first to comfort you."

"I'm so tired of this couch! If you would hold me on your lap, and read out of the 'Wide, Wide World,' I think it would rest me."

She was small for a child of ten years, and her little frame, wasted by disease, was a light burden for my strong young arms; but I lifted with awe that which I knew must soon receive the mysterious seal of death, and communed reverently with that gentle spirit which would soon stand in the presence of angels.

An hour later, when Mr. Hamlin came in from school, the child still lay in my arms, but the low singing and reading had soothed her into a blissful unconsciousness of her pain and weariness.

"I am glad to find you so employed, Miss Kendall; but let me remove your charge to the couch. She will rest quite as well there now." And almost before I was aware of his intent, Mr. Hamlin had lifted the child from my arms, and placed her upon the couch so gently that her light slumber was not broken.

"Come out for a walk. I want to show you a bit of landscape which is lovely in this hazy light."

"My shawl is not thick enough for a long walk, and my aunt will expect me."

"I will take you to your aunt's, where you can exchange your shawl, while I gain her permission to escort you."

The words were spoken with a gentle authority, and just enough of persuasion in the voice to prevent me from rebelling against that authority.

"Thank you," he said, with a quiet smile in his brown eyes, as he held the door open for me to pass. "I think I can reward you for the favor you are showing me."

It was provoking to see Aunt Lydia's complacent smile, when Mr. Hamlin asked her permission to take her niece to Brier Hill for a walk.

"Hope will be glad to go; she has been sitting in the house too much this week, and I was telling her this afternoon that to-morrow we would go and see your sister. How is Mrs. Craig?"

"Much as usual, thank you; always a little dispirited; but the care of little Phil is enough to sadden any woman. Miss Kendall, are your boots thick enough for a rough road?" he asked, as I appeared, equipped for the walk.

"Oh, yes; Hope's walking-boots are thick enough for a man. Stop and drink tea with us, on your way home, Mr. Hamlin?"

"Not to-night, Miss Hastings;" and the next minute I found myself walking by Mr. Hamlin's side, obliged to listen to his words, and occasionally to answer, though I made my replies as short as possible. I could not help confessing to myself that he talked well—his language was abundant and choice; there was no apparent desire to show off his knowledge of books, for he rarely quoted; and yet his conversation showed that he was a well-read man, familiar with the literature and history of his own country; and then, struggle against the feeling as I would, my vanity was not a little pleased that a man of Mr. Hamlin's cultivation should choose such themes to talk to a young girl upon, and I wondered if he could talk such nonsense to the Blakes as I had heard William Fairchild and Carey Chapman.

Mr. Hamlin had picked up a bit of limestone soon after we had gained the highway, which, leaving the village, wound up a long and rugged hill; and as we slowly walked up the ascent he spoke of its formation, and of the different fossil remains which were found in the Connecticut River valleys. I forgot the strict reticence which I had resolved to show, no matter what might be the theme of Mr. Hamlin's conversation, and was soon drawn into a discussion of Hugh Miller's books. I had read two or three of them carefully with mother, only a few months before; and geology being with her a favorite science, she had inspired me with something of her own enthusiastic love for it. I hardly knew how freely I was talking, until I met my companion's pleased eye resting upon my face. With a confused blush, I paused.

"Why did you tell me you were a poor talker?" he asked, with a smile.

"Because I only talk about such things as I have seen and read, and my acquaintance with the world is much less than that of other girls."

"I am glad of it; and that is one reason why I wish to make you my friend. There! do you think Hugh Miller and his Lydia ever saw a more delicious sunset from the summit of Ben Nevis than is laid out before us?"

I turned to follow with my eyes his outstretched hand, and stood speechless—almost transfixed. The village of Hebron lay in the shadows of the valley, at the base of the hill upon which we stood. The windings of the stream could be seen for several miles, and the golden light of the sinking sun, mellowed by the haziness of the October day, rested upon a circle of hills, which stood like watch-towers around the village and the Twin-basins. The dreamy beauty of Autumn's loveliest mood lay upon village, lakes, forests, and hills. Only here and there were the month's brightest tints of red and golden to be seen, where an occasional maple sturdily resisted the season's coquettish changes, and refused to doff its gorgeous mantle for one of pale yellow or russet brown.

I was roused from the rapt, abstracted mood in which I had stood gazing at the picture, by the sound of Mr. Hamlin's voice, repeating:

> "'O, Autumn! why so soon
> Depart the hues that make thy forests glad?
> Thy gentle wind, and thy fair, sunny noon,
> And leave thee wild and sad?'"

"For the first time in my life, Mr. Hamlin, I have felt the truth of another stanza in that poem."

"Please repeat it."

> "'The mountains that enfold,
> In their wide sweep, the colored landscape round,
> Seem groups of giant kings, in purple and gold,
> That guard the enchanted ground.'

Do not the distant hills look like sentinels clad in kingly robes? and does not the valley, seen in this smoky light, look like enchanted ground?"

"'Tis a beautiful picture—fair enough to have inspired Bryant. He could catch the perfect harmony of an hour like this, and weave it into music, and so paint it in words that thousands could see the smoky light, and almost hear the sound of dropping nuts. I see that you have read Bryant, and appreciate him, too."

"I know a few of his poems, but none as well as 'Autumn Woods' and 'The Death of the Flowers.' I had taken them up to make a study of just before leaving home. Mother loves Bryant's poetry."

" You are fortunate in having a mother so competent to instruct you. I would like to know her."

" I wish you might. She is said to have a very thorough acquaintance with English literature and history. Look at the purplish mist which is shrouding those hills to the right, Mr. Hamlin, and see how lovely the contrast to those distant mountains, which are still bathed in sunlight! And the village is in shadow, too. It will be quite dark when we reach it, and then you will have a long walk beyond. We must return at once, but I'm much obliged to you for showing me this view at this hour."

" Goethe says we should read a poem, see a picture, and listen to good music, if possible, every day. Have we not enjoyed the poem, picture, and music during the last hour?"

" I think so; and when I read 'Autumn Woods' hereafter, this picture will always rise up before me."

A minute more of silent gazing at the gathering shadows in the valley, the purple hills, and golden mountain-tops, and we turned to retrace our steps over the rugged path.

Mr. Hamlin said little as we walked toward the village, but my tongue for this evening hour was unloosed, and I talked of Sherbrooke, my mother, and our school. I told him of our conquered difficulties, our escape from poverty's shackles, my studies and my aspirations for the future; and bidding him good-night at the gate, I lingered under the old poplars, to select and lay away the sweetest memories of the hour. And then I remembered that I had spoken with Mr. Hamlin more freely of our affairs than I had ever spoken with any one else. Was it that his face and bearing inspired confidence? and was I beginning to like and trust Aunt Lydia's favorite?

No, I would not like him, and I would set a strict guard over my tongue when next we met. With this newly-registered resolve I entered my aunt's parlor. Mr. Hopkinson sat by her side upon the straight-backed sofa, and seeing at a glance that my presence would be an incumbrance, I walked into the kitchen, where Jane was preparing supper.

But the tea was destined to lose its fragrant aroma, while the muffins cooled and Jane's temper grew cloudy; for Aunt Lydia and the minister had evidently forgotten the meat that perisheth, in the discussion of some topic more interesting than the Sanborn and Perry case. When Aunt Lydia appeared, she made no allusion to the insipid tea and cold muffins, but ate and drank in a silence quite unnatural to her; and not until the tea things were removed and we sat alone by the glowing embers upon her parlor hearth, did she find her voice.

"'A man's heart deviseth his way, but the Lord directeth his steps,'" she quoted with a sigh, and indeed my aunt almost always finished her quotations thus, as "some people always sigh in thanking God." "I had made my plans for the last of December or first of January, but Caleb needs me now, and I've about made up my mind to be married next week. People will talk, I dare say, for Mrs. Hopkinson hasn't been dead only ten months; but Caleb says if we can see a straight path we should walk in it and not turn aside for babbling tongues. I had planned on getting a new black silk and purple merino made up before I changed my situation in life, so that folks shouldn't say I was wasting the minister's salary on new gowns, and then my fall's work isn't half done yet, though I must say, Hope, you've helped it along wonderfully by the way you've taken hold."

Here I managed to slip in a "Thank you," for my aunt's

compliment, but she was too much absorbed in her own thoughts and plans to heed it.

"I must go over to Mrs. Craig's to-morrow and get her to cut and make the dove-colored silk that father brought home for Emily. It has laid in my camphor-wood trunk for more'n seventeen years, but it will be just the thing for a woman of my age to be married in; and then if the Sunday after is pleasant, I can wear it with a real India shawl that was given to father by the owners of the ship. I've never worn it, because I knew father meant it for Emily, but I've somebody to please now besides myself. Of course everybody will be staring at me the first Sunday after I'm married, just as if I hadn't walked regularly into church every Sunday for so many years, though to be sure I've never walked up the broad aisle leaning on the minister's arm."

It was said with a sigh, but one could easily see that the contemplation of herself in the dove-colored silk and India shawl, leaning on the minister's arm, was not a disagreeable picture for the mind's eye to rest upon.

"Poor little Ellen is getting weaker every day, and it won't be long she'll need my nursing, even if I go there next week, and I shall have the satisfaction of seeing that she is well cared for, besides getting Matilda Crockett out of the way. I told Caleb to-night that I should want to keep Jane, and he'd better give Matilda notice to leave. You see, Jane is a sort of relation of ours; her father was cousin to your grandma Hastings' first husband, and when she was left an orphan, without a cent in the world, I took pity on her and gave her a home for the few chores she does; but I shall pay her wages after I'm married."

"What will you do with your house and farm?"

"I shall let the farm to Adoniram Staples, and I suppose his family will have to move into the house, though it will be amazing hard to see strangers under this roof. And now, Hope, as I find you are bent upon going back to your step-mother, and after talking the matter over with Caleb and your Uncle John I've made up my mind not to oppose you, though I've hoped all along you'd stay with your mother's relations; but as I was going to say, I don't want you to go back till after it's all over with poor Ellen, for she has taken a great fancy to you. If Ellen was likely to live, I should feel a sight more like insisting on your staying with me; but after she dies I shall have Mary sent off to school. Caleb says her mother's relations somewhere in York State want her to board with them, and I shall persuade him to let her go."

Aunt Lydia talked on about the alterations she should have made in the parsonage and in the minister's style of living, what she should do in the parish, and speculated upon what people would say, until the clock struck nine, when I was dismissed to my room, wondering how Aunt Lydia's heart could have been turned from its fixed purpose of retaining me in Hebron. Perhaps little Ellen's removal would make me less useful in her new family relations—and perhaps Uncle John and the minister had persuaded her to leave me free to select my own home; but I was too grateful for the prospect of returning quietly to mother, without an open rupture with Aunt Lydia, to speculate long upon her motives. "When a man's ways please the Lord, he maketh even his enemies to be at peace with him." Had I chosen a way pleasing to the great Searcher of hearts? Humbly trusting that I had, I sought His blessing with a greater peace and happiness in my heart than could be painted in words.

CHAPTER XXXIII.

MR. HAMLIN'S LIBRARY.

"Dwell I but in the suburbs
Of your good pleasure?"
SHAKESPEARE.

"HOPE, I'm going into the attic to look over the things in my camphor-wood trunk. You may come along, if you're curious to see how your gran'ther Hastings spent his money."

The permission to look into that trunk, which I had heard my aunt guarded with such jealous care, surprised me not a little, and I gladly threw down the heavy quilt, which I was binding, and followed her up the narrow staircase. She had hardly drawn the paper shade away from the window and dusted the lid of the trunk preparatory to opening, when we heard a quick step springing up the stairs, and Cousin Lydia stood before us.

"Jane said I should find you here, and I'm so glad I happened to come just now, for you've always been promising to show me what's in that trunk, aunt, and I'm sure you're just on the point of opening it."

"'Childhood and youth are vanity,'" sighed my aunt, as she turned the key in the lock, and raised the lid. "I can remember when the vain and perishable things of this world had a greater charm for me than they have now."

"But you like to wear pretty things once in a while now, aunt, and you musn't blame young girls for having just a little bit of pride."

"'When pride cometh, then cometh shame.' I should

be sorry to see any of my kin brought to shame by the indulgence of sinful pride."

Here Aunt Lydia took from its wrappings of old linen the India shawl, and shook out its folds, glancing with much satisfaction at its rich material and lovely colors.

"What a beauty!" exclaimed Cousin Lydia. "Why have you never worn it, aunt?"

"I have never needed it before; the cashmere shawl I've worn for fifteen years is still as good as new. Your gran'ther brought this home the last time he came, and though he never said so, yet I knew he meant it for Emily; and this too," she added, producing the dove-colored silk, which was destined for such honorable service. "Poor Emily never lived to see them," she sighed, and hid her face for a minute behind her kerchief; but when it was withdrawn her black eyes were bright, dry, and hard.

"I have always intended to make a present of some of these things to you both, when you were old enough to take good care of them;" and she drew out from the trunk two patterns of silk muslin, delicate and pretty.

"They are lovely," said Cousin Lydia, "and the pink will make Hope a charming dress. You will give them to us, of course, because a minister's wife can't wear such gay things."

"Well, may the Lord forgive me if I am fostering your foolish pride. I hope you will take good care of them, and remember your gran'ther brought them all the way from Canton. Here are a couple of embroidered aprons, which you may as well take; they'll never be of any use to me."

The aprons were pretty, and our thanks profuse.

"Oh, aunt! I see a bit of something wrapped up in that old table-cover, and it looks lovely. What is it?" asked my cousin.

"Only a couple of silks, which your gran'ther brought

home for Emily and me after she died, and I was in mourning. After I laid off my mourning for Emily and father, I had not the heart to make up such a handsome silk; and, besides, blue never was becoming to my complexion, and I doubt if it would be to either of you."

"Do let us try the effect. It's such a shame to allow such pretty things to moulder away in this old trunk!"

"They'd better turn to dust here than nourish vanity in your hearts," said Aunt Lydia; but she allowed the little brown hands of her namesake to draw out the folds of silk and fling an end around my shoulder.

"There! who says blue isn't becoming to Hope? The white forget-me-nots are so lovely on this blue ground, and look just like Hope! Come, aunt, you can afford to be generous as long as you are going to marry a minister. Give us these silks to wear at your wedding."

"There won't be time enough to make them; and besides, I shall have no wedding—but you may have the silks. I'm glad that I have it in my power to do something handsome for my nieces."

Aunt Lydia's generosity almost deprived me of speech for a minute, until I remembered that at least half the articles in the old chest were intended for my mother, and had become valueless to my aunt, which remembrance somewhat modified my gratitude. Cousin Lydia had much more daring and assurance than I could summon, and was evidently bent upon making the most of her aunt's generous mood, for she sent her plump arms into the depths of the trunk, and brought up duplicate patterns of embroidered muslin, which she laughingly declared were brought home by her grandfather expressly to make wedding-dresses for Aunt Lydia's nieces.

"You foolish child! they were brought home before either of you were born. But take them, and go off now, both of you. I can't waste any more of my precious time upon this trunk," and the lid came down between the treasures and our admiring eyes, but not before the India shawl and dove-colored silk had been removed.

"It is a good morning's work for us, anyhow," whispered Cousin Lydia as we retreated to my room with our spoils; "and how fortunate for us both that I happened in! You never would have asked for a thing."

"No; and I wondered how you dared."

"Well, when I saw that old trunk, I said, Now or never! You see, I've always been teasing aunt for a sight of the things that grandpa brought home, but she has managed to put me off, and it's lucky for us that she was seized with a generous fit this morning. We may thank Mr. Hopkinson for the gifts, however, for if she hadn't the prospect of marrying a minister, all this pretty finery would have mouldered in that old attic."

And Cousin Lydia, as she spoke, threw first a fold of the pink muslin and then of the blue silk around her neck, trying the effect of each before my little mirror.

"It will astonish father to know how aunt has opened her heart; for though he thinks she's a wonderful woman, he often says she's as close as the bark of a tree. But after all, she has only given us things that are useless to her, and glad as I am to get them I am not going to feel under any obligations to her. Indeed, I don't believe she has given you half of what really belonged to your mother. I longed to tell her how that handsome shawl would be much more becoming to you than to her."

"Hush, Lydia! She may hear you. I'm sure I'm very grateful for what she gave me, and think the shawl would be much too costly and handsome for me."

"I can only say you are a queer girl, Hope. Now I never see a handsome thing but I want it for myself.

You'd never see me in any thing old, faded, or commonish, if I could have my way; but father has always been afraid to buy me any thing pretty, because Aunt Lydia would say such sharp things about it, and look as severe as if she expected to see every thing turning to dust and ashes under her eyes."

It was impossible not to be amused with my cousin's pleasure in her new possessions, and quite natural for me to share it in a measure. I found myself wishing that an opportunity might soon occur to show the Blakes that I did not always wear white at parties; and then I wondered if Carey Chapman liked pink or blue best—not very profitable speculations, certainly, and my better nature quickly thrust them aside.

"Hope, I want this quilt finished before dinner," called my aunt from the bottom of the flight of stairs.

"Yes, aunt, I'm coming directly," was the answer, as the silk and muslins were carefully laid away.

"I came over on purpose to help this morning, but I declare my head has been so turned by my aunt's generosity, that I came near forgetting that I could use a needle."

The lively girl ran down-stairs, and, seizing the quilt, made her needle fly much more rapidly than her tongue. In Aunt Lydia's presence she was generally quiet; but this morning she could not resist the temptation of whispering now and then to me of our unexpected good fortune, and asking questions about the most becoming styles of making muslins and silks.

Aunt Lydia's gifts had deprived me of the power of refusing to accompany her to Mrs. Craig's.

"You will go, of course, Hope," she said, soon after dinner, and though I disliked the putting of myself in Mr. Hamlin's path, yet I answered: "If you wish it, aunt; but I'm afraid little Ellen will want me."

"You can spend an hour with Ellen before we need to

start, and as soon as Jane has finished her ironing she's going in to amuse Ellen for a couple of hours. Jane has a nice tact with children, and is just as handy as an old nurse." And remembering that aunt had told Mr. Hamlin I was going to call upon his sister, I had not courage to make further resistance.

But the soft beauty of the Indian summer day did not possess the same charm for me, when walking by Aunt Lydia's side, that it had the previous day, when Mr. Hamlin's intelligent conversation had given life and harmony to the landscape. Aunt Lydia saw nothing beautiful in the gentle decay of the season—a cold, practical, utilitarian spirit seemed to pervade her entire nature.

"Look, Hope, and see what a quantity of nuts are left on those beech-trees; they are worth three cents a quart for oil. I mean to send Adoniram and Jane out here to-morrow to gather them, for it's an awful shame to let them run to waste! You and I might come, too, if we were not so busy just now. And that pasture is white with life-everlasting, just in the right state to gather! It makes an excellent bed, almost as good as feathers; but poor folks are so shiftless! they never know how to make the most of what Providence has left at their doors. Adoniram's wife was complaining only last week because her children had nothing but straw to sleep on, and she has two girls and one boy old enough this minute to be picking that life-everlasting!"

Aunt Lydia saw nothing but an excellent and economical dye in the scarlet-berried sumach—nothing but a medicinal wine in the purple clusters of the elderberry. The white, silvery stems of the beech were so many cord-feet of wood to feed her stove; and the majestic maples were valued only for their yield of sap, which made sugar for her daily wants. Its pendulous yellow blossoms in spring and its crimson tints in autumn were unheeded by her, or looked upon as an extravagant waste of Nature's resources.

While my aunt was still commenting upon the utility of the beech, maple, and sumach, as well as upon the want of thrift in all poor people, we reached Mrs. Craig's cottage, a low, yellowish-brown house, with a neatly-kept greensward in front, shaded by a large maple and a mountain ash. The warmth and beauty of the autumn day had tempted Mrs. Craig to bring her invalid boy out upon the greensward, and she sat in a low chair under the maple with her foot upon the wicker cradle, humming a sad, dreamy tune, with an air so abstracted that she did not hear our steps upon the turf.

"How do you do, Mrs. Craig? and how is little Phil?" called my aunt, within a few feet of the woman's chair.

"Oh, it's you, Miss Hastings! Philip said you were coming. Will you go in, or sit here in the shade till you are rested?"

"I'm not tired, and can't sit a great while anywhere to-day. No, don't move Phil's cradle. We can talk here as well as in the house. This is my niece, Hope Kendall, Mrs. Craig."

Mr. Hamlin's sister only bowed, and made some common remark about the autumn day, and turned toward my aunt, whose black eyes were sharply scanning little Phil. I moved away from the group under the maple-tree, and seated myself upon the stone step of the cottage door, but near enough Mrs. Craig and my aunt to hear their words, and to note the expression of each face.

Little Phil's physical condition was first carefully investigated by my aunt, and I heard her recommending a vigorous daily rubbing of his limbs with mud-turtle's oil, followed by a bandage of mullein-leaves.

"Does he ever try to use his legs?" inquired Aunt Lydia.

"No—never."

"What a pity! and he's nearly six years old! I can see that he's failed since I was here last; but like as not he'll live to wear you out. It's a mysterious affliction, and I hope you'll bow to it. Solomon says, 'Despise not the chastening of the Lord, neither be weary of His correction.' Have you as much sewing on hand as you can do at present?"

"More than Philip is willing I should do."

"But I want you should fit and make a dress for me in just a week. Your work always suits me, and there's nobody else I can get to do it but Esther Davis, and she spoilt a green merino for me the last winter you were in Montreal. It was too short-waisted, and too small in the arm-size, and the skirt was too long;" and while my aunt spoke she unrolled the dove-colored silk, and held it out for Mrs. Craig's inspection.

"I should like to oblige you, Miss Hastings, but this is such a nice silk, and I know so little about new styles, that I'm afraid I shall disappoint you if I attempt it."

"You've always fitted me well, and I don't care for the newest fashions, though, to be sure, when one is having a nice dress it is well enough to make it in good style. I, of all persons, must hereafter set an example of plain, neat dressing to my sisters."

"Then this is your wedding-dress?"

"Yes; if nothing happens, I shall be married to our minister in a week from to-morrow. He needs some one to take care of his house and nurse Ellen, and I have promised to do my best. I should like for you to see Mrs. Houghton's green silk before you cut mine. She had it made in New York last May, when she went to visit the doctor's sister, and it has three ruffles around the bottom of the skirt, and the sleeves are made to match, with narrow ruffles. It's an awful shame to cut such thick silk up into ruffles, but I shall have no other trimming. Save as much of the silk as you can, for I should like a mantle of the same to wear next summer, if I live. Ah me! 'the fashion of this world passeth away.' I never thought, one year ago, when I was waiting on poor dear Mrs. Hopkinson, that I should be called to fill her place."

Here Aunt Lydia hid her emotions for a few brief minutes behind her handkerchief, while Mrs. Craig's large, hopeless eyes wandered off to the brown fields and orchards. But with such interesting business on hand as the cutting of her wedding-dress, it was not to be expected that my aunt's face would remain long behind her handkerchief, no matter how tender and sacred the memories which called for its shield. She was quickly engrossed in the important details of the dress, arranging for its fulness, length, ruffles, and cape, with as much interest as if no shadow had crossed her memory, and the fashions of this world did *not* pass away.

"It is lucky there's a large pattern of the silk, for I had quite set my heart on a cape like the dress. Father always did buy a sight more'n enough for a pattern; but, poor man! he couldn't be expected to know just how much it would take to make a dress." And then Aunt Lydia gave a circumstantial account of the numerous patterns which had been brought home by her indulgent father—told the style in which they had been made, how long they had lasted, and the final disposition made of the worn-out garments. And when the theme was at last exhausted, she went in-doors with Mrs. Craig to be measured for the new dress, while I remained near the wicker cradle where lay the little helpless boy.

Hearing a fretful wail, I approached the cradle and bent down to soothe the occupant. Never had I seen before such large, expressionless eyes, such wan cheeks and lips, and such pitiable weakness. A nervous fluttering of the hands seemed the only motion it was capable of making, and a plaintive "Mam, mam," the only sound which resembled speech. I moved the cradle to and fro, softly humming one of the hymns which had often soothed little Ellen; and while thus employed, Mr. Hamlin approached me, with a frank smile that showed his pleasure in meeting me.

"I am fortunately at home earlier than usual to-day," he said, in greeting. "But where is my sister? and why are you left in charge of poor little Phil?"

"Mrs. Craig and Aunt Lydia are in the house, busy with dress-making, but I chose to remain out. Little Phil was asleep when his mother left him."

"'Tis getting late for the child to be out. I will take him in, and show you my home. I am glad to have that pleasure."

"I only came with Aunt Lydia for a walk," I stammered out, determined that he should not be encouraged by my presence, and making no movement to follow him into the house.

"But after so long a walk you must need rest. Do not refuse my hospitality."

It was said with that mingling of entreaty and authority which I had obeyed once before; and I was conscious that obedience to his will came easier to-day than yesterday, as I followed him into the low-ceiled parlor, where Aunt Lydia and his sister were employed over the dove-colored silk.

While Mr. Hamlin was arranging the child on a low, cushioned couch, and greeting my aunt, my eye took in with a few quiet glances the simple appointments of the room. It was evidently the common sitting-room, but it had an air of taste and neatness that made it almost elegant. The carpet was of home manufacture, woven in stripes of green and crimson, while the low walls were covered with a delicate buff paper and ornamented with several pretty crayon drawings. Choice plants filled the southern window, and English ivy fell in grateful luxuriance from a hanging basket. Bouquets of autumn leaves, ferns, and blue gentian stood upon the mantel and table.

I knew, before my eye had completed its survey, that a generous, loving hand had endeavored to make this room so beautiful and cheerful that sad memories could not shadow it; and when I saw the grateful smile with which Mrs. Craig greeted her brother, I knew whose heart had devised and whose hand had executed.

"Philip, take Miss Kendall into your room, while I finish fitting Miss Hastings' dress," said Mrs. Craig; and I had no choice but to follow Mr. Hamlin across the narrow entry to another room, much like the one we had left. The furnishing was even more plain and simple, with the exception of a well-filled book-case and a cabinet of shells, minerals, stuffed birds, etc. Crayons and engravings also decorated this room. One—a child's face—I recognized at a glance. It was a most truthful likeness of little Ellen Hopkinson.

"Are these your own drawings, Mr. Hamlin?"

"Yes—they are simple sketches, thrown off as a recreation after close application to study. I've never had a teacher in drawing, but my pictures please my sister and our friends, so I enjoy making them."

"This is an excellent likeness of Ellen."

"I'm glad you think so—I wanted to make a faithful copy of her face, if possible. She came to see me last summer, and while she was looking at these shells, she was unconsciously sitting for her picture. I shall give it to her.

father when her face is hid from his sight. Do you recognize this sketch?"

" 'Tis the old meeting-house at the 'four-corners,' where Uncle John says my mother used to sing. It would make a beautiful picture if you could color it with some of those tints we saw yesterday. Do you paint as well as draw?"

"I have been experimenting a little since I made the acquaintance of a New York artist, who spent the summer in this vicinity sketching. He taught me how to mix paints, and gave me many valuable hints about colors, but I have not found much time to profit by his instructions this autumn. Much as I admire pictures and reverence the genius of true artists, I do not think I have enough of talent in that direction to justify me in spending more than an occasional hour in sketching."

"I wish I knew that I had as much talent for drawing as you have."

"You will very likely find you have more. Have you read this?" he asked, taking from the table "Aurora Leigh."

"No; I've never seen it before."

"It is a recent publication—a poem full of vigorous life and thought, and bears the impress of a strong, masculine intellect."

"Cannot a woman have as much strength of intellect as a man?" I asked, ready at once to contradict Mr. Hamlin, though I had never given a minute's serious thought to the question of difference between masculine and feminine minds.

"I think I honor and reverence the intellect of your sex as much as any man or woman can, but there is only one Mrs. Browning, and her greatest charm is in the pure and delicate womanliness with which she uses her pen—the tender, thrilling power with which she moves the waters in all human hearts. She sanctifies and crowns with a rare beauty the common incidents of our every-day life, but when she leaves these and soars away into a region of classical and mythological lore she becomes pedantic and obscure. You see that a plodding earth-worm like myself may find fault even with this 'Shakspeare of women.' Shall I lend you ' Aurora Leigh?' "

"Thank you, I would like to read it, if Aunt Lydia does not keep me so busy, during the week which remains of my visit, that I can find no leisure for reading."

"One week only? Then your aunt has not persuaded you to find a home with her?"

"Oh, no, nothing could induce me to remain away from mother and Sherbrooke."

"Nothing?" he questioned, taking my hand, and looking into my eyes with an honest manliness. "Forgive me, but I have been presuming enough to hope—"

It was not decreed that I should learn what he had hoped that day, for at this moment Aunt Lydia opened the door of the parlor and approached Mr. Hamlin's room, talking loudly in a business like way to Mrs. Craig about the making of her dress. She did not find me standing with my hand in her friend's, waiting for the finishing of that sentence, but steadfastly gazing at the picture of little Ellen, while Mr. Hamlin was absorbed in searching for a choice shell, which he told Aunt Lydia was given him by her father.

"Ay, here it is, Miss Hastings—I was not more than eight years old when your father brought that home. I think I must have been a favorite of his, for he often brought me some trifle."

"He was a generous man and fond of children, and he spent a deal more money in buying little nick-nacks for them than he ought to. If he'd been more careful of his earnings, he needn't have made so many voyages, and might have left his children a sight better off. What heaps of books you have here, Mr. Hamlin! Do you ever expect to read them all?"

"I trust so, and many more, if my life is spared."

"Dear me! much study would be a weariness to my flesh, but I have a great respect for those who like books. Sister Emily was almost always reading something, and your father, Hope, was a wonderful scholar; but if he'd spent more time in work and less in reading, he might have left his family with a shelter for their heads. Remember, Mrs. Craig, I shall want that dress next Wednesday—when shall I come to try it on?"

"Come in Friday, if convenient."

"No, no, Friday is such an unlucky day with me—the dress would be sure to set like a fright if you finish fitting it on Friday. I'll come Saturday after dinner."

"Very well."

"Come, Hope, it's quite time we were walking toward home. You look at those drawings as if you never saw a picture before."

I started nervously, turning toward my aunt a flushed, confused face, and, saying something about my fondness for pictures, I bade Mrs. Craig "good-evening," and endeavored to pass her brother with only a bow, but I could not evade his outstretched hand, nor resist the consciousness that his firm clasp of mine spoke of more than ordinary friendship.

CHAPTER XXXIV.

AUNT LYDIA'S WEDDING.

"And I pray thee, now, tell me, for which of my bad parts didst thou fall in love with me?"

It was a busy week which preceded my aunt's wedding. What with sewing, preserving, waiting on little Ellen, and assisting in the dismantling of the red cottage, I was almost too busy to think of myself.

The parsonage must be thoroughly scrubbed before Aunt Lydia's carpets and furniture could be transferred to it, and Matilda Crockett couldn't be trusted to do it—Jane or I must superintend.

At last, with a grateful feeling of relief, I saw Aunt Lydia deliver up the keys of her cottage to Adoniram Staples, and then climb into the wagon which was to convey her and her bridal paraphernalia to Uncle John's, where she was to spend the last night of her spinster life. She was to promise love, honor, and obedience to the minister, in the large square parlor of Uncle John's farm-house on the following morning, and go from there directly to the parsonage. And in what a practical, business-like way was every thing done! There was no lingering under the roof which had sheltered her for nearly forty years, and no pause in the garden, except for a few words of caution to Adoniram.

"Be sure and not let your children pull up my caraway and spearmint; they musn't play in the garden—there's room enough back of the house. Come, Hope, jump into the wagon—there's no time to waste."

"If you please, aunt, I'll walk—the air will refresh me, and I can look in upon Ellen on the way."

"Very well, child, but don't linger, for I want you to finish making the button-holes in my morning wrapper." And with that she drove off, while I walked slowly forward, crushing the faded maple-leaves that lay upon the path, and thinking of home. Uncle John and his family had urged me with so much hearty kindness to spend a few days with them after Aunt Lydia's marriage, that I had found it impossible to refuse. And then Mr. Hopkinson had entreated me to remain until his child no longer needed me. Mother wrote cheerfully, advising me to stay while my services were useful to my aunt and my little friend; and turning these things over in my thoughts, I saw no way of escape to Sherbrooke for several weeks. But crushing back my homesick longings, I prayed for strength and patience, and walked into little Ellen's room with as much cheerfulness as I could summon. I was rewarded for my self-denial by the bright look of welcome which the child always gave me.

"I was sure you would come," she said, as I took her from the couch and held her against my breast, "though papa said you would be too tired. I will not ask you to sing but just one hymn."

"And what shall that be?"

"Oh, the best of all your hymns!—

'Rock of Ages, cleft for me,
Let me hide myself in Thee.'"

I sang the first stanza tremulously, but with the second my heart was in unison, and my voice rose clear and exultant, until a rich bass voice joined in the melody, and I knew that Mr. Hamlin had come in and was standing behind my chair; and then only for a moment did the words and music tremble upon my tongue—the spirit of the hymn had so permeated my thoughts that self was forgotten.

"Aunt Lydia needs me this evening, Ellen. Shall I put you back now upon the couch?"

"Yes; but after to-morrow you must stay with me all the time. Mr. Hamlin said you would."

A quick, impulsive feeling of resentment against Mr. Hamlin's authority struggled for a moment to find expression in words, but was repressed with an effort, and bidding Ellen good-night, I turned and exchanged greetings with Mr. Hamlin. I had not seen him alone since the conversation in his library; the hurry and bustle of the past week had favored my avoidance of him. I had not given him an opportunity to finish that broken sentence, and tell me what he "hoped," and as we stepped out of the parsonage into the gathering twilight, and I knew that I must walk by his side for a long half mile, I determined to keep his tongue far away from that unfinished sentence. But though I summoned to my aid all the light artillery of talk which I could command, words did not flow freely when there was enough of the lingering daylight left to assure me that his eyes were bent gravely and searchingly upon my face.

"Have you found time to read 'Aurora Leigh?'" he asked, when I paused for breath and to rally my forces.

"I have run over it hastily, just to get the story, but I don't think I like it very well."

"It requires a careful reading to be appreciated. Certainly your mother never allowed you to run over your reading in a hurry."

Kindly, earnestly, but yet reprovingly, his eyes still read my face.

"No; mother never allowed me to read in a hurry, but you must remember that she did not ask me to read 'Aurora Leigh,' and then you don't know how busy my aunt has kept me. However, I don't believe I should like the book if I read it ever so carefully."

"Tell me why."

Gentleness, persuasion, and authority were blended in that short sentence.

"Well, I think Romney Leigh was very dictatorial— there was too much authority in his love-making, and his cousin Aurora was very blind, and cold, and perverse ; but, dear me ! I know nothing of love, and not enough about men and women and books to criticise. There were some passages that seemed beautiful to me."

"Will you quote them?"

> "'A face flashed like a cymbal on his face,
> And shook with silent clanguor brain and heart,
> Transfiguring him to music. Thus, even thus,
> He too received his sacramental gift
> With eucharistic meanings, for he loved.'

"And speaking of her own poetical gift, Aurora says :

> 'Alas ! near all the birds
> Will sing at dawn, and yet we do not take
> The chaffering swallow for the holy lark.'

"In another place, she says :

> 'Get leave to work
> In this world. 'Tis the best you get at all ;
> For God in cursing gives us better gifts
> Than men in benediction.'"

"You have quoted some choice passages, and I am confident that many more might be drawn from the storehouse of your memory, despite your hasty reading of 'Aurora Leigh.' My own experience has proved the truth of your last quotation. I was willing to work a few years since, but not as God directed. The work which then seemed a burden, almost a curse, is now a blessed gift—a daily benediction. Once I thought it hard that my ambition should be clogged by such labor as was necessary to support my poor sister and her invalid child; and for many months I rebelled against the circumstances which had thrown them upon me, and refused to see God's hand in the shaping of events. Now I can thank Him daily for the privilege of working as He directs."

"I am glad, too, that I have got leave to work, for now I can help mother support and educate the younger children. I sometimes wonder how people can be happy who have nothing in the world to do, and yet there never was a happier or more cheerful person than my friend Virginia; and her father is so rich that she need never touch a bit of work, and doesn't know the meaning of self-denial."

"Then I should suppose she would be so selfish and frivolous that your love for her would have no foundation on which to rest."

"You do not know how kind, and sensible, and amiable she is—and beautiful, too," I added, after a moment's pause.

"The gods must have been uncommonly lavish of their gifts, to bestow upon one person wealth, beauty, good sense, and amiability. You must see her through rose-colored glasses, my little friend."

I was glad that the shadows of twilight would not permit him to see the bright flush which spread over my face, when that phrase, "My little friend," slipped from his tongue, but I knew the unusual glow was not caused by Mr. Hamlin's words; they were almost sacredly associated with Carey Chapman.

We had just reached the farm-house gate, and I was congratulating myself upon the skill with which I had kept my companion from referring to the interrupted interview in his library, when he arrested the hand which I had reached out to open the gate—the same hand which Carey Chapman had kissed—and, holding it firmly, he said, almost abruptly:

"Miss Hope, I must detain you a minute, while I ask one question. Would the knowledge of my love make it easier for you to remain in Hebron until Ellen no longer needs you?"

The something which I had feared and avoided had burst upon me now in words—and words, too, that must be answered. But how? I did not love him, though I revered his character and admired his intellectual strength, and would gladly have retained his friendship; but womanly instinct told me that I must lose him as a friend unless I could retain him as a lover.

My right hand trembled in his, and my tongue refused its office; but that silence must be broken; and then another low question, which I instinctively felt came from a great, loving, generous heart:

"Hope, is there no answer for me?"

"Oh, Mr. Hamlin, not such an answer as you wish! I like you—but—" Here I broke down in sobs; and drawing my hand from his, hid my face; for though the twilight would have concealed my blushes, it did not my tears.

Gently, tenderly as a woman might, he drew my hands away from my face, holding them in his own, while he stooped and touched my forehead with his lips, and then said:

"I see that you have not thought of love, dear Hope, and I have been too hasty; but I can wait. God knows that the hope of winning your love will make life very precious to me. Do not be afraid of me. I will not thrust my love upon you. You shall be only my very dear little friend, until such a time as the knowledge of my love will be a comfort and a blessing to you."

And raising my hands to his lips with tender reverence, he opened the gate, led me through, and leaving me upon the farm-house steps with a whispered "God bless you!" he turned and walked rapidly in the direction of his home. And there I stood, by my uncle's threshold, so confused, so filled with contrition because I had not found courage to tell Mr. Hamlin plainly that I did not and never could love him, that I was ashamed to open the door and look my rough and honest uncle in the face.

There was such a tumult of strange and conflicting thoughts in my brain! Why could I not take for my shield and rest the love of that noble Christian heart, which had just been offered me?

And then came up the memory of the few tender phrases which Carey Chapman had whispered in my ear—phrases which stern common sense told me, as I stood there questioning my heart in the darkness, had slipped from his smooth tongue without thought. Oh, if Carey Chapman had only spoken as Mr. Hamlin had, so earnestly and plainly as to leave no doubt of his honest love! and perhaps he would when I returned, and he saw I was no longer a child! I was growing old upon those steps—counting time by heart-throbs, not by years. Love and sorrow—and they almost always come to us hand in hand—mature the heart in its spring-time of years. And, standing there, I compared the two young men, and wished Carey had Mr. Hamlin's earnestness of purpose, his Christian faith, and his noble self-denial. I felt that the literary culture and polished manners of the former hardly compensated for the want of certain traits of character; and while sober reason was getting the victory over girlish fancy, memory must needs bring up that brook-side scene, and

I saw again those pale, handsome features, and those drenched, motionless limbs, which had been so indebted to his dog and myself. I felt the warm glow that thrilled me when his lips had touched my poor, scratched hand; and with a blush of shame, though I was alone with the darkness, I remembered that that same right hand had been kissed by Mr. Hamlin within the last hour—kissed, too, with a warmth and fervor that carried a strong conviction of his love to my poor heart, while Carey Chapman's carelessly tender words had always left me doubtful whether he regarded me as still a child, who had earned the right to be petted because of her courage, or as a woman, to whom he owed a great debt.

My reverie was interrupted by the sound of footsteps approaching the door, and the next moment Aunt Lydia's voice brought my thoughts down to the practical affairs of this life.

"Hope, I declare you've frightened me half to death! standing like an owl in the dark! Where have you been, child?"

"I called on Ellen and stayed to sing for her a little while, and then I've been standing on the steps to think."

"And catching your death in the night air, you foolish girl! Just as though your thinking couldn't be done in the house."

Uncle John came to my defence.

"Come, come, Lyddy, I won't have Hope scolded any more. I dare say you've kept her too busy to think for a whole week. She shall do as she likes under my roof. Come right to the kitchen and get some supper, for I'll be bound your thinking hasn't taken away your appetite."

But I had no relish for Aunt Abby's hot biscuits and fragrant tea; and after making a vain effort to eat, that I might gratify my kind relatives and silence their questionings, I moved from the table and took up the sewing which Aunt Lydia wanted finished. It was a difficult thing to keep my thoughts so far controlled as to join in the conversation which flowed glibly around me; and my weariness and headache being taken as sufficient excuse for my unwonted silence and paleness, I was sent early to my share of Cousin Lydia's bed.

Painfully confused and uncertain thoughts banished sleep from my eyelids for many hours, and not until I could leave the direction of my life-path to the Beneficent Father, who had so kindly and wisely led me hitherto, did I find that rest which my tired heart was needing. I slept so late on my aunt's bridal morn that Cousin Lydia was sent to rouse me, and her hearty laugh awoke me to a consciousness of the importance of the day.

"Come, Hope," she called, "you've lost the cream of the morning now by your laziness; but father wouldn't let me call you before, because he said you were tired and needed a morning doze."

"What do you call the cream of the morning?"

"Why, the best part of it, of course—and there's been plenty of cream this morning; you've missed a walk with me over the frosty stubble to gather holly and gentians, not to mention the fun of seeing Aunt Lydia eat buckwheats and drink coffee."

"Why shouldn't she eat her breakfast as usual?"

"Well, to be sure! Why shouldn't she? Getting married is just as much a matter of business with her as laying out farm-work for Adoniram Staples, but I don't believe I shall eat and drink on my wedding-day. Hope, are you in love?"

"In love with whom?" I tried to look at my cousin's bright, questioning eyes steadily, but I knew there was a tell-tale color in my face.

"Oh, with me, of course," she replied, "but I'll tell you why I asked. I've always fancied that if I were in love, I should be sober and thoughtful just as you are; and when you said last night that you had been stopping on the steps to think, I said to myself, 'Hope is in love'—and then I watched you in the evening, and I knew you didn't care for any thing that father and Aunt Lydia were saying, though you pretended to listen."

"What a wise head and heart you must have! but you needn't act the spy over me any longer, nor watch for any symptoms of love-sickness about me; my life will be too busy for any indulgence in romance or sentimentality."

"Then I wouldn't give a straw for it—I might as well be a machine for sewing, sweeping, and washing dishes, if it were not for the romance of expecting a grand lover to come along one of these days, who would help make me wiser and better than I am now. But make haste, Hope; it's nearly nine o'clock, and we want you to trim the rooms and help dress the bride. There's a young parson from Eloth coming over to tie the knot, and he'll be here directly; he spent a Sabbath with us last summer when he exchanged with Mr. Hopkinson, and he's a right pleasant young man, if he is a minister."

"May be he is the grand lover you are expecting, who is to make you so wise and good."

"Who knows?" responded my cousin, with a bright blush as she skipped from the room, humming a lively air.

Twelve o'clock came, and found gathered in Uncle John's square parlor, Deacon Sanborn and his prim wife, Dr. Houghton and his showy one, Mr. Hamlin and the young clergyman, with several other prominent supporters of Mr. Hopkinson, whom my aunt wished to witness the ceremony.

Mr. Hamlin met me with so much ease and frankness,

that for a moment I half believed the conversation of the previous evening to be the memory of a troubled dream. What a relief it would have been to find it only a dream! But no! the very hand he had kissed was trembling now in his, while his honest eyes were bent upon my face, kindly and searchingly—only for a moment, and then he presented me to the clergyman, Mr. White, from Eloth, a pale, spare young man, just released from his preparatory studies, who seemed more than willing to be entertained by his host's daughter, and after a few commonplace remarks to me, turned to listen to my cousin's voice.

Mr. Hamlin talked to me in his quiet way about the evergreens which decorated the plain room, until the door opened and Mr. Hopkinson led in his bride. I am almost certain that no woman ever made her responses in a clearer tone, or with an air that said more plainly, " Whoso findeth a wife, findeth a good thing, and obtaineth favor of the Lord;" and had Solomon written " husband " instead of its corresponding feminine, I believe Aunt Lydia would have crowned the ceremony by quoting the passage. She took refuge behind her whitest and finest handkerchief during the prayer; but her face wore such an expression of cheerful resignation when the services were concluded and the handkerchief withdrawn, that I couldn't help wondering why it had been used.

The dove-colored silk and tasteful head-dress took the impress of at least ten years from my aunt's face, or perhaps the thought that she would now be able to do her duty by Caleb and his children helped efface time's footprints; or more than all, her joyful release from the watch-tower of single-blessedness, where she had so long looked anxiously for the coming man, might have softened her features by filling her heart with a more kindly charity toward all men. However, there was still enough of the stern, uncompromising maiden lady left about the new Mrs. Hopkinson to place her identity beyond question, and to keep alive much anxiety in my own mind as regarded the future of the minister and his little girls. The old matter-of-fact element in the bride's character enabled her to receive the congratulations of her friends with remarkable self-possession, as well as to partake of Aunt Abby's abundant refreshments with as much apparent relish as any of the guests. Neither did it forsake her when, later in the day, she had exchanged the dove-colored silk for a dark print, and was making a mustard-draught for her little step-daughter's side; nor yet when she took the vacant chair opposite the minister at table, and poured for him a cup of tea.

Sipping the beverage with as much of a business-like air as if she had been employed by an importer of teas to decide upon their quality and value, she asked abruptly:

" Where did you buy this tea?"

" I think it came from Smith Perry's; but really I don't know. Matilda has ordered the groceries for some time," answered the minister.

" It's poor stuff, at any rate—not much better than old hay I shall tell Jane not to use any more, for I'm very particular about my tea. Deacon Sanborn bought me a small chest of real Ning Yong when he went to Wiltshire last summer, and I've but just made a beginning on it. You'll soon know the genuine article after using that."

The good man smiled an acknowledgment of her prophecy in his favor; but I fancied his smile grew a little forced and troubled as the supper progressed, and my aunt commented freely on the quality of the biscuits, sugar, preserves, etc.

" Never mind, Lydia," responded Mr. Hopkinson, after listening patiently to his bride's remarks on the meanness of men who would sell inferior groceries, and the shameful incapacity of Matilda Crockett in her cookery, "never mind; you shall have every thing your own way as soon as possible."

"I don't care for my own way, but I want to see you and the children made comfortable."

"Always thinking of others, dear Lydia; but you must remember that your own comfort and happiness are not to be set aside. Your presence in the house will be a great relief to me—so great, that I trust I may soon be able to resume my work on the essay I have told you about. I am endeavoring to prove the equality of the human races, both morally and intellectually, in this essay, and the subject being such an important one, I am trying to give it my best thought."

"I hope you'll be able to finish it to your satisfaction," said my aunt; "and I shall take good care that your study hours are not broken in upon as they have been."

She didn't feel quite at home on the subject of the essay, which the minister was intent on explaining to us, and turned with evident relief when, from the next room, little Ellen's voice feebly called "Mother." The beautiful, almost sacred title, given her for the first time, did not appear to unlock any very deep emotion in her woman's heart, for, with a steady hand and unmoved face, she poured a cup of tea and prepared a bit of toast for the invalid before answering the summons. Alas! I thought, "Nature thrusts some of us into the world miserably incomplete on the emotional side."

CHAPTER XXXV.

REJECTED LOVE.

"Nothing is our own: we hold our pleasures
Just a little while, ere they are fled;
One by one life robs us of our treasures;
Nothing is our own except our dead."
Miss Procter.

THE faded leaves of November moaned and rustled as the bleak winds swept them across little Ellen's grave. The tears that I shed over her still, cold face and closed eyelids fell for those who were left, and not for the pure child called so early to her Father's home. She had grown very dear to me during those bleak November days, when her pure, pale face had rested against my bosom, and her frail form had grown lighter in my arms; and I wept because those trusting blue eyes would never look lovingly into my own again, because that hushed voice would never claim from me another hymn. I wept for the awkward, unlovely sister, whose grief even did not draw out the sympathy which a fairer child's would, but sobbed itself away in a lonely corner, and for the father, who, kneeling by the still form, moaned, "If I be bereaved of my children, I am bereaved." "Surely, the Lord hath sorely afflicted me. He hath taken the wife of my youth and the children of our love. Rachel is not, and Samuel hath He taken, and now my pet lamb." And then followed earnest petitions for submission, till the bowed head was raised, and almost triumphantly he exclaimed, "Even so, Lord, for so it seemeth good in Thy sight."

Aunt Lydia's proverbs did not forsake her at this most opportune moment for quoting, and with an audible sigh she withdrew her handkerchief from her eyes and said:

"'The Lord will not suffer the soul of the righteous to famish.' Caleb, this is no place for you and Mary; take her to your room and leave me to do all that remains to be done for Ellen." The tired and grief-stricken minister suffered his new wife to lead him away, and I trust her strong presence and her quotations comforted him.

A long month of weary watching had passed since Aunt Lydia had worn her new honors. The larger part of my time had been spent by the bedside of my little friend; but now that she no longer needed my care, my heart turned yearningly toward my mother's home.

Mr. Hopkinson, had added his gentle entreaties to those of my relatives, that I would at least spend the winter in Hebron; but I had met all persuasions with one answer: "Mother needs me, and father wished me to be her help and comfort."

"You are despising the counsels of your elders, Hope, but you must remember that 'he that hath a froward heart findeth no good.'"

"I think Hope has no intention of despising our counsels, Lydia," answered the minister, "and God will surely bless her for the unselfish obedience which she renders to her father. May He give thee all earthly good, my child, and an inheritance incorruptible, undefiled, and that fadeth not away!"

The last sentence was spoken with tender solemnity, his hand resting upon my head, and from that minute I knew Mr. Hopkinson would be my friend, whatever might betide. I kissed the hand which he had laid in blessing upon my head, and thanked him with such words as my trembling tongue could command.

14

It was the evening after we had laid little Ellen under the brown sods, that, sitting in the parsonage parlor, I heard a step which I had learned to know full well, and which for once I was sorry to hear fall upon the gravelled path. Mr. Hamlin's entrance brought only fear to my heart. The greetings were all quiet and subdued, because of the recent presence of death in that room, but the minister grasped his friend's hand in a way that left no doubt of his welcome. Even Aunt Lydia's hard voice had a mellower, more womanly tone than usual, when she inquired for little Phil.

My aunt soon found an excuse for leaving the parlor, and directly after Mr. Hopkinson remembered something which required his personal attention, and I was left alone with the man whom I honored so much. I had seen him every day since he first spoke to me of love, but though he had never alluded to that theme in words again, I had read the story in every look of his clear, honest eyes, in the clasp of his hand when he greeted me, in the tones of his voice, even though he addressed me upon the most commonplace subject; and, from my confused want of self-control in his presence, I was sure he had gathered hope and assurance.

Mr. Hopkinson had been sitting by my side on the old-fashioned sofa, and when he left the room Mr. Hamlin came forward and took the vacant seat, saying in his characteristic, straightforward way—

"I wanted to see you alone once more before you left Hebron, Miss Hope, and I told your aunt that I did, and why I wished it. My love for you has her sanction, and I trust it may have your mother's, if you will give me permission to call upon her during the Christmas holidays. Hope, you are not afraid of me?" It was not strange that he asked, when the hand he had taken trembled so in his clasp, but my tongue could not find an answer for his question.

"I wish my love to bring you only pleasure and happiness. What has it brought you, Hope?"

"Not happiness, because—because I only like you, Mr. Hamlin." I looked up at him, that he might see I was in earnest, and draw no false conclusions from my agitation and my tears. What a look of regret met mine! What a cloud of disappointment instantly shadowed his face! He did not speak for several minutes, neither did he relinquish the hand he had taken, but sat looking at my tearful face. I knew it was a pitiful and loving as well as a regretful look which was bent upon me, and I dreaded to hear his next words; they came at last, tender and tremulous, but freighted with a noble, generous manliness, that increased the honor and respect I had before felt for him.

"Do not weep, my little friend. I know your kind heart is grieved for my pain and disappointment, but may you never know how great it is! I have been so blind and presuming as to think my love might be returned. I mistook your tears a month ago, and thought you did not know your own heart. I see now it was only for my disappointment that you wept. Be comforted, dear Hope, for God will help me bear this, as He has helped me in lesser trials; at least, I'll try to think so."

"And you will still be my friend?"

"Always: you are the first woman that I've ever loved, and you will be the only one. But, Hope, if I must put away all tenderer thoughts than friendship for you, we must not meet again for many months, until I've learned self-control."

That would not be an easy lesson I knew, when two or three large drops fell from his eyes upon the hand he held.

"God only knows how dear you are to me, and how hard it is to believe that you are not the woman He made for me; but forgive me—this knowledge only grieves and troubles you."

He looked at me a minute longer, then laid his hand tenderly and reverently on my head, bent forward and touched my hair with his lips, and instantly quitted the room.

I ran to the little chamber which had been set aside for me in the parsonage, afraid to meet Aunt Lydia's eyes. Tears of grief and mortification flooded my face, when I thought of the sorrow and disappointment I had brought to Mr. Hamlin. How tender, reverent, and forbearing he had been! not a single reproach had escaped from his tongue, and scarcely a tinge of the regret, which had been so plainly stamped upon his face, had been allowed to color his words. What a noble, generous love I had cast aside!

Aunt Lydia looked in upon me on the way to her own chamber, to assure me that she would call me in time for the stage, but she made no comments upon my swollen eyes, and I marvelled that she asked no questions. My slumbers had been so broken for the last month that sorrow for my friend's pain could not succeed in banishing sleep entirely from my eyelids, and then my heart was quieted with the hope of meeting mother so soon. To-morrow night, please God, I would rest in her arms.

In the gray light of the November morning I left Hebron, with Mr. Hopkinson's blessing treasured in my heart, poor, lonely Mary's tears upon my hands, and Aunt Lydia's quotations ringing in my ears. "Thine own friend and thy father's friend forsake not," had been her last injunction. Surely I had, and so had my father, dearer friends than Aunt Lydia, whom I would never forsake.

Two hours' riding in a stage-coach, over a country which the desolation of November had so changed that I could hardly recognize a familiar feature in the landscape, and we reached the nearest railroad station. Mother had written that Mr. Chapman would meet me at the end of my journey by rail. I knew she meant the father, but I could not help thinking it would be pleasant if by some chance the son came instead; and the thought, which I dared not make a wish, caused the color to flush and pale upon my face.

It was the gray hair and calm, sober face of my elderly friend that met my expectant eyes, when the train stopped at Brierfield, only five miles from my home. There was no need of the anxious, nervous fluttering at my heart.

"Ah, little truant, we have you at last!" he exclaimed, holding me at arm's length, and gazing with almost a fatherly tenderness into my face. "Bless me! what a woman you've grown since leaving home! Jump into the chaise, my dear, and I will look after your bundles."

"I'm very glad to see you, Mr. Chapman, and glad to be in Sherbrooke again. Are they all well at home?" I asked, as he wrapped me in fur robes. The short day was drawing toward twilight, and a cold, drizzling storm of rain had just set in.

"All well; but I think you are very much needed by your mother. Why have you stayed so long?"

"I could not come before; at least, it seemed better that I should not, and mother approved of my staying."

"Yes—I've no doubt; and has concealed from you all knowledge of the sickness which has visited her family. I dare say, now, she has written as cheerfully as if her days and nights had been spent in luxury and ease."

"Who has been sick?"

"Willie, Sophie, and one of the Mayhews have been down with scarlet fever more than half the time since you left."

"Why didn't she send for me?"

"I told her she ought, but she said the fever was contagious, and you were doing a good work in Hebron, and must not be told of her necessities. Hope, do you know there is scarcely another woman in the world as self-sacrificing as your mother?"

"Yes—I know; indeed, no one can know her as I do; but what help has she had during all these weeks?"

"Mrs. Chapman says that Jones girl has been a host in herself, and Jonas Gould's wife has been there; but still your mother has had a hard time. Do not fret now, for all the patients are doing well, and there is no longer any danger of contagion."

So I tried to put back this new grief, and ask cheerfully after the villagers and the objects of neighborhood interest. Mr. Chapman had always, since my father's death, talked to me upon business matters, such as other girls of my age would not have cared to understand; and now he told me of the new county buildings, which were in process of erection, the certain prospect of hearing the whistle of the steam-engine in Sherbrooke before winter had fairly set in—only a few days more of work were needed—and how Mr. Clark had failed to secure capital for the rebuilding of his factory.

"But what will the poor folks do, who have depended upon him for work?"

"I have heard that Brown and Son, of Wiltshire, will build in the spring, but it will be a hard winter for our poor. Mr. Clark has opened a small grocery; and I am afraid it will be more of a drinking-saloon than an honest place of business."

And now the orchards, fences, and farms began to look like old friends in the dim and uncertain light, and I knew that just ahead, not a half mile distant, stood our own brown house. Mr. Chapman's words were lost upon me; I heard nothing distinctly until the clasp of my mother's arms, and her voice of welcome, roused me to the delightful consciousness of being at home.

CHAPTER XXXVI.

HOME AGAIN.

"It is a very miserable epoch, when the evil necessities of life first get the better of us, so far as to compel us to attempt throwing a cloud over our transparency."—HAWTHORNE.

"You look so tired, mother, that I shall insist on your resting for as many weeks as I have been gone."

Mother answered only with a smile—a smile full of content, even though the lines of her face quickly settled again to their usual grave quiet. We were sitting hand-in-hand, as we had so often sat after the children were in bed, watching the fading embers on the hearth. Mother had told me of the sickness which had prostrated three members of her family. Willie was attacked first, and suffered least; he was almost well, when Sophie and Annie came down together. They had been very sick for more than a month, but were rapidly recovering now—would be able to resume study again when the Fairchilds came in December.

"You will at least give me the hardest work to do. I feel just like grappling with, and conquering all sorts of difficult things."

Mother's face was again lighted for a moment with that cheerful, contented smile; but as she looked up at me, I think she must have seen in my face something which she had not seen there before—a shadow, perhaps, of the womanliness which the experiences of the last three months had given me.

"You shall have plenty of work, my child; I feel already as if the burden of the autumn were more than half lifted from my heart and hands by your presence. I expect soon to find myself leaning upon you much as I did upon your father. Your face is more like his than it was three months ago. What has given you such a womanly air?"

"I suppose absence from you and reliance upon myself has wrought some change in my character, and of course gives expression to my face. Then it made me feel womanly to find how little Ellen clung to me in her sickness, and how useful I could be to my aunt, and—"

"What else, Hope?" Mother questioned, with her clear, steady eyes upon my face, as I paused, stammering and confused, conscious of withholding a part of the truth. I meant to tell her at some time all about my acquaintance with Mr. Hamlin, and why not now?

It was always a relief to share my troubles with her, and the knowledge of my friend's love had surely been a trouble to me; but I sat gazing at the whitening embers, not knowing how to speak, even to mother, upon the subject. I honored Mr. Hamlin so much that his love seemed too sacred a thing to be spoken of to any one; but if mother could only teach me how to put all remembrance of it away—and yet I didn't quite wish to forget his love, for it had been an honor to me, if I could not return it—and I thought I should always be a purer and more unselfish woman for having known of it.

"Have you kept from me any thing which has troubled you, Hope?" mother asked, after a few minutes of quiet waiting.

"I do not know as I should feel troubled, mother, but

I was obliged to disappoint some one, and I am very sorry for the pain I caused."

"It was a disappointment to your aunt, of course, not to keep you in Hebron; but, Hope, you were free to stay with her."

"Oh, Aunt Lydia was not so very loath to give me up after she was married, and especially after little Ellen died, but some one else wanted me to stay in Hebron." Another pause, while my nervous fingers toyed with the buckle of my belt, and my eyes were employed in watching the white ashes that fell from the dying coals.

"Well, Hope, I would like to hear about this mysterious 'some one.'"

"Mother, did ever a person whom you only liked very much as a friend, wish you to love him more than that?"

"Is this your trouble, Hope?"

"Yes—but I never thought he would care for me until it was too late. He was Aunt Lydia's friend, and I didn't mean to like him at all, because she was always praising him; but it happened somehow that we saw each other very often, and he knew a great deal about books, and was so much older and wiser than myself, that I liked to talk with him until—until I knew he loved me."

"I am sorry that such knowledge and such pain should have come to you so soon, dear child; I have wished to keep you with me many years yet, as long as we both live, if it could be for your happiness. Perhaps I am very selfish in feeling pleased that you could not return this man's love, yet I think there is scarcely a man living to whom I could give my child."

"I am sure you would have liked Mr. Hamlin, mother, because he never seemed to think of his own pleasure, but was always trying to make everybody happy. And then he is very scholarly and has pleasant manners, and such an agreeable way of saying things that one cannot help talking with him—and more than all, he is a Christian."

"And you liked him very much? Are you sure that you do not love him, Hope?"

"Oh, very sure; but still, mother, it grieved me to know that he was pained and disappointed, and I should so like to have him for a friend!"

"If you want to bury your sorrow for your friend's disappointment in hard tasks, I should advise you to take up some interesting study with a strong and vigorous will, and not give your memory time to dwell upon your acquaintance with Mr. Hamlin."

"I will plunge into German with my whole heart, and please let us never speak about this matter again. Tell me now about Virginia. Has she called often since I went away?"

"She has not been here since the fever broke out, but I have found our friends very attentive. Mrs. Chapman, Mrs. Blake, and Mrs. Eveleth have been like sisters; there was no danger to them from contagion, and I think there would have been none for you."

"Then you should have sent for me, and not have tired yourself so with nursing and housework."

"Martha Jane managed the housework much better than any one could have believed possible. I had succeeded in teaching her self-respect before Willie was taken sick, besides giving her some thorough lessons in work, and with a couple of hours' help from Jonas Gould's wife each day, she managed very well. Kind, patient instruction and encouragement have so changed her, that I think, with Mrs. Gould's assistance, we shall want no other help at present."

"Not if you allow me to do as much as I can. Are the new rooms finished?"

"Yes—but not furnished, and I am sorely puzzled to

know how to get the simplest furniture which will be suitable without getting in debt. The finishing of those rooms has used up nearly every dollar that I have saved from Mr. Mayhew's payments, and sickness has made our expenses much heavier than usual this fall."

"And worrying about it all has made you look pale and careworn, mother. I am sure Mr. Chapman will contrive a way to help us get the furniture. We have got safely through difficulties that seemed greater than this."

"I know it, and do not mean to be over-anxious; Mr. Chapman will probably help us, but I do not like to receive too many favors even from him. But we will not talk of these things any more to-night; I ought not to have mentioned them so soon. God will provide all things necessary for our comfort and well-being."

For several days after my return the weather was so bleak and uncomfortable, and the mud so deep, that a walk or a ride to the village was out of the question; so I busied myself with housework, reading, and sewing, and was so happy in resuming my pleasant duties, that I was quite content to let the pleasure of seeing Virginia wait. Sophie and Annie were still prisoners within the house, and though rapidly recovering strength, would not be able to resume their studies for several weeks. Scarcely a month was left us now for finishing our preparations for the reception of new pupils; and if each hour of the day was freighted with work, it was made pleasant by mother's happy faculty of making all labor a delight. Even the dark, short days of early winter were rendered bright and cheerful by her smile and voice.

After much thought and consultation with me as to how money could be raised for purchasing necessary furniture for two new rooms, mother had decided to part with a valuable watch which had been given her by a brother, long since deceased. She had retained it during all our hard struggles with poverty, because of its associations with her girlhood; but now she would dispose of it, rather than have the shadow of a debt hanging over her again.

"It ought to bring a hundred dollars," she said; "and then, if I could borrow another hundred of Mr. Chapman, I think I could manage to make the rooms neat and comfortable."

"Make them look pretty too, if possible, mother, because the Fairchilds will come from such a handsome home that we shall not want the contrast to be too great. You may take all the money you have laid aside for my winter cloak, I can make the old one last."

"Will you be just as happy in the old cloak, Hope?" mother asked, raising her eyes to my face, while her sewing dropped for a minute upon her lap.

"I shall at least be content, if going without a new cloak will take the weight of one care from you."

"Dear, generous Hope—so like your father!" she said, and bent forward to kiss my cheek—a caress which was ample payment for any self-denial.

In the afternoon of a December day we walked over the frozen ground to the village, to consult with Mr. Chapman; and, reaching the gate, mother bade me go on and spend with Virginia the half hour which she would consume at the Chapmans'. My willing feet needed no urging, but carried me very swiftly to Squire Thornton's handsome library and Virginia's hearty welcome.

I was too much absorbed with the pleasure of meeting my friend, for the first minute, to notice that a gentleman had risen from the sofa, and was an amused spectator of our school-girlish embraces. The tones of his voice sent the blood in quick, tingling pulsations to my heart, and made me conscious that Carey Chapman had looked on, while I had kissed the cheeks, forehead, and lips of Virginia.

"There, Miss Kendall, your friend has had quite her share of your caresses, until my presence is duly recognized;" and he took the same hand which had been scratched in his behalf, and led me across the room, placing me in a chair by the western window, talking all the while in such an easy, unembarrassed way, that I gained coolness and courage enough to answer the questions which my friends poured out upon me, and to catch an occasional hurried glance at his face. What a proud and handsome face it was, with its regular features, steel-blue eyes, and faultless whiskers! and what an elegant figure leaned carelessly against the window draperies, while his hand toyed with the silken tassel!

And as I sat listening to the smooth flow of talk, my eye could scarcely have helped noting Virginia's bright beauty, enhanced by something, I knew instinctively, besides the lovely soft folds of silk that fell around her, and the scarlet geranium blossoms which lay against her white throat. Her face wore a new and softer look, a tenderer charm. I dared not ask myself what flower had blossomed in her soul to lend such beauty to her face. My gray merino, plaid shawl, and silken hood seemed suddenly out of place in that handsome room. They belonged to the real, working-day world, as well as my plain self; and what part or lot could they have with so much beauty, polish, and wealth?

The old, hard question, "Who maketh thee to differ?" which I thought answered and forever silenced, was again rapping at my heart. Could it be possible, I queried, that my own vanity had over-estimated the attentions of Carey Chapman? that only gratitude to one who had rendered him timely service had prompted his delicate consideration for me? that his own distant kinship to my step-mother had been the reason for his polite interest in me?

I had suffered an affection for him to take root in my heart, and already the buds of the forbidden flower were just ready to open—they needed only the sunshine of his encouragement; and I blushed when I thought that perhaps his keen eye had already discovered my secret.

"What is the matter, Hope?" exclaimed Virginia. "You are red as my geraniums one minute, and the next a veritable pond-lily. Are you ill?"

"No—only a little faint; perhaps the walk has been too long for me, and your room is rather warm," I answered, opening my shawl and hood, only to refasten them with nervous haste, when Virginia left the room, and I was alone with Carey Chapman.

"I have noticed your changing color, and am afraid your friend's fears are not groundless," he said, coming forward to my side, and taking my hand. "You have grown nervous and injured your own health in your attentions to the child whom you have written Virginia about. You should have remembered that the old friends have claims upon you as well as the new," he said, with one of those looks which seemed to imply a deeper meaning than he dared put in words. I could not answer, with his eyes upon my face.

"Has the memory of our pleasant walks, rides, and conversations faded from your heart, as well as the ugly scratch upon your little hand?" he asked; and again the hand was raised to his lips.

The action gave me strength to draw it from his clasp, and courage also to say:

"No, Mr. Chapman; I never forget my friends, nor their kindness to me."

The next moment Virginia entered the room, to find

him standing by the window, playing with the silken tassel of the curtain as carelessly as if his hand had never touched a more sentient thing.

"Hope, you must drink this glass of cordial—Aunt Sallie made it, and always administered it when we had colds, or were fatigued; it is her sovereign balm for all physical ills."

I drank the cordial, and in as few words as possible declared myself sufficiently strong to go.

"Not until you have promised to spend the whole of to-morrow with me," said Virginia, not only in words but with persuasive looks.

"I cannot come to-morrow—mother is going to Wiltshire, and I must stay with the children."

"Then come on Thursday."

"Perhaps, if I can be spared."

Mother did not appear to notice my unwonted silence as we walked home in the wintry twilight. She talked with more than usual cheerfulness of our brightening prospects—told me of Mr. Chapman's willingness to loan two hundred dollars and take her watch for security, and that if we were well during the winter the watch could be redeemed when our payments from Mr. Mayhew became due. She little guessed that the half hour in Squire Thornton's library had given me glimpses of a cloud which threatened to overshadow my whole life, that—

> "Some sudden qualm had struck me at the heart,
> And dimmed mine eyes that I could see no further."

CHAPTER XXXVII.

DREAMS OF HAPPINESS.

"Fancy made me dreams of happiness,
For hope grew round me like the twining vine,
And fruits and foliage, not my own, seemed mine."
COLERIDGE.

SLEEP had done much toward "knitting up my ravelled sleeve of care," but it had not been sufficiently sweet and undisturbed to clear my brain of all anxious thoughts, neither had it driven off a headache which was with me, the usual accompaniment of anxiety.

Mother had noticed my unwonted paleness, and the want of alacrity in my movements, but had been assured that only a headache was troubling me, and had driven off to Wiltshire for a day's shopping, with Jonas Gould for an escort.

It was one of those soft, bright days of early winter, when the Indian Summer returns coquettishly to smile upon the brown fields and leafless trees, as if loath to resign them to the cold caresses of Winter. My morning's work was performed in so spiritless a manner as to draw from Martha Jane the ejaculation—

"Laws, Miss Hope, you must have an awful headache! You're as white as them pillowcases; and my goodness! if you ain't ironing of 'em wrong side out! You'd better go to bed this minute, and leave me to finish that ironing."

"You may finish the ironing, but my head is not so bad as to oblige me to lie down; I must remain up, to keep the children amused."

"You promised to read us a story to-day, Miss Hope. You are not too sick to read?" asked Annie Mayhew.

"No—come into the parlor; you shall have the story."

"Read one of Fanny Forester's, please. Miss Thornton gave me 'Alderbrook' just before I was taken sick, and I like the stories ever so much, but Carey Chapman says they are trash."

I knew the mention of that name brought color to my cheeks, but fortunately my back was turned toward the fireside group in searching for the book, so that the foolish, tell-tale tint faded unnoticed. The story was one of absorbing interest to the girls, and gave me some pleasure, inasmuch as it brought them enjoyment, and served to divert my own thoughts.

The reading was interrupted by Dora's glad voice, exclaiming, "Here's Carey Chapman! I'm so glad! It's been an age since we've seen him," and the delighted girl flew to admit him.

"You see that I'm a welcome guest to your pupils, Miss Hope, but I suppose I need not feel complimented, as they would be glad to see almost any one after their long confinement."

"Indeed! you know there is no one we should care half as much to see, unless 'tis Virginia Thornton. Tell her that Miss Hope has got back, and there is no danger of catching the fever now, and we all want her to come." Dora's ready words gave me time to collect my thoughts.

"Then you mean to affirm that Miss Hope's return frightened off the contagious fever? I was not aware that she had so much power."

"You are quizzing me now, Mr. Chapman, and I suppose I have been careless as usual in the use of words, but you see I have missed your instructions." The child was really putting on coquettish airs. 'Tis true she was nearly fourteen.

"I do not mean that you shall lack for a Mentor in future—I shall call more frequently after next week, when the cars will be running from Sherbrooke to Wiltshire. What book have you, Miss Hope?"

"Fanny Forester's 'Alderbrook.' I was reading to the girls."

"Were you interested?"

"Yes, I think so; at least, my auditors were."

"'Tis a splendid book," exclaimed Dora, "and Miss Thornton gave it to me; she says you called it trash, but you couldn't have read it when you said that."

"No, I had only glanced at a few pages; I should think Fanny Forester would be a favorite with young people; but your teacher does not look greatly benefited by the morning's reading. Ask her if she will do me the honor to ride in my chaise."

He still stood, leaning against the mantel, carelessly twirling his glove, but scanning my changing color intently the while.

"Thank you, I must not go out to-day; I am left in charge of the young people—and besides, I have a bad headache."

"That's the very reason why you should drive in this clear, wintry air; come, I must take no excuse—allow me to be dictatorial. These young people can amuse themselves for an hour; I will not keep you out longer than that."

"Yes, make her go, Mr. Chapman; she hasn't had a ride since she came back; we can manage to amuse ourselves for an hour," said Dora, while Sophie and Annie ran for my cloak and hood.

It seemed foolish to resist the combined entreaties of

Mr. Chapman and my pupils; so I donned cloak and hood, and allowed Carey Chapman to assist me to a seat in his chaise.

"I shall not give you the choice of a road this morning, Miss Hope, for I must drive over to North Sherbrooke on business," Mr. Chapman said, as he turned his horse in that direction.

There was certainly pleasure in listening to his nicely modulated voice, his easy flow of words, and I soon found that the exhilarating ride and conversation were banishing from memory the troubled thoughts which had haunted me since the day before. It was simply natural that he should call often upon Virginia, they were such near neighbors, and she was so bright and agreeable, I thought; and after all, I might have been mistaken in thinking they were more than friends. I would at least enjoy this hour's pleasant talk with him, watching meanwhile to keep my interest in him properly checked—and more, I would carefully compare his conversation with that of one whom I knew loved me.

He scarcely obliged me to talk at all during our rapid drive to North Sherbrooke, a small village distant about three miles from our farm, but talked easily and continually about the improvements in our town and his own settlement in Wiltshire.

"The practice of law will be monotonous to me, I foresee, but I shall make it only a stepping-stone to political preferment. I am ambitious, and nothing shall satisfy me until M. C. is written after my name. What do you think of such an ambition?" he asked.

"I suppose 'tis commendable; at least, if one is ambitious to occupy a high position for the sake of enlarging his sphere of usefulness."

"Ay, my little friend, you look at every thing in such a utilitarian way! I'm afraid you would hardly consent to share the fortunes of an honorable senator, or an ambassador to foreign lands, if they were laid at your feet." He paused, as if waiting a reply. None came; and he added, much as if he were alone, and communing with his own spirit, " Yes, I would be one of the great ones, whom

> 'We build our love around, like an arch of triumph;
> Whose thoughts possess us like a passion—
> Whose words haunt us, as eagles haunt the mountain-air;'

and if I have a friend envious as Brutus, I will give him more occasion to stab me than Cæsar gave; for it shall never be said of me—

> 'And thrice I offered him a kingly crown,
> Which thrice he did refuse.'

Here we are at Squire Follet's office. Will you hold my horse while I go in? My business will not occupy more than five or ten minutes."

He placed the reins in my hands and sprang out of the chaise, disappearing in the office, while I sat thinking of his ambition, and comparing it with Mr. Hamlin's. I knew that the latter had refused honorable positions—Mr. Hopkinson had told me so—for the sake of cherishing and supporting a broken-hearted sister and her invalid boy. One lived to make himself an honorable position in society, and the other thanked God for work, without seeking a reward.

" You look as if the cares of a nation were resting upon you, Miss Hope," said Mr. Chapman, in a light tone, as he took the reins from my hands. " Were you considering ways and means for my promotion?"

" No; I am not a political *intriguante!*"

" Women should never know any thing about the diplomacy and intrigue necessary to gain political distinction. Polite and general literature, with the accomplishments which make a home pleasant, ought to satisfy a woman's ambition. Am I right?" he asked, after waiting for an answer.

"I think a woman should know something about politics, and she ought to have knowledge enough of the solid branches to make her useful and respected."

"But not enough to make her a blue. Don't go and make yourself so wise that I shall be afraid of you! What are you studying now?"

"I have not commenced study since my return; but immediately after the holidays I shall take up French and German."

"A knowledge of both those languages is most desirable for a lady. You will learn music too?"

"If I can find the time. I must take the heavier part of teaching from mother this winter. She is looking worn and tired."

"And your visit to your aunt has not proved the best tonic for your health or spirits," he said, looking at me so searchingly, and yet so kindly, that I knew my face was instantly dyed. "I know your head is better for this short drive; and the day is so remarkably fine that if it were not for my promise to your pupils, I would take you around by Cameron pond. I want to see the old light in your eyes before leaving you at home."

I think his wish must have been gratified, for the flow of conversation was very smooth during the remainder of the drive, and he left me at my mother's gate, too bewildered with happiness to ask my heart a reason for its joy. Most certainly, "fruits and foliage, not my own, seemed mine."

Mother came home in the evening, refreshed by her little journey and a call upon the Fairchilds. She gave us an animated account of her shopping and introduction to her new pupils. "They will be here the first Monday in January," she said; "and Mrs. Fairchild has secured two more for us, so that we shall begin the year with eight boarding-pupils. I am glad to see you looking brighter, Hope. Is your head quite relieved?" asked mother.

"The pain is all gone."

"She may thank us for it, Mrs. Kendall, for we made her go and ride with Mr. Chapman. He said the air and exercise would cure her head, but she wouldn't have gone if we had not teased her," said Dora.

"A drive must have been invigorating in such delightful air; it was almost like a September day. But what brought Carey from the city?"

"He had business in North Sherbrooke."

"And oh, Mrs. Kendall! he promises to call often as soon as the cars are running!"

Mother did not look particularly delighted with Dora's last bit of information. I could not help seeing that she would prefer Carey Chapman's calls should not be frequent.

The bright days of December brought plenty of callers from the village to congratulate me on my return. Virginia was in almost every day, sparkling, attentive, and beautiful as ever, with a shade more of thought in her eyes, and a softer grace in her manners. She was making preparations for a Christmas party, and would not be denied the pleasure of expecting me; and so mother and I contrived to add to our many cares the making of Aunt Lydia's present, my blue silk dress.

CHAPTER XXXVIII.

HOPE KENDALL'S CHRISTMAS.

"It was a happy thought to bring
To the dark season's frost and rime,
This painted memory of spring,
This dream of summer-time."
WHITTIER.

"MISS HOPE, I've a mighty big box here, sent from Hebron to you. What in the world could that stingy old aunt of yourn find to fill a box three foot square with?" asked Jonas Gould.

"A box from Aunt Lydia! well, the contents of her camphor-wood trunk must have been troubling her conscience, or the minister may have taught her the blessedness of giving. Wait a minute, Jonas, and I'll find a chisel and a hammer for you to open it."

The noise of opening brought mother to the kitchen. "Do I hear aright?" she asked; "is there a box from your aunt? Why, Hope, you must have found the door to her heart."

"If her heart is softened, 'tis the minister's work, not mine; but what have we here?" I asked, as the nails yielded to Jonas' strength, and revealed the back of a picture and frame; "Aunt Lydia hadn't a single picture in her house," I exclaimed, removing the wrappings, and, lifting the uppermost frame, I looked upon the innocent face and dreamy blue eyes of Ellen Hopkinson. I knew at a glance whose hand had drawn those lovely features; whose heart, even in pain and disappointment, had planned for me this pleasant Christmas greeting; but I stood before it in silence. I could only answer mother with a quiet yes, when she asked if it was the face of my little friend; and dimly through tears, I read the lines inscribed beneath the portrait—

> "The blessing of her quiet life
> Fell on us like the dew;
> And good thoughts, where her footsteps pressed,
> Like fairy blossoms grew."

" My goodness! it looks more like an angel than a real flesh and blood child!" exclaimed Jonas, whose acquaintance with pictures was not extensive.

" Such a pure and trusting expression, and such lovely features, are rarely combined in one face," said mother, too intently gazing upon the picture to notice my emotion. " Hope, do you think your aunt had this picture painted on purpose for you?"

" No." The tones of my voice caused mother to turn, but I was assisting Jonas to lift another picture from the box and place it in an upright position against the wall, and she could not see my face.

" Two pictures? Why, Hope, how rich you are! Is that bit of landscape to be seen in Hebron?"

" Yes—that old meeting-house is where my mother used to sing, and she taught her first school in that little brown house under the maples."

" There's nothing else in the box—shall I clear it away with all them old papers? It seems kinder strange that yer aunt should use so many in packing two picters, when old paper is worth two cents a pound."

" Wait a minute, Jonas," and I bent over the box, lifting each paper and searching carefully for a note. No—there was none, and I turned away disappointed. Even though I read forgiveness and continued friendship in these products of Mr. Hamlin's pencil, my perverse heart craved something more. I would gladly have seen in words, what I already knew so well, that these pictures were painted expressly to give me pleasure.

"Can you guess who sent these pictures, Hope?" asked mother, when Jonas had carried the box away, and left us alone.

"Yes—Mr. Hamlin, the friend I told you of."

"Is he an artist?"

"Only an amateur—he will never make painting a profession."

"Then I think the art will lose a masterful hand; that head of your little friend seems to me beautifully executed, and before I was married I was familiar with good paintings in New York. Was there really so much of soft, tender, spring-like beauty in little Ellen, or is this painted from memory, and exaggerated?"

"He painted it last summer, when she was first beginning to droop ; 'tis a faithful copy."

"Your friend has given us all a joy, but you must not look at your treasures with such an April face, or I shall think there is more pain than pleasure for you in receiving them."

"There are, of course, some sad memories associated with these gifts, but they bring me much real joy; I do not deserve to be so kindly remembered by Mr. Hamlin. Shall we hang them in the parlor?"

"It would be a pity not to place them where our friends can enjoy them with us—unless you particularly wish to keep their possession a secret."

"I have no such wish—and I'll call Jonas to help hang them while the children are out."

"Such a face as that, always looking down upon us, ought to strengthen our faith in all things pure," mother said, when we had adjusted the pictures in the most favorable positions on our low walls, and still stood admiring them.

"I wish you could have known little Ellen and the friend who has painted her likeness."

"It is not impossible but I may yet know the friend."

"I can hardly see how knowing him will ever be possible for you, as you are not likely to visit Hebron, and there is nothing to bring Mr. Hamlin here."

Mother only answered with a quiet smile, and I took up my sewing, thinking how very pleasant it would be to meet my friend again, if only to thank him for his beautiful Christmas gift; but not now—not while there were any traces of the pain I had last seen in his face.

The blue silk was finished for Virginia's party, and proved more becoming than Aunt Lydia had predicted; but I think mother must have seen something more in my face than pleasure in wearing my aunt's gift—a light which came only from within.

I would much rather have accepted the offered escort of Carey Chapman than ride with our awkward, matter-of-fact Jonas, in the farm-wagon, but mother had very decidedly rejected Carey's proposal to come for me, telling him that our hired man was a trusty escort.

I was the first arrival, and had several minutes for quiet admiration of my friend, before others came to claim her attention. She was more lovely, in her dress of white, with buff trimmings, than I had ever seen her, and I could not help exclaiming:

"Oh, Virginia, how beautiful!"

"Am I pretty, dear Hope?"

"Much more than pretty, in my eyes; you are positively lovely to-night!"

"You are a partial little friend, but it pleases me to

know that you think I'm lovely. I care much more about my looks than I used to. Some day I shall tell you why, only don't think me vain and silly now. You are looking uncommonly well, too, and have a very becoming dress."

"It is a present from Aunt Lydia, though I believe it was bought for my mother by Grandfather Hastings, and has lain in my aunt's trunk for eighteen years."

"Well, I'm glad she had the good sense to give it you at last; but it must have cost her a severe heart-ache to part with so valuable a silk, even if it was useless to her! Come down now, and see the parlor and library, before they are filled with guests: they are beautifully trimmed with holly and flowers, and Captain Wynne and I did it all!"

It was like fairy-land to one who had seen so little of the gay world; and the wreaths and festoons of flowers, and the glitter of lights in the handsome rooms, almost dazzled me, and quite deprived me of speech; but the volubility of Virginia, and the kindness of her father and Captain Wynne and his happy wife, soon released my tongue, and directly my eyes and thoughts were engaged with the entrance of guests, most of whom were familiar to me. Belinda and Esther, dressed in showy, vulgar taste, were fluttering noisily around, talking loudly about a concert which they had attended in Wiltshire the evening before. Their knowledge of music was paraded on every occasion.

"You here, Mr. Chapman? I'm glad to see that you are not a fixture in Wiltshire!" said Belinda, with her prettiest drawl, as the person addressed came toward her.

"You could not expect me to remain away from Sherbrooke to-day, especially when I knew how many attractions Squire Thornton's rooms would offer!"

"Oh, you men always flatter us so!" answered Belinda,

who had appropriated the compliment, as Carey Chapman meant she should; else why did he accompany his words with such a meaning smile and bow? I knew that he thought her shallow, frivolous, and vain, and I could not help thinking he had no right to foster her vanity with words which, addressed to her, were untrue and heartless. Esther was pouring into my ear an exaggerated history of her recent visit to Wiltshire, but she needed no answers, so that more than half my attention could be given to the conversation of Belinda and Mr. Chapman, who stood near us.

"Aren't your old law-books horridly stupid?" Belinda asked, with a little shrug of her bare shoulders.

"Not quite so entertaining as some things I've read; Dickens' novels, for instance."

"You don't pretend to think Dickens is entertaining? I never could get through with one of his books, he writes about such common characters—old fishermen, and paupers, and prisoners. I want the books I read to give me descriptions of the best society."

"What books are favorites with you?"

"Oh, I dote on Mrs. Southworth's novels, and Marian Harland's! Esther and I often sit up till midnight reading. We are fond of poetry too."

"I thought so."

"Pray, tell me why, Mr. Chapman?"

"Do we not almost instinctively know from one's face when the mind is fed

'upon the soft and sweet
And delicate imaginings of song?'"

"Only a clever person like yourself could read a face so correctly. There are so few people here in Sherbrooke to appreciate our fondness for books, and sympathize with our endeavors to rise above the common herd! Oh, Mr. Chapman, you cannot think how often we pine for cultivated society!" It was said with a most languishing droop of the eyelids, appealing pathetically to the sympathies of the young man.

"But, Miss Blake, you are more fortunate than many of your friends; you are not confined to Sherbrooke for your society. You and your sister have a world all to yourselves in your books, poetry, and music; and then you have the variety of frequent visits to Wiltshire. Did I hear you say that you were there last week?"

"Yes; we only came home to-day for the party, though Gov. Fairchild and his wife are going so soon to Washington, that we couldn't conveniently stay with them any longer. We have such nice times there, going to parties and concerts, that our village seems more dull and stupid than ever when we get back! Every thing is so slow and old-fashioned here, I quite envy you the happiness of living in Wiltshire."

"Miss Belinda and Esther, please give us that duet you promised for this evening?" asked our fair hostess, coming forward and laying her hand on Belinda's thin, jewelled arm.

"Not now, Virginia; don't ask us to play first. Get Mrs. Eveleth to sing some of her musty old songs!" answered Belinda.

"You see, Miss Blake wishes to enhance her own charms by contrast," said Mr. Chapman, with a look which the fair sisters failed to interpret, for they chattered noisily on, about never wanting to play first, and classical music like theirs not being appreciated in mixed company; and then they whispered and laughed while Mrs. Eveleth sang "Do you remember Sweet Alice, Ben Bolt?" declaring the song was as old as the May-Flower.

At last, after much affected hesitation, the Misses Blake were induced to favor the company with some of their classical music, and Carey Chapman turned the pages, making flattering comments, I was almost sure, from the delighted tosses of the pale-brown ringlets, and the satisfied look on the insipid faces, when the young man bent to make some whispered remark.

The evening was fast waning; and though there had been no lack of kind attentions to me from Virginia and her guests, still I was conscious of a slight feeling of disappointment and dissatisfaction. Must I go without one word from Carey Chapman? No; he was approaching now, in his own peculiarly easy, graceful way, and I knew that my fast-changing color gave him just the welcome which he wished to see. " My little friend is gathering up only beauty and perfume from her second party, without getting warped by the world's air, I trust," he said, retaining the hand which I had offered in greeting, much as if he had an especial ownership in it.

"I think I have seen more of the world's air—more insincerity this evening than ever before, but I hope I shall not imitate or become warped by it."

" I am sure you will not, nor allow your faith in goodness and truth to be diminished. You have yet to learn, Miss Hope, that there are some natures so shallow, self-conceited, and artful, that a man never feels like dealing otherwise with them than in their own coin. I saw you were shocked with the flattering attentions which the fair sisters wheedled out of me, but you must have noticed that my compliments would have been vapid and meaningless to more sensible ears."

" Have we any right to pamper the vanity of persons whose perceptions are so blunted by self-conceit that they cannot detect the hidden sarcasm, concealed in flattery?"

"You are a severe moralist, my little cousin, and I am justly rebuked, and almost penitent enough under your displeasure to promise solemnly never to use merely pretty compliments again. But you will admit the temptation was great?"

"It might be for some—perhaps for all men."

"You think not for women, I infer from your emphasis on the word men."

"I cannot see how a truthful woman could ever be tempted to foster the vanity of a vain one."

"You will not think I am dealing with you as with the fair Belinda, when I tell you that your straightforward honesty is perfectly charming? Come, now, Miss Hope, let us make a bargain: I will give you an hour's instruction in German twice a week, if you will give me as many lessons in moral philosophy."

"I have never studied moral philosophy, and if I had, I should not dare teach you."

"But you would like the German lessons?"

"Oh, so much! But you are not serious?" I asked, venturing to raise my eyes to the handsome face which was bent over me.

"Never more so—but mind, I shall expect to get a full reward for my German lessons in the moral and religious instructions which you and your excellent mother will give me."

"Won't it be very inconvenient for you to come twice a week from Wiltshire?"

"Not if I choose to make it convenient. Can you not persuade your friend Virginia to join you in the study of German?"

"I hope so. Yes, I am very sure she would like German. Where shall we meet?"

"Sometimes in your mother's parlor and sometimes in

Squire Thornton's library, as you and your friend can agree. Is Jonas Gould coming for you?"

"Yes."

"Then I suppose it will be needless for me to offer you my protection?"

"Thank you, but Jonas can take care of me."

"At least you will give me the pleasure of taking you to the supper-room; you see a movement is making in that direction."

I allowed him to place my hand upon his arm, and walked with him across the room. Passing Belinda, I saw a shrug of her shoulders, and distinctly heard her whisper to Esther, "The impudent little thing, always in the way!"

"She won't be asked to our whist-party next week," Esther whispered in reply.

How strange, I thought, when Belinda and Esther are always so gracious and patronizing to me when at home!

"Only a whiff of the 'world's air,' my little friend," said Carey, looking at my flushed face; he had heard the remarks and seen my annoyance. "Some people do not like to see the budding roses of their neighbors, when their own are getting faded," he added, when we were at a safe distance from the sisters. "You must not allow those jealous remarks to spoil your evening's pleasure."

There was no danger of my evening being spoiled when I met such approbation and encouragement in his eyes; when he took such pains to make me forget and to interest me in conversation.

And then when Jonas Gould came for me, it was Carey Chapman who met me in the hall and led me to the old farm-wagon, lifting me in with more than brotherly care, and raising my ungloved hand to his lips under cover of the darkness, with such deference as might have been given to a princess. And was it strange that a girl, scarcely nineteen, should hold the hand which had received such honor to her flushed cheek, and turn over in her bewildered, happy thoughts, the looks and words which had so dazzled her?

"He's a smooth-tongued chap," said our honest, outspoken Jonas, when we had rode in silence more than half way home. Jonas had served us faithfully several years in my father's lifetime, and was privileged above his position.

"Who? What did you say?" I asked, roused from my sweet reveries.

"I say that Carey Chapman is a smooth-tongued chap, and you mustn't mind nothing about his soft sayings. If you had a father or a brother, may be I wouldn't dare say as much, but there never was an honester man than David Kendall, and he told me just afore he died always to serve you true and faithful."

"And you've given good heed to his words, Jonas," I replied, when the blunt man's voice became husky, and there was an awkward pause.

"Wa'al I've tried to, but I shouldn't be more'n half doin' my duty, if I saw a young gal like you gettin' in love with a harnsome feller as is courtin' half a dozen may be besides. Ezra Smith, the Square's hired man, says as how young Chapman is there hangin' round Virginny as often as twice a week, and Sam Atkins that used to go to the same district school with Carey and me, and is workin' at his trade now in Wiltshire, says he may be seen a'most any day gallivantin' round with old Judge Southby's harnsome daughter. You see there are plenty of young men now-a-days that want to get all the girls in love with them, and then they've only to go and pick out the harnsomest and richest, and all the rest may whistle."

I made no reply, but the words of Jonas had brought

my thoughts for the minute down from the rose-colored clouds. Mr. Chapman might like Virginia and admire her beauty and vivacity, I thought; and it was only natural that he should often be Miss Southby's escort—he was her father's partner in business; but I was too happy in the young love and strong faith of my dawning womanhood to believe that Carey Chapman could have just such another "little friend" as he was pleased to call me. Doubt might for an hour eclipse my sunshine, but it was only truth's shadow. "Who never doubted, never half believed."

CHAPTER XXXIX.

FIRST ATTEMPT AT AUTHORSHIP.

"He who could not sit
And sing contented in a desert isle,
His audience the mute trees and wandering winds,
His joy the grace and beauty of his song,
Should never lift his voice 'mong mortal men."
ALEXANDER SMITH.

I SAW that mother did not quite approve of the proposed German lessons, when I told her of Mr. Chapman's willingness to instruct Virginia and myself, and thought it wise to make no mention of the moral philosophy which would be taken in payment.

"You know Professor Roeder will give you lessons in German as well as in French and music, if you have time for so many studies," mother said, with one of those searching looks which seemed to read my very thoughts.

"Then I ought to make remarkable progress, if I have two lessons a week from a professor, and review them under such a scholarly eye as Carey Chapman's. I am sure Virginia will feel disappointed if I do not find time to study with her, and I would rather get up an hour earlier each morning than not take those lessons."

"You must not attempt so much that nothing can be well done, Hope; and remember, I shall rely upon you for more help in teaching than I did last year."

"You will always find I shall have time to give you all the assistance that you need."

There was a short pause, and mother sat with a shadow of troubled thought resting upon her face and veiling her eyes, while I sewed upon my old blue merino, which mother had cut over for Sophie, furtively glancing now and then at the dear face opposite me. There was a tender tremor in her voice when she spoke:

"Hope, I'm anxious to see you a self-reliant, independent woman—" I knew mother had not finished her sentence, by her abrupt pause.

"And you've always done your best to make me one Have I not profited by your instructions?"

"Yes; but I have often doubted, during the last year, whether a teacher's profession will develop your best capabilities. Your father said once, when speaking of your letters to him, 'Hope has a very agreeable and easy way of saying things, and might make her pen of great use;' and while you were at Hebron your letters reminded me of your father's expression. Has it never occurred to you that your thoughts might be made marketable?"

"Once, last summer, when we were reading of Jean Paul Richter, I thought that perhaps some time our own poverty might be a stimulus for me, and that thought has haunted me ever since. But, mother, teaching will make me self-reliant, and I am sure it will always be an agreeable profession."

"But the time may come when we shall need more

means than we can earn in teaching, or when you will need some more stimulating and exciting employment, in which to bury your dead hopes."

"I have none, mother."

"No; and God grant that you never may have! but I have known very few women to whom Sorrow did not come sooner or later; 'tis said to be the twin-sister of Love. You know that in a few years Willie must be sent from home to school, if he shows any desire for an education, and that will greatly increase our expenses. With the limited number of pupils which we can take in this house, we can do little more than meet our yearly wants, without setting aside any thing for sickness or old age."

"You have been overworked, dear mother, and that is why you are less hopeful than usual."

"I am not wanting in hope or courage, but it is well for us sometimes to look at bare facts; if looked at in the right spirit, they will only prove incentives to cheerful exertion. Why not try your skill in writing a little sketch this week?"

"What shall I write about?"

"You could hardly do better than write a simple description of Ellen Hopkinson's short life."

"But, mother, I should be so ashamed and discouraged, if no publisher would accept my offerings."

"You should not be, but only whet the sword of your spirit anew; and then, if you entirely fail in your attempts to write, you have still teaching left as a resort. I have a school-friend in Philadelphia, who has earned an enviable reputation with her pen, and she has a most generous heart, as well as an extensive acquaintance with editors and publishers. I could intrust your sketches to her; and if she could not find an editor willing to pay a small sum for them, she would at least keep your secret."

I dared not show mother what bright and beautiful visions her words had called up; but as we sat by the glowing wood-fire, I saw many a possible castle in the future—many comforts and luxuries, which might be purchased with the products of my pen; and then, crowning all, I even dared hope that I might leave "footprints in the sands of time," might make a name worthy of being written on the same page with Mrs. Stowe's, Miss Warner's, and Miss Cummins's. I even went so far as to lay the warp of my first story, and wonder how it would look in print.

"Mother," I said, throwing down the blue merino, "if my attempts in writing are successful, I mean to write a story one of these days, and my best character shall be a step-mother; not a selfish, disagreeable one, as every novel-writer makes. You shall be my heroine."

"Thank you for the compliment, Hope, but you might find a more worthy subject for your pen."

"I doubt if I could find a more abused and misrepresented subject. Did you ever know a step-mother to figure in print who was not artful, jealous, ill-natured, and cruel?"

"They are too frequently unwomanly in character, else they would not so often suffer in print. If a woman is naturally selfish, the position of step-mother will develop that trait, and every one will be watching for its manifestations and exaggerating the fault; but if she is a warm-hearted, sensible, self-sacrificing woman, loving her husband, his children will be dear to her, and their helpless, half-orphaned dependence will draw out all the tender, motherly instincts of her better nature. I have seen unjust, intriguing step-mothers, but they were women who would have been so in any position; and I have seen noble, Christian women, patiently fulfilling a mother's mission, striving to gain the confidence of children who had been poisoned with tales of cruel step-mothers."

"Won't it be pleasant to step aside from the beaten path of story-writers, and show that a woman can be tender and loving and generous to children that are not her own? What a busy winter we shall have!"

And what a busy, bright, and beautiful winter it proved! There were cares and trials, to be sure, connected with our teaching, but we brought courage and cheerfulness and willing hands to the work. German and French were learned with an eagerness and facility which quite astonished mother; she did not know that my ambition was prompted and inspired, and every faculty of mind quickened, with the sweet hope of pleasing Carey Chapman. I could have overcome much greater obstacles, encouraged with his approbation.

Virginia took up the German language with a will and relish quite inexplicable to me, unless, indeed, as sometimes I fancied, she too was desirous of pleasing our mutual friend. His attentions to us both were so alike, so brotherly, that, had I not been favored with an occasional clasp of the hand or tender phrase when we were left for a minute alone, my quiet happiness would have been ruffled with jealous doubts.

Was this new, sweet, delicious joy in the friendship and companionship of Carey Chapman, love? I often questioned my heart, but its answer was unsatisfactory. That my self-love was flattered, my fancy dazzled, and my affections interested, I was sure; but while there was a want of confidence in Mr. Chapman's honesty, the deepest fountains of my nature were not likely to be moved. And, fortunately, my mind was so agreeably and constantly occupied during the winter, that my affections had less time for taking deep and permanent root.

My first attempt in writing was commended by mother's friend, and her influence secured its acceptance in a respectable magazine. With what intoxicating joy I learned of its success! what a flower-crowned and gold-bespread path of usefulness seemed open to me! And yet the article upon which I had spent days of thought and many hours of mechanical labor, only brought me three dollars, and a copy of the magazine for a year, in what the world would call payment; but I received the richest of all remunerations for a young aspirant, encouragement to climb the hill.

Mother's friend wrote: "Tell your daughter that I think her little story very pleasantly and gracefully told, in fact, extremely well written; and that I trust I can dispose of as many articles as she will find time to produce, if they are all written in as natural, artless, and graceful a style as her first."

Those encouraging words were worth vastly more to me than money; and in the fulness of my grateful joy I could only lay my head upon mother's lap and weep. My joys crowned each other in such completeness that they "waded in tears."

"Have you thanked God, my child, for the gift of a ready pen?" asked mother, as she lifted the brown hair from my forehead, and kissed it.

"I have tried to."

"Now, in the very beginning of your career, entreat Him for a blessing on every line you write, and resolve that, however great the temptation, you will never utter a sentiment unworthy the pen of a Christian woman; and never throw off an article hastily, for the sake of the price it will bring, but write with such earnest thought and care that your talent may honor the Giver."

"Mother, I would like to tell just one person what a pleasant and useful future seems opening to me, because I had so many talks with him last fall about books and work, and the right way of using our powers; and as I have never thanked him for his Christmas gift, do you think I might send the magazine in such a way that he would know who wrote the article about little Ellen?"

"Certainly, if you would like to give him a pleasant surprise; and then, as you took the same stanza for your text in writing which he took for the subject of his brush, it would be only just for you to give him the picture you have painted in words. Shall you tell Virginia and Carey Chapman?"

"Not yet—not until I feel more certain of my ability to write acceptably. I could not endure Carey's sarcastic raillery about the 'indigo tinge,' as I have heard him call articles from a woman's pen. He thinks it much more important that a woman should be ornamental than useful."

"There is no reason why use and ornament, or good common sense and accomplishments, may not be found in one character, and I trust that some day you will be an example of their happy combination."

The spring brought changes to our household. Mr. and Mrs. Mayhew returned from Europe in April, and took up their residence in Philadelphia, and Dora and Annie, who had become very dear to us, were taken home. They were so much pleased with the improvement in their daughters, that I was invited to become their governess, but declined, thinking I could be more useful to mother by remaining with her to teach in our family school, and also secure more time for writing. Our family school was getting so favorably known through the influence of Mrs. Fairchild and other friends, that we had no difficulty in keeping our rooms full of pupils; and as long as we had work enough of this kind, we could give our anxieties about money matters to the winds.

Mr. Mayhew had added one hundred dollars to his last payment in consideration of mother's increased care during the illness of his daughter; and this, with what she had been able to save from her winter's earnings, enabled her to redeem the watch, and pay for the furnishing of our new rooms. But my ambition was far from satisfied—the parlor carpet was faded and worn, the cane-seat chairs gave abundant testimony of their long service, and almost every article of household furniture told tales of Poverty's harsh reign. The addition to our family of eight frolicsome young girls had not improved the appearance of the furniture, which was showing signs of hard usage before their advent. I longed to see the dear old rooms in a new and tidy dress; the floors so covered and the walls so ornamented, that the eye would be pleased and cheered whenever it rested upon them.

The removal of Mr. Mayhew's piano was a severe loss to us. Music was the only study or accomplishment which my dear half-sister could hope to excel in. She was so delicate in health, and her eyes had suffered so severely from the effects of scarlet fever that any thing like a severe course of study was not to be thought of; a piano, then, was almost a necessity, inasmuch as we had several pupils who wished to practise music besides Sophie and myself, and the expense of buying one and refurnishing the south chamber from which Mrs. Mayhew's furniture had been removed, was all that mother dared incur during the spring—and that involved the anticipation of quarterly payments not due until June. Debt was still our great bugbear, and much as we desired to improve and beautify our home, we purchased only such articles as were necessary for the prosperity of our school.

Spring brought me more than its accustomed gifts of freshness and bloom—it brought me many rainbow-hued fancies and ribbons of thought, which gushed forth sometimes in metrical numbers, but more frequently were woven into prose tales, which, if they lacked finish, depth, and maturity of thought, were at least fresh and artless. Poverty and a warm, unselfish love for my step-mother and her children, were the only stimulants which my pen needed.

CHAPTER XL.

DEMOLISHED AIR-CASTLES.

> "I've waked and slept through many nights and days
> Since then,—but still that day will catch my breath
> Like a nightmare. There are fatal days, indeed,
> In which the fibrous years have taken root
> So deeply, that they quiver to their tops
> Whene'er you stir the dust of such a day."
> MRS. BROWNING.

It was the last of May, and the month wore its loveliest crown of apple-blossoms—beauty and freshness everywhere met the eye, while the woods were all astir with a flutter of wings and a twitter of songs. The air, too, was laden with the sweet month's most bewildering odors, and my young heart, beating in harmony with the music of the day, my feet naturally turned into the by-path which led to the village. I was going to Squire Thornton's library for the weekly German lesson which had become one of my chief delights, and my thoughts were busy with the poem which was our lesson for this day.

"Ich habe geliebt und geleibet," I repeated, as my feet lightly touched the tender new grass, keeping time with the rhythm of the poem.

"Hope, you gray bird, how dare you mope through this lovely old wood with your eyes fastened on that book?" and Virginia sprang forward from a mossy knoll by the old log bridge, where she had been waiting for me.

"I was just looking over the poem we were to translate to-day, but I have been giving the woods their full share of my time and thoughts."

"As if you could, and read a German poem too! Why it is the most perfect day that ever I have known, and my birthday too. You should have paid me the compliment to remember it, and have worn a holiday dress in honor of the occasion. That old gray gown isn't in keeping with the season's blossoms, and yet you are looking well, dear Hope, so bright and happy that you need no ornaments. Sit down here on this knoll; I want to tell you something."

"Hadn't we better walk along? You can talk as we go, and then Mr. Chapman won't be kept waiting."

"No—I told him not to wait for us; I'm not going to spend any part of this beautiful day in reading German," and Virginia pulled me to a seat beside her on the bank, while I looked at her fair face to see if I could read there the "something" which she had to tell. It was full of sunshine as the day, and crowned with a fairer, tenderer beauty than I had ever noted before; the blue depths of her eyes seemed softly shaded by some happy thought, and with a blushing, conscious hesitation, she toyed with a diamond ring upon the white fore-finger of her left hand.

"Hope, do you see my birthday present?" she asked, holding up the finger for my inspection.

"I see, and 'tis very beautiful; I am glad that your twentieth birthday is made so pleasant for you."

"Oh, you are so matter-of-fact! Can't you guess what this ring worn on my forefinger means?"

"It means that your beautiful present fits only that

finger," I answered, though a dim perception of another significance to the ring was beginning to fill my thoughts with vague fears.

"I came out here on purpose to meet you and tell you something, and now you won't help me by asking a single question, and I've been longing to tell you ever since Christmas."

"What, dear Virginia?"

"I am engaged to Carey Chapman."

I had just time to see the droop of her lids and the deepening color of her cheeks, when, with a sudden impulse, she threw herself forward and hid her face in my neck. It was well perhaps that she had not the courage to lift her eyes to my face before she hid them; she would have seen no tears, but a sudden eclipse of all the joyous light which had flooded my soul a minute before, when walking over the green wood path I had softly murmured the words of a German poem. There was a sudden cessation of my heart's pulses—a choking sob in my throat, as my woman's nature rose up in rebellion against the hard fact.

What right had Carey Chapman to love another, when for months he had never met me without a look or a word which had seemed to claim me as his own. He had never said that he loved me, or that I was dearer to him than others were; but he had shown such a delicate consideration for me—such a tenderly protective bearing ever since that summer's day when I had brought him back to life, that my heart had almost instinctively turned toward him. For a few minutes the friend, whose happiness till then I had thought dear to me as my own, was repulsive and hateful. I could have thrust her from my arms. It was not enough that she was beautiful while I was plain—that she was rich and I was poor, but she had come between me and the love which might have blessed me.

Alas! what a gulf of separation yawned between us now! On her side beauty and fragrance without stint, love and happiness without measure; on my side a barren waste, a hard, matter-of-fact struggle with poverty. Tears would have been a relief, or even words; but only that dry, gasping sob, which threatened to choke, came instead.

Virginia, in the fulness of her joy, did not miss my words, but still hiding her blushing happiness against my bosom, she softly whispered:

"I have known that he loved me since Christmas. Do you remember that I was glad because you said my dress was becoming, and that I looked beautiful to you? Well, Carey had told me that day for the first time that he loved me, and I never cared so much before about my looks. I did so want to tell you, but father said I must not, for he wasn't quite satisfied with Carey, and didn't wish us to be engaged. It was not until to-day that he gave him permission to put this upon my finger, and you are the first person I've told about my great happiness. Dear Hope, kiss me and wish me joy."

Could I refuse the request of such a timid, tearful pleader! No; I lifted the golden-brown hair from her low, white forehead, and touched it with my lips. The act unloosed my tongue; and, with a half sob, I exclaimed, "God bless you!"

"I knew you would be so glad, dear Hope, for we've always been such friends. Carey has been a little jealous of you since I gave him the right to think of me as his own; but I tell him that you are my sister and best friend, next to father and himself, and I shall always claim the privilege of loving you just as dearly as when we were little girls and gathered flowers and nuts in these old woods.. You'll never love me any less, dear Hope?"

"No, never;" and I lifted my heart in prayer for help to keep that promise.

"It has been so hard sometimes for me to keep my secret from you, because I had no mother to talk over every thing with, as you have; and when my heart is so full of happiness, I want some one to share it with me. I began to like Carey as long ago as when we rode to Switzerland, and I more than half believed that he liked me too, though he never said so in words until Christmas morning, when he came into our library, which I was trimming with holly, and asked me if I would accept a Christmas gift from him; and I said 'yes,' not thinking what he meant, till he said I must give him something in return; and when I looked up at him I knew just what he was going to say. You are crying, dear Hope!"

"Never mind;" but the drops that fell upon her hair softened the bitterness of my grief, and washed from my heart all resentment against the dear friend who had so unconsciously stolen what I had coveted as my heritage.

Words can never paint the miserable humiliation and disappointment of that hour, nor the great effort necessary to sit upon that bank and listen to the shyly told happiness of Virginia. It would require strength of will and charity to meet calmly the woman who had been blessed with a boon denied yourself, but to hear from her lips the story which was filling your own heart with darkness and desolation required almost more than human strength; and while my friend's joy rippled forth in music, my despairing cry went up to heaven, "Help, oh, help me drink this cup!"

When the blushing face was raised, and the happy eyes looked up into my own, they could read there nothing of the last hour's history. My face had never much color, and if it were paler than its wont, Virginia saw it only through the rose-tinted veil of her own sweet joy.

"You do not seem quite as glad as I thought you would, Hope, but I suppose you are tired. Some day you will know what a great joy it is to be loved."

"Perhaps; but I expect nothing."

"You are so grave and quiet, I dare say you could live on, studying and teaching, and never dream of a sweeter life; but I should die without love."

"May you never feel its want, Virginia!"

"Thank you for the prayer. I wish I was as good and sensible as you are, and then I should deserve to be happy. I wonder Carey should have chosen me, for he knows just how superficial my education has been; but he says there'll be great pleasure in teaching me. 'Tis fortunate that I cared enough for music to learn that thoroughly, because he's so fond of it, and has such a well-cultivated ear and such fastidious taste. Now, Hope, there'll be no time for German to-night, and I'm going to walk home with you. I told Carey that he might call at your mother's for me this evening."

So soon! If I could have put off meeting him until I had had a little longer time to look my sorrow in the face —time to bury my dead hopes and roll a stone over their grave; but now pride and a woman's strength of will must be my shield. If, in my simplicity, I had almost unconsciously shown a pleased interest in his lightest words, if my flushed face and drooping eyes had often given him the welcome which his vanity desired, he should now see that only the surface had been moved by fancies lighter than a summer breeze. I had yet to learn that "the price one pays for pride is mountain-high."

We walked back over the forest-path, which I had trod so lightly an hour ago; but where was the scent of blossoms? where was the fresh beauty of the day? and why had the birds ceased twittering in the trees?

Virginia's words rippled in waves of music, but she never dreamed that they were ploughing deeply into the tender soil of my heart, or that love and happiness, looked at through her eyes, were to me only the ghosts of what "might have been."

"Come, Hope, help me gather a bouquet. It is a pity to leave so many blossoms to waste their fragrance. I thought you never went over this path without stopping to gather something."

"I always stop unless I am greatly hurried, because mother is so fond of flowers; and when there are none, she likes to have ferns and leaves in our vases. I saw great quantities of blue and yellow violets as I came along."

"And where are your eyes now? We can find oceans of them on every sunny bank!"

I went to work, mechanically gathering the delicate little wild flowers, blue, and white, and yellow, enriching the cluster with pink lady's slipper and fragrant fern. When we reached home, the arrangement of them, with Virginia's lively flow of words, so diverted mother's attention from me that she saw no heavier shadows on my pale face than fatigue or headache often left there; and taking refuge behind my friend's volubility, my silence was unheeded.

Carey Chapman came in with even more than his accustomed easy assurance. His distant cousinship to mother had been accepted most unwillingly by her as an excuse for the familiarity with which he came and went.

"Cousin Hope is losing her roses," he said, retaining my hand as he often did; but very seldom had he called me cousin before. If the address were intended to show me that any previous little tendernesses were but the prerogatives of cousinship, he was rewarded; for I seized upon the hint to control my actions and words.

"And the loss of them being but the fulfilment of your prophecy, must in a measure gratify you," I replied, with as much of Virginia's light, playful manner as I dared attempt to imitate. "You will soon be reminding me that 'the world's air has warped my way.'"

"But why should I be gratified to see the fulfilment of my prophecy?"

"A man's self-esteem would be shocked if his predictions were not verified, and he would soon begin to doubt his own infallibility; which, to say the least, would not be pleasant."

"Behold what the world's air has already accomplished! Six months ago my little Cousin Hope did not deal in sarcasm."

"Please remember that I had not been favored with your instructions six months ago."

"Have I taught you any thing not found in German text books?" The question was asked with that steel-blue eye of his scanning the changing color of my face.

"I have been told that a good teacher is never confined to text-books, and I should certainly be a dull pupil if I had learned only German from you."

"You have learned nothing which you regret?"

"Only this morning I read in one of Miss Proctor's poems, that 'Life has nobler uses than regret.' Mine, at least, if it has not noble uses, will have stern, practical ones."

"And you will meet every duty with the same brave courage that prompted you to follow the leadings of my dog one summer day?"

"With more real courage, I trust."

"Did you translate the poem selected for this evening's reading?"

"Yes: and liked the poetry, not the sentiment. The

German maiden should not have prayed for death because she had lived and loved. True heroism accepts pain as a necessary part of life's discipline. But speaking of German reminds me, Mr. Chapman, that I shall have no more time for our evening lessons."

" Why not?"

" Professor Roeder gives me quite enough to do in German, and I need my evenings for practice."

" And for the weaving of such pretty fancies as I find in the last number of Harper? You need not turn away your face to hide its tell-tale color, for I became possessed of your secret lawfully. The lady who disposes of the products of your pen is visiting at Judge Southby's; and, meeting her in company last evening, I had the unspeakable happiness of hearing my little friend's talents eulogized in a most gratifying way. You were very fortunate in being introduced to publishers by so successful and generous a woman as Mrs. Gordon."

" Please do not speak of what I am doing."

" Then you are not writing for fame?"

" No. You are well aware that poverty makes it necessary for mother and myself to turn every available talent into money."

" And 'fine thoughts are wealth, for the right use of which men are accountable.' I expect to say of you, as Festus said of his friend:

> 'One there was,
> From whose sweet lips elapsed, as from a well,
> Continuously, truths which made my soul,
> As they sank in it, fertile with rich thought.'"

" You are not serious; and I remember that 'praise undeserved is satire in disguise.' I only hope, with diligent study and practice, to write so acceptably that we may not be entirely dependent on teaching; and, if God permits, I should like to have the satisfaction of knowing that a few hearts are strengthened and cheered by my pen."

Virginia's playful reminder that our conversation was too exclusive was very welcome, as my forced calmness was fast ebbing away under the searching eyes that seemed to read my very thoughts.

Carey Chapman turned toward mother, saying:

"Your friend Mrs. Gordon is visiting at Judge Southby's, and proposes spending a day with you, if agreeable, before returning to Philadelphia. I will take your answer to her to-morrow."

"Tell her it will give me great pleasure to see her. She was a dear friend of my school-days, and will always be a welcome guest."

At last they were gone, and I was free to seek the solitude of my own room, where I might look unshrinkingly at my withered hopes. Not only my present pain, but the desolate, barren path of the future, threw its dark shadows around me. I did not know that the soil of the heart, after pain has burnt out its weeds, produces an abundant harvest of peace, nor that

"Grief is joy misunderstood."

CHAPTER XLI.

RACHEL SHAW'S STORY.

> "I thank Thee more that all our joy
> Is touched with pain;
> That shadows fall on brightest hours,
> That thorns remain;
> So that earth's bliss may be our guide
> And not our chain."
>
> MISS PROCTOR.

IF mother saw that a great sorrow lay heavily upon my heart she wisely kept silence. I could not have borne sympathy even from her for the first few days after I had learned of Carey Chapman's want of truth and honor. My heart was in the furnace of pain, and I prayed that God would bring it forth purified as gold by heat. During those days of darkness and desolation, I despised myself for the vanity and presumption which had so blinded me, quite as much as I blamed Mr. Chapman for his flattering and meaningless attentions. My womanly instincts told me that he had no right to take advantage of my simplicity, and win my love just for the poor and pitiable triumph of testing his power; but still I blushed when I thought how I had magnified his cousinly attentions—what trifles I had seized to build my hopes upon. And when I had learned to look back calmly upon our acquaintance, tearing from my eyes the veil through which I had gazed, I saw that

> "When faith is lost, when honor dies,
> The man is dead."

He, whose easy and polished manners had captivated my fancy, whose scholarly attainments had won my respect, was suddenly bereft of more than half his attractions because I saw that vanity and self-esteem were the warp of his character, and that ambition was fast filling in the woof, while there were not threads enough of truth and noble purpose to give the web consistency and coloring. Was my vision cleared by seeing that the grapes were too high, and as a matter of course sour? Had Carey offered me the love in which my friend was rejoicing, should I have seen through the cold, steel-like polish of his exterior, and detected the lack of honesty and manliness?

Doubtless I should have gone blindly forward until some accident had shown me that only perfect confidence in a man's stability and integrity can be taken by woman as a foundation to build her love upon. If I moved about mechanically during those days, still every duty was bravely met, and many hours were found to sit with old Mrs. Shaw, whose life was quietly ebbing away. Her poor tired daughter was much in need of all the assistance which friends and neighbors could give. She had passed the noon-time of life, and all its freshness and strength had been given to her invalid mother, whose age and feebleness were soon to be exchanged for eternal youth. The patience, cheerfulness, and piety of Miss Shaw under the crushing hand of poverty and sickness, taught me lessons which the history of a lifetime can never efface. She might have seen with that keenness of vision which suffering brings to woman, that my heart was under a cloud, that the buoyancy and elasticity of my life was crushed, for she told me once when we sat watching the restless sleep of her mother, some passages from her own sad history, which I intuitively felt were brought out from the storehouse of her memories, only to comfort and strengthen me.

"Is it the first day of June, Miss Hope?" she asked, turning from the window where her faded eyes had been resting on the golden clouds of sunset and the blossoming trees.

" Yes; the first of June."

" It is always a beautiful season, but the scent of apple-blossoms brings up very vividly the memory of a great trial, which has left its coloring on my whole life."

She gazed silently upon the wan face of her mother for a few minutes, and my reverence for her was so great that I dared not break the silence. Presently she spoke—

" I feel moved to tell you a little of my history, and it may do us both good if I can bring myself to speak of it. Thirty years ago—I was young then, Hope, not much older than you are now, and very unlike what you have ever known me—a young man came into our village to spend a summer. He came from Savannah, to recover from the effects of a fever, and boarded with his uncle, old Dr. Howe, who died long before you were born. Mother had just injured her spine by a fall, and everybody knew she must be confined to her bed as long as she lived; and as we were poor, I was teaching the village school, and sewing after school hours to support her. All the neighbors loved mother, and tried to lighten the burden of her confinement, and I suppose Dr. Howe brought in his nephew more to amuse her than because the young man needed such humble society as ours. Sherman Howe was a good reader and well-supplied with such books as we rarely saw in our village, and after a few visits he proposed to read aloud to mother and myself while I sewed. Well, he soon grew so familiar with us that he would come to my school-room door to walk home with me; and before the summer was over, Hope, I knew that he loved me, and that my own heart was far from indifferent to him. But much as I longed for the support and protection of his love, I dared not allow my affections to go out toward him, for something told me his love was too selfish to be burdened with my invalid mother. He went back to Savannah late in October, without having said in words that he loved me, but his looks and manners had not left me in doubt. He gave me the books we had read together, and if it had not been for those and the letters which came twice a month, I should have had a dreary winter. He wrote such beautiful letters, dear Hope, and praised the industry with which I read, until his commendation became so sweet and pleasant, that the loss of it made my trial very bitter at last. He came again in May, when the apple-trees were white with blossoms and the spring was just as beautiful as now, and asked me to be his wife.

"'I cannot leave mother,' was my only answer.

"'But, Rachel, your mother cannot travel, and I want to take you to Paris, that while I am finishing my medical studies, you may be acquiring accomplishments, so that I shall not fear to introduce you to my sisters and my Southern friends. I can afford to hire a nurse for your mother, and I am sure she would never ask you to spend your life in attendance upon her.'

"No; if mother had known that love and wealth and protection had been offered me, she would have added the weight of her own entreaties to Sherman's; but I determined to spare her the pain which a knowledge of my sacrifice would give her. I knew that even with his love I could not be happy, if she were left to strangers; and no matter how strongly my heart plead for him, I was firm. And then he accused me of want of love, and in his disappointment said harsh things and left me in anger. For months my poor heart seemed crushed with its weight of sorrow, and in its hunger for the love which had been laid aside, cried out against my judgment. But the merciful Father pitied my weakness and brought me out of the cloud, purified, I trust, but certainly so strengthened that I have been able to bear the burdens of life with patience and cheerfulness." Miss Shaw paused, and I ventured to look up at her face, in the new light which her words had thrown over it. She was past fifty, and her long years of watching and hard struggling had left their traces on her hair and face; but I saw that in youth she might have been handsome. That she was intelligent and lady-like I had long known. How beautiful and heroic her faded features looked to me now, and how insignificant my own trials seemed, compared with hers! And while we watched the fluttering breath of the sleeper, hushed and awed by the mysterious Presence which we felt to be so near, Rachel Shaw spoke of the blessedness which her great sacrifice had brought her—of the peace and rest she had found under the shadow of God's wings.

"I have never mentioned this portion of my history since the death of old Dr. Howe," she said in conclusion; "and I think one reason why I've been moved to tell you to-night, is that you may be surer of the promise that, though 'weeping may endure for a night, yet joy cometh in the morning.'"

I thanked her for the confidence, and walked home in the soft gray twilight, rejoicing in the strength which her words had inspired. If my heart had lost its animating hopes, if the light which had been my beacon during the winter and spring had suddenly vanished, I found that I had strength and courage enough left to grapple with the realities of life—light enough to warn me of its shoals and quicksands.

During the night, while Mrs. Eveleth watched with Rachel Shaw, the death-angel came and released the weary invalid. The poor, patient daughter folded the still hands and closed the eyes of her dead mother, and sat down uncomplaining with her grief. What had she to live for now? I wondered if her thoughts did not wander off to that beautiful Southern home, where a strong man sat with his fair wife and children, and if she did not sigh for the love which had once been offered her. But no murmurs escaped from her thin lips, and but few tears fell from her faded eyes. Trust and submission were the guests that occupied the otherwise empty chambers of her heart. After a few days she took up her needle again, patiently working for her own bread; but wherever there was a sick child, or an overworked mother, or suffering of any kind, there might the quiet face and tender hands of Rachel Shaw be found. Life, for her, had lost its sweetness and bloom; but, looking forward with strong faith to the "fulness of joy in Christ's presence," she was

"Only waiting till the shadows
Were a little longer grown."

Mrs. Leigh Gordon made her promised visit; and, next to mother and Rachel Shaw, I was more largely indebted to her for my returning cheerfulness, than to any one else. She was a charming woman, in the prime of her summer-time, with a face not so remarkable for its features as its expression. The light of a pure, truthful spirit and noble purpose animated it. She had been left a widow while yet a girl in years, and having been the wife of a literary man, and extensively known in literary circles, the fruits of her ready, graceful pen never begged for a market; and when she had won for herself a comfortable income, and one of the most honored and loved names in American literature, it was her pride and delight to assist others, especially young women, by her own encouragement, and by sending their efforts, with a note of commendation, to some editor of her acquaintance.

It was my pleasant privilege, during the week of Mrs.

Gordon's visit, to be the companion of her walks, and with the assistance of Mr. Chapman's horse and chaise, which had been generously offered for the use of our guest, to show her the beautiful scenery in and around Sherbrooke. Mother must have known that I needed the refreshing and cheering of just such a person as Mrs. Gordon, else she would not have contrived for us so many solitary walks and drives; and Mrs. Gordon, seeing me, as she supposed, a little weary and overworked, strove to refresh me and divert my thoughts from their every-day channels. She gave me the history of her own girlhood, and many charming descriptions of city life—told in a racy way of her first interviews with editors and publishers, and of the books, persons, and incidents which had helped form her character and shape her life.

"You know, my dear, that one of our best authors says, 'Men may rise on stepping-stones of their dead selves to higher things,'" said Mrs. Gordon as we were slowly returning by the forest-path from the village. "I was just reminded of that quotation by seeing those fresh twigs of willow, growing out of that old stump. I know that a new life may often spring from the ashes of an old one, and the new growth may be as unlike the old, as those tender sprouts of willow are unlike the decayed branches which were cut away. I had lived very carelessly and uselessly until I met Mr. Gordon, and then I was too happy during my short married life to think of being more than attractive and pleasing to him. When God took from me the idol I was worshipping, I thought for many months that I could not live without the love, the protecting tenderness, which he had given me. Tennyson says:

> 'When love is grown
> To ripeness, that on which it throve
> Falls off, and love is left alone.'

For many months love and grief only were left to me; but in God's own good time, grief wept itself away, and to the earthly love were added Hope, and Faith, and Charity, and out of that charity grew strength to endure, and courage to work for others. You have a great gift, Miss Hope, and it pleases me to see you using it so cheerfully and self-denyingly."

"I should never have thought of writing, if the necessities of mother's family had not been so great; and then, had it not been for your encouragement, I doubt if I could have gained sufficient courage to have sent an article to the papers."

"The merit of your sketches alone, without any introduction of mine, would have procured them a market. Have you ever thought of writing any thing longer and more pretending than these magazine articles?"

"I have hoped that when I have read and studied more, and have had the experience of two or three more years, I might attempt greater things."

"How old are you?"

"Nineteen."

"But remarkably mature for that age, as indeed almost any girl would have been, trained by such a mother; and then your surroundings have helped mature and develop your character earlier than if you had seen no necessity for courage and exertion. I have noticed the tact and judgment with which you instruct and amuse your mother's pupils, and I think you may excel in writing a book for young girls, something that would be suitable for Sabbath School Libraries. If you succeed as well with it as you have with your sketches, I think there will be no difficulty in obtaining a publisher."

Mrs. Gordon went on talking in her pleasing, encouraging way, until we reached mother's door, when she paused, and looking into my face with her earnest eyes, said half playfully:

"You must lay aside your German for the present, as I shall only give you until the Christmas holidays to write the first two hundred pages of your book for girls, and then you must come to my home in Philadelphia for a visit, and I will review the manuscript with you before you copy or rewrite it."

And so it was settled, before Mrs. Gordon left us, that if we were prospered, I should go to Philadelphia for the holidays.

Before the fading of the June roses I was at work upon a story for girls, seizing every spare hour for this purpose, and always carrying about with me a scrap of paper and a pencil, that I might be prepared to add a few lines or even words, when a minute's leisure permitted. When a chapter was finished mother listened to the reading of it, commending where she could, but faithfully pointing out inaccuracies and exuberancies of style; and as little by little the pages of manuscript increased, I gained in strength and courage, for I found that new hopes and joys were springing from the ashes of my buried love. I was rising on the "stepping-stone of my dead self to higher things," and found that I had no place for regret in my busy life.

CHAPTER XLII.

NEWS FROM HEBRON.

"Neither call the giddiness of it in question, the poverty of her, the small acquaintance, my sudden wooing, nor her sudden consenting; but say with me, I love Aliena; say with her that she loves me."—SHAKESPEARE.

"HEBRON, June 28, 185-.

"MY DEAR HOPE:

"You have not heeded my last injunction, 'Thine own and thy father's friend forsake not.' It has been more than three months since I have heard from you, or seen any thing from your pen, excepting two or three articles in 'Harper's,' which Mr. Hamlin says are yours. I'm sorry you didn't consult Caleb or me before you commenced writing; but then I ought not to expect you to show any deference to our wishes when you are under your stepmother's influence. Caleb thinks well of your articles, but says you are very young to write for magazines, and that you ought not to publish any thing until it has been written at least a year. Your Uncle John is very much pleased with your writings, because, as he says, they are not made up of high-sounding phrases without any meaning, but are filled with common thoughts that people can understand.

"You ought to have good abilities, for both your father and mother were remarkable scholars. David used to write for the 'North American' and the 'Evening Courier;' but he was never half paid for the time he spent. I've always thought that writers were to be pitied. You know Job says, 'Oh, that mine enemy had written a book,' which shows plainly to my mind that he wouldn't have wished his friend to write one; and even Solomon says, 'He that increaseth knowledge, increaseth sorrow.' This passage probably refers to writers, for Solomon generally commended knowledge and wisdom to the young. I want you to write just as soon as you get this, and tell me how much you are paid for each article, and how many scholars Mrs. Kendall has, and how you manage to get a minute for study or writing, with all the work which must fall to your hands.

"I have an uncommon amount of news to tell you, or I shouldn't have taken a half day in strawberry time to write. In the first place, we have sent Mary to her mother's relations in York State. She was such a queer-tempered child that I never could understand her, and then her moping and idleness were worrying my life out; so Caleb was at last persuaded to give her to her mother's sister, a woman who has only one child, and so much property that she'll be likely to do well by Mary. There's one great load off my shoulders! You remember how much talk there was last fall about Deacon Sanborn and Smith Perry? Well, it came to such a pass in March that Smith was excluded, and of course he has left the sanctuary and taken his children from the Sabbath-school; but more than all, he refuses to pay his pew-tax, and as he gave more liberally for Caleb's support than any other member, it is rather hard work to raise the salary. In fact, Caleb would resign, because there's been such marked opposition to his antislavery views by a few prominent members; but I insist on his remaining, for, as I tell him, 'truth must conquer in the end.' It would be a pretty muss for me to leave my little property here, and go to a new field of labor, where, like as not, Caleb's views might clash again with some world-hardened politicians, who don't care a fig for the poor, down-trodden negroes, and who'd just as soon commune with men who buy and sell their own children and brothers, as not! I tell Caleb to remain upon the watch-towers here, proclaiming the truth, whether men will hear or not; and if bad comes to worse, I can use my own private income in helping out the salary, though, to be sure, I would much rather be laying it up for a rainy day.

"Adoniram Staples is working my farm again this year, and the crops look well. The grass is heavy and nearly ready for the scythe, and the fruit-trees promise a good yield; but there may be a drought or an early frost to disappoint our hopes. Adoniram's wife died in April and left five poor, helpless children. She'd been complaining for more'n a year; but folks thought she was only nervous and shiftless, and perhaps she didn't get all the sympathy she needed. Poor thing! she's better off now, for Caleb says she gave good evidence of a change of heart before she died. Whom do you think Adoniram has got to take care of his children? That very Matilda Crockett, with her long curls, who pretended to do Caleb's housework last year; and I've good reason to believe that she tried to catch Caleb too, the bold, impudent thing! a pretty minister's wife she'd have made! Folks will talk, you know, and Deacon Sanborn's wife told me yesterday she'd no doubt that Adoniram would marry Matilda before winter. She's been seen more than once carrying the baby into the field where Adoniram was hoeing, and I saw her hold it up for him to kiss one day when I was over there. I was so shocked that I could hardly help giving her a piece of my mind right on the spot; but you may be sure I gave her such a look as she'll remember to her dying day.

"Poor little Phil Craig is dead; and, if you'll believe it, his mother seems to feel as bad as if he'd been a promising child! Susie Staples went over to Mrs. Craig's just as she was coming down with the measles, and of course she gave them to the child, and Dr. Houghton said he hadn't vitality enough to throw off the disease; it appeared to settle on his lungs, and made short work with him. But I think 'tis a mercy he was taken, especially as there was no prospect of his ever making any thing. It was beautiful to see how devoted Mr. Hamlin was to his sister in her affliction; he certainly strives to fulfil the law of Christ by helping bear her burdens. She has seemed more than ever the light of his eyes since you served him so shamefully last fall; but as Caleb has always advised me not to scold you about that affair, I will let it drop now, only I must say your stubbornness provokes me not a little.

"Mr. Hamlin is going to spend the fall and winter in Philadelphia studying something, though for the life of me I can't see why he needs to study any more.

"Our trustees are looking for a teacher, but I've no faith to believe they'll ever find another as good and as faithful as Mr. Hamlin has been. I often tell him he's made the academy more like what it was when your father taught here than it has ever been since. I've already written a long letter, but I've kept the best piece of news for the last. Your cousin Lydia is going to be married in September to Rev. Jotham S. White of Eloth. She has been so foolishly shy, and has made so much fun of him ever since he exchanged with Caleb last January, that I never suspected she'd have him, though we knew he had taken a fancy to her. Your cousin Lydia is a good girl, but she gives no evidence of having chosen the better part, and for a minister to be unequally yoked with an unbeliever is a great pity! What an example he is setting for his brethren! But as I tell Caleb, 'every tub must stand on its own bottom,' and I've cleared the skirts of my garments by speaking my mind freely to both. There's no doubt the match will be a good one for Lydia; Mr. White is a rising man and well educated, Caleb says, and besides he's the only child of a deacon very well to do, but he has chosen a wife who'll be no helpmeet for him. She never has been willing to go to prayer and conference meetings, nor to the Sisters' Aid Society, and she's always making light of serious things, and putting off the day of grace till a more convenient season.

"It frightens me to think of her unfitness for such a sphere as a minister's wife is called to fill. Just think of her taking the lead in a sisters'-meeting, as I did yesterday, with twenty present all older than herself!

"But I've tried in vain to turn her from her purpose, and now I shall take hold and help her get ready. She'll be married in that embroidered muslin that your gran'ther brought from India, and I've a pattern of gray pongee that has been lying useless in my camphor-wood trunk ever since father's last voyage, which I shall give her for a travelling dress. It's so foolish to spend money in travelling as young married folks do now-a-days, but Lydia has set her heart on going to Niagara. She says she'll have to settle down into a grave minister's wife soon enough, and she's bound to see a little of the world first. She'll find it a vain show. Brother John is able to give Lydia a good fitting out, and he'll do it too, for he sets his eyes by her with all her flightiness. Such a stew as she has kept that minister in since last January! I've no doubt he's come clear from Eloth, a good ten miles, more'n twenty times if he has once, and never got a decided answer till last week, and she a-laughing about his pale face and hungry looks all the time!

"But she's sober enough since the thing was settled, and I can't help hoping she has a realizing sense of her unworthiness. Who knows but what ' her own works may yet praise her in the gates?' I've set together a patch-work quilt of buff and pink in a star pattern since you were here, which I shall give to Lydia, and I'm going to get our young members to make another, writing texts of scripture on the white squares—it will be such an appropriate gift to a minister's wife. You might send her a present of your own work, if your life wasn't worried out of you with so much teaching and fagging. Lydia says she shall write you herself in a few days. Caleb sends his regards; he's hard at work on an article for the 'Progressive Age.' I shall expect to hear from you next week, and mind that you tell me just how you are spending your time, and when we may expect to see you in Hebron.

"Your affectionate aunt,
"LYDIA HOPKINSON.'

This was my aunt's second letter only since her marriage, which fact accounts for its length and the amount of its news. The announcement of my cousin's engagement surprised me not a little. It seemed strange that she, so lively and fun-loving, should have been the choice of one so serious and grave as Mr. White had appeared to me. I tried to rejoice in my cousin's new happiness, and the effort brought a measure of cheerfulness to my own heart. A note from Lydia telling me how bright her future looked, soon followed my aunt's letter.

"Mr. White is not just the kind of man whom I've always fancied I should fall in love with," she wrote; "but then he's vastly too good for me, and I hope his wisdom and goodness will be sufficient for two, as I have taken especial pains to show him how entirely wanting I am in both these qualities, ever since he cared for me. What could have attracted him toward such a sinner as I am, will always be a mystery to me; but I hope I have enough of love and reverence for him, and a sufficient amount of common sense, never to make him repent of his choice. Strictly between you and me, Hope, I've always liked him better than any other young man ever since I first saw him; but I've been a great plague to him through the winter and spring, partly because I wanted him to see what I am, and partly because it was really very hard for me to decide that I could be tied to a minister and a country parish all my life. I'd like to live in a handsome, generous way, and be able to invite plenty of company to my house, and dress prettily, and go and come as I choose without feeling accountable to the whole church for every dollar I spend. And I suppose I could have lived very much as I liked, if I had married somebody else who took a fancy to me last winter; but I had seen Mr. White, and his pale face and serious eyes haunted me, and I couldn't get rid of the impression that his strength would be a shield for my weakness, and that with my hand in his I should be more likely to find 'the pearl of great price,' than I should alone, or with the guidance of a worldly man. Now, really, Hope, I mean to set about getting religion seriously as soon as our honeymoon is over, and I wouldn't wonder if in two or three years you should find me a pattern minister's wife, presiding at all sorts of sisters'-meetings in a gray gown and a gray bonnet without a flower or a feather, and with a face looking sober enough to be responsible for all the sins of the parish. Jotham says I can get religion without being so prim and disagreeable as a great many pious people are; and when I think how cheerful you and Mr. Hamlin and some other professing Christians are, why then I long to know your secret.

"What a lovely wife you'd make for a minister, Hope; such an excellent helpmeet, as Aunt Lydia would say.

You don't know how delighted we all are with the beautiful things you write for 'Harper's.' Father could hardly believe Mr. Hamlin when he told us what your signature was; but he's just as proud of you as he can be, and says, 'Tell Hope she's beholden to her step-mother's training for the ability to write so well,' and he sent another message too, something about your keeping clear of new-fangled notions of women's rights, but I don't exactly remember it.

"Now, Hope, I'm going to be married on my twentieth birthday, the tenth of September, and I want you should be my bridesmaid, and come at least a month beforehand, so that I can depend upon your taste in finishing up my dresses. Mother has hired a woman to help make quilts and blankets and all sorts of house-keeping things. She and Aunt Lydia seem bent upon filling the parsonage at Eloth so full that we shall never need any thing more if we live threescore and ten years. It seems to be such a comfort and pleasure to father and mother to be doing for me now, that I let them have every thing their own way. I know it will be hard enough for them to give me up, even if they do like Jotham, and think he's such a splendid match for me. You shall stand up with Mr. Hamlin, for he won't go to Philadelphia until after the tenth of September, especially if he thinks there'll be any chance of meeting you here. He's a great friend of Mr. White's, and if you and he could only just come to an understanding, it would be the loveliest arrangement and quite complete my happiness; for now that I'm really in love, I cannot bear to think of your spending your life in teaching and writing, without knowing the blessedness of loving and being loved, even if the world does praise you. I thought of you last night when Jotham was reading to me something out of 'Aurora Leigh' about—

'How dreary 'tis for women to sit still
On winter nights by solitary fires,
And hear the nations praising them far off,'

and I shuddered with fear lest you should be so wrapped up in your studies and writings, that at last you'd be left to a solitary fire and a desolate life. Come by the first of August, and leave all your books and gravity at home, for I mean to make my last month under my father's roof a merry one. Oh, I mustn't forget to tell you that my devoted minister is constantly setting traps for my improvement, requesting me to read this, that, and the other book; just as if there wouldn't be dull, mopish days enough after I am fairly caught, for him to use in improving my mind, till every thought will run in just such a narrow groove as Aunt Lydia would cut for it. It would be great fun for you to see how our good aunt leads her Caleb about. She's thrown so many proverbs at his head and so much chaff in his eyes, that he hardly dares wink without her permission; but they say he will write what he has a mind to when he gets his study to himself, the strongest articles on Equal Rights, Progress, Freedom of the Will, etc. I'm sure they look musty and disagreeable enough, but I never read them, and I do sincerely hope Jotham won't blossom out into a reformer, and feel called upon to be making war against every thing that other people like.

"Wish me joy, dear Hope, and pray that I may be worthy of my great happiness.

"Your affectionate cousin,
"LYDIA."

CHAPTER XLIII.

SWITZERLAND.

"Memories dwell like doves among the trees,
Like nymphs in gloom, like naiads in the wells;
And some are sweet, and sadder some than death."
ALEXANDER SMITH.

THE beautiful scenery and pure air of our hills had drawn several families to Sherbrooke for a summer vacation, and picnics, boating, driving, and horseback excursions made the days fly swiftly. It was midsummer, and our pupils had gone for a vacation, so that mother and I were more at leisure to join parties of pleasure than we were the previous summer; yet, for some reason which I could hardly have explained, parties had lost much of their former zest for me; and, had it not been for exciting mother's solicitude, I should have refused all invitations, and given up my entire vacation to writing.

I had already become so much absorbed in my story for girls, as to lose nearly all consciousness of pain and disappointment, and could meet Carey Chapman, not without a momentary flush of color and trembling of the heart, but with sufficient coolness to hide my weakness from observers, and I devoutly hoped from his eyes also. He called rarely, except when accompanied by Virginia, and talked much more with mother than with myself.

If any thing were needed quite to dethrone the idol I had cherished—quite to obliterate all traces of the love which had taken root in my heart—it was a revelation of his selfish vanity at Switzerland. A picnic party had been arranged, which mother and I had been persuaded to join,

Several of the party were to go on horseback, and Mr. Chapman offered me a gentle, well-trained animal to ride— a horse that had become familiar to me, so that I sat quite at ease upon his back. Two carriages filled with ladies followed the equestrians, and later in the day Mr. Chapman, Captain Wynne, Squire Thornton, and Mr. Eveleth proposed joining us. It was a day full of beauty and promise, and our party were in excellent spirits. The pleasant, agreeable movement of my horse brushed from my thoughts every shadow; and if Carey Chapman did not see in my eyes just the light which pleased his vanity, he saw at least quiet enjoyment of the ride, the scenery, and the conversation; for, riding between Virginia and myself, he had never exerted himself more to talk well.

We had trotted gayly over three miles of our way, when we saw a woman standing in the door of a forlorn-looking shanty, a few rods from the road, endeavoring to hail us by waving a colored apron. The Blakes and their cousin, William Fairchild, trotted past, without appearing to notice the woman's signal or words.

"What can she want?" asked Virginia, checking her horse by the rude bars which separated the lane from the main road.

"She is only a common Irish beggar," answered Carey, searching in his pockets for loose change. "Just trot along, while I throw her this."

"No—she seems in distress," I suggested. "Allow me to wait and hear her story."

"Quixotic!" I heard Carey mutter, in an aside for Virginia's ear; but by this time the woman had reached the bars, where, panting for breath, in a half-scream and half-moan, she burst forth:

"Lord save yez, good folks, my swate leetle Norah is kilt entirely, she is, all alongst of fallin' into a pot of bilin' hot wather, whiles I ran for a minute to drive the pig from the cabbages, the unlucky beast! It's an hour agone, bad luck to me, since the childer went to school, away off in the red house over the hill, and Dennis is diggin' a drain for the Square, and won't be back till dark; and all the whiles my darlint is scramin' for a docther, and niver a sowl have I to sind! Now, saints presarve us, young man, but surely yez will run straight back for a docther?"

"If your child is killed, a doctor will be of no service."

"Och! not kilt entirely, to be sure! but scalded from head to foot, and fallin' jist from one fit into anither, as fast as iver she can, poor dear! and no one to bring me a docther!"

"You see, my good woman, we are started on a pleasure excursion, and I cannot leave these ladies and ride an hour in the hot sun to bring a doctor; but when we reach Switzerland I will send back a servant, who has gone ahead with our hampers, for Doctor Blake."

"May the blessed Virgin kape us! and may the ghost of my swate child haunt yez, if the breath laves her body without a docther or a praste!"

I saw Virginia make a movement as if she would turn her horse back toward the village; but a firm hand was laid upon her check-rain, and a whispered remonstrance, uttered with a pair of steel-blue eyes bent upon hers, arrested her.

"Wait patiently, my poor woman, while we ride forward and send back our man; it will not make an hour's difference in the doctor's coming," said Virginia.

I did not wait for the finishing of her sentence, but, turning my horse, touched him with my whip, and his willing feet carried me swiftly back toward the village. I did not look to see if Carey were following, for I had caught an encouraging look from mother's eye as I started, and knew that she approved of my mission. She and Mrs. Chapman had alighted from the carriage, and were preparing to follow the distressed woman into her miserable cabin. I trotted as rapidly toward the village as I dared ride alone, until I reached the road that diverged toward North Sherbrooke, when I suddenly remembered that Esther Blake had told me her father had been summoned thither very early in the morning, and had not returned when they left home, an hour previous. If I rode on to his office in the village, I might lose time in bringing him to the suffering child; but if I should ride up to North Sherbrooke, I might fail to meet him, as there was an old and a new road, connecting the village with this part of the town. I sat a minute, deliberating what course to pursue; and deciding that the safer one would be to ride directly to the doctor's office, I again gave my horse an intimation that she might go forward as fast as she chose, which was so quick a-trot as to bring nearly every woman and child to the windows and doors as we flew along. Arriving at Doctor Blake's, I learned that he had not yet returned from his early morning call, and therefore I at once turned back toward North Sherbrooke. As I was repassing the bank building, Mr. Chapman's kind voice arrested me. He had been standing just within the door when I passed up the street, and was awaiting on the steps my return, to learn the object of my call at the doctor's office.

"Hope," he called, "Hope Kendall, what has happened to bring you back?"

"An Irish woman, who lives three or four miles from here, was in great distress for a doctor to see her scalded child, and I rode back for Doctor Blake; but he has been gone to North Sherbrooke since five o'clock this morning."

"Ah, that's a pity. What do you propose doing now?"

17

"If you think 'tis safe, I shall go on toward North Sherbrooke to meet him."

"It may be safe, but I don't like to trust you alone on that road. My horses have gone to Switzerland, and 'tis impossible for me to accompany you.—Hulloa, we're in luck! Here's Farmer Hutchins, bound for North Sherbrooke, I'll warrant. Good-morning, Mr. Hutchins; are you on your way home?"

"Wa'al, I reckon so—have done up all my business, except just leaving this basket of my old woman's at Widow Reed's."

"You are just in season, for we wanted to send a messenger to your village for Doctor Blake, that he may call on an Irish family who live about a mile this side of Switzerland, before he returns home. Hope Kendall—you remember David's girl—was riding past there this morning, and hearing of the woman's trouble, she rode back for the doctor, and now proposes to go on to North Sherbrooke for him; but if you can find the doctor, Hope will ride along in your company until you reach the cross-roads, and then she'll go on alone to Switzerland to join her picnic party."

"I'll engage to find the doctor, and take keer of David's gal as long as she's a mind to ride in sight of my old mare."

It was not the easiest exercise that one might have chosen to keep up with Farmer Hutchins' mare, when her head was turned toward home, but I managed to ride within talking distance of the farmer, and to make short replies to his quaint remarks. I quickly found out that he knew the Irish family which was needing the doctor.

"So it's Dennis McCarthy's little Norah that tumbled into the tub, is it? Wa'al, I'd drive my mare a long way to find a doctor for her. She's a bright little thing, and my old woman has taken a great fancy to her. You see, Dennis often does a day's work for me; and sometimes, when his wife is going to the village to wash, he'll bring little Norah on his back and let her play around while he's at work. They moved into that old shanty when the railroad was bein' built, and Miss Hutchins soon found 'em out. I tell ye she's a master hand to find out poor folks, and she managed, with a little help from your village gently to clothe up three of the little McCarthys so that they could go to school. They're hard-workin' folks, and Dennis seems to be honest and temperate; but somehow they do contrive to be awful poor."

Before reaching the cross-roads, the well-known horse and chaise of Doctor Blake appeared, approaching us, and I was glad to wait at the turning, to make explanations to him.

"Well, I declare, this is hard on a man!" exclaimed the good doctor. "Ten o'clock and no breakfast, but an imperative summons from a young lady to ride two miles further before breaking my fast, to dress an Irish child's burns, with only a 'thank yez' and 'God bless yez' for my pay! But I suppose my steak and coffee will have a better relish, if I perform a deed of charity before returning home, will they not, Miss Hope?"

"I should think no person knew better than yourself the sweets of self-denial."

"Well, I must confess 'tis not a very self-indulgent life that a doctor leads," he answered, turning his horse toward the Irish shanty. "What with hard riding and broken slumbers and irregular meals, he needs an iron constitution and a good temper to stand the fatigue and irritation. But you haven't told me yet, Miss Hope, how it happened that you came for me?"

So I told him in as few words as possible how we

learned of the accident, and that Carey Chapman was the only gentleman escort, and there were five ladies left under his protection, four in the carriage and one on horseback.

"So, so! and it was much easier and pleasanter for my fine young man to ride leisurely along and chat with the ladies than to turn back and hunt up a doctor? And surely he was in a strait 'betwixt two,' having, no doubt, a desire to ride back in your stead, or at least to accompany you, and yet not willing to leave his lady and four other women exposed to the dangers of an unprotected ride over so wild a road as leads to Switzerland. He deserves our sympathy!" said the doctor, with a comical smile in his usually grave eyes.

I made no answer, but called his attention to the delicately beautiful hedge-roses, which, with the clover-blossoms, sweetened the summer air.

"Yes, I see them; but you mustn't expect a man whose thoughts are always occupied with fevers, dropsies, consumption, and broken bones, and whose olfactories have become so accustomed to the smell of drugs that he hardly knows the difference between a hedge-rose and a burdock, to go into raptures over flowers like a sentimental young lady."

"I didn't go into raptures, and I'm not sentimental."

"Are not? why, I thought all young ladies were; though, to be sure, I knew you had been educated in a sensible way. But here we are at Dennis McCarthy's lane, and I've got to climb those bars and travel through that mud to see your patient."

"Not my patient, but yours, doctor."

"I see you are disposed to be pugnacious this morning, and I suppose you've a right to be, in consideration of the self-denial you've practised in staying away from the picnicking party so long. What are you going to do now?"

"Dismount, and go in to see the poor child."

"Well, if you've a fancy to do so, it will be useless for me to oppose you, and I'll even go so far as to help you off your horse, but who'll put you on again?"

"You will probably be so kind."

"Why, child, I haven't lifted a lady into the saddle for more than twenty years. And now you'll oblige me to help you over these bars, I dare say."

"No—only fasten my horse, and I'll be no further trouble."

I heard him grumbling in his own pleasant way about the trouble that women always were, while I was unfastening the bars and gathering up my riding-skirt. I picked my way through the muddy lane where Mrs. McCarthy's pig and cow were entirely at home, and entered the low door. As I expected, mother and Mrs. Chapman were with the poor woman, assisting to soothe the suffering child.

"The Lord love yez, Miss, and save yez from sich a trouble as is breakin' me own heart! May yez never want for a docther nor any other blessin'. Shure now, docther, an I'm afraid it's too late to save the darlin'?"

"I hope not," answered the doctor, taking the child from mother's arms, where it lay quite still, until it was moved by the doctor, when its screams were heart-rending, and the poor mother's agony was almost equal to the child's. Her groans and ejaculations filled the house, until told by the doctor that she was adding to the child's sufferings by giving such noisy vent to her grief, and then she went into the yard, covering her head and face with her apron. Dr. Blake dressed the child's burns, and administered soothing opiates, but told us the injuries were so great that he saw no probability of saving her. He suggested that it would be best for him to return at once to the village and summon Dennis and a strong Irish woman to aid Mrs. McCarthy, and that I had better ride on to Switzerland and send back a carriage for mother and Mrs. Chapman; and so I was lifted awkwardly into my saddle by the doctor, who scolded vigorously all the while about the impropriety of sending me off for another solitary ride.

"However, 'tis not a bad road, and your horse is well-behaved; you understand how to manage her if she should attempt to run?"

"Yes; Mr. Chapman has taught me, and I have no fears."

"You are a good, sensible girl, and worth more than forty boarding-school misses," said the doctor, as he placed the reins in my hand, and turned my horse toward Switzerland.

I reached the rendezvous of our party without mishap, and was lifted from my saddle by Mr. Chapman's servant—the gentlemen of our party were engaged in escorting the ladies around the ruinous old mill.

The fatigue and excitement of the morning had been so great, that I was very glad to seek a sheltered nook, where I might enjoy the beautiful prospect and rest for a half hour before joining the merry, pleasure-seeking group of girls, whom I could see at a distance. The old pines around me were made musical by the summer winds, which in return were laden with the aromatic perfume of the trees, the fern, and the flowering laurel, which stood in queen-like beauty against a dark back-ground of evergreens.

I was getting quite in harmony with the soft loveliness of the day and the musical swaying of the pines, when a step upon the crackling underbrush arrested me, and a hand parted the branches of laurel which I thought screened me from the view of the party.

"I saw Henry with your horse, and he told me you had returned, so I took advantage of my cousinly prerogative to hunt for you," said Carey Chapman, carelessly seating himself on the bank by my side. "I wished to apologize for what might have seemed ungallant in my behavior this morning before you were discovered by the rest of our party, as after that I can hardly hope to catch your ear alone. In the first place, I did not half believe the woman's story—that class of people always exaggerate so—and I supposed a half hour's delay could make no essential difference. Then I was not really aware of your intention until you had galloped off at so swift a pace that I should have found some difficulty in overtaking you; and if I followed you, I must leave Miss Thornton and four other ladies unprotected. I chose the least troublesome horn of the dilemma, but the awkwardness of my position has annoyed me ever since the noisy Irish woman hailed us. Are my excuses accepted?"

"Certainly."

"Is that my only answer? Give me your hand in token of forgiveness."

"You do not need any such assurance," I answered, but without extending my hand.

"One year ago you would not have hesitated to place your hand in mine. What has wrought the change?"

"Perhaps I am grown a little wiser, but I should not hesitate now to use my hand in your behalf if your necessities required my service."

"That admission, small as it is, comforts me. But I have sometimes thought you would do more for me than others—that you would be my dearest and most faithful friend—did I think correctly?"

"'Tis not generous nor manly in you to question me in such a way," I answered, while my face and throat felt hot with the quick rush of blood, and I rose, attempting to walk away.

"Wait a minute, Hope, while I do myself the justice to say that I have found it would be an easy thing to love you, if wealth and beauty had not been placed in the scale against you; and often have I sighed;

> 'Oh, why was woman made so fair? or man
> So weak as to see that more than one had beauty!'"

"Say no more, lest I learn to despise the man whom I have so honored, and pity the friend whom he has chosen," I exclaimed, breaking away from his detaining hand, and, running from the laurel-sheltered nook, I gained the path which led to the old mill. There was no need of such speed as my exasperated feelings urged upon my stumbling feet, for Carey Chapman was in no mood to follow. If his self-complacency had been flattered by my tell-tale color, it had as surely been wounded by my last words. He was not the kind of man to show pique or annoyance when he joined the party, but zealously tried to make the day pass pleasantly to all, while his devotion to Virginia was such, that an observer might have questioned whether he was not an exception to the class of men 'who could see that more than one had beauty.'

My annoyance at the ungenerous way in which Carey Chapman had endeavored to draw from me a confession of the love which he had probably seen in my eyes and in my manner for a whole year, soon passed off in self-congratulation that love for him was entirely uprooted, and that my lack of wealth and beauty had at least saved me from being the companion of selfishness and vanity.

"Ah, Hope Kendall, you have managed to make yourself the heroine of the day, I understand," drawled Belinda Blake, approaching me with her cousin. "As for me I never care to distinguish myself by mingling with such lowbred people as must live in that shanty. I saw the woman trying to hail us, but I wouldn't look that way again, and I succeeded in keeping Cousin William from seeing her, by pointing out the laurels on the other side of the road."

Cousin William did not look quite so delighted as the circumstances and Belinda's enjoyment of her ruse seemed to demand.

"I hope your long ride did not fatigue or incommode you seriously," said Mr. Fairchild.

"Oh, she'll make the morning's ride pay, Cousin William, I dare say," said Belinda, with a disagreeable emphasis on the word pay. "Come, Hope, confess now that you'll weave the incidents into a magazine story, making yourself the heroine who saved the child's life."

"I performed only a simple act of kindness, Miss Blake, without thinking whether it would be known; it was not worthy the prominence your words give it;" and seeing mother and Mrs. Chapman coming up the path, I joined them, avoiding Belinda and her set as much as possible through the day.

The incidents of the morning somewhat sobered for me the pleasure of the party, so that in retrospect, they looked less enchanting than in anticipation; yet there had been enough of enjoyment to counteract the pain, and I had learned that one may gain—

"Even from the bitterest part,
A stronger heart."

CHAPTER XLIV.

WHAT MIGHT HAVE BEEN.

> "My bounty is as boundless as the sea,
> My love as deep; the more I give to thee
> The more I have, for both are infinite."
> SHAKSPEARE.

SEPTEMBER filled the air with delicious odors of ripening fruits, when I was lifted from the lumbering old stage-coach by my uncle John. "Your relatives will expect you," mother had urged, "and the change of scene will benefit you, and your aunt will find fresh cause of complaint against me if you do not go."

The last reason was weightier than the others, and thinking of my cousin's disappointment if I failed to be her bridesmaid, I left home less unwillingly than last year. My stay had been limited to one week, because of the school duties which would demand my return.

"Bless my eyes! you look more like David than ever!" exclaimed my uncle, lifting me from my feet and kissing me with rough cordiality. "Take care, Lyddy, and leave enough of Hope for your mother to kiss," he continued, as my cousin flew to the gate and welcomed me in her own demonstrative way.

"I knew you would come," she said, "though Aunt Lydia persisted in saying your mother wouldn't let you," and she half pulled me up the path to the door where Aunt Abby stood, her quiet face lighted with a welcoming smile.

"I am as glad to see you as Lydia is, if I do not make quite as much noise," she said, "and your aunt and Mr. Hopkinson, and some one else, will thank you for coming."

I knew the "some one else" meant Mr. Hamlin, and inferred at once that he was still in Hebron; and I could not help acknowledging that the little hamlet would hardly be as pleasant to me without his presence. I was conducted to my room by Lydia, whose tongue flew from one subject to another so rapidly that my thoughts could scarcely follow.

"Only a week, you miserly Hope," she exclaimed, "when I wanted you so much for the whole month of August. Why couldn't you come before?"

"Because I was so busy. You remember I wrote."

"Yes! but just as though you could be busy about any thing of half as much importance as my wedding clothes!"

"I knew that I could be of little use in your preparations. I am not expert with my needle. Are you all ready?"

"Dear, no! the embroidered muslin and the travelling-dress have not been touched, but Mrs. Craig begins upon them to-morrow. Oh, Hope, I am so happy at last!" she said, flinging her arms around me for another embrace.

"At last? why you've been happy all your life."

"Yes—happy in a quiet way, but not positively, blissfully happy until I was sure that I loved Jotham as he deserves to be loved. 'Tis such a luxury to know that a good man loves me."

She whispered the last sentence, hiding her blushing face in my neck, much as Virginia had done, and when she raised it, I thought

> "The cataracts of her soul had poured themselves
> And risen self-crowned in rainbow,"

so joyfully radiant were her eyes.

"We shall keep you to ourselves this evening, Hope," said Uncle John, as he gave me a seat by himself at the supper-table, "and try to get a good look at you before your Aunt Lyddy finds out that you're here. She'll be wanting you there to-morrow, and by the next day Jotham will come, and the house will be turned topsy-turvy in preparations for the wedding. You'd no idee that our Lyddy would pick up a beau so soon when you saw her last?"

"Not the least."

"Now, father—" commenced Lydia, raising a warning finger.

"No, child, I'll not tell how you took us all by surprise, after worrying Jotham's life out of him, by coming round at last and saying as how you'd have him. I reckon you've had too much to do to think of the beaux, Hope, since you was here. A girl's head must be pretty clear of silly notions, if she finds time to write so many clever things as you do—and teach too. But somehow you don't look worried and fagged as I expected you would. What's your secret, Hope?"

"I have none, uncle, excepting a strong desire to be useful; and in our house, mother always contrives to make work so pleasant that it never frets us."

"I'll tell you what, Abby," exclaimed Uncle John, "we'll go down to Sherbrooke when Lyddy is fairly off our hands, and see this wonderful mother of Hope's. We shall need something to cheer us up a little after her noise and clatter are out of the house." Uncle John paused to look tenderly at the child, who was so evidently his pride and pet, and who would so soon go from his protection. "After all, I tell her mother she isn't going but ten miles from us, and I have a colt that only asks an hour and five minutes to go over the ground in; we can ride there any morning to breakfast."

I lost no time the morning after my arrival in walking to the parsonage, knowing my aunt would be sure to find fault if I delayed coming. I saw her in the garden before I reached the house; and her back being turned to the street, and her face shielded by her large sunbonnet, she did not see me until I laid my hand upon her arm, saying:

"Aunt Lydia, I've come."

"Goodness! why, how you have frightened me, child! Where did you come from, at this hour of the day?"

"From Uncle John's; the stage left me there last evening. You know Cousin Lydia particularly wished me to spend this week with her, else I should have come directly to you."

"That would have been the best way; but I'm glad to see you in Hebron again;" and the greeting that followed, though prim and formal, convinced me that Aunt Lydia had spoken truly. "'A merry heart maketh a cheerful countenance,'" she said, scanning me attentively. "You can't have had time to be merry, but your face has a cheerful look. You may as well take hold and help pick a mess of beans for dinner, as it's ironing day, and Jane hasn't time. Be careful and not pull and trample the vines when you are picking off the pods."

"Mr. Hopkinson is well, I hope?"

"Yes; but it would sound much more respectful in you to call him uncle. He has a father's love for you, and you might at least call him Uncle Caleb."

"I will gladly, if it will be agreeable to him."

"Of course it will; and you would do well to ask his advice, and not rush headlong into writing and publishing without consulting your best friends. 'The words of a man's mouth are as deep waters, and the well-spring of wisdom as a flowing brook.' You saw enough of Caleb last fall to know that his heart was a well-spring of wisdom, and that he would be your safest counsellor."

"I have great confidence in his judgment, and hope I shall never write any thing that will not merit his approval."

"Whatever made you think of writing in the first place? and what do you get for your trouble and time?"

So, while we picked and shelled the beans for dinner, I told my aunt what first prompted me to use my pen, what encouragement I had received, and what were my future prospects.

"'The hope of the righteous shall be gladness, but the expectation of the wicked shall perish,'" quoted my aunt with a sigh, when I had concluded; and the sigh plainly intimated that my expectations would share the fate of the wicked. "You may possibly get a living by writing," she continued, "but you must remember that Solomon says, 'The talk of the lips tendeth only to penury;' and for my part I see no difference between talking and writing."

I listened patiently to many more old maxims and proverbs, of which my aunt seemed to have an inexhaustible store; but having so satisfactorily disposed of her by way of marriage last year, 'tis not my purpose to quote freely from the long conversations in which she honestly tried to improve my tastes during my week's stay in Hebron. 'Tis enough to say that the channel through which her thoughts flowed had not become essentially widened and deepened by the daily companionship of so truly good and generous a man as Mr. Hopkinson; and though he still listened politely when she quoted, I thought he wore an air of abstraction, as if her words failed to make the impression they had made one year ago. He showed a warm interest in my pursuits and studies, and gave me many excellent hints about style, which were not increased in value because of my aunt's oft-repeated assurances that "in a multitude of counsellors there was safety."

My short visit was drawing rapidly to a close, and I had not seen Mr. Hamlin. He had called once at Uncle John's when I was out, and though he was still very intimate with Mr. Hopkinson, I did not happen to meet him at the parsonage until the evening before the wedding, and I had only two more days to remain in Hebron. It had been arranged that Mr. Hamlin should be groomsman for Mr. White, and of course I must see him on the morrow; but I could not help thinking it would be much pleasanter to meet him first in a quiet way, when I should dare look in his face to see if there were any shadows of the disappointment which had once clouded it.

I had walked to the parsonage late in the day previous to the wedding, and Aunt Lydia having been peremptory in her wishes for me to remain to supper, I had thrown off my hat and was sitting by her side, telling her of the completed arrangements for the morrow, when Mr. Hamlin walked in. I saw him through the open window coming up the garden-path, and had time to overcome a foolish, nervous fluttering of my heart before he entered. The first glance at his honest eyes, as he approached me, told me that if he had failed to seek me during my visit in Hebron, it was from no lack of the old interest. His face was for a moment lighted with gladness when he took my hand in greeting, but he turned directly from me after having said a few commonplaces, to talk with Aunt Lydia. She occasionally drew me, by questions, into the conversation, but I was left quite at liberty to study the speakers. A year had left Mr. Hamlin's face unchanged, unless, indeed, the lines were deeper and graver around the mouth, and smiles came less frequently into his eyes;

and then perhaps his constant forgetfulness of self had softened and refined his features. Altogether, it seemed a more pleasing and agreeable face than when I had last seen it, and I congratulated myself that I could call him friend.

When Aunt Lydia left the room to look after her supper, I summoned courage to tell him that his Christmas gift had given me great pleasure.

"I hoped it would be an assurance to you of my continued friendship."

"It was, Mr. Hamlin, but I did not know how to tell you so, only by sending the magazine."

"I hoped you would write and tell me if the pictures were more acceptable than the gift you had previously declined."

"I should have written but—"

"I understand, Miss Kendall, you did not wish to hold out even a straw for my drowning hope to cling to. I ought to be manly enough to thank you for your honesty."

Aunt Lydia came in to announce supper, and Mr. Hamlin was persuaded to remain and partake of it, and when the meal was finished and I took up my hat and stepped out into the soft September twilight to return to Uncle John's, I knew Mr. Hamlin would be my companion for the walk. For several minutes the anticipated events of the morrow gave us a theme to talk upon, and somewhat thawed the icy barrier which I had built between us.

"When do you return to Sherbrooke?" Mr. Hamlin asked, when I allowed the conversation to flag for a moment.

"The day after to-morrow."

"Then lest I should not find another opportunity so favorable, let me tell you how much I have been gratified to see the productions of your pen in print. You do not need my commendation, yet I can hardly forbear telling you that your articles are all so stamped with simple truth and grace, that I have often thought I must have recognized your spirit in them, even if you had not been kind enough to send me your first sketch, signed with your initials."

"You are the only one besides mother and Mrs. Gordon to whom I have given any intimation of what I am doing. Several others have discovered my secret by accident."

"Thank you for the confidence."

And what was there in his eyes when I caught their expression in uttering that last sentence, that so unloosed my tongue, and prompted me to tell him what encouragement I had received in writing, and what were my aspirations for the future?

Only quiet interest in my lightest words, and that truthful, honest, intelligent manliness, which wins a woman's love—only these; but when we reached Uncle John's door and I was left alone upon his steps as I had been once before, I remembered how freely my thoughts had shaped themselves into words in his presence, and again congratulated myself that I had such a friend.

Lydia's lively, rattling gush of laughter did not provoke the echoes on her bridal morn; she was hushed, sober, and white as any bride could be in her embroidered muslin.

"I should be perfectly happy this morning, dear Hope," she whispered, just before leaving her chamber to join Mr. White, "if it were not for two ungratified wishes."

"What are they?"

"One is the wish to take father and mother with me, and the other is that you may know the happiness of loving and being loved."

"Both very natural wishes at this hour, I suspect, dear Lydia, but you must be comforted by remembering how near your parents will be to your new home; and then as for my happiness, you don't know what a multitude of resources I have. Let no thought of me cast a shadow upon your heart to-day."

Aunt Abby came in to summon us into the presence of Mr. White and his friend, and in a brief ten minutes more Mr. Hopkinson had pronounced the solemn words which made Lydia Hastings Mrs. Jotham White; and during the congratulations that followed, I escaped from Mr. Hamlin's side, glad of an excuse to entertain some other guests, and in this way quiet my own foolish heart, which had been strangely disturbed by the looks and manners of my friend.

Had it not been for Aunt Lydia's timely quotations, the company would have made but a sorry appearance for a festive occasion; but her proverbs were not likely to fail on such an auspicious day as witnessed the union of her namesake and a clergyman.

"I hope, Lydia, you'll be one of those women 'whose price is far above rubies, so that the heart of your husband can safely trust in you," she quoted, after having touched the bride's cheek with her thin lips, and then followed a few words of admonition to Mr. White, so formal and so provocative of smiles, as quite to banish sentiment and tender demonstration from the room.

Immediately after the early dinner, Mr. White and his bride left in a carriage for the nearest railroad station, *en route* for Niagara, and I packed my simple wardrobe for a return to Sherbrooke on the following day. If I had any regrets in leaving, it was because I had seen so little of Mr. Hamlin, and because I had found it was so very difficult a thing for him to be simply a friend, and wondering why I cared so much for his conversation and his encouragement, and why he had left Uncle John's so suddenly, after seeing Mr. White and Lydia off, without so much as a simple good-bye for me; I only half-listened to Aunt Abby's words, as we walked leisurely through the orchard-paths near sunset. Some domestic duties called my aunt in-doors, and I still lingered under the fruit-laden trees, enjoying the fragrance and the sunset, which sent long arrows of golden light in amongst the mossy old trunks, when I saw Mr. Hamlin approaching me.

"I remembered that I did not bid you good-bye when I left your uncle's this morning, and seeing you in the orchard as I was passing, I took the liberty of joining you."

"Thank you; I have just been thinking how sorry I should be to leave Hebron without having had one pleasant talk with you. Last evening you allowed me to do nearly all the talking, and to-night I wish to be a listener."

"What shall I talk about?" and his manner in asking the question showed me that only one theme was uppermost in his thoughts; but I was not willing to be told again of his love, so I answered lightly,

"Oh, I would like to know what books you have read since last fall, and what pictures you have painted."

"My reading has been chiefly confined to chemical and medical studies. I am preparing myself to practise medicine, and shall spend the autumn and winter in Philadelphia for that purpose. I should have been off ten days ago, but the trustees wished me to remain until my successor arrives. He could not be here before next Monday, and 'tis an old-time custom for the school in Hebron to open the first of September."

There was an embarrassing pause, which Mr. Hamlin did not seem inclined to break, and for some reason the subjects which I had wished to converse with him about, did not present themselves readily; but the silence growing awkward, I asked:

"Will Mrs. Craig live alone?"

"No; the new teacher and his wife will board with her."

"She must miss little Phil."

"We both missed him and mourned for him, but I think Elizabeth is beginning to feel that God acted wisely and mercifully in removing Phil from his sufferings."

"It will be a great trial to your sister, this separation from you."

"Yes—but 'tis only a temporary one, and that remembrance comforts us both. I shall be prepared to commence my life-work when I return from Philadelphia, and shall probably take Elizabeth with me to one of our large Western cities, where we shall make a home. We have only each other to live for now, and very few persons will inquire what we are doing."

"Only each other to live for now"—it was said in a cheerless tone, and with a want of hope and courage in his face that saddened me. Yet why should I care how or for what purpose Mr. Hamlin lived? I only knew that I *did* care. We had reached the gate that separated the orchard from the garden, when Mr. Hamlin held out his hand, saying:

"I would ask you to prolong this walk, but I am a dull talker to-night. I supposed myself prepared to meet you again as an ordinary friend, but I find I am not. Good-night and good-bye. May God's blessing go with you and abide with you!"

"Good-bye;" it was the only word I dared trust upon my lips, though the appealing, almost despairing look of Mr. Hamlin's eyes, seemed to crave something more.

I knew that he loved me as well as when he first declared his love, but the knowledge did not give me the same unhappiness as it did a year ago. I did not feel quite sure but in time I might learn to return it, if he should ever ask me again; but thinking such an event improbable, I tried to dismiss the whole matter from my mind and think only of the work God had given me to do—wisely concluding that the dream of love, which for a few months had seemed to me the substance instead of the shadow, would be the only knowledge I should have in this life of that

"Sweetest joy and wildest woe,"

which makes either an Eden or a workshop of this world.

CHAPTER XLV.

PREMONITIONS OF SORROW.

"'Tis always morning somewhere, and above
The awakening continents, from shore to shore,
Somewhere the birds are singing evermore."
LONGFELLOW.

My journey home was uneventful, and the haven of peace and rest at its end was more delightfully agreeable than ever before. Mother's quiet, cheerful presence always soothed my restlessness, and her conversations and the books we read together gave tone and vigor to my thoughts. She had arranged a pleasant surprise to make my coming home as joyous as possible. The old worn and faded carpet had been replaced by a new one in my absence, and a couple of pretty easy-chairs quite changed the aspect of our parlor.

"You can't guess what has happened," shouted Willie, before I had alighted from the wagon which brought me from the depot.

"Don't tell," whispered Sophie, "let us see if she notices at once;" and both children clung to my neck in tender greeting, as soon as my feet touched the ground. I was led into the parlor by Willie, who insisted on having my eyes blinded until he had opened the door and given me permission to look.

"There now!" he exclaimed in gleeful triumph. "What do you see?"

"The work of some benevolent fairy, I'm sure! Why, Willie, we shall hardly dare step on such a beauty of a carpet!" and I tried to make the real pleasure I felt demonstrative enough to suit the child's notion of joy.

People whose every wish is gratified, whose eyes have always been accustomed to the beauty which wealth creates, can hardly understand the pride and pleasure that we took in our new possessions. They were the fruits of our own honest endeavors, and enjoyed with a zest known only to those whose luxuries are the reward of exertion.

When mother and I were left alone for the hour's communion which we always had before separating for the night, I gave her a history of my visit and my cousin's wedding.

"And you did not find it so very unpleasant as you feared to be bridesmaid for your cousin?" mother asked.

"I only enjoyed it because I knew that I was giving Lydia pleasure, and I hope I may never be asked to be bridesmaid again."

"I think you will be. Virginia was here yesterday, and she made me her confidante."

"She is going to be married?"

"Yes—on Christmas eve; and she says your experience in Hebron will just fit you for the service she shall require of you."

"Virginia has so many friends who would be proud to

have the honor, that she must excuse me." I knew there was a color in my face which mother misinterpreted, for her face was grave, and her voice more than usually tender, when she spoke again.

"Hope, there is one subject on which I have never sought your confidence, trusting if you needed my sympathy you would ask it. You must not think, dear child, because I have never spoken, that I did not know you received a great blow when the knowledge came to you that Carey Chapman was engaged to Virginia. I saw that you met the trial bravely, and I was sure victory would finally be yours. I have hoped ever since you were so interested in writing, that you had found a balm and gained a conquest."

"I am sure I have, mother. I do not envy Virginia now the love I was foolish enough to believe mine all through last autumn and winter, nor do I look back with any regret on my acquaintance with Carey. His conversation and encouragement have been a great stimulus to me; but, thanks to your teachings, I have been able to see through his selfish ambition, and to feel sure that I could not have been a happy or suitable companion for him. I only feel chagrined that I allowed myself to be flattered by his attentions, till I really believed he loved me, and I am afraid he thinks I loved him."

"Then let me advise you to accept Virginia's invitation, and act the part of bridesmaid in your own natural, unembarrassed way. If you refuse your friend's request, Carey will very likely believe you have loved and still love him, and I would not allow his self-conceit to be further flattered by any marked avoidance of him. Show him by your manner that if your girlish fancy was captivated for a short time, your woman's heart is reserved for the honorable man who comes in an open, honest way, to win it."

"Do you remember, mother, when you were urging me last winter to try what power there was in my pen, you said I might some time need the occupation of writing to bury my dead hopes in? and then I was so confident I should never have any to bury."

"Yes; my very anxiety about the growing interest which I saw you felt in Carey's society, induced me to urge upon you the cultivation of a taste for some employment more engrossing and stimulating than teaching. I foresaw then the result of an intimate acquaintance with him, but I dared not forbid the German lessons, lest you should feel that I had robbed your life of one of its innocent pleasures. I knew that the wife whom Carey would choose must have either wealth, beauty, or such influential friends as would help him up the ladder he is climbing; and fortune has not favored my little girl with any of these gifts, though she has been blessed with an excellent intellect and a truthful, loving heart."

"And the best of instruction you may add, mother; for if I ever accomplish any thing worth mentioning, it will be owing to your careful education and the cheerful patience which you have shown in your own life."

Mother's only answer was the touch of her lips to my forehead; and after a minute's silence I spoke again.

"If you think my refusal to be Virginia's bridesmaid will be misinterpreted by Carey Chapman, or will be a disappointment to the bride, I will try to oblige her; but I cannot afford to buy any new finery for the occasion. If I visit Mrs. Gordon this winter, I must have a new cloak and bonnet, and that will take every dollar which ought to be spent on my wardrobe. The embroidered muslin must serve again."

"And it will be very pretty and appropriate. I have laid aside enough so that your wardrobe can be made neat and becoming for a short visit to Mrs. Gordon, and she is too sensible a woman to expect much from you in the way of dress, knowing as she does that almost our entire income depends upon our teaching. And 'tis probable, Hope, there will be a greater necessity even for our exertions in the future than there has been. Do you know that Sophie's eyes are not getting any better, but rather worse?"

"I thought Dr. Blake spoke hopefully the last time he saw them."

"He does not profess to have much skill as an oculist. I have noticed ever since her sickness of a year ago, that she has great difficulty in reading fine print; and yesterday I found her crying, and when I questioned her, she said she could not see the notes clearly upon the sheet of music before her."

Mother's voice was tremulous, and her eyes filled with tears, while my own were overflowing. We had known for many months that Sophie's eyes were seriously diseased, but had been unwilling to admit to each other the extent of the calamity we feared; and now to dread for this dear child total darkness—she, who had been our sunshine, it was almost more than we could bear. Mother was the first to speak calmly:

"My anxiety may have exaggerated the difficulty, but I have decided to send her to Philadelphia with you in the winter, and have her eyes examined by the best oculist there. Meantime we must try to keep her cheerful and employed with something that will not tax her sight severely. We must remember, too, that our griefs will come to us so tempered that we can bear them. An old adage says, 'Fortune never comes to us with both hands full;' and though she has dealt so kindly with us of late, we must not expect to glide on so smoothly all through life.

18

But it will be one of the hardest of all my trials to see my dear Sophie blind."

So we went to work again that autumn with every incentive for exertion doubled; not only our present wants, but the probable future of a blind daughter and sister, "pricked the sides of our intent."

We had nine boarders and several day pupils from the village; but as we had two strong servants in the kitchen, it was not necessary for me to take more of the housework upon myself than sufficed for exercise, so that I found several hours each day for writing and amusing Sophie. The story for girls progressed rapidly, and by the middle of December was finished. There were three hundred pages of manuscript, and I calculated there would be at least two-thirds as many in print. It had been read to our pupils as a weekly serial during the fall term, and the enthusiastic manner in which they listened and applauded, considerably increased the confidence with which I regarded it.

It was a busy autumn too in Squire Thornton's handsome house. Virginia's bridal paraphernalia was in the hands of dressmakers and sempstresses, and kept several of the rooms in a delightful flutter of ribbons, laces, muslins, and silks. I was often seized by my friend in her own pretty, imperative way, and almost forcibly taken to the scene of action, to witness the triumphs of art which Madam Hermiér achieved.

Virginia was very happy in anticipation of the winter's gayeties. She was going to Washington to spend the first few weeks of her honeymoon, and would then return to a handsome house in Wiltshire, the gift of her generous father.

When I chanced to meet Carey Chapman at Squire Thornton's, his manner toward me was that of easy, cousinly assurance, while the most tender empressment marked his demeanor to his bride elect. His watchful eye never permitted her to open a door, to turn her music, or provide for herself a seat; but underneath this too manifest devotion, I often fancied there lurked an abstracted air, a half-wearied look, as if he were not entirely satisfied with the heritage that had fallen to him. It might be all a fancy of mine, and I devoutly hoped it was.

The eventful evening came at last, and Virginia was radiant with her own sweet beauty and the soft white draperies of silk and lace which floated around her. ' I forgot myself, my simple muslin, and my much dreaded service—forgot that ever a thought of the handsome bridegroom had ruffled the quiet waters of my own heart, as I looked upon the fair creature, whose life had been such a jubilant spring morning, and prayed that her future might be crowned with all beauty, fragrance, and joy. Nor even when the promises were made and the prayers said, and in my turn I had greeted the bride, did the pulses of my heart quicken, as Carey bent down and touched my lips with his own.

"'Tis my cousinly right," he whispered so that only my ear and Virginia's caught the words; but I determined that the opportunities should be rare for the exercise of such a prerogative, even though the bride smiled her glad approval of the act.

Jonas Gould came for mother and myself, and when we were fairly turned toward home, he took occasion to " clear his mind."

" So the knot is ra'ally tied, is it? Wa'al I hope it's strong enough to keep Carey in the traces. If he does go galivantin' round in the style he's kept up for the last year, he'll get a pretty plain piece of my mind, and I can't say but as how he'll feel the strength of my right arm too.

Virginny's a terrible nice girl, a sight too good for Carey, and if he don't treat her well, he'd better take keer of his handsome face, for it may get some ugly bruises. They do say that old Judge Southby's daughter is in a decline, all owing to her disappointment, and the judge started for Europe with her last month."

"How did you come by your news, Jonas," mother asked.

"Wa'al, I met Sam Atkins last week, when he came home to see his mother. Me and Sam and Carey used to go to the district school when we was boys, and Sam's living in Wiltshire now, a-working at his trade, and he keeps a pretty sharp eye out on Carey. You see Sam used to have a likin' for Mary Ann Reed, but she thought herself a heap too good for an honest blacksmith, and Sam says if any one can tell Widder Reed where Mary is now, Carey Chapman's the man."

"Heaven forbid!" ejaculated mother.

"Wa'al, it's no concern of mine, only I've always had a mighty fancy for Virginny, and the man as gets her oughter be true as steel."

No more words were exchanged with Jonas on this topic; but when we reached home, mother took both my hands in hers, and looking in my eyes, which shrank not from her scrutiny, said:

"Thank God, Hope, for the strength He has given you, for the refuge of His love, and pray that Virginia may learn to rely on the very present Help we all have in trouble."

"I will, mother."

CHAPTER XLVI.

OLD AND NEW FRIENDS.

> "How a great love becomes
> Its own reward, how its most holy flame
> Warms, purifies, expands the heart and brain;
> Makes a man godlike with the sacred force
> And elevation it accords to him."

THE winter months rolled away, each day crowded with cares and duties, before I could be spared from mother's school, and before a suitable escort could be found to accompany us as far as Philadelphia. Early in March Mr. Chapman's business took him to Washington, and he kindly offered to place us in Mrs. Gordon's care. He beguiled the journey of much of its tediousness by his pleasant conversation, and in New York devoted a whole day to our entertainment, showing me for the first time some really good pictures. Words would give but a faint idea of the enthusiastic delight with which I first gazed at Hildebrandt's "Othello and Desdemona," "The Martyrdom of John Huss," and Church's "Heart of the Andes." I was familiar with Shakspeare's "Othello," and could easily fancy that I heard the gentle Desdemona entreating the Moor " to teach the friend that loved her to tell his tales so that she might be won." The "Heart of the Andes," with its rich beauty, so gorgeous in coloring that the gallery seemed scented with the fragrance of flowers, filled me with rapt, admiring wonder. So life-like was the picture that I almost expected to see the trembling branch of a giant forest tree, upon which a condor rested, break and fall beneath his weight—and the light, fleecy clouds to float and assume new forms on the canvas; while the shrubs, trees, and flowers seemed swaying in the breeze that wafted to me tropical perfumes.

Never did short winter day seem to me so brief as the one spent in this great city, when every thing was veiled in the charm of novelty to my young eyes, and each pleasure was enhanced by the intelligent conversation of my friend. In the evening of the third day after leaving Sherbrooke, I found myself with Sophie quietly domiciled in Mrs. Gordon's pleasant, unpretending home in Arch Street. The welcome extended by that hospitable lady could hardly have been warmer had we been near relatives.

"You shall not tell me this evening what you have accomplished since I saw you last June, Miss Hope," said Mrs. Gordon, after we had been refreshed with tea, and all her kind inquiries about mother and the prosperity of our school had been answered. "You and Sophie are much too weary with your journey and sight-seeing in New York to talk, so I shall send you early to bed. To-morrow I shall keep you both in my own room, secure from all excitement and company; and then, if you are sufficiently rested, you may read to me your story for girls."

"I do so hope you will like it, Mrs. Gordon; I have written it very carefully, and there is a great deal depending upon its success."

"I dare say I shall be pleased with it, but the question with publishers will be, 'Will it sell?' You must not be sanguine of success in disposing of your manuscript. I infer from the expression of your face that you have achieved a nobler victory in writing this story than could be reaped from pecuniary gain. The worth of any work which has called out and strengthened our faculties and ennobled our aspirations, can never be reckoned in dollars and cents."

No; I had already learned the truth of Mrs. Gordon's words, and I well knew if my little story never saw the light of day in any other shape but its present—a neat manuscript, tied with pink ribbon—that the peaceful rest, the healing which my heart had found in the occupation of my brain, would be through life of more worth to me than any pecuniary consideration. And yet, as I lay awake in my strange bed, and turned the subject over and over in my thoughts, I longed for just such a field of usefulness as might be opened to me if this story could only serve as a key to unlock the heart and purse of some publisher, and through him gain the ear of intelligent and generous readers.

The day succeeding our arrival in Philadelphia was ushered in with a disagreeable storm of wind and rain; and for once I was glad to see the dripping clouds and drenched streets, for I trusted they might secure Mrs. Gordon's attention to my manuscript; nor was I mistaken. Soon after breakfast she joined me in the library, saying:

"Now, Miss Hope, if you are not too tired to read, we will give this day to your manuscript, as it seems likely to be one of quiet. Sophie may amuse herself with this game of *solitaire*, and I will take a piece of plain sewing, but my mind will be free to enjoy your reading. I believe you expect me to use a pruning knife wherever my taste suggests it?"

"Certainly; I shall be very grateful for any hints and corrections which you may make."

Mrs. Gordon was an attentive and judicious listener; not a superfluous adjective or adverb but received the condemnatory stroke of her pencil, and many ambitious sentences, which I had considered highly ornamental, her riper judgment persuaded me to erase; but when the reading was completed, and I found my friend could find in the story much more to commend than condemn, hope whispered many sweet possibilities to my heart.

"You had better entrust your manuscript to me, and I will do the best I can for you with publishers; and let me advise you to banish it from your thoughts during the remainder of your visit. I see that you need recreation and freedom from work for a few days. I have made an appointment for to-morrow morning with Dr. Daniels, the most celebrated oculist we have in our city; and if any thing can be done for Sophie's eyes, I feel confident he will know what to do. I have invited some very pleasant and intelligent people to visit me this evening, and I would like to introduce you to several whom it may be well for you to know hereafter."

I was truly grateful to Mrs. Gordon for the interest she manifested in my pursuits, and for the assistance she had rendered; but when I attempted to express my thanks, she protested against them, saying:

"Any help which I can give to young women who are trying to be useful, I give most cheerfully, regarding it as a thank-offering for my own success."

I dressed Sophie carefully in her best gown, a pretty shade of soft blue merino, and then with little thought about my own personal appearance, I put on Aunt Lydia's present, the blue silk with clusters of white flowers upon its ground, and before the arrival of company led my sister into the most obscure corner of Mrs. Gordon's parlors and found a seat for us both, where the ample draperies of a bow window would partially screen us.

In my efforts to keep Sophie amused and happy I soon forgot my own embarrassment, and was able to exchange the usual commonplaces of conversation with several agreeable people whom my hostess introduced.

I was beginning to talk quite freely with an elderly professor about Sherbrooke and the pictures I had seen in New York, when suddenly the familiar voice of a gentleman who had just entered and was talking with Mrs. Gordon, arrested me. I could not see his face, but I knew at once that the broad shoulders and clear, healthy voice of the new comer, belonged only to Philip Hamlin. A thrill of pleasure sent the blood to my face and as quickly withdrew it, for the question which instinctively and instantly presented itself was, "How shall I meet him?" It had hardly occurred to me as possible that in so large a city as Philadelphia accident would bring Mr. Hamlin into my presence. I had determined not to seek him, and I knew of no way in which he could have been apprised of my visit to Mrs. Gordon.

Professor Harriman's reminiscences of a summer tour to the Berkshire hills fell monotonously upon my ear, but fortunately he was too much engrossed with his own pleasant memories to notice my inattention. My ears were intent upon catching every sentence that fell from Mr. Hamlin's lips, and my eyes were eager to read his face. At last it was partially turned toward me, while he conversed with a young lady who appeared to be familiarly acquainted with him. It was marked with the same high and noble purpose—the same quiet self-reliance—the same frank, honest manliness, that had once made me glad to call him friend. If I only had just such an intelligent brother, I sighed.

Professor Harriman having finished his account of a month in Berkshire, looked around probably to find some more sympathizing listener than I had proved, and discovered Mr. Hamlin.

"Ah," he exclaimed, "Mrs. Gordon has succeeded in

drawing out my favorite. That young man, Miss Kendall, who is conversing with my daughter, the young lady in a gray dress, will make his mark in the world. He is a faithful, persevering student, and has just the brain and temperament for a successful man. By the way, he's from your part of the world too, and I'll bring him up and introduce him."

It was of no use for me to tell the kind old Professor that I was very pleasantly occupied, and would wait for an introduction to his friend; he did not comprehend my meaning, but walked off toward Mr. Hamlin, and directly I saw him returning with the young man's arm in his.

"Miss Kendall, here is my friend Mr. Hamlin, a native of New England."

I rose and offered my hand, glancing timidly at his surprised face.

"Miss Kendall! Is it possible? I did not expect the pleasure of meeting you."

"You did not know Mrs. Gordon was a friend of mine?" I stammered, more at a loss for words than I was willing for his quick ears to detect.

"Certainly not. I have only had the honor of meeting Mrs. Gordon a few times at Professor Harriman's, and the charm of her conversation, together with her gracious treatment of me a stranger, tempted me to accept the invitation this evening. May I ask what brings you to Philadelphia?"

"Mrs. Gordon's invitation, and the need there was for some one to attend my sister Sophie, who is needing medical advice. Mr. Hamlin, this is my sister," and I took Sophie's hand, and drew her up by my side.

I did not like Mr. Hamlin less because he gave the delicate, shrinking girl much more of his time and conversation during the evening than he gave me, and I was pleased and glad that Sophie appeared to turn almost instinctively toward him, trusting in his kindly strength much as little Ellen Hopkinson had formally.

My acquaintance with the Chapmans, Fairchilds, and Thorntons, and more than all my daily companionship with mother, had taught me to appreciate the kind of people whom I met at Mrs. Gordon's. I soon learned from the conversation that her guests were chiefly authors, artists, and professors, and that once a week they were in the habit of meeting to discuss books, works of art, and the great political questions of the day.

"You will observe, Miss Kendall, that Mrs. Gordon's friends all have an object in life, from the earnest and spirited tone of the conversation," remarked Mr. Hamlin.

"I have already inferred that many of them must believe with Goethe that 'a useless life is a lingering death.'"

"I think the most discouraging thing to a true nature would be the fear of uselessness—of being a mere weed, condemned to be nothing and do nothing."

"Might not a man of abundant wealth become so engrossed in the pleasures of it, as to forget whether he is useful and therefore his uselessness will be no hindrance to his happiness?"

"Doubtless many persons become so absorbed in selfish pleasures and luxuries as to forget that there is any thing required of them here or hereafter; but happiness under such circumstances, would be simply a negative kind of animal, enjoyment. Surround any true soul with all the sumptuous trappings of wealth, and condemn him to a useless life, and it will be but a gilded prison-house."

"Well, I am glad that I've never been called to choose between a gilded prison-house and a useful life. It is difficult for me to believe that any thing could compensate for the loss of the pleasures which toil for those we love brings to us."

I had inadvertently touched a chord that in its vibrations brought sadness to my friend, for his face was instantly clouded, and when he spoke it was to change the current of his thoughts.

"Have you heard from your cousin Mrs. White recently?" he asked.

"Only once since I saw her, and that was soon after her return from Niagara, She wrote a long letter, describing in her own lively way the pleasures of her journey and the reception which her husband's parish gave her."

"Her cheerful companionship will be invaluable to my friend White. He is somewhat too grave and scholarly, and needs to be drawn away from his books to mingle more freely with his parish. How long will you remain with Mrs. Gordon?"

"Not more than a week I presume, unless the oculist finds it necessary to see Sophie's eyes more than once. We shall consult him to-morrow."

"May I call in the evening to ask what his opinion is?"

"Certainly; both Sophie and I will feel more at home in Philadelphia because we have found a friend."

He looked searchingly in my face as I spoke, and must have seen the color come and go in my anxiety to show him that I regarded him as a friend. He had risen to leave, but after a moment's hesitation seated himself again by my side, and as Sophie had been carried away by Mrs. Gordon, he asked:

"What do you fear for your sister's eyes?"

I told him of the dimness of vision which had been creeping stealthily but surely over her eyes for the last year, of the severe sickness which had preceded it, and of all our anxieties; and though he said little in reply, and soon left me to join the group whom Miss Harriman's brilliant conversation had drawn around her, I felt strengthened and comforted by his words.

I was near enough to catch part of Miss Harriman's words, and to find that she was defending Mrs. Gaskell's "Life of Charlotte Brontë" from the attacks of a young man who declared that—

"Mrs. Gaskell had ruthlessly entered the sanctities of private life, exposing foibles which in no way added to the lustre of the Brontë family."

"But a truthful biographer should expose the foibles as well as the virtues of his characters."

"Then let Mrs. Gaskell confine herself to the weaknesses of Charlotte Brontë, and not dress up ill-founded rumors of the father's violence and the brother's dissipation, not to mention her most unwarrantable and unladylike attack upon the privacy of another home, so that her biography descends to mere gossip and scandal."

"I will admit that Mrs. Gaskell erred against good taste in two or three instances, but I still insist that she meant to be truthful, and only to expose such weak and wicked traits in the Brontë family as would show the obstacles her favorite Charlotte had to contend with."

I could not hear the young man's reply, for a sweet-voiced middle-aged lady had been introduced by our considerate hostess, and in conversing with her I could only catch occasional scraps of sentences which were wafted to me.

I found myself eagerly watching Mr. Hamlin's face and movements during the remainder of his stay in Mrs. Gordon's parlor, and wondering if the bright intelligent face and agreeable conversation of Miss Harriman would not so attract him as to cause forgetfulness of the dream which had visited him in Hebron more than a year ago.

She was dressed in simple elegance, and carried about with her the unmistakable air of a person accustomed to refined society; and more than all, she seemed to my foolish fancy bent upon making Mr. Hamlin sensible of her charms. Yes; I thought, and she is succeeding too, for see how he is bending over the hand she has offered in saying good-night; and how unnecessarily long he is holding that small fair hand as if parting from her were "such sweet sorrow." And when he was gone I still furtively watched the lady and thought I saw

> "Her eyes of violet gray were colored rich
> With gloom of tender thought, and mirrored large
> Within them, starry futures swam and shone."

CHAPTER XLVII.

BEHIND THE CLOUD.

> "One by one thy griefs will meet thee;
> Do not fear an armed band;
> One will fade as others greet thee,
> Shadows passing through the land."
> Miss Procter.

I HAD sent word to Mrs. Mayhew that we were in Philadelphia, and had received from her a note, inviting us to dine with her on Saturday; and we had arranged to drive there directly from the doctor's office. Mrs. Gordon accompanied us, and when the long and critical examination of Sophie's eyes was finished she took her down to the parlor, while I remained to hear the doctor's decision. It was useless for him to obscure his meaning in scientific and professional terms, for the truth must be told in such language as I could comprehend.

"Are we to understand that my sister must be blind?" I asked tremblingly, when the oculist paused for a moment in his description of the different causes for blindness.

"Blindness is inevitable, miss. The present dimness of vision is caused by a paralytic affection of the optic nerve, which was doubtless submitted to the pressure of a tumor during the illness that you told me of. In her case the pupil will gradually become more and more insensible to the rays of light, and in less than a year she will probably lose the power of discriminating objects. You are ill, young lady; the change from the frosty air of the out-door world to my office has been too sudden for you."

He led me to a sofa and attempted to remove my bonnet, when tears that could no longer be checked flowed so freely that he saw I was in no immediate danger of fainting; and muttering something half audibly about sudden attacks of hysteria and the nervous irritability of some people, he turned from me and prepared a cordial, which he bade me drink. I obeyed, because I did not wish to explain to him that I was not needing a mere physical cordial, and as quickly as could be dried my eyes, summoning all my courage to meet the certainty of this new trial.

I did not know, until I heard the fatal decision of Dr. Daniels, how strongly hope had struggled with my fears. Mrs. Gordon and Sophie were waiting for me in the parlor; and knowing they would suspect the cause of my long delay, I bathed my eyes, and, assuming a cheerfulness that I was very far from feeling, went down to them, trying to frame some sentences by which I could evade telling them the truth until we reached home. But Mrs. Gordon saved me from the pain of evasion, by saying, as soon as I entered the room:

"You need not tell us what the doctor has said, Hope. Sophie and I have decided that she had better not know until she reaches home. I shall send you to Mrs. Mayhew's in the carriage, and walk back now. Gather just as much pleasure and enjoyment from this visit to your friends as you can. My carriage will call for you as early as six o'clock this evening." And Mrs. Gordon bent over my fair young sister, and kissed her forehead with that tenderness which we feel for one upon whom some great calamity has fallen.

We found Mrs. Mayhew formally polite in her greeting. She had paid in gold the debt she owed my mother, and her whole bearing showed that she did not intend for us to presume on an intimate acquaintance with her young daughters. Dora and Annie felt the restraint of their mother's presence, and imitated her cool politeness; and during the entire day the conversation was confined almost entirely to commonplace inquiries after the welfare of mother's school and the neighbors whom they knew. Dora seemed interested in my account of Virginia's wedding; and, in asking questions about it, came near forgetting her studied formality. Indeed, they both forgot it when Mrs. Mayhew was called from the room for a half hour, and clung around my neck, kissing me in their old, demonstrative way.

"Dear old Sherbrooke!" exclaimed Dora, "I wish I was there studying with your mother; but we are kept under the eye of a stupid governess, who scarcely allows us to wink naturally; and then we have such horrid cross masters in music and French and dancing, that we don't care to learn. Nothing is made pleasant for us here, as it was at your mother's; and then we both get cross, and mamma says 'tis because our manners have been neglected. We don't see anybody, because we haven't come out, and we never shall come out if June doesn't get married. She and father are in Washington, so you won't see them."

I murmured some formal expression of regret, and then Mrs. Mayhew entered, and Dora fell back into the lines of etiquette. Dinner in this elegant mansion was a cold, stately ceremony, with two colored servants in waiting; and poor, timid Sophie was so much embarrassed as to drop her soup-spoon on her new blue merino, to drink from the finger-glass, and to commit various other little improprieties, so that on the whole we were very glad to hear Mrs. Gordon's carriage announced immediately after we had risen from the formal dinner. The invitation for this day, and one call from Mrs. Mayhew and her daughters while we were at Mrs. Gordon's, and the lady of fashion had discharged her obligations to the daughters of a woman who had been for three years mother and teacher of her children.

When I reached Mrs. Gordon's I could no longer restrain the grief that had been locked within my heart all day; and shutting myself in my friend's chamber, where I should not be discovered by Sophie, I permitted its violence to escape in tears, until Mrs. Gordon knocked for admittance, and attempted to soothe me by bringing to my remembrance many things which would in some degree soften and atone for blindness.

"I have sent Sophie to bed; she complained of weariness and headache. And do you know what a long time I have allowed you to remain here alone?"

"I haven't thought much about time; I wanted to learn how to bear the weight of this new sorrow before I met Sophie again."

"Carry it where you have learned to carry all your sorrows, my dear Hope, and remember to be grateful that God has made you so capable and efficient an aid to your mother. You will have a stronger incentive to exertion now than ever before. But Mr. Hamlin is waiting for you in the parlor; he tells me that he is an old friend of yours."

"Yes, I used to meet him often when I was visiting my aunt in Hebron."

"Well, go down, please, and entertain him while I finish some letters that ought to be mailed to-night."

I found Mr. Hamlin reading a magazine contribution from Hugh Boyd, and for several minutes he talked only of this author's quaint and humorous style—his charmingly novel way of presenting common truths and beautifying the every-day incidents of life, until he saw that I was more at ease, and could join in the conversation.

"I have never seen you look so fatigued before, Miss Kendall," he said, abruptly changing the current of our talk, "and I infer from your face that mental depression has more to do with it than physical weariness. Am I right?"

"Oh, Mr. Hamlin, it will be a relief to tell you how very wretched Dr. Daniels' decision has made me. How can I ever tell Sophie that she must be blind?"

"I was afraid you had heard unpleasant news," he said, after a moment's pause. "Try and be comforted, Miss Kendall, by remembering Who has been eyes to the blind, and that His grace is sufficient for us in the darkest hour of trial."

"I know, but 'tis so difficult to submit just now, when my heart is full with this one thought, that my dear sister must be forever shut out from all the pleasures of sight."

"Not forever. You forget how short is time, and that in our eternal home there are no physical infirmities—no need of the sun, for the Lamb is the light thereof."

"And my dear, patient, long-suffering mother! I shall have to tell this new grief to her."

"The same Hand that held a bitterer cup to her lips will hold this; and moreover, she has learned not to look at life's long sorrow, but to bear patiently each moment's pain."

"If I could only suffer instead of Sophie! She is so clinging and dependent, and to think she can never see the faces of those she loves again!"

Here my voice could no longer be controlled, and the delicately appreciative nature of Mr. Hamlin allowed me to weep several minutes undisturbed; and when he spoke, it was in a low tone of tender sympathy for my sorrow.

"Miss Kendall, you are forgetting, in the newness of your grief, how many pleasures remain to those who are deprived of sight. I think you have told me that your sister has musical tastes, and there is almost an inexhaustible source of pleasure and amusement in the study of that science, which you are aware may be learned nearly as well without as with sight. Then the loss of one sense sharpens and quickens all others, and the pleasures of hearing and memory will be so enhanced as to compensate in some measure for the loss of sight. There are books printed for the blind, which she will very quickly learn to read by the sense of touch; and crocheting, knitting, and several kinds of fancy work, which multitudes of young ladies with good eyes find very engrossing, may be successfully learned by the blind. You must think of the pleasures that remain to your sister, and remember that we have a very present Help in all our trouble."

His words comforted me, and before he left I could see some light behind the dark cloud—if I only dared ask Mr. Hamlin to tell Sophie the decision of the oculist; but no, I had no right to ask favors of him.

What a tower of strength he seemed, and yet as gentle and tender in his sympathies as a woman!

"It has been a relief to talk this trouble over with you, Mr. Hamlin, but I have been very selfish in entertaining you in this way."

"I called for the very purpose of listening to your griefs; I gathered, from what you told me last evening of your sister's eyes, that you had the worst to fear. You may remember that I once promised to be your friend, if I ever found you in need of one. Mrs. Gordon says if the weather is favorable next Monday, she will accept my escort to Laurel Hill cemetery. Will you and your sister accompany us?"

"Thank you: I shall be very glad that Sophie will have such a pleasure to remember."

"Good-night." He went without another word; without any of his old lingering in my presence, or any of his former half-playful, half-authoritative commands. I was strangely perverse. One year ago I had rebelled against his dictatorial spirit—now I rather longed to hear him say "you ought" and "you must," and thought it might be very pleasant for the woman whom he loved to obey him. And then I remembered Miss Harriman's pleased attention when he talked the evening before, the charming deference she gave to his opinions, and the tender, half-abstracted look she wore after he left; evidently his authority would be no heavy chain for her.

Sophie and I shared the same bed during our visit at Mrs. Gordon's; and creeping softly into the room, I found her sleeping so quietly that I trusted my unpleasant message might be kept from her a few hours longer. I had not yet become so familiar with the certainty of the great affliction which threatened us as to cast my burden on the Lord, therefore my unreconciled heart made me restless and wakeful, and the morning light that rested on my sister's quiet face, saw upon mine the traces of a struggle which had failed to make a Penniel of my chamber; I could not see God's purpose in this new affliction.

"Hope, you needn't be afraid to tell me what the oculist said," whispered Sophie, laying her fair cheek against mine. I had assisted at her morning toilet in unusual silence, and we both stood looking out upon the clean, quiet streets of the city, waiting for the summons to breakfast. "I know if there had been good news for me, you would have told me last night; but I saw that you looked sad and kept your face turned from me, and once in the night I heard you sobbing. Don't mind so much about it, dear Hope, for I think I've learned, in whatsoever state I am, to be content."

What could I say? and what could I do but fold the simply trusting, innocent girl to my heart, and let the last of my unsubmissive tears fall upon her golden hair?

"If I had good strong eyes, they would never be of as much use to mother as yours," she said, in her confiding way; "and you know I never cared half as much for reading as you always did, and never should know enough to teach and write as you can. The only thing I care very much about is music, and Mrs. Gordon told me last night that she knows several blind persons who can play the piano beautifully. It will be very terrible at first not to see mother's face, or yours, or Willie's; but then I shall always remember them just as they are now, young and fair, and shall never see the wrinkles and gray hairs that must come."

She said this with a smile so serene, and a look so nearly radiant, that I knew she had a deep fountain of peace and joy in her heart, that would help her to accept any trial, even blindness, as one of God's messengers. The delicate, timid young girl, whom mother and I had always shielded from every rough encounter with hardships, had suddenly become stronger than I—she, the sufferer, had become the comforter.

"I shall see everything through your eyes, dear Hope," she added, after a minute's thoughtful pause, "and if mother should be taken away, you will never let me be separated from you?"

"Never, never—God will give me strength to take care of you."

"Then my heart is at rest. But I mustn't forget to tell you that I have discovered something about myself that will give you and mother pleasure." She hesitated, as she always did in speaking of herself.

"What is it, darling?"

"I think my memory is remarkably good—ever since I have had this to fear," touching as she spoke the drooping lids that fell over her blue eyes. "I have tried very hard to remember what you have read aloud, and I can repeat a great many short poems, that I have heard more than once. You read Bryant's 'Snow-storm' twice to Mrs. Gordon the other day, and when you had finished I found that I could recall every line of it."

And partly to assure me of her gift, but more I was sure to comfort me and divert my thoughts from her, she repeated the beautiful poem.

We went hand-in-hand into the breakfast parlor, where Mrs. Gordon awaited us, and after one searching glance at our faces, I saw that she knew the agony of the conflict had passed, and that both our hearts were submissively waiting God's will. She bade us good-morning, and then, as if continuing a strain of thought which our entrance had interrupted, she repeated—

"'All that seems but darkness here,
When thou hast passed beyond it, haply shall be crystal clear.'"

That Sabbath in Philadelphia was one of peace and rest to my heart—one of the stepping-stones upon which I rose to higher and purer things—a day wherein pride and selfishness was more thoroughly washed from my nature than ever before.

CHAPTER XLVIII.

LAUREL HILL.

"Into what little space
May the concentrate essence of a life
Be love-condensed!"

"Hope, this is more like an April day than any thing March usually brings us," said Mrs. Gordon, coming into her sunny breakfast parlor on Monday morning; "I trust your spirits and Sophie's are as bright and buoyant as the weather. If they are, I think we way promise ourselves an agreeable excursion."

"You may rely on our being in harmony with the outdoor world, Mrs. Gordon, and on our thorough enjoyment and appreciation of all the pleasures your kindness provides for us. The only hindrance to my enjoyment will be the thought that you are wasting so much of your precious time in entertaining us."

"Don't let that thought trouble you. I am needing the recreation almost as much as you are, and we have all earned our holiday I am sure. Mr. Hamlin is a very diligent student, and I doubt if he has taken one whole day for pleasuring before since he came to our city. We can see Girard College and Fairmount water-works to-day, as well as Laurel Hill; and to-morrow I shall take you to 'Independence Hall,' the United States Mint, and to one or two picture galleries."

I attempted to express a tithe of my gratitude in words, but was quickly interrupted by my friend:

"No—you need not thank me. I understand what you wish to say. If all things work together right, I shall beg an invitation to spend a couple of weeks with your mother, next summer, and then you will more than repay my present hospitality by showing me your beautiful hills and woods. Have you decided that you must return to Sherbrooke this week?"

"Oh, yes, on Thursday—mother can hardly spare me from her school till then, and she will be impatient to get Sophie back. Besides, I should not like to travel without an escort, and on Thursday Mr. Chapman will return from Washington, and will call here to take us in charge."

"I have received an invitation this morning from Mrs. Harriman to meet a few friends at her house to-morrow evening. I am invited to bring my guests—shall I accept for you?"

I hesitated—my desire to see Miss Harriman in Mr. Hamlin's presence again was very strong, but I had only the one evening dress in which Mrs. Gordon's friends had seen me, and I was not sure that my hostess would like to introduce it into polite society twice in one week.

"Thank you, Mrs. Gordon, I would like to go, but—"

"What is the 'but,' my dear?"

"You know I have but one evening dress."

"And a very pretty and becoming one it is; so that question is settled, and I will write a note of acceptance while you and Sophie are getting ready for our excursion.

Mr. Hamlin will come with the carriage in less than half an hour."

My heart had recovered its usual quiet tone of cheerfulness since I had seen Mr. Hamlin; and as both he and Mrs. Gordon seemed bent on making the hours pass agreeably, I joined in the animated conversation, thinking only of making this day so pleasant for my dear sister that golden memories of it would reach far into her blind future. Mr. Hamlin devoted himself to Sophie until we reached Laurel Hill, explaining the architecture of the college buildings to her, and telling her many amusing peculiarities of their founder; his manliness had never seemed greater or nobler than when stooping to amuse a young, sensitive girl. Sophie appeared quite at ease with her new friend.

It was mid-day when we reached the cemetery grounds, and leaving the carriage at the gates, we strolled on foot through the dry paths, that we might more carefully examine the statuary and monuments. It so happened at last that Mrs. Gordon and Sophie were left behind, and I found myself walking beside my friend, and talking with something of the freedom of one year ago.

Mr. Hamlin's first inquiry was how Sophie had borne Dr. Daniels' decision.

"Bravely, wonderfully—as well as if she had been preparing for such a calamity all her life. Instead of needing comfort from me, she has shown herself more capable of administering it."

"I gathered as much from her face; it is a remarkably peaceful, trustful one. Indeed, I may say it rests and soothes me only to look at her. And you, Miss Kendall, can you say 'all my springs are in Thee'?"

"I can at least accept submissively and unquestionably to-day what seemed so darkly mysterious on Saturday."

"I doubt not in time you will see behind the veil of cloud which shrouds so many of God's dealings with His children. You had better rest upon this seat, and wait for our companions."

We had reached an eminence that overlooked several paths, and I sat down upon a rustic seat, while my companion stood by my side. He did not talk as freely with me to-day as he did with Sophie, and I soon lost my easy, cheerful flow of words, and sat silent and grieved because of Mr. Hamlin's grave abstractedness, and allowed my eyes to rove in quest of Mrs. Gordon and Sophie. I quickly discovered them, seated also on a sunny knoll not far from us. Two grave-diggers were throwing up fresh sods within the range of my eyes, but so far off that I could not hear the sound of their spades; and a solitary snow-bird alighted on a leafless branch of a locust, directly in front of me. This was destined to be a memorable hour—an hour which would reveal to me the hidden secrets of my own heart, and into which would be condensed such passions, struggles, hopes, and fears as I had never known—therefore each sight and sound of that hour are engraven upon my memory with a diamond point. For a brief space the sands of life seemed slipping from beneath my feet, and only a black gulf of unmitigated horror and despair opened before me.

While I sat gazing upon the wintry landscape, noting how slowly the red tinge of spring's new life was creeping over the trees, a sight met my vision which almost froze my blood.

A large dog bounded over the stone wall which separated the cemetery grounds from a field, and his singularly frantic movements at once riveted my gaze. Instinct whispered to me almost instantly that the animal was mad—and oh! he had turned toward our eminence—he had evidently scented us, and scarcely a hundred yards lay between his rabid fury and our defenceless selves.

"My God!" exclaimed Mr. Hamlin, whose eyes seemed to have detected the furious animal at the same instant as mine, "that dog is mad! and he is making directly for this seat! Hope, as you value your life, for the sake of your blind sister, spring over this seat and crouch behind it;" and while uttering the words he was drawing off his thick overcoat, and with extended arms holding it in front of me to keep the animal at bay. No— my feet would not move—I was paralyzed with fear! but not for myself.

The moment's awful peril showed me that one was exposed whose life was infinitely sweeter to me than my own.

In the blind, rushing, furious haste of the rabid animal, when he was so near that we could see his inflamed eyes, and the disgusting white foam that clung to his distended jaws, he became momentarily entangled in a low shrub of buck-thorn; and quick as thought Mr. Hamlin sprang forward, throwing his coat over the dog's head, and at the same instant, seizing him by the neck, he held him so muffled and blinded that while the man's strength lasted, the brute could not injure us. But how long would a man's strength resist the furious struggles of the enraged animal?

I did not wait to ask, for if fear had frozen my life-current a minute before, love and anxiety had thawed it and lent my feet the speed of wings. I stopped an instant by Mr. Hamlin's side as I flew past—long enough to lay my hand upon his shoulder and say, "Take courage, Philip! keep the dog down a little while, and I will bring you help."

The word Philip sprang to my lips involuntarily, and even in that moment of fearful peril I saw that his eyes had gathered just the kind of hope and courage from my face and words which would lend his arms almost superhuman strength—which would quicken every self-preserving instinct of his nature.

A minute's rapid running over sunken graves and low shrubs of hemlock and thorn, brought me near enough to catch the ear of the grave-diggers.

"Come! Bring your spades, a mad dog is upon us! follow me!" I shouted, and waiting only an instant to see that they caught my meaning and were coming with rapid steps toward me, I ran back, thinking no longer of danger to myself, but hoping if my friend's strength were failing, that mine might avail to keep the dog in check for a few brief seconds.

"Hope! keep back, not a step nearer—you can do nothing but pray! God helping, my strength will last a minute longer. Keep Mrs. Gordon and Sophie away from the danger."

God forgive me, but in my selfish terror for the man I loved, I had hardly thought of them before, and glancing toward the seat where I had last seen them, I saw they were aware of Mr. Hamlin's peril; but probably conscious that their presence on the scene would be useless to him and increase their own danger. I could only kneel with uplifted heart, entreating God's help, while my eyes were riveted on Mr. Hamlin's pale face, on which I could see large beaded drops of agony, and the knotted veins in his temples told the fierceness of his struggle.

"Keep hold of the brute, but stoop forward so as I can aim at his head." I heard the grave-digger's words, but for the next ten minutes I was unconscious. I did not see the well-timed and vigorous blows which the laborers were obliged to wield before the dog lay prostrate and powerless, his mad sufferings mercifully ended.

My first consciousness assured me that my head rested against Mr. Hamlin's shoulder—that Mrs. Gordon and Sophie bent over me—that one of the workmen stood by with a tin pail of water in his hand—while the other turned Mr. Hamlin's ruined coat over and over with his spade, commenting upon its condition.

"I declare, there ain't two pieces as big as my hand but what have the marks of that brute's teeth. It's lucky 'twas such a mighty thick one, and lucky that you thought of blinding him with it, and lucky that you have a pair of strong arms, young man; else you and that girl would have had an awful death to look forward to."

"Yes," answered his fellow-laborer, as no other member of the party had yet found language even for the outward expression of thankfulness. "And it's lucky you and me was a-working near by, where the young woman could find us, for I reckon one man's strength couldn't have held the dog a minute longer. I wonder, Joe, if we hadn't better bury the poor beast away in that holler?"

"Do so at once, my good friends," said Mr. Hamlin, "and bury that coat with him; you must manage to remove him without bringing your hands in contact with him. Hoist him into a wheelbarrow with your spades. Here is a trifling reward for the great service you have rendered me, and you will have my lifelong thanks and good wishes."

The men moved off, with profuse thanks for Mr. Hamlin's bits of gold, and we still sat upon the bank, silent from that excess of grateful emotion which rarely finds expression in words. At length Mrs. Gordon spoke.

"Hope, if you are strong enough to walk, I think we should move toward our carriage. Mr. Hamlin has no overcoat, and this exposure, after such an unusual exercise of strength, will be dangerous."

"Let us start at once," I said, rising to my feet, and attempting to move forward; but my trembling limbs would have made little progress, had it not been for the arm I was compelled to lean upon—that arm which had not lost all its strength in the desperate struggle which had so severely tested it, though every nerve and muscle in it appeared to me still quivering with the strain they had received.

Very few words were spoken as we rode back toward Mrs. Gordon's home, and those few were in hushed and subdued tones, as if we were still standing in the presence of Death. Mr. Hamlin made but one allusion to the perilous incident of the day, after he had described to Mrs. Gordon at her request the attack of the dog, and then it was to express the hope that the incident would not be made public.

"You must let me prescribe for you to-day, Mr. Hamlin, if you are a physician," said Mrs. Gordon, when we reached her door. "You must ride to your boarding-house, take a cup of hot coffee and a bath, and go directly to bed, and if possible to sleep. I shall send to-morrow morning to inquire for you, and in the evening, if you please, you may call upon us."

"Thank you, but do not take the trouble of sending to inquire for me; rather give me the privilege of calling in the morning to report myself and learn if you or the young ladies have received injury from the fatigue and excitement of the day."

"Well, come in the morning if you are able;" then she held out her hand to him while she added, "I do not know how to express my gratitude and admiration for the strength and courage you have shown to-day. You have probably saved yourself and others from the most terrible death."

I did not trust myself with words when Mr. Hamlin

lifted me from the carriage, but I did venture to raise my eyes a moment to his, that he might read the gratitude that dared not seek audible expression.

I went at once to my chamber, glad of its solitude, that I might analyze the emotions which the hour of peril had awakened. What was this new feeling that had so suddenly burst into life, overpowering for a minute my maidenly reticence, and drawing from my timid lips the familiar household name of the man I had taught myself to believe was only a friend? I ran over in my thoughts the history of my acquaintance with Mr. Hamlin, recalling his every word of endearment, his slightest expression of interest, and I knew that I loved him now, and had loved him even when my heart was so dazed and bewildered by a sickly fancy, that it accepted the shadow for the substance. For a brief space I opened all the doors and windows of my heart, that it might bask in the warmth and sunshine which the blessed consciousness of loving worthily brought to it— that a sweet perfume of budding hopes might creep softly into its quiet chambers. I remembered only the fact that he had loved me, forgetting that I had cast his love aside, and that for many months he had been acquainted with the elegant Miss Harriman, exposed to the charm of her accomplishments too, at a time when he was seeking a grave for his first love. But dark memories came quite soon enough to cloud my happiness, to remind me that I had most unguardedly shown my love to a man who perhaps no longer valued it.

A tingling sensation of shame crept through my veins and flushed my face, though I was alone with the darkness. And then my great selfishness in thinking for an hour of my own happiness, when hardly two days since I had resolved to devote my whole life to the dear sister whose blindness would make her dependent, rose up before me, and made my brief dream of love look like a premeditated crime.

But if Mr. Hamlin should ask for my love again—if I had not mistaken the expression of his eyes when he was struggling for his own life and mine—might it not be possible to accept it and divide the devotion of my life between him and my mother's family?

Would not the knowledge of his love so strengthen and inspire me that every faculty of my heart and soul would become purified, ennobled, and quickened into new life? Would Mr. Hamlin accept a divided love? Conflicting waves of thought swept over me, as if the still, deep river of my being had suddenly met an impetuous, rushing mountain torrent, and the two forces, instead of blending and flowing onward in a deeper, broader channel, with a swifter current, were struggling for the mastery. Summoned to meet Mrs. Gordon and Sophie at the supper-table, I thrust the contending tides of feeling back into my heart, closed the flood-gate upon its waters, and met them with a face that told no tales of my struggles; at least I hoped so.

CHAPTER XLIX.

HOPE'S JOY AND REFUGE.

> "Oh, speak not lightly of
> A lady's love. It is her paramount,
> Especial jewel, over which keep guard
> All things most rare in her tenacious sex."

"HERE's some flowers for yez, miss, and a letther; they was brought by the man as took yez to ride yesterday, and the mistress says as how ye must be ready to go out in jist an hour, plase, and Miss Sophie is to go to her now in the librerry."

Were ever rose-buds, mignonette, and geraniums sweeter than those which I pressed to my lips as soon as Sophie had left me alone? I knew, as I drank in their beauty and fragrance, that in mystic language they heralded the mission of the note; and with eager, tremulous fingers, I tore open its envelope and read:

"MY DEAR MISS KENDALL:

"For more than a year I have been trying to forget you, believing that my love would never find an answering echo in your heart; and could you know the strength, depth, and tenderness of my passion for you, you would believe that such efforts have not been made without great pain. Until I met you last week I supposed I had acquired at least patient acquiescence in my fate; but the trustful way in which you spoke to me of your sorrow, showed me that you and confidence in my friendship; and showed me, too, that my love for you could never be crushed out. But I did not mean to be so selfish as to plead with you again for a gift you had once refused; I meant only to seek a few hours of enjoyment in the society of the only woman I have ever loved, thinking it could in no way disturb her quiet heart, until the awful hour of peril yesterday, when, for a brief moment, you touched my arm and looked into my eyes, saying, 'Take courage, Philip!' then I did take courage, for I thought I discovered in your face and words a deeper, an intenser feeling than mere friendship, and the trembling hope which your touch and words inspired gave strength and nerve to my arms; the remembrance of them has made me so presuming as to ask you to reconsider your decision of a year ago.

"Hope, what does the assurance of my love and constancy bring you now? If only friendly emotion, if your touch and words yesterday were only wrung from you by the intensity of our mutual danger, do not hesitate to tell me so. But if the peril of the hour revealed to you the possibility of loving me, I should accept such an assurance as the sweetest earthly blessing God could bestow, and the purest love man ever offers to woman should shield and protect you, and help bear your burdens. Think of this renewed offer of my love calmly and carefully during the day; and if, oh, Hope! if you can give me any encouragement, if you can permit me to try and win your love, wear the flowers I have sent to Professor Harriman's this evening.

"Always yours,
"Philip Hamlin."

I could no longer mistake the language of my heart; the warm, exultant thrill of happiness which the renewal of Mr. Hamlin's love gave me was more than mere friendship —was vastly deeper, stronger, and more satisfying than the girlish fancies which I had permitted to come between my heart and happiness once before. There was no longer any doubt or question whether I could love and honor this man; now I only asked myself, would it be right to admit any new claims, when more than ever before mother needed my undivided strength and duty? At last I resolved that it was at least due to Mr. Hamlin's constancy to tell him of my love; and I had such entire confidence in the noble generosity of his great heart, that I was sure he would know just what I ought to do—that he would not ask for any love or duty that would conflict with what I owed my mother's family.

Mrs. Gordon, though she raised a pleased and somewhat searching look to my face when I entered the library, equipped for a walk with her, had too much delicacy and refinement to seek an explanation of the light which must have shone in my eyes; she only said:

"Mr. Hamlin made a hasty call of inquiry this morning; he would not stop to sit, but I suppose he told you in his note that he has not suffered from his great exertions yesterday?"

"Yes, indeed! I don't know—" I stopped, confused, stammering, and blushing. I was sure Mr. Hamlin had made no mention of physical discomfort, and I had forgotten my own anxiety on his behalf.

"Yet I gather from your face that you have received no unpleasant message," she said, smiling at my embarrassment.

I bent over Sophie and busied myself with the readjustment of her cloak, hat, and scarf, that my blushing face might not be too easily read. If I say that the curiosities in old Independence Hall did not receive quite as much of my attention as they might, had I visited them a week earlier, those who remember their first sweet joy in loving and being loved, will not be surprised. Nor do I believe Mrs. Gordon wondered at the half-abstracted, mechanical way in which I spent this day of sight-seeing.

When the hour for visiting the Harriman's came, I was still happy and exultant over my new hopes, but uncertain about the propriety of wearing Mr. Hamlin's flowers— doubtful whether I ought to accept his love without consulting mother; and yet she had taught me to be independent in my thoughts and acts, and if I might only venture to give him this little reward for his generous love and constancy, it would be very pleasant. I would at least try the effect of a bit of ivy and some geranium flowers in my hair, and two or three rose-buds at my throat; and when I timidly glanced at the reflection of my unusual adornments, I decided to wear them, though I knew that in so doing I was riveting chains that could not be lightly broken. I entered Mrs. Harriman's parlor, clinging closely to Mrs. Gordon, too self-conscious and shy to raise my eyes until I was obliged to in response to the greetings of our host and his cordial, talkative lady; and then for several minutes I did not allow them to wander from the group that stood near, but listened to Miss Harriman's sparkling conversation as eagerly as if the room could contain nothing of greater interest for me. But my ear soon detected the tones of a voice that had health, clearness, and authority in it, and made me deaf to all other sounds—a voice that sent a thrill of tender emotion through my veins, and cleared up any lingering doubt which still remained about the propriety of wearing Mr. Hamlin's flowers. And if his voice had not given me assurance his eyes would have, when I ventured shyly to seek them. He came eagerly forward as soon as I had glanced toward him, and though he accosted me only in the common phrases of an every-day greeting, yet there was something in his voice and words that quieted my trembling heart and gave me courage to reply.

He drew from me a history of the day's pleasures, and then talked about what I had seen in such a way as to require but few words from me. I knew he was trying to make me feel quite at ease with him, and I felt very grateful for his delicate consideration. Much as I liked to listen to his talking, I was so embarrassed by the consciousness of my new position toward him, that it was something of a relief when Miss Harriman joined us. She talked uncommonly well—not with Virginia's careless, rippling flow of words, but with more dignity and grace. She amused us for half an hour with a description of a summer tour in western New England, and then was led away by her father to entertain his guests with music, and I soon found that she could play and sing as brilliantly as she could talk.

"The music has drawn so many people from the library, that you will find this a favorable opportunity to see a new picture by Champney which hangs there. Shall I take you to it?"

I assented by placing my hand on his offered arm, and was led across the long parlor to the spacious library, which occupied the lower floor of an entire wing, and talked to by Mr. Hamlin about its books, pictures, statuary, and elegant ornaments, till I could speak naturally. When the music had drawn the guests all away from the library, Mr. Hamlin asked:

"Hope, may I venture to thank you for the great favor you have shown me?"

"What favor?" I asked, forgetting in my confusion that I had granted any thing.

"Didn't you wear these flowers because I asked you to?"

"Yes," but it was a faint little affirmative, scarcely audible.

"And as an assurance that I might in time win your love?"

"Yes—I suppose so."

"Thank you a thousand times for the blessedness of that assurance. But have you nothing to say to me?"

"Oh, so many things! but not now. Every thing is so new and strange, that I hardly know myself."

"But you know that by wearing these flowers you have given me certain rights, and one of them is to know something of your heart. I ought to be satisfied with what you have already granted, but you see I am selfishly craving more. If you can tell me that you are happy, and that my love makes you so, I will wait patiently for further knowledge."

"I am very happy."

"And what causes the happiness, Hope?"

"What you have told me and what I have discovered about myself."

"May I ask what new knowledge of yourself you have gained?"

"No—you said you would wait patiently; and besides, I cannot talk for fear some of those people may be within hearing."

"Look up at me, Hope; I have scarcely seen your eyes once to-night."

I obeyed—obedience to that gently-authoritative voice was not hard; and as I permitted him to read for a moment in my face and eyes that story which I could not tell in words, I knew that I had chosen a master, whom to obey would be a pleasure rather than a duty.

"My Hope!" he whispered, bending low his proud head—"my very own! to love, and cherish, and protect! God bless you, dearest!"

We stood side by side with clasped hands, silent for a minute, until the cessation of music in the adjoining parlor brought to us the remembrance that this room might be invaded, when Mr. Hamlin drew my hand within his arm, and led me slowly from picture to picture, descanting upon the characteristic merits of each artist with as much apparent calmness as if we had thought of nothing else during the evening.

"Have you decided when to leave Philadelphia?" he asked, as we stood a little apart from the rest of the company.

"Yes, we leave on Thursday."

"So soon?"

"The object for which we came is accomplished, and mother cannot well spare me from her school any longer, especially as Sophie's eyes cannot be benefited by remaining."

"You do not intend to travel alone with your sister?"

"No, Mr. Chapman, who accompanied us here, went on to Washington, and returns Thursday; we shall meet him at the depot."

"May I spend to-morrow evening with you, at Mrs. Gordon's?"

"I shall want to see you. I cannot explain some things to-night that you ought to know."

"And I may tell Mrs. Gordon what rights you have given me, so that my attentions to her guest will not surprise her?"

"If you think 'tis necessary."

"There may be no absolute need to tell her, but much satisfaction in speaking of my new rights," he said, with a merrier smile than usually lighted his clear, brown eyes. "Do you know I am going to sacrifice my own pleasure in standing near you and talking to you, lest the exclusiveness of my attentions should draw upon us unpleasant observations? I shall leave you with Miss Harriman and contrive to get a few minutes' conversation with Mrs. Gordon."

And soon after I saw him standing in a window recess with my friend, his honest face aglow with the earnestness of his words. He did not seek me again during the evening, and I was glad of the opportunity to watch him furtively as he moved about amongst the guests, conversing fluently. I could see that his opinions were sought and respected here, much as in the little hamlet of Hebron, and I was proud and pleased that my friend, my lover, should be so esteemed.

I was no longer jealous of Miss Harriman, though she leaned upon his arm in walking to the refreshment-room, and appeared to find his conversation much more interesting than any thing the supper-table furnished.

Mr. Hamlin met us in the hall, as we came down cloaked and hooded for our departure, and led us to the carriage, but his only language was a firm, tender clasp of my hand, and a common "Good-night." Yet the echo of his words, "My very own! God bless you, dearest!" made sweet music in my heart long after the streets of the great city were silent.

Mrs. Gordon drew me tenderly to her arms, when bidding me good-night.

"Mr. Hamlin has told me something which explains the abstracted look of happiness your face has worn to-day," she said. "I know very little of your friend, only that his face is stamped with the patent of nobility. It has impressed me every time I've seen him as the mirror of a most generous, intelligent, manly soul, and Professor Harriman's family are quite enthusiastic in his praises; they have seen a great deal of him since he came to this city. I can congratulate you most heartily and warmly."

"Dear Mrs. Gordon, isn't it wrong and selfish in me to accept his love, when mother and Sophie need me so much?"

"You must settle that question with Mr. Hamlin; if your love has flowed out to him almost without your permission, in a strong tide, I think it will inspire you with new strength to labor for others. No doubt he will contrive a way in which he can help bear the burdens of your mother's family, and you may go to rest now, thinking only of the strength and blessedness which your new happiness gives you."

I accepted her advice, for I was

> "A woman like the rest,
> A simple woman who believes in love,
> And owns the right of love, because she loves,
> And, hearing she's beloved, is satisfied
> With what contents God."

CHAPTER L.

GOLDEN THREADS.

> "Let no one ask me how it came to pass;
> It seems that I am happy, that to me
> A livelier emerald twinkles in the grass,
> A purer sapphire melts into the sea."
>
> TENNYSON.

"HOPE, you said last evening that you had many things to tell me, but you are very silent to-night." Mrs. Gordon had sent me into the library to meet Mr. Hamlin, and after I had received the greeting which he said it was his right to give, I sat by his side, listening to his words, but too happy and too timid to talk.

"You can trust me?"

"Entirely, as I never trusted any one before, but oh, Mr. Hamlin!"

"I must correct you there; you called me Philip once; call me so to-night, Hope."

That word had leaped to my lips unconsciously in the sudden revelation which terror had made to me, and it was not easy to speak it now with Mr. Hamlin's eyes upon my face. I hesitated for a moment.

"Call me Philip, Hope," he said once again, with that mingling of tenderness and authority in his voice which I had heard more than once.

"Philip."

"Thank you, dearest, and now before you tell me any of the terrible things of which you've hinted, tell me what were the discoveries of yourself that you spoke of yesterday."

"I found, when you were in such great peril, that your life was very precious to me."

"Why?"

"Because I loved you."

"Since when, dear Hope?" and my face was so held beneath his eyes, that he could read every fitful blush, every changing expression.

"Since I met you last September."

I was drawn within his arms, held close against his breast, and his lips were pressed first upon my hair, then my forehead, eyes, and lips, while he whispered the fond words which ever since have been

> "My heart's sweet scripture to be read at night
> When weary, or at morning when afraid."

"Now, dearest, I will hear all your explanations. I am strong for any thing."

Then I told him of mother's dependence upon me in

her school, of the greater need for my assistance which Sophie's blindness would create, of my father's repeated injunctions to me to aid and comfort mother. "Would it be right," I asked, "to allow even my love for you to come between me and the duty I owe to mother?"

"I believe in an overruling Providence, dear Hope, and trust that in time all obstacles will be removed from our paths. I shall not ask you to make any sacrifices for me; only give me the privilege of sharing your burdens. Your love will be an inexhaustible mine of strength and courage in my heart, giving me something to make life precious, helping me to surmount all difficulties. Will not the knowledge of mine do something for you?"

"Oh, Philip, it will be such a comfort to come to you for advice, to lean upon your strength! such a sweet privilege to love you, if 'tis only right!"

"My darling! my own sweet wife, in the sight of God! Ever since I first knew you I have believed if you did not come to me in time, you must in eternity. It may be many months, perhaps two years, before I can claim you; and I trust by that time your love and duty will in no way conflict. Are you quite content?"

"Quite."

"Yet I fancy there is a cloud in these truthful eyes— these eyes that first unconsciously told me what depths of tenderness, what capacities of loving there were in your nature. What causes the shadow, dearest?"

"Something about myself that perhaps I ought to tell you. You may not care as much for me when you know."

"I'm not afraid to hear any thing you can have to tell, since you have said that you love me."

And with many blushes, many confused pauses, I told him of my acquaintance with Carey Chapman, of all his meaningless attentions, of the foolish fancy which for so many months bewildered me and captivated my senses, so that I mistook it for genuine love—of my grief and shame when I discovered my mistake.

"Had you this preference for Mr. Chapman when you first visited Hebron?"

"Yes; and that was one reason why I did not listen to your love then."

"What other reason had my little Hope?"

"I didn't mean to like you, because you were Aunt Lydia's favorite; and yet, after I knew you well, I longed to keep you for a friend, and I was very sorry to give you so much pain as I did. Will you care as much for my love, now that you know all?"

"I shall prize it more highly, if you can say it springs from a deeper fount than was ever stirred before."

"I think I loved you all that dreary while; but I did not know how much until I met you at Lydia's wedding, so cold and formal and hopeless."

"Why didn't you tell me then that you could care for me?"

"You didn't ask me."

"Foolish little woman! allowing the chances for happiness of two lives to float past her, and not holding out a hand to stay the tide! How shall I forgive her?"

"You have no need to ask how. I can see absolution in your eyes." And I felt it in his tightened clasp, and in the lingering touch of his lips. There was so much to say! he must needs be told what I had read, what written, and what were my plans and expectations, stopping me very often to ask if I were quite sure that I loved him, if I were quite content; lifting the heavy waves of hair from my forehead with such a loving, reverent touch, and looking in my eyes and face as if he would never tire of reading in them a language sweeter than words.

When the little French clock on the mantel struck ten, he rose abruptly, saying—

"My selfishness is detaining you from the preparation for your morrow's journey. When may I come to Sherbrooke?"

"Whenever you please, I suppose."

"But when will my coming please you?"

"Our pupils have a week's holiday in May."

"Then I shall come in May; and as a reward for the great favor you have shown me, I shall ask you to wear this;" and he slipped upon the forefinger of my left hand the tangible token of our engagement, and left me standing alone in Mrs. Gordon's library, looking at the bright gem upon my finger and thinking of all it implied, the added zest-and beauty to life, the new incentive to earnest action, and the strength, refuge, and protection so dear to every woman.

Mr. Hamlin came in the morning to accompany us with Mrs. Gordon to the depot, where we met Mr. Chapman; and with a tell-tale color in my cheeks, which both gentlemen must have noticed, I introduced my friends. There was time but for a few hurried words, and those, spoken in the presence of others, were such as any friend might have said; yet there was a whispered "My own," and a clasp of the hand that spoke volumes, and the choicest, sweetest bouquet as a parting gift that ever whispered love's language to a maiden's heart.

It was pleasant to be so cared for, and the temptation was strong to sit in silence and think over every look and word of love that Philip had given me; but such an indulgence would not be in accordance with the self-forgetfulness which I had tried to make the law of my life, so I chatted merry nonsense to keep Sophie amused, and read paragraphs from the morning paper to Mr. Chapman, who sat in front of us, and told him of the pleasures which our visit had brought to us—all but that greatest pleasure, which words could hardly have painted, but which I think my elderly friend must have guessed, for he more than once rallied me on the brightness of my face and the buoyancy of my spirits.

We reached home, tired and glad, in the waning light of a soft March day. Mother held first one and then the other of us in her arms, as if her eager, hungry love would never be satisfied, looking into my face and then into Sophie's with her searching eyes, saying but little in words, but much in a more eloquent language of the lips.

At Mrs. Gordon's suggestion I wrote mother from Philadelphia the decision of Doctor Daniels, so that she might have time to become acquainted with her grief before meeting Sophie, and I saw the marks of the conflict through which she had passed in the heavy, purple shadows under her eyes, in the quivering muscles of her face, and in the loving, tearful tenderness with which she looked upon her stricken child; in the trustful, appealing confidence with which she turned to me. She was a long time absent with Sophie in her bed-chamber; and when she returned for the talk which we rarely failed to enjoy before separating for the night, I saw that something had calmed and quieted her grief.

"Sophie's cheerful submission is so wonderful, so unexpected to me, Hope," said mother, seating herself beside me, "that I can only say 'tis God's doing, and marvellous to me. I have been afraid, until this last hour's conversation with her, that she did not comprehend the magnitude of her affliction; but I find her cheerfulness does not spring from ignorance or false hopes, but from her entire submission. Now tell me, Hope, more fully than you could write, all the oculist said."

So, while the glowing embers faded upon the hearth, I

told mother every particular of the oculist's examination, and the ground for his conclusions; and then, to soften her grief, I told her of every little thing that helped atone for the loss of sight which Mrs. Gordon and Mr. Hamlin had brought to my remembrance. I meant also to tell her of my new happiness, but not to-night. I must wait until she could look at it with less tearful eyes, or until circumstances favored the development; and meantime Mr. Hamlin's ring lay in my pocket-book. But I did not wait long, for the next evening's mail brought mother a letter from Mr. Hamlin, which made my communication easy—a letter so full of delicately-expressed sympathy for her affliction, so deferent in the manner of his asking for her sanction to our engagement, and so manly and generous in its whole tone, that it proved a successful pleader in his behalf. "I shall not ask for Hope," he wrote, "until you can give her to me without making too great a sacrifice—until you can rely upon my being to you a son."

"And you love him, Hope?" mother asked, after she had read and re-read that letter.

"Yes, mother."

"How long since?"

"Since I met him last September; and I sometimes think ever since he first asked me."

"I more than half believed so, when you told me of your grief at his disappointment, and again when his present of pictures arrived, and I noticed your emotion. Perverse child! how near you came to wrecking your life's happiness! But how shall I ever live without you?"

"Perhaps Mr. Hamlin will make a way for us all to live together."

Mother's face showed her want of faith in any such probability. It was not likely that Sherbrooke would need another physician, nor likely that mother could be induced to leave the dear old farm we had redeemed from debt with so many sacrifices.

But I took up the cares and labors of our daily life with a lighter heart than ever before, having great confidence in Mr. Hamlin's resources, and great faith in God's loving kindness and tender mercies.

Mrs. Gordon had expressly enjoined upon me, before I left her home, the need of daily practice in writing, if I wished to form a clear, healthy, and vigorous style; and now, in addition to her advice and mother's commendation, I had the powerful stimulus of Mr. Hamlin's loving encouragement and the strong incentive of procuring for Sophie every pleasure that would throw light upon her darkness. And, without waiting to hear the fate of my first venture, I seized eagerly every spare hour for study and writing, and during the spring months finished a couple of magazine stories, which added a few dollars to my purse, and brought joy, gratitude, and inspiration to my heart.

In May, when the orchards were aglow with blossoms, and the woods trembled with their burden of song, and the old Earth smiled as if conscious of her own exceeding loveliness, just when the coy, girlish beauty of the month was gliding onward to the riper glories of June, Mr. Hamlin came. Did I love him less because I saw that mother learned, almost before the close of his first day, to lean upon his strength and seek his advice, and that Sophie turned intuitively toward his generous protection—that her quick ear detected at once his approaching footsteps? for, alas! she now only saw "men as trees walking."

Willie sought his help in making bows, arrows, popguns, and kites, and Jonas Gould complimented his knowledge of farming. In less than a week the people of Sherbrooke seemed to regard him as especially belonging to the town. He rode with Doctor Blake to call on the sick, and walked with mother into many a poverty-stricken home, and with Mr. Chapman and Squire Thornton he discussed the political interests of the town and county. Men respected his judgment and strength, and women trusted in his truth.

The familiar landscape of Sherbrooke never looked so lovely to me as when his well-trained, artistic eye discovered to me new shades of beauty, and new points of interest; and in walking, riding, talking, and reading with him during the fortnight of his visit, I learned that he was one of those

> "Whose hearts have a look southward, and are open
> To the whole noon of nature."

CHAPTER LI.

CONCLUSION.

> "She is so conjunctive to my life and soul,
> That as the star moves not but in his sphere,
> I could not, but by her."
> SHAKSPEARE.

THE year that followed my engagement to Philip Hamlin was not cloudless. Life had still its petty trials and its carping cares. Mother was prostrated in the autumn with a low fever, and for three months the entire burden of the school and family fell upon me. We had ten boarders and twice that number of day-pupils; and though I had efficient aid in the kitchen, and an assistant teacher in the school, and Rachel Shaw to nurse mother, yet the care, the responsibility was mine, and often it seemed as though my aching head and limbs must have refused to bear their burden, had not my spirit been comforted and buoyed up by Mr. Hamlin's letters. He was an assistant physician in a hospital in Philadelphia.

My poor little waif of a story was still wandering from one publisher's office to another, and its want of success sorely troubled me, and hung a heavy weight upon the wings of my ambition. It was too short a story for one publisher, and too unpractical for another; the third found it " charmingly written, full of vivacity and fresh young life, showing a highly-cultivated and poetical imagination, but wanting in thrilling incident and dramatic power. It was too quiet to suit the present tastes."

The fourth, after keeping the manuscript two months, said " their house had so many manuscripts on hand, they had no leisure to examine it."

The fifth recognized in the young authoress " decided talent, poetic tastes, a pure and graceful style, but the story was not exactly in their line; better suited to the wants of the Tract Society, or the Massachusetts Sabbath-School Publication Society." These comments were duly forwarded by Mrs. Gordon, and always accompanied by an encouraging word from herself, playfully reminding me of Bruce's spider, and the often-rejected works of authors, who in the end were successful. And at last the sixth publishing house, more than a year after the completion of the manuscript, found it " a pleasant story, well written, showing an intimate acquaintance with the wants of young girls; and though the times were not particularly favorable to the publication of so quiet a story, yet, on the whole, they had decided to publish, if the author would accept eight per cent. on the retail price of the books sold."

The authoress was quite ready by that time to accept any thing, and hailed the proposition with delight and eagerness. Not even Philip Hamlin was permitted to share the honeyed sweetness of my triumphant joy until the printed proof of my success could be laid beneath his eyes.

Mrs. Gordon, mother, and Sophie were my sympathizers and advisers while the book was in press.

How lovingly and reverently that semi-weekly bundle of proof-sheets was examined! What an important matter seemed the size of the page, and the type and the general appearance of the title-page!

What grave consultations we held over the color of the muslin bindings! I wanted them all brown. Mother preferred green—and Sophie's choice wavered between blue and green.

And when the advent of the little book was announced in the city papers, and our Sherbrooke "Chronicle" noticed the appearance "of an excellent, healthy book for girls, author unknown, though evidently written with a lady's pen," I feared even to meet the eyes of the staid old worshippers in our village church, lest they should read the secret in my face, when, bless the good, honest souls! not one in twenty ever saw an advertisement of the book. I am older now, and have seen more than one cherished brain-child petted, praised, criticised, and found fault with by the press, but to feel once again the elastic, absorbing freshness of that first joy in authorship, I would write many a weary day and night, endure many a fatigue and hardship.

Mother was able to resume the direction of affairs in the school-room by the first of the new year, and in April my book was fairly launched, and I was at work upon a more ambitious one. Mother and Philip Hamlin were urging me to rest; Mrs. Gordon was begging me to come to the city for change of air, and Virginia wanted me in her beautiful home, but I resolutely said nay to all entreaties; not till the summer holidays, when I would find rest and change of air in Cousin Lydia's parsonage. But how long my physical energies would have endured the strain of the past year, if circumstances had permitted my ambition to carry me forward in the path I had marked out, I cannot tell. The May which ushered in my twenty-first birthday had blossomed again, when our village was tossed into a troubled sea of excitement and consternation by the loss of our good Doctor Blake. He was not dead, thank God! His sixty years sat gracefully upon him, but he had accepted a professorship in a medical college, and our village was without a doctor, or would be in a month's time. Doctor Blake had been a successful practitioner in Sherbrooke for more than a quarter of a century, and had a strong hold on the hearts of the people.

Every one said he would not have been induced to leave but for the persuasions of Belinda and Esther, who were tired of Sherbrooke, and anxious to display their attractions in more appreciative circles.

I knew that Mr. Chapman, Squire Thornton, our minister, and many others, had expressed a strong desire that Philip Hamlin should be Doctor Blake's successor; I knew they had consulted with mother, that she had written and they had written, but I had not dared add the weight of an expressed wish to Philip, lest he might be tempted for my sake to accept a field of labor to which his sober, better instincts did not call him.

But one day when I sat at work in the deserted school-parlor, correcting the most unpromising school-girlish exercises in composition, Philip Hamlin walked in, and with a bold sweep of his hand, scattered the papers before he took me in his arms.

"Philip! I'm so glad to see you! but why didn't you tell me you were coming?"

"Why didn't you ask me to come?"

"I knew you would, as soon as it was right and best."

"I see now I ought to have come before, and exercised a little wholesome restraint and authority over you. Why have you worked so hard, Hope?"

"Who has told you that I have worked hard?"

"I have been sitting with your mother for a whole hour, too conscientious to call you away from the school-room until the last class was dismissed; and meantime your mother and I have settled some very important questions. Put on your hat, Hope, and come out of this stifled room, and we'll walk as far as the old log bridge before I tell you what has brought me so suddenly to Sherbrooke."

I obeyed the voice I loved so well, glad and happy to be by my master's side.

"So my little Hope has blossomed into an authoress since I've seen her," he said playfully, as we walked through the fern-scented pastures to the bridge; "I'm half afraid to claim an ownership in her now, she has been so complimented by the wiseacres."

"Don't laugh at me, Philip."

"But isn't there a large part of yourself given to the public that I've no claims upon?"

"Not unless you choose to have it so."

"I choose to have you mine—only mine, and I know you will be, even if you give an occasional book to the world. Your love for writing can never conquer your craving for human love."

"Don't be too confident."

"Don't tempt me to forbid the use of your pen."

"You have no right, and I have not promised to obey."

"Obedience shall never be exacted from my wife, only such as love makes spontaneous. Hope, aren't you going to ask why I've come to Sherbrooke?"

"You said you would tell me."

"Can't you guess?"

"For a holiday—a breath of spring, that could not be found in the city?"

"Just that—for a breath of spring that will sweeten every winter of my life. Hope, I have come for my wife!"

"A wife isn't always to be had for the asking," I blushingly answered.

"Yet I have courage to ask. Hope, will you be my breath of spring, my help, my comforter, my own wife?"

"When mother—"

"Your mother says yes, now, as soon as I can gain your consent."

"Not to leave her?"

"Hope, is she preferred before me?"

"No, no, you should know better than to ask."

"Then why not come to me now?"

"Oh, Philip, she needs me so much."

"So do I."

"But you—you could wait."

"I have waited a long time now; but Hope, I think I know why you hesitate, and I will not test your love any further, but tell you some of the reasons why I wish for you now. I am coming to live in Sherbrooke."

It was just what I had hoped and prayed for, but I could not tell him so, though he must have read a satisfactory answer in my face and eyes.

"I have yielded to the persuasions and representations of some of your townspeople, and have decided to succeed Dr. Blake. Your mother says I may add a wing to her house large enough for a parlor, library, and two or three chambers, and I have promised that my wife may spend a couple of hours each day in the school-room, and always be near enough to comfort Sophie, and be, as she has been for

CONCLUSION. 463

so many years, the light and blessing of her mother's home."

"Dear Philip—so generous and thoughtful!"

"Do you think so? Well, before the end of June I want to take Mrs. Hope Hamlin to Hebron and Lake George, for a week's holiday. Have I permission?"

"'Tis very soon," I stammered. But I will not tell how his eloquence prevailed; nor how soon a modest wardrobe, suitable for a country doctor's wife, was prepared with the help of Virginia's taste, and Wiltshire dressmakers; nor how the June skies looked lovingly down on my wedding morn, and the June roses filled the air with perfume, and our good neighbors smiled on David Kendall's Hope, as they gathered around the door of the church to greet Philip Hamlin's bride.

I will not tell what joy, and rest, and peace Philip's tenderly-spoken "sweet wife" brought to my trusting heart; with what patience I listened to Aunt Lydia's assurances that "a gracious woman retaineth honor;" and with what humility and gratitude I received the benediction of Caleb Hopkinson, the rough congratulations of Uncle John, and Cousin Lydia's glad and often-repeated "I knew it would be so."

I will only hint that mother's school still prospers—that her patient heart, pure, self-forgetful life, and generous culture, are still helping mould young girls—that Sophie, in her blind weakness and cheerfulness, is often the help and comforter of our stronger lives—that my great happiness has not been allowed to drown my plans for usefulness—and that never was village doctor busier or more beloved than my Philip Hamlin.

THE END.

www.ingramcontent.com/pod-product-compliance
Lightning Source LLC
Chambersburg PA
CBHW031954300426
44117CB00008B/763